Lecture Notes in Computer Science   11698

More information about this series at http://www.springer.com/series/7408

Alexander Romanovsky ·
Elena Troubitsyna · Friedemann Bitsch (Eds.)

Computer Safety, Reliability, and Security

38th International Conference, SAFECOMP 2019
Turku, Finland, September 11–13, 2019
Proceedings

 Springer

Editors
Alexander Romanovsky ⓘ
Newcastle University
Newcastle upon Tyne, UK

Elena Troubitsyna
Åbo Akademi University
Turku, Finland

Friedemann Bitsch ⓘ
Thales Deutschland GmbH
Ditzingen, Germany

ISSN 0302-9743 ISSN 1611-3349 (electronic)
Lecture Notes in Computer Science
ISBN 978-3-030-26600-4 ISBN 978-3-030-26601-1 (eBook)
https://doi.org/10.1007/978-3-030-26601-1

LNCS Sublibrary: SL2 – Programming and Software Engineering

This Springer imprint is published by the registered company Springer Nature Switzerland AG
The registered company address is: Gewerbestrasse 11, 6330 Cham, Switzerland

Preface

This volume contains the proceedings of the 38th International Conference on Computer Safety, Reliability, and Security (SAFECOMP 2019) held during September 10–13, 2019, in Turku, Finland. The European Workshop on Industrial Computer Systems, Technical Committee 7 on Reliability, Safety, and Security (EWICS TC7), established the SAFECOMP conference series in 1979. It has since contributed considerably to the progress of the state of the art of dependable computer systems and their application in safety-related and safety-critical systems, for the benefit of industry, transport, space systems, health, energy production and distribution, communications, smart environments, buildings, and living. It covers all areas of dependable systems in the Smart World of Things, influencing our everyday life. Embedded systems, cyber-physical systems, (industrial) Internet of Things, autonomous systems, systems-of-systems, safety and cybersecurity, digital society, and transformation are some of the keywords. For all of the ICT upcoming trends, safety, reliability, and security are indispensable, and SAFECOMP addresses them properly from a technical, engineering, and scientific point of view, showing its increasing relevance for today's technology advancements. The special themes of SAFECOMP 2019 were Safety and Security of Autonomous Systems.

We received a good number of high-quality submissions (65), and the international Program Committee (more than 50 members from 14 countries) worked hard to select 21 papers for presentation and publication in the SAFECOMP 2019 proceedings (Springer LNCS 11698). The review process was thorough and each paper was reviewed by at least three independent reviewers. The merits of each paper were evaluated by the Program Committee members during the on-line discussions and face-to-face meetings. Three renowned speakers from the international community were invited to give keynotes: Marco Vieira (University of Coimbra, Portugal) "Trustworthiness Benchmarking of Safety Critical Systems"; Ross Anderson (University of Cambridge, UK) "The Sustainability of Safety, Security and Privacy"; and Jack Weast (Intel, USA) "An Open, Transparent, Industry-Driven Approach to AV Safety". Following tradition, the conference was organized as a single-track event, allowing for intensive networking during breaks and social events, and participation in all presentations and discussions. This year again we had five high-quality workshops running in parallel the day before the main conference: SASSUR – International Workshop on Next Generation of System Assurance Approaches for Safety-Critical Systems, DECSoS – International ERCIM/EWICS/ARTEMIS Workshop on Dependable Smart Embedded Cyber-Physical Systems and Systems-of-Systems, STRIVE – International Workshop on Safety, Security, and Privacy In Automotive systems, WAISE – International Workshop on Artificial Intelligence Safety Engineering, and ASSURE – International Workshop on Assurance Cases for Software-intensive Systems. These workshops covered a diverse range of topics related to safety and security. The proceedings of the workshops are published in a separate SAFECOMP workshop proceedings volume (LNCS 11699).

We would like to express our sincere gratitude to many people whose contributions made SAFECOMP 2019 possible: the authors of the submitted papers and the invited speakers; the Program Committee members and external reviewers; EWICS and the supporting organizations; the sponsors; and last but not least, the local Organization Committee, who took care of the local arrangements, the web-master, and the Publication Chair for finalizing this volume. We hope that the reader will find these proceedings interesting and thought provoking.

September 2019

Alexander Romanovsky
Elena Troubitsyna

Organization

Committees

EWICS TC7 Chair

Francesca Saglietti   University of Erlangen-Nuremberg, Germany

General Chairs and Program Co-chairs

Alexander Romanovsky   Newcastle University, UK
Elena Troubitsyna   KTH Royal Institute of Technology, Sweden
     and Åbo Akademi, Finland

General Workshop Chairs

Ilir Gashi   CSR, City University London, UK
Erwin Schoitsch   AIT Austrian Institute of Technology, Austria

Publication Chair

Friedemann Bitsch   Thales Deutschland GmbH, Germany

Local Organizing Committee

Elena Troubitsyna   Åbo Akademi, Finland
Minna Carla   Åbo Akademi, Finland
Christel Engblom   Åbo Akademi, Finland
Inna Vistbackka   Åbo Akademi, Finland

International Program Committee

Uwe Becker   Draeger Medical GmbH, Germany
Peter G. Bishop   Adelard, UK
Friedemann Bitsch   Thales Deutschland GmbH, Germany
Jean-Paul Blanquart   Airbus Defence and Space, France
Sandro Bologna   Associazione Italiana Esperti Infrastrutture Critiche,
     Italy
Andrea Bondavalli   University of Florence, Italy
Jens Braband   Siemens AG, Germany

Martin Törngren	KTH Royal Institute of Technology, Sweden
Mario Trapp	Fraunhofer Institute for Experimental Software Engineering, Germany
Tullio Vardanega	University of Padua, Italy
Marcel Verhoef	European Space Agency, The Netherlands
Jonny Vinter	RISE Research Institutes of Sweden, Sweden
Hélène Waeselynck	LAAS-CNRS, France

Sub-reviewers

Mehrnoosh Askarpour	Politecnico di Milano, Italy
Zeinab Bakhshi	Mälardalen University, Sweden
Philipp Berger	RWTH Aachen University, Germany
Matthew Fernandez	Intel, Austria
Peter Folkesson	RISE Research Institutes of Sweden, Sweden
Jelena Frtunikj	BMW Group, Germany
Mohammad Gharib	University of Florence, Italy
Tim Gonschorek	Otto-von-Guericke Universität Magdeburg, Germany
Robert Heumüller	Otto-von-Guericke Universität Magdeburg, Germany
Dubravka Ilic	Space Systems Finland Ltd., Finland
Ramneet Kaur	University of Pennsylvania, USA
Björn Leander	Mälardalen University, Sweden
Naveen Mohan	KTH Royal Institute of Technology, Sweden
Sebastian Nielebock	Otto-von-Guericke Universität Magdeburg, Germany
Thomas Noll	RWTH Aachen University, Germany
Viorel Preoteasa	Space Systems Finland Ltd., Finland
Ashur Rafiev	Newcastle University, UK
Clément Robert	LAAS-CNRS, France
Ivan Ruchkin	University of Pennsylvania, USA
Behrooz Sangchoolie	RISE Research Institutes of Sweden, Sweden
Rishad Shafik	Newcastle University, UK
Irfan Sljivo	Mälardalen University, Sweden
Joel Svensson	RISE Research Institutes of Sweden, Sweden
Lars Svensson	KTH Royal Institute of Technology, Sweden
Xin Tao	KTH Royal Institute of Technology, Sweden
Kimmo Varpaaniemi	Space Systems Finland Ltd., Finland
Inna Vistbakka	Åbo Akademi, Finland
Fredrik Warg	RISE Research Institutes of Sweden, Sweden
Teng Zhang	University of Pennsylvania, USA
Xinhai Zhang	KTH Royal Institute of Technology, Sweden

Supporting Institutions

European Workshop on
Industrial Computer Systems –
Reliability, Safety and Security

Kungliga Tekniska högskolan –
Royal Institute of Technology

Newcastle University

Åbo Akademi

Austrian Institute of Technology

City University London

Thales Deutschland GmbH

Intel

Lecture Notes
in Computer Science (LNCS),
Springer Science + Business Media

Austrian Computer Society

ARTEMIS Industry Association

Electronic Components and Systems
for European Leadership - Austria

Verband österreichischer
Software Industrie

European Research
Consortium for Informatics
and Mathematics

Invited Talks

Trustworthiness Benchmarking of Safety Critical Systems

Marco Vieira

University of Coimbra, Portugal
mvieira@dei.uc.pt

Abstract. Some recent incidents and analyses have indicated that possibly the vulnerability of IT systems in railway automation is increasing. Due to several trends, such as digitalization or the use of commercial IT and communication systems the threat potential has increased. This paper discusses the way forward for the railway sector, how many advantages of digitalization can be realized without compromising safety. In particular topics like standardization or certification are covered, but also technical issues like software update.

The Sustainability of Safety, Security and Privacy

Ross Anderson

University of Cambridge, UK
ross.anderson@cl.cam.ac.uk

Abstract. Now that we are putting software and network connections into cars and medical devices, we will have to patch vulnerabilities, as we do with phones. But we can't let vendors stop patching them after three years, as they do with phones. So in May, the EU passed Directive 2019/771 on the sale of goods. This gives consumers the right to software updates for goods with digital elements, for the time period the consumer might reasonably expect. In this talk I'll describe the background, including a study we did for the European Commission in 2016, and the likely future effects. As sustainable safety, security and privacy become a legal mandate, this will create real tension with existing business models and supply chains. It will also pose a grand challenge for computer scientists. What sort of tools and methodologies should you use to write software for a car that will go on sale in 2023, if you have to support security patches and safety upgrades till 2043?

An Open, Transparent, Industry-Driven Approach to AV Safety

Jack Weast

Intel, USA
jack.weast@intel.com

Abstract. At Intel and Mobileye, saving lives drives us. But in the world of automated driving, we believe safety is not merely an impact of AD, but the bedrock on which we all build this industry. And so we proposed Responsibility-Sensitive Safety (RSS), a formal model to define safe driving and what rules an automated vehicle, independent of brand or policy, should abide to always keep its passengers safe. We intend this open, non-proprietary model to drive cross-industry discussion; let's come together as an industry and use RSS as a starting point to clarify safety today, to enable the autonomous tomorrow.

Contents

Interactive Systems and Design Validation

Formal Verification

Towards Zero Alarms in Sound Static Analysis of Finite State Machines

Josselin Giet, Laurent Mauborgne, Daniel Kästner[(✉)],
and Christian Ferdinand

AbsInt GmbH. Science Park 1, 66123 Saarbrücken, Germany
kaestner@absint.com

Abstract. In safety-critical embedded software, the absence of critical code defects has to be demonstrated. One important class of defects are runtime errors caused by undefined or unspecified behavior of the programming language, including buffer overflows or data races. Sound static analyzers can report all such defects in the code (plus some possible false alarms), or prove their absence. A modern sound analyzer is composed of various abstract domains, each covering specific program properties of interest. In this article we present a novel abstract domain developed in the static analyzer Astrée. It automatically detects finite state machines and their state variables, and allows to disambiguate the different states and transitions by partitioning. Experimental results on real-life automotive and aerospace code show that embedded control software using finite state machines can be analyzed with close to zero false alarms, and that the improved precision can reduce analysis time.

1 Introduction

During the past years the size and complexity of embedded software has sharply increased. Contributing factors have been trends to higher levels of automation in various industry domains, cost reduction by shifting functionality from hardware to software, and generic interfaces imposed by standardization frameworks, such as the AUTOSAR architecture for automotive software.

A significant part of embedded software deals with safety-relevant functionality. A failure of a safety-critical system may cause high costs or even endanger human beings. With the growing size of software-implemented functionality, preventing software-induced system failures becomes an increasingly important task. It becomes paramount when fail-operational behavior is required, which is the case for systems providing highly automated driving capability.

One particularly dangerous class of errors are runtime errors due to undefined or unspecified behaviors of the programming language used. Examples are faulty pointer manipulations, numerical errors such as arithmetic overflows and division by zero, data races, and synchronization errors in concurrent software. Such errors can cause software crashes, invalidate separation mechanisms

© Springer Nature Switzerland AG 2019
A. Romanovsky et al. (Eds.): SAFECOMP 2019, LNCS 11698, pp. 3–18, 2019.
https://doi.org/10.1007/978-3-030-26601-1_1

in mixed-criticality software, and are a frequent cause of errors in concurrent and multi-core applications. At the same time, these defects also constitute security vulnerabilities, and have been at the root of a multitude of cybersecurity attacks, in particular buffer overflows, dangling pointers, or race conditions [10].

The absence of such code defects can be shown by abstract interpretation, a formal methodology for semantics-based static program analysis [4]. It supports formal soundness proofs, i.e., it can be proven that no error is missed. Abstract interpretation-based static analyzers provide full control and data coverage and allow conclusions to be drawn that are valid for all program runs with all inputs. Such conclusions may be that no timing or space constraints are violated, or that runtime errors or data races are absent: the absence of these errors can be guaranteed [8]. From a methodological point of view, sound static analyzers can be seen as equivalent to testing with full data and control coverage. Nowadays, abstract interpretation-based static analyzers that can detect stack overflows and violations of timing constraints [9,18] and that can prove the absence of runtime errors and data races [16] are widely used for developing and verifying safety-critical software.

Safety-critical functionality is often related to control-and-command functions. A straightforward way to implement control functions is by using finite state machines, in particular when automatic code generators are used. At the model level formal methods are available which are able to prove correctness properties of such finite state machines. However, at the code level, finite state machines are typically represented by a sequence of if- or switch statements, possibly distributed over many source functions. Since the behavior of the automaton is determined by the transitions and the states, the control flow at the code level becomes dependent on the data flow, in particular on the values of the state variables of the automaton. The values of those variables must therefore be known very precisely for specific control paths. For large-size programs, the abstractions necessary to scale up depend heavily on the structure of the code. That means that when analyzing code generated from state machines, using legacy abstractions, the analysis is either very imprecise or very slow and memory demanding, sometimes both. Hence the required precision used not to be feasible, typically resulting in high false alarm rates.

In this article we present a novel abstract domain for finite state machines, implemented in the abstract interpretation based static analyzer Astrée. The key idea is to keep as much information as if the structure of the state machine was explicitly reflected in the control flow of the program. To achieve that, the new domain keeps, for each possible value of the state, separate abstract values (corresponding to sets of possible values) for all other variables. The main difficulty is that in a modern and precise static analyzer, abstract values contain also memory information and points-to relations which may change how the state is referenced. This is tackled with a dedicated domain tracking changes on the state references. The second difficulty is the efficiency of the approach: keeping separate invariants may be very costly, especially memory-wise. This is mitigated by the data sharing capabilities of Astrée, and the introduction of directives providing explicit control to select the parts of the program for which the state machine abstraction may be relevant. The case distinctions then are only performed when analyzing these parts. These directives can be inserted manually or under control of tailored heuristics.

After a brief overview of related work in Sect. 2 we introduce the concept of abstract interpretation and its application to run-time error analysis in Sect. 3. The structure and design of the analyzer Astrée is illustrated in Sect. 4. Section 5 gives a concrete example to illustrate the challenges of analyzing finite state machine code and the key contribution of our approach. The state machine domain is formally defined in Sect. 6, Sect. 7 sketches its implementation within Astrée. The precision gain and efficiency of the new domain are measured on industrial examples in Sect. 8, Sect. 9 concludes.

2   Related Work

In static analysis, disjunctions have long been observed to be key to precision of the analyses. One of the first practical work on the subject is the development of dynamic partitioning by François Bourdoncle [3], which was implemented for analysing the LUSTRE language, allowing partitions on boolean variables [7]. The main limitation of the approach was scalability. Techniques based on reduced cardinal power of abstract domains [5] were proposed and implemented in [14], allowing dynamic partitions relating boolean variables to numerical variables (still used in Astrée). The main limitation of those works is that they cannot partition memory layout and points-to information, which are parts of the state machine implementation in modern programs.

Another approach consists in verifying properties expressed as state machines. In the typing community, these properties are known as typestate properties [19]. An advanced analysis of such types was proposed by [6], based on flow-insensitive pointer analysis. For large-scale Java programs, CLARA [2] is a framework for specifying and verifying finite-state properties of programs, combining static analysis and insertion of dynamic monitoring code instrumentation. The main limitations of this line of work, compared to our approach, is the need for explicit specifications. Some other lines of work, such as [20] could extract the finite state machines from the code, using machine learning techniques. But such a technique, based on a set of actual executions, may miss rare states, and would only be a first step in providing specifications covering all possible unwanted undefined behaviors of some C or C++ code that Astrée is now able to exclude using the new state machine domain.

3   Abstract Interpretation

The semantics of a programming language is a formal description of the behavior of programs. The most precise semantics is the so-called concrete semantics, describing closely the actual execution of the program on all possible inputs. Yet in general, the concrete semantics is not computable. Even under the assumption that the program terminates, it is too detailed to allow for efficient computations. *Unsound* analyzers may choose to reduce complexity by not taking certain program effects or certain execution scenarios into account. A *sound* analyzer is not allowed to do this; all potential program executions must be accounted for. Since in the concrete semantics this is too complex, the solution is to introduce a formal abstract semantics that approximates the concrete semantics of the program in a well-defined way and still is efficiently computable. This abstract semantics can be chosen as the basis for a static analysis. Compared to an analysis of the concrete semantics, the analysis result may be less precise but the computation may be significantly faster.

Formally, for a given concrete domain D, the abstract semantics require specifying an abstract domain $\mathbb{D}^{\#}$, transfer functions which specify the effect of each statement on the abstract values, and a join function $\sqcup$ which specifies how to compute the union of several abstract values at control flow joins. Together, these functions allow to define the abstract semantics $[\![s]\!]_{\mathcal{A}}^{\#}$ for each statement s. The abstract semantics defines an abstraction function α which converts concrete values into abstract values, the concretization functions γ does the opposite. In order to be able to reason about approximations, the abstract domain must be equipped with a partial order ($a \sqsubseteq b$ means that a is more precise than b). When the abstract domain is a complete lattice which satisfies the ascending chain condition [1], and transfer and join functions are monotonic, the abstraction and concretization functions form a Galois connection [4]. In this case, the definition of the abstract semantics is simplified and the abstract interpretation framework automatically implies termination and soundness of the involved operations [4]. Quite often, though, to be precise enough the abstract domain does not satisfy the ascending chain condition. In such cases, one must also define a widening operator ∇ [4], which ensures termination of all computations in the abstract domain, at the cost of extra approximation. The widening operator may be thought of as a way to introduce extrapolations in the analysis.

4   Sound Static Runtime Error Analysis

In runtime error analysis, *soundness* means that the analyzer never omits to signal an error that can appear in some execution environment. If no potential error is signaled, definitely no runtime error can occur: there are no false negatives. When a *sound* analyzer does not report a division by zero in a/b, this is a proof that b can never be 0. If a potential error is reported, the analyzer cannot exclude that there is a concrete program execution triggering the error. If there is no such execution, this is a false alarm (false positive).

In the following we will concentrate on the sound static runtime error analyzer Astrée [11,17]. Its main purpose is to report program defects caused by unspecified and undefined behaviors according to the C99 norm. The reported code defects include integer/floating-point division by zero, out-of-bounds array indexing, erroneous pointer manipulation and dereferencing (buffer overflows, null pointer dereferencing, dangling pointers, etc.), data races, lock/unlock problems, and deadlocks. The analyzer also computes data and control flow reports containing a detailed listing of accesses to global and static variables sorted by functions, variables, and processes and containing a summary of caller/-called relationships between functions. It reports each effectively shared variable, the list of processes accessing it, and the types of the accesses (read, write, read/write). Astrée is widely used in safety-critical systems, and provides the necessary tool qualification support, including Qualification Support Kits and Qualification Software Life Cycle Data reports. Practical experience on avionics and automotive industry applications are given in [11,13,16]. They show that industry-sized programs of millions of lines of code can be analyzed in acceptable time with high precision for runtime errors and data races.

4.1 Basic Design of Astrée

Astrée uses abstractions to efficiently represent and manipulate over-approximations of program states. One simple example of abstraction used pervasively in Astrée is to consider only the bounds of a numeric variable, forgetting the exact set of possible values within these bounds. However, more complex abstractions can also be necessary, such as tracking linear relationships between numeric variables (which is useful for the precise analysis of loops).

As no single abstraction is sufficient to obtain sufficiently precise results, Astrée is actually built by combining a large set of efficient abstractions. Some of them, such as abstractions of digital filters – and now of finite state machines –, have been developed specifically to analyze control-command software as these constitute an important share of safety-critical embedded software. In addition to numeric properties, Astrée contains abstractions to reason about pointers, pointer arithmetic, structures, arrays (in a field-sensitive or field-insensitive way). Finally, to ensure precision, Astrée keeps a precise representation of the control flow, by performing a fully context-sensitive, flow-sensitive (and even partially path-sensitive) inter-procedural analysis. Combined, the available abstract domains enable a highly precise analysis with low false alarm rates.

Astrée directives, e.g., for specifying range information for inputs, or tailoring the finite state machine domain as described in Sect. 6.2, can be specified in the formal language AAL [12] by locating them in the abstract syntax tree without modifying the source code – a prerequisite for analyzing automatically generated code.

To deal with concurrency defects, Astrée implements a sound low-level concurrent semantics [15] which provides a scalable sound abstraction covering all possible thread interleavings. The interleaving semantics enables Astrée, in addition to the classes of runtime errors found in sequential programs, to report data races, and lock/unlock problems, i.e., inconsistent synchronization. The set of shared variables does not need to be specified by the user: Astrée assumes that every global variable can be shared, and discovers which ones are effectively shared, and on which ones there is a data race. Since Astrée is aware of all locks and spinlocks held for every program point in each concurrent thread, Astrée can also report all potential deadlocks. The analyzer takes task priorities into account and, on multi-core processors, the mapping of tasks to cores.

5   Analyzing State Machines – An Example

Consider the code fragment in Fig. 1a. It implements the state machine described in Fig. 1b whose state is represented by variable state. One major difficulty on this simple code, is to recognize that in state 3, the pointer p always points to the variable state. Using standard abstract domains, we get the result shown in Fig. 2: the analyzer cannot distinguish between individual iterations of the endless loop, it can only compute invariants which hold for any possible loop iteration. That means that the analyzer will (correctly) determine that at the beginning of any iteration of the loop p being either uninitialized (invalid) or pointing to state. After executing the statements of case 0 the value of p did not change, but state can be in 1, 2. After case 1, p points to state, and state must be 3. However, as the information at the beginning of the loop body is imprecise the analyzer cannot infer that when execution reaches case 3, it must have been in case 1 in the previous iteration. Therefore it cannot exclude that p may be invalid and will raise an alarm in line 17 (possibly invalid pointer dereference).

```
1   int *p; int state = 0;
2   while (1) { env_get(&E);
3      switch (state) {
4         case 0:
5            if (E) state = 1;
6            else state = 2;
7            break;
8         case 1:
9            state = 3;
10           p = &state;
11           break;
12        case 2:
13           if (E) state = 0;
14           else state = 1;
15           break;
16        case 3:
17           *p = 4;
18           break;
19        case 4:
20           return;
21     }
22  }
```

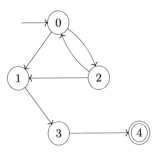

(a) C Code fragment   (b) State machine

Fig. 1. State machine with corresponding C-code implementation

Using the Astrée option for activating the state machine domain (Sect. 6) and indicating that the variable state stores the state of the state machine, Astrée is able prove that the program contains no error (pointer p is always well

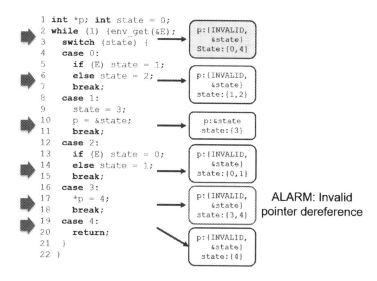

Fig. 2. Result with traditional abstract domains

defined in line 17), and also to precisely know the state after state 3, even though variable state is not directly mentioned in that case.

In addition, activating the option for automatic detection of the state machine (Sect. 7), Astrée can discover by itself the state variable and automatically prove the absence of runtime error on this piece of code.

6 The State Machine Domain

The state machine domain allows us to map each relevant program variable to an own abstract value for every possible value of a state variable in a finite state machine. This works by partitioning the abstract value of the memory domain according to the state variable.

Let us first assume we already have a basic abstraction for sets of memory states, which we assume to be sound and terminating. Such an abstraction introduces an abstract domain that will be referred in the following as the *underlying domain*. We denote this domain $\mathbb{D}^{\#}$, $\top$ its maximal element, $\sqsubseteq$ its approximation partial order, $\sqcup$ its join operator, and ∇ its widening operator (see Sect. 3). The meaning of an abstract element is described by the concretization function γ, such that for any abstract element a, $\gamma(a)$ is the set of memory states represented by a. This is summarized by the following notation:

$$\left(\mathbb{D}^{\#}, \top, \sqsubseteq, \sqcup, \nabla\right) \xrightarrow{\gamma} \left(\mathcal{P}\left(\mathbb{M}\right), \subseteq, \cup\right) \tag{1}$$

In order to formally define the state machine abstract domain, we introduce the sets: $\mathbb{L}$, of expressions of a program which are valid destinations of assignments (left-values), and $\mathbb{V}$, of integer values. Our goal is to define a new abstraction where we can have a separate abstract value of the underlying domain (i.e. a set of memory states) for each integer value that the state variable may take. For reasons of efficiency this partitioning must not be applied in cases where it is not relevant (i.e. when we are outside the scope of a finite machine implementation), or unnecessarily costly. Then the state machine domain $\mathbb{D}_{\mathcal{A}}^{\#}$ is defined as follows:

$$\mathbb{D}_{\mathcal{A}}^{\#} := \left((\mathbb{V} \to \mathbb{D}^{\#}) \times \mathbb{L}\right) \cup \left(\mathbb{D}^{\#} \times \{\top\}\right) \tag{2}$$

An abstract value of the state machine domain is either a value of the underlying abstract domain combined with $\top$ to denote cases when we do not partition. Or it is a function $f^S : \mathbb{V} \to \mathbb{D}^{\#}$, called partitioning function, from integer values to abstract values in the underlying domain, combined with an expression $l \in \mathbb{L}$ that is currently partitioned. Here l is an lvalue of a state variable S, and the integer values in $\mathbb{V}$ are the values S can take. This allows us to have different abstract values in the underlying domain for each different value of S. As mentioned before, the underlying domain is the memory domain which keeps track of the values of all program variables. Hence we can separately keep track of the values of all variables for each possible value of the state variable.

6.1   Abstract Operators

The invariant maintained by the domain is that the image of an integer value s by the partitioning function f^S is an abstract memory state representing abstract values for all variables in the program, but where the only possible value of the state variable S is s. In order to maintain this invariant, we define three new operators, **guard**, **trans** and **forget**, used to compute the abstract semantics of program statements.

The first operator, **guard**, aims at reducing the value of an expression according to a given value. Its purpose is to do an abstract evaluation of the guard in an if-then-else statement, a while loop statement or an assertion statement. We assume $\mathbb{E}$ to be the set of all possible program expressions. Then, for any expression $e \in \mathbb{E}$, value b and abstract value d, **guard**(d, b, e) filters the set of memory states represented by d, keeping only those in which e evaluates to b. Of course, this may introduce approximations.

Let's assume we have an abstract value $d = (f, S)$ with the partitioning function f being defined on values 0 and 1, i.e., S is a state machine variable and we distinguish between program states where it is 0 and 1. Let's further assume that at a given program point we have $f(0) = \{S = 0, x \in [0, 10], ...\}$ and $f(1) = \{S = 1, x \in [5, 8], ...\}$ ("..." represents the values of all other variables, which are irrelevant for the example). If the next statement is **if** (x<2) s1; **else** s2;, then, to determine the abstract memory state in the *then* part, we can apply the guard function **guard**$(d, true, x<2)$ which returns $d' = (f', S)$: f' is a partial function only defined on element 0 with $f'(0) = \{S = 0, x \in [0, 1]\}$ (since $x < 2$). In particular the value $f(1)$ has been filtered out since in that case $x \in [5, 8]$ which is not compatible with the condition. As a consequence, e.g., the analyzer will know that the *then* part can only be executed when the state machine is in state 0.

The second operator we use to compute the abstract semantics is called **trans**. It is needed when performing transitions on the state machine: for any abstract value d and expression ℓ that can be used as left-value, $\mathbf{trans}(d, \ell)$ computes a new abstract value where the different values taken by ℓ are separated (i.e. represented by different underlying abstract values, through use of the **guard** function). Note that d and $\mathbf{trans}(d, \ell)$ represent the same set of concrete values, just the representation is different.

There are two main usages for this operator: when we first want to track a state variable (upon encountering the __ASTREE_states_track directive, see Sect. 6.2), we apply the **trans** operator on an lvalue ℓ of the state variable $(\mathbf{trans}((d, \top), \ell))$ to create f^S, i.e., the partitioning according to the current possible values of the state variable S. In the case that a state variable can take values $\{0, 1\}$ according to the abstract state of the underlying domain, the *trans* operator creates the partitioning $f^S(0) = \{S = 0, ...\}$ and $f^S(1) = \{S = 1, ...\}$. Second, when there is an assignment to a state variable, i.e. the value of the state variable changes inside a partition, the partitioning must be updated and "re-sorted" by computing the appropriate joins, so that the partitioning remains consistent. Changes of state variables are detected by a dedicated domain (see Sect. 7).

The final basic operator needed for the state machine abstract domain is the $\mathbf{forget}(d)$ operator, which simply computes the join of all partitioned abstract values, forgetting the relationships with the state variable. This is useful to keep the domain efficient, and only keep the extra information inside the state machine implementation, where it matters.

For reasons of space we skip the formal definition of the ordering $\sqsubseteq_A$, the join $\sqcup_A$ and the widening ∇_A operators of the partitioning domain. The termination properties of the widening operator can be proven assuming we put a limit on the number of partitions (corresponding to a limit on the number of states of the underlying state machine), and assuming there can be only a finite number of expressions seen during a given program analysis. Note that such limits are enforced independently of the number of states actually declared or automatically found (see Sect. 7): any statement that would lead to more states than the limit is handled as **forget**.

6.2 Abstract Semantics

Semantics for Atomic Statements. The abstract semantics of atomic statements (such as assignments) on partitioned abstract values consists in applying the semantics of the underlying domain to each sub-value, and to reapply the partitioning according to the variable using **trans**. In the case of a *top* value, the underlying semantics is simply applied to the value.

$$[\![s]\!]_A^{\#} (d, \top) \longmapsto \left([\![s]\!]^{\#}(d), \top \right) \tag{3}$$

$$[\![s]\!]_A^{\#} (v \mapsto d_v, \ell) \longmapsto \mathbf{trans} \left(v \mapsto [\![s]\!]^{\#}(d_v), \ell \right) \tag{4}$$

When the statement s does not make any assignment to the expression we do not have to make any repartitioning, hence the simplified formula:

$$\llbracket s \rrbracket_{\mathcal{A}}^{\#} (v \mapsto d_v, \ell) = \left(v \mapsto \llbracket s \rrbracket^{\#}(d_v), \ell \right) \tag{5}$$

Directives for the Partitioning Domain. Moreover we add two new directives, that do not have any effect on the concrete semantics, but trigger the partition in the new domain:

- `__ASTREE_states_track((` ℓ `));`, where $\ell \in \mathbb{L}$, and
- `__ASTREE_states_merge(());`

The effect of `__ASTREE_states_track((` ℓ `));` in the abstract domain is simply to apply the **trans** function. So, given an abstract value d, it returns **trans**(d, ℓ). The variable given as argument is the new state variable that controls the partitioning.

The directive `__ASTREE_states_merge(());` is used in order to stop a partitioning by merging all partitioned sub-values. Given an abstract value d, it returns **forget**(d).

Semantics for Complex Statements. For non atomic statements (e.g., conditionals, loops, statements blocks), we follow the basic framework of abstract interpretation (Fig. 3).

$$\llbracket s_1 s_2 \ldots s_n \rrbracket_{\mathcal{A}}^{\#}(d) = \left(\llbracket s_n \rrbracket_{\mathcal{A}}^{\#} \circ \cdots \circ \llbracket s_2 \rrbracket_{\mathcal{A}}^{\#} \circ \llbracket s_1 \rrbracket_{\mathcal{A}}^{\#} \right)(d) \tag{6}$$

$$\llbracket \texttt{if}(e)\{s_t\}\{s_f\} \rrbracket_{\mathcal{A}}^{\#}(d) = \llbracket s_t \rrbracket_{\mathcal{A}}^{\#} (\textbf{guard}_{\mathcal{A}}(e, true, d))$$
$$\sqcup_{\mathcal{A}} \llbracket s_f \rrbracket_{\mathcal{A}}^{\#} (\textbf{guard}_{\mathcal{A}}(e, false, d)) \tag{7}$$

$$\llbracket \texttt{while}(e)\{s\} \rrbracket_{\mathcal{A}}^{\#}(d) = \textbf{guard}_{\mathcal{A}} \left(e, false, \lim_n d_n \right)$$
$$\text{where } d_n \text{ is } \begin{cases} d_0 = d \\ d_{n+1} = d_n \nabla_{\mathcal{A}} \llbracket s \rrbracket_{\mathcal{A}}^{\#} (g_n) \end{cases} \tag{8}$$
$$\text{and } g_n = \textbf{guard}_{\mathcal{A}} (e, true, d_n)$$

Fig. 3. Abstract semantics for complex statements

The abstract semantics of a sequence of statements is defined as applying the abstract semantics of each statement in order. In case of a conditional statement we apply the semantics of the statements in the *then*-part (resp. *else*-part) on the abstract value compatible with evaluating the condition to *true* (resp. *false*) and compute the join of the results. The most intricate statement is the while loop statement: on the abstract, the semantics of the statement is computed as the least fixpoint for the function which takes an abstract value d_n (representing the accumulated set of possible states at the head of the loop), refine it so that it only represents concrete states on which the loop guard is true (using the **guard** operator, yielding g_n), then apply the abstract semantics of the loop body ($[\![s]\!]_A^{\#}$). The new value is compared to the value accumulated in the previous iteration d_n, using the widening operator ∇_A to extrapolate to d_{n+1}. The sequence $d_0, d_1, \ldots, d_n, \ldots$ is guaranteed to reach a fixpoint, which we call $\lim_n d_n$, and on which we can apply the loop guard again to only keep those states on which the guard evaluates to false, which are those leaving the loop.

The proof that the abstract interpretation in the partitioning domain $\mathbb{D}_A^{\#}$ terminates and is sound is by induction over the syntax of the program. The interesting case is the one for the atomic statements, and it is a straightforward consequence of the soundness of the abstract interpretation in the underlying domain and the soundness of the **trans** operator.

6.3 Putting It Together

The result of the analysis using the FSM domain on the working example of Sect. 5 is shown in Fig. 4. Let's call an abstract value of the underlying memory domain an *environment*. Using the heuristics described in Sect. 7, the analyzer automatically detects the finite state machine in the code and is aware that the variable state represents its states. Therefore it maintains a full partitioning of state which means that it keeps a separate environment for each possible value of state. The environment includes full information about the abstract value of all relevant program variables. In particular, this allows the analyzer to

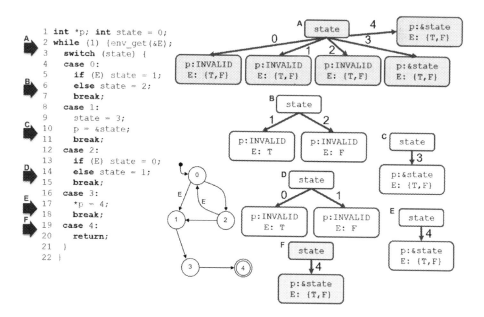

Fig. 4. Result with novel FSM domains

be aware of the fact that when state is 3 at the beginning of a loop iteration, p must point to state. Figure 4 depicts this partitioning, i.e. the environments associated with every possible value of state at the beginning of the loop (A), immediately before the **break** statement in each switch case (B-E), and immediately before the **return** (F). More precisely, the tree structures of Fig. 4 represent the partitioning functions. For example, the tree shown at location (B) represents the abstract value $d = (f, \texttt{state})$, where state is the state machine variable, and f a partitioning function such that $f(1)$ is the abstract memory value (i.e. the environment) in which state is 1, p is *invalid* and E is *true*. $f(2)$ is the abstract memory value in which state is 2, p is *invalid* and E is *false*.

7   Implementation

As described in Sect. 4, Astrée combines a lot of abstract domains to achieve precision, parameterization and efficiency. There is a global hierarchy in the implementation, which determines what kind of information each domain may access, and what level of abstraction they can use.

The State Machine Domain builds on the Memory Layout Domain, which abstracts memory locations and pointer information, and associates memory locations to unique keys. All value domains only see the keys and compute sets of possible values for those keys. A dedicated helper value domain tracks which keys must be considered as state machine variables, and warns the State Machine Domain when such a variable is modified. Then, and only then, does the State Machine Domain trigger a call to **trans**, which is key to the efficient implementation for that domain.

While state machine state variables can be declared by an end-user using a simple directive, we always aim at the maximum automation of Astrée. In order to avoid this end-user declaration, we also have implemented automatic discovery of state machine state variables. It works in the following way:

– Identify integer variables used in switch statements
– keep those variables which are also assigned in at least one case of the switch, possibly following function calls
– keep only the switch statements appearing inside possibly infinite loops

That heuristics captures some commonly generated state machines, and allows for a fully automatic and precise analysis of codes using this pattern. When the heuristics misses a state machine, the analysis will just miss the expected precision gain, which can still be achieved using directives. When the heuristics wrongly identifies a state machine, if the number of supposed states is small enough, the analysis will just be imprecise, and if the number of supposed states exceeds a built-in threshold, it will be rejected by the heuristics. Generalizing the heuristics to cover more complex patterns is subject of future work.

8   Experimental Results

We have tested our approach on multiple examples. The summary of these experiments is displayed in Table 1. In this table, we used the following notations:

- (∗) means the state machine variable was automatically detected by Astrée,
- (I) denotes industrial code (avionics/automotive),
- (TL) denotes code generated by TargetLink,
- (Sc) denotes code generated by SCADE.

Table 1. Experimental results

Benchmark	Code size (LOC)	#Errors		#Alarms		Memory		Time		#States max
		wo/	w/	wo/	w/	wo/	w/	wo/	w/	
B1 (I)	348 530	1	0	45	4	814	424	24′34″	9″	4
B2 (I)(∗)	11 646	2	2	82	80	482	647	5′22″	8′50″	3
B3 (TL)	2 335	0	0	34	34	215	230	16″	3′15″	24
B4 (Sc)	4 442	0	0	15	3	156	159	2″	3″	3
B5 (I)(Sc)	8 733	0	0	57	48	173	243	6″	30″	14
B6 (I)	2 044 805	6	6	1787	1787	12 729	15 167	4h07′	3h32′	4

The tables indicates the code size measured in lines of preprocessed code without comments and blank lines, the number of states discovered, as well as the number of alarms, definite runtime errors, time and memory consumption with vs. without finite state machine domain. For reasons of confidentiality we cannot disclose further information about the industrial examples.

8.1   Number of Errors and Alarms

The performance of the abstract interpretation is strongly correlated with the place of the state machine in the code. For example, in the second benchmark, the state machine is only a small part of the code. On the contrary, in the first example the state machine is central in the design of the code.

At this point, one has to make a remark about the difference between alarms and errors raised by Astrée. In Astrée, an error is raised when all traces in an abstract value leads to a definite run-time-error. In the first example the error disappears since with the finite state domain Astrée is able to recognize that the context leading to the definite alarm was infeasible, i.e., it was actually a false alarm.

The performance also depends on the explicitness of the transitions. Indeed, in the third example all transitions are explicitly guarded. Therefore no improvements are made in the analysis since the partitioning previously performed by Astrée is enough to handle the state machine.

In order to determine the false alarm rate in the code parts related to finite state machines, we performed a manual review of code and findings. The result is that with the state machine domain, all alarms related to the implemented state machine could be disproved by the automatic analysis in all investigated benchmarks. In the last example, the state machine implementation did not induce any alarm in the analysis, which explains why we get the same number of alarms with and without the state machine domain activated.

8.2 Efficiency

As expected, the required analysis time typically increases, and the observed increase depends on the number of combined states possible at a given program location during the run of the program. For example, the third and fifth examples show that such an increase can be significant. Still, the local approach achieved with our abstract domain is much more efficient than a full partitioning of the control flow. This is confirmed by experiment $B6$, which shows that activating the finite state domain is feasible for code sized above 2 million lines of preprocessed C code.

On the other hand, in the first and sixth example we observe a significant decrease of analysis time. The reason of that is a reduction in the size of the state space Astrée has to explore to cover all possible program behaviors, and thus be sound. The increased precision allows Astrée to exclude infeasible paths it could not recognize as infeasible before. In particular, in the latter case, the finite state domain does not reduce the number of alarms, but there is still a positive effect due to the reduction in analysis time.

In general, the memory needed for the analysis increases when we do an analysis with state partitioning. In the benchmarks under investigation the maximum observed increase in RAM usage is 40% ($B5$), with RAM usage decreasing by 48% in $B1$. The moderate increase in memory consumption illustrates how the intrinsic sharing enforced by Astrée allows for keeping memory overhead low, validating our approach.

9 Conclusion

The work described in this paper solves the long-standing problem of statically analyzing finite state machines at the C code level. In the past, due to a lack of efficient abstractions, static analyzers suffered from high false alarm rates and/or high analysis complexity. This article presents a novel abstract domain which allows a highly precise analysis of finite state machines implemented in C programs. State variables can be automatically detected, and are disambiguated by state partitioning in the relevant program scope. The novel abstract domain is sound and enables highly efficient implementations, making the analysis applicable on large-scale industry-size software projects. Experimental results with the static analyzer Astrée on real-life software confirm both the precision and the efficiency of our approach.

References

1. Atiyah, M.F., Macdonald, I.G.: Introduction to Commutative Algebra. Addison-Wesley (1969)
2. Bodden, E.: Verifying finite-state properties of large-scale programs. Ph.D. thesis, McGill University (2009)
3. Bourdoncle, F.: Abstract interpretation by dynamic partitioning. J. Funct. Program. **2**(4), 407–423 (1992)
4. Cousot, P., Cousot, R.: Abstract interpretation: a unified lattice model for static analysis of programs by construction or approximation of fixpoints. In: Proceedings of POPL 1977, pp. 238–252. ACM Press (1977)
5. Cousot, P., Cousot, R.: Systematic design of program analysis frameworks. In: 6th POPL, pp. 269–282. ACM Press, San Antonio (1979)
6. Fink, S.J., Yahav, E., Dor, N., Ramalingam, G., Geay, E.: Effective typestate verification in the presence of aliasing. ACM Trans. Softw. Eng. Methodol. **17**(2), 9:1–9:34 (2008)
7. Jeannet, B.: Dynamic partitioning in linear relation analysis: application to the verification of reactive systems. Formal Methods Syst. Des. **23**(1), 5–37 (2003)
8. Kästner, D.: Applying abstract interpretation to demonstrate functional safety. In: Boulanger, J.-L. (ed.) Formal Methods Applied to Industrial Complex Systems. ISTE/Wiley, London (2014)
9. Kästner, D., Ferdinand, C.: Proving the absence of stack overflows. In: Bondavalli, A., Di Giandomenico, F. (eds.) SAFECOMP 2014. LNCS, vol. 8666, pp. 202–213. Springer, Cham (2014). https://doi.org/10.1007/978-3-319-10506-2_14
10. Kästner, D., Mauborgne, L., Ferdinand, C.: Detecting safety- and security-relevant programming defects by sound static analysis. In: Rainer Falk, J.-C.B., Chan, S. (eds.) The Second International Conference on Cyber-Technologies and Cyber-Systems (CYBER 2017). IARIA Conferences, vol. 2, pp. 26–31. IARIA XPS Press (2017)
11. Kästner, D., et al.: Finding all potential runtime errors and data races in automotive software. In: SAE World Congress 2017. SAE International (2017)
12. Kästner, D., Pohland, J.: Program analysis on evolving software. In: Roy, M. (ed.) CARS 2015 - Critical Automotive Applications: Robustness & Safety, France, Paris (2015)
13. Kästner, D., Schmidt, B., Schlund, M., Mauborgne, L., Wilhelm, S., Ferdinand, C.: Analyze this! sound static analysis for integration verification of large-scale automotive software. In: Proceedings of the SAE World Congress WCX2019 (SAE Technical Paper). SAE International (2019)
14. Mauborgne, L.: Astrée: verification of absence of runtime error. In: Jacquart, R. (ed.) Building the Information Society. IIFIP, vol. 156, pp. 385–392. Springer, Boston, MA (2004). https://doi.org/10.1007/978-1-4020-8157-6_30
15. Miné, A.: Static analysis of run-time errors in embedded real-time parallel C programs. Logical Methods Comput. Sci. (LMCS) **8**(26), 63 (2012)
16. Miné, A., Delmas, D.: Towards an industrial use of sound static analysis for the verification of concurrent embedded avionics software. In: Proceedings of the 15th International Conference on Embedded Software (EMSOFT 2015), pp. 65–74. IEEE CS Press, October 2015
17. Miné, A., et al.: Taking static analysis to the next level: proving the absence of run-time errors and data races with Astrée. Embedded Real Time Software and Systems Congress ERTS^2 (2016)

18. Souyris, J., Le Pavec, E., Himbert, G., Jégu, V., Borios, G., Heckmann, R. : Computing the worst case execution time of an avionics program by abstract interpretation. In: Proceedings of the 5th International Workshop on Worst-Case Execution Time (WCET) Analysis, pp. 21–24 (2005)
19. Strom, R.E., Yemini, S.: Typestate: a programming language concept for enhancing software reliability. IEEE Trans. Software Eng. **12**(1), 157–171 (1986)
20. Walkinshaw, N., Taylor, R., Derrick, J.: Inferring extended finite state machine models from software executions. Empirical Softw. Eng. **21**(3), 811–853 (2016)

Graceful Degradation Design Process for Autonomous Driving System

Tasuku Ishigooka[1]([✉]), Satoshi Otsuka[1], Kazuyoshi Serizawa[2], Ryo Tsuchiya[2], and Fumio Narisawa[2]

[1] Research and Development Group, Hitachi Ltd., Tokyo, Japan
`tasuku.ishigoka.kc@hitachi.com`
[2] Hitachi Automotive Systems Ltd., Tokyo, Japan

Abstract. An autonomous driving system requires the safety and availability of automated driving. For example, an autonomous driving system with automation level 3 requires the functions to request the driver to take over driving and to sustain safe automated driving until the driver accepts the request if a hardware failure occurs. However, there is a demand to continue automated driving if the system maintains sufficient performance for automated driving after the failure occurs. Therefore, we propose a graceful degradation design process to improve the automated driving continuation rate by defining degradation functions against performance limitation and hardware failure. The process integrates and extends ISO/PAS 21448 and ISO26262 and carries out these tasks in the order of system-level, ECU-level, and microcontroller-level degradation design. Furthermore, we propose a framework to calculate worst-case mode switch time (WCMST), which means the time duration from failure detection to degradation processing, by utilizing degradation design results. To evaluate the proposed process and framework, we applied them to the prototype system with automation level 3. The evaluation results showed that the designed system can sustain automated driving against 86.1% of performance degradation factors and that the framework can improve the calculation accuracy of WCMST by 35.3%.

Keywords: Graceful degradation · Autonomous driving · Fail-operational

1 Introduction

An autonomous driving (AD) system requires a fail-operational function, that sustains safe automated driving and stop the vehicle in a safe place, if a failure occurs during automated driving. The functions that the system requires are defined by SAE J3016 as automation levels according to the driver assistance level [1].

For example, an AD system with automation level 3 (AD-Lv3) requires a fail-operational function to request the driver to take over driving if a hardware

A. Romanovsky et al. (Eds.): SAFECOMP 2019, LNCS 11698, pp. 19–34, 2019.
https://doi.org/10.1007/978-3-030-26601-1_2

failure occurs. If the request is accepted by the driver, the autonomous driving operation of the system will terminate. If the request is denied due to time-out, the system with AD-Lv4 has to guarantee safety. For example, the system moves the vehicle to a safe place and stops. In this paper, we assume even AD-Lv3 supplies safety functions like the above for a frequently encountered part of the specific driving situation.

Meanwhile, as the system consists of multiple sensors and a microcontroller (MC), an increase of the frequency of hardware failure occurrence may cause a decrease of availability. Therefore, if failure propagation is protected and the system still has sufficient performance to guarantee safe automated driving, continuation of automated driving is demanded instead of requests to take over driving or stop the vehicle in a safe place.

As a method to select degradation functions (DFs) according to the running system performance, graceful degradation is proposed [2]. The DF provides a limited function compared with a full function executed in the normal state. The system with graceful degradation monitors its own running performance. If it detects a failure of hardware such as sensors, actuators, and electronic control units (ECUs), it selects a DF (the execution condition of which can be satisfied by the current system performance) from candidates and carries out the function [3]. Graceful degradation enables the improvement of availability while guaranteeing safety by selecting the DF with the highest performance among the candidates. Graceful degradation is mainly studied in the avionics domain [4] and recently has been studied in the automotive domain [5].

The factors that reduce system performance are classified as hardware failure or performance limitation of sensors, actuators, and algorithms. In the automotive domain, safe design against hardware failure is performed according to the functional safety standard ISO26262 [6]. Most fail-operational architectures apply at least double modular redundancy to sensors, actuators, network buses, ECUs, and power supply devices. Furthermore, regarding ECUs, the AD function executed in the normal state and the DF executed after a failure are allocated to different ECUs [7]. For example, if the autonomous driving ECU (AD-ECU) for AD-Lv3 fails, another ECU with a DF submits the request to take over driving, sustains driving while waiting for takeover acceptance, and stops in a safe place if the request is denied by time-out, and so on. On the other hand, in the automotive domain, safety design against performance limitation is performed according to ISO/PAS 21448 [8]. This standard defines the analytic process for the performance degradation of the sensor, actuator, and algorithm caused by the weather and road conditions. Furthermore, it defines the process to improve the system specification by adding a sensor or updating the algorithm to prevent performance degradation.

To achieve the coexistence of safety and availability in the AD system, graceful degradation taking into account both hardware failure and performance limitation is necessary. A design methodology for ISO26262 and ISO/PAS21448 has already been proposed [9]. However, it does not focus on graceful degradation.

Therefore, we propose a graceful degradation design process against hardware fault and performance limitation.

The proposed process consists of system-level, ECU-level, and MC-level degradation design. In system-level degradation design, DFs against performance limitation and DFs against hardware fault of sensors and ECUs are independently defined. After that, DFs against the combination of both are defined. Consequently, all of the DFs for an AD system can be defined. In ECU-level degradation design, DFs against ECU internal hardware failure are defined. For example, DFs are clarified for when a failure of an MC among multiple MCs occurs or when multiple sensor inputs stop due to an Ethernet switch failure. In MC-level degradation design, defined DFs and a function to select a DF according to the failure factor are designed. Thus, the process enables the development of an AD system based on graceful degradation with safety and availability by analyzing multiple factors causing performance degradation and defining DFs against these factors.

ISO26262 requires evidence about that mode switch time, which shows the duration time from failure detection to DF execution, and the mode switch must finish by the deadline. An existing method [10] based on execution flow can calculate WCMST. However, the calculated WCMST is pessimistic because the combination of the failure factor and the DF may not actually happen. To analyze the actual combination and calculate the WCMST, a method using model checker is proposed [11]. But, if the WCMST does not satisfy the deadline, the re-designing efforts may be huge because the function specification and software design must be changed.

Therefore, we propose a framework that enables accurate calculation of the WCMST by utilizing state machine information of degradation design results. In particular, the framework finds failure factors requiring maximum fault detection time at each MC for each DFs. Then, it determines the WCMST by comparing the mode switch time of each factors. The major contributions of our paper are as follows:

(i) AD system concept based on graceful degradation
(ii) graceful degradation design process for AD system
(iii) integration of proposed process into ISO26262 and ISO/PAS21448
(iv) calculation framework of WCMST
(v) evaluation results through the AD-Lv3 prototype

In Sect. 2, we present the proposed design process. In Sect. 3, we explain the detail of the calculation framework of WCMST. In Sect. 4, we explain the evaluation result through a case study using the AD-Lv3 prototype. In Sect. 5, we conclude with a brief summary and mention future work.

2   Graceful Degradation Design Process

In this section, we explain the proposed AD system concept based on graceful degradation and the design process.

2.1 Autonomous Driving System Concept with Graceful Degradation

In this section, we present the AD system concept based on graceful degradation against performance limitation and hardware failure. The concept improves availability because the system can sustain automated driving instead of requesting the driver to take over or stopping in a safe place if performance limitation or hardware failure occurs.

In this paper, we classify performance limitation and failure as different events. The reason is that performance limitation is an event (such as certain weather or a road condition) that lead to a transient state, but hardware failure is an event that leads to permanent state. Regarding temporary failure of the hardware such as neutron ray, we assume that it is masked or corrected. Furthermore, regarding software failure, the factors are eliminated at the development process.

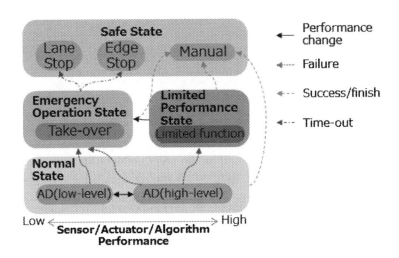

Fig. 1. System concept based on graceful degradation

We show the system concept by using a state machine diagram, as shown in Fig. 1. This figure shows the system behavior expressed by a hierarchical state machine, which consists of four groups. They are safe state (SS), guaranteeing safety from the AD point of view, normal state (NS), running by automated driving without failures, limited performance state (LP), running by automated driving with failures, and emergency operation state (EO), moving to SS due to failures. States that execute a DF for performance limitation are defined as a lower layer of NS.

For example, in AD-Lv3, if a performance limitation or a hardware failure occurs and the system requires the driver to take over driving, the system state changes from *AD state* of NS to *take-over waiting state* of EO. If the driver accepts the request, the system state transit from EO to *manual driving state* of SS. If the driver does not accept within the deadline, the system state transit to *safe stop state* of EO.

On the other hand, if the system can sustain automated driving after the failure occurs, the system state transit from NS to LP. Consequently, the proposed concept can guarantee both safety and availability by utilizing LP.

2.2   Clarification of Factors to Transit to EO

This section clarifies the factors to transit to EO. As mentioned in the previous section, the EO of AD-Lv3 requires sustaining automated driving during the takeover procedure to a driver. In this paper, the effects of performance limitation or a hardware failure are classified into two groups: effects that immediately complicate the automated driving or effects that complicate the arrival at the destination although guaranteeing the automated driving.

An example of a factor that causes the former effect is performance degradation caused by a single point of failure of a mission-critical sensor, such as a camera, for the automated driving or a performance limitation. A safety measure is required against performance limitation and hardware failure because EO cannot be achieved if the automated driving is difficult. In this paper, we assume that the system applies heterogeneous redundant sensors and ECUs against performance limitation and hardware failure caused by mission-critical factors. Furthermore, we do not focus on an additional failure after a failure occurs because the frequency of this occurring is negligibly small [6]. The definition of DF for the redundant system is presented in Sect. 2.3.

An example of a factor to cause the latter effect is hardware failure of sensors, such as the GNSS, or hardware failure of the ECU to provide map information. In this case, the redundant design is not mandatory in AD-Lv3 because the automated driving can continue for a short duration. However, the system must take over the driving operation to the driver by EO because it cannot receive the map information to arrive at the destination.

2.3   Proposed Design Process

We propose a graceful degradation design process according to the concept mentioned in Sect. 2.1. Figure 2 shows an overview of the proposed design process. This process consists of system-level, ECU-level, and MC-level degradation design phases. The process proceeds by stages in the order of DF definition, clarification of state transition condition, and DF implementation.

The system-level degradation design independently defines DFs against performance limitation and against hardware failure of sensors, acutuators, and ECUs. Subsequently, DFs against both are defined. The DFs of an AD system are determined by integrating each defined DF. The ECU-level degradation design defines DFs against ECU internal hardware failure and verifies that the WCMST satisfies the deadline. The MC-level degradation design defines the failure factor that causes MC failure by analyzing MC internal failure and updates the state machine developed by system-level and ECU-level design. The state machine is implemented as a state management module to select a DF according to the detected hardware fault.

The details of each design process are explained by using an example of AD-Lv3 for highway from next subsection.

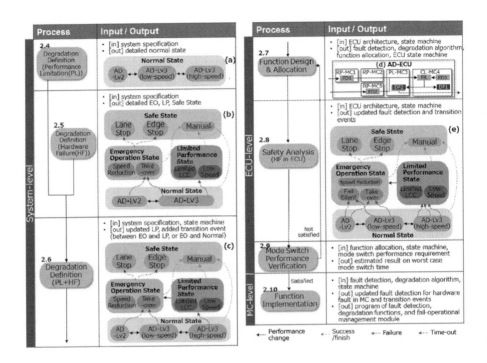

Fig. 2. Proposed design process

2.4   System-Level Degradation Process: Degradation Definition Against Performance Limitation

The AD system recognizes lane and other vehicle by camera and measures the distance from them by Lidar or Radar. It provides automated driving by collision avoidance by controlling steering and braking according to the traffic condition. The performance limitation of these sensors, recognition algorithm, and actuator may occur according to the weather or road conditions. According to ISO/PAS 21448 [8], the factors triggering performance limitation are bad weather, such as fog, rain, and snow, or bad road conditions such as faint white lines and tunnels.

Table 1 shows the characteristics of major sensors for AD systems. For example, the camera can recognize objects that are far away. However, the performance decreases due to bad weather. On the other hand, Radar is not affected by weather. Radar is useful to accurately measure the distance from obstacle, but has problems to classify objects or recognize lane position. Thus, a sensor alone cannot handle various driving situations. Therefore, the AD system has redundant sensors by using different sensors for all directions to complement the characteristics of each other.

Table 1. Example of sensor characteristic

Target	Recognition classification	Range	Weather condition		Road condition	
			Bad weather (fog, rain, snow)	Bad condition (backlit, reflection)	Bad road (faint white lane)	Tunnel
Camera	object, lane, signal, obstacle distance	middle or far	range decrease	noise	difficult to detect	--
Lidar	obstacle distance	middle or far	range decrease	--	--	--
Radar	obstacle distance	middle or far	--	--	--	--
Sonar	obstacle distance	near	range decrease	--	--	--
Surround Camera	lane, obstacle distance	near	range decrease	noise	difficult to detect	--
GNSS	location	--	--	--	--	noise

Table 2. Example of impact analysis matrix

(a) Part of Impact Analysis Matrix for Performance Limitation   -- : none

Situation	Performance Degradation Device	Sensing Direction	Change of Performance			Degradation Function (in NS or EO)
			Map Update	Obstacle Detection / Sensing Range	Lane Detection / Sensing Range	
Fog	Camera	Front	--	Radar / --	Camera / short	AD-Lv3(low-speed)
Fog	Camera	Left or Right	--	Radar / --	--	--
Fog	Camera	Rear	--	Radar / --	--	--
Tunnel	GNSS	--	-- (supported by odometry)	--	--	--

(b) Part of Impact Analysis Matrix for Hardware Failure

Failed Device	Sensing Direction	Change of Performance			Degradation Function (in LP or EO)
		Map Update	Obstacle Detection / Sensing Range	Lane Detection / Sensing Range	
Front Camera	Front	--	Lidar / Short	Side Camera / Short	AD-Lv3(low-speed)
Left or Right Camera	Left or Right	--	Lidar / --	--	--
Rear Camera	Rear	--	--	--	--
GNSS	--	stop	--	--	EO

(c) Part of Impact Analysis Matrix for Hardware failure and Performance Limitation

Situation	Performance Degradation Device	Failed Device	Sensing Direction	Change of Performance			Degradation Function (in PL or EO)
				Map Update	Obstacle Detection / Sensing Range	Lane Detection / Sensing Range	
Fog	Camera, Lidar	Front Radar	Front	--	Lidar / short	Camera / short	EO
			Left or Right		Radar / --	--	
			Rear		Radar / --	--	
Fog	Camera, Lidar	Left or Right Radar	Front	--	Radar / --	Camera / short	AD-Lv3(low-speed without automatic lane change)
			Left or Right		Lidar / short	--	
			Rear		Radar / --	--	
Fog	Camera, Lidar	Rear Radar	Front	--	Radar / --	Camera / short	AD-Lv3(low-speed)
			Left or Right		Radar / --	--	
			Rear		Lidar / short	--	

To define DF against performance limitation, we focus on the kinds of sensors and sensing direction of a target system architecture. We analyze the change of recognition contents or range in each direction against each factor causing performance limitation and define DFs if necessary (see Table 2(a)).

For example, in an AD system whose both camera and Radar sense the front of an ego vehicle, if the weather is fog, as the Radar is not affected, the AD system selects automated driving based on Radar. However, the camera can only recognize white lanes that are a short distance away due to the fog. Therefore, the AD system needs a DF for driving at a low speed to avoid the situation when the traffic lane deviates during a sharp curve.

We can define DFs against performance limitation by analyzing all sensing directions in all situations. Weather or road conditions may recover during automated driving. Therefore, states to execute DFs against performance limitation are sub-states of NS (see Fig. 2(a)).

2.5   System-Level Degradation Process: Degradation Definition Against Hardware Failure

As mentioned in Sect. 2.2, to continue automated driving after the failure occurs, hardware redundancy is necessary. For example, regarding sensors, redundant heterogeneous sensors are applied, as mentioned in Sect. 2.4. Furthermore, the AD-ECU also must be redundant. In this step, DFs against hardware failure of sensors and ECUs are defined.

A sensor failure may affect recognition distance or content. However, the effect of the failure is prevented by the redundant sensor; otherwise the effect occurs. Moreover, if the vehicle is equipped with sensors of the same kind, the required DFs depend on the sensing direction, such as the front, left, right, and rear of the vehicle. Therefore, the definition of DFs is conducted by taking into account the sensing direction affected by each sensor failure (see Table 2(b)).

In particular, the system sensing the front by camera and Lidar conducts the automated driving by using a camera with a long recognition distance in NS. If a camera failure occurs, the system can sustain automated driving by using Lidar for front obstacle detection. However, as the recognition distance becomes shorter, the DF to reduce the speed according to the changed recognition distance is necessary for collision avoidance. For lane detection for sustaining automated driving, the side camera or rear camera can be substituted for the front camera.

In the system duplicated by AD-ECU and degradation ECU, if the failure of AD-ECU occurs, the AD function degrades. For example, if the failure of AD-ECU with passing function occurs, the degradation ECU without the passing function sustains the automated driving for EO. If the failure occurs during passing a vehicle, the degradation ECU does not work because of the impossible situation. Therefore, a DF to fill the function gap is necessary. For example, the trajectory information of AD-ECU is stored as backup in the degradation ECU in NS. If the failure of AD-ECU occurs, the backup is utilized until the automated driving of the degradation ECU is available.

2.6   System-Level Degradation Design: Degradation Definition Against Performance Limitation and Hardware Failure

In Sects. 2.4 and 2.5, DFs against performance limitation and hardware fault are defined independently. In this section, DFs for both are defined. The important point of the analysis is to define DFs when the failure of one of the redundant sensors occurs when the performance of the other sensor is degraded (see Table 2(c)).

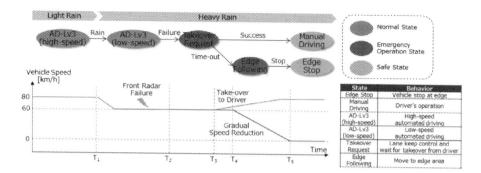

Fig. 3. Example of degradation function against performance limitation and hardware failure

For example, in a system sensing the front by camera and Radar, if the performance degradation of the camera due to heavy rain while driving on the highway occurs, the system switches to automated driving based on Radar and conducts a DF to reduce speed according to the sensing distance (T_1 of Fig. 3). Furthermore, if the failure of the front Radar occurs during low-speed automated driving, the system must drive at a slower speed because the system must rely on the degraded camera. However, this produces an unacceptable risk of rear-end collision. Hence, the system decides to request the driver to take over driving (T_2 of Fig. 3). If the take-over request is accepted, the operation becomes manual driving by the driver (T_3 of Fig. 3). On the other hand, if the request is not accepted by the deadline, the system will stop at the edge of the road (T_4 and T_5 of Fig. 3).

The state machine of the system is established by integrating the DFs defined in this section, Sects. 2.4, and 2.5 (see Fig. 2(c)).

2.7 ECU Level Degradation Design: Function Design and Allocation

The AD function and DFs are implemented in AD-ECU or the degradation ECU. In this step, before the definition of DF against ECU internal hardware failure, we design the algorithm of DFs and allocate each DF to the MC.

In this paper we assume that AD-ECU consists of MCs called RP-MC, PL-MC, and CL-MC. For example, RP-MC performs recognition processing for camera, Lidar, or Radar, and failure detection (FD) for the hardware of sensors and other ECUs. PL-MC performs a function to integrate recognition results, localization, trajectory generation, and DFs. CL-MC performs a decision-making function to select a DF as fault reaction (FR) if performance limitation or hardware failure occurs. Furthermore, CL-MC performs a function to translate the trajectory information to control command for the actuators (see Fig. 2(d)). The degradation ECU may consist of an MC because the ECU has minimum functions.

2.8 ECU Level Degradation Design: ECU Safety Analysis

In this section, DFs against ECU internal hardware failure are defined. The analysis target is an ECU internal device such as the communication bus between sensor and MC, the bus between MCs, a network switch, a power supply device, and MC.

If a failure of network switch occurs, it causes multiple point failure of the sensors. Therefore, additional DFs may be necessary according to the new performance degradation. The DFs against multiple point failure of sensors can be defined at the system-level degradation design step. However, it is not efficient because of the huge number of the potential combination. Thus, in this step, only the actual combinations are analyzed.

2.9 ECU Level Degradation Design: Verification of Mode Switch Performance

In this section, the real-time performance of the system is verified. In particular, the WCMST of the system can finish by the failure time to interval (FTTI) [6] to avoid hazards and is verified by referring to the specification information. If it does not finish, the design process must return to Sect. 2.7, and the function allocation must be re-designed. This process is conducted before the software or hardware development. Therefore, the process is efficient to reduce efforts if specification refinement is necessary.

The calculation method of WCSMT is specified in Sect. 3.

2.10 MC Level Degradation Design: Function Implementation

In this section, DFs against MC internal hardware failure such as CPU and memory are defined. Furthermore, the functions defined in this proposed whole process are implemented on MCs. Consequently, we can develop the AD system based on graceful degradation.

2.11 Integration into ISO26262 and ISO/PAS 21448

In Sect. 2.3, we explained the design process for graceful degradation. In this section, we explain the position of the proposed process in the whole process based on ISO26262 and ISO/PAS 21488.

Figure 4 shows the overview. Section 2.4 is contained in the process on improvement of function and system specification. Section 2.5 is contained in the process for functional safety requirement definition. Section 2.6 is not clarified in the standards. Therefore, we establish it as the independent process. Section 2.9 is contained in the process for technical safety requirement definition. Section 3 is originally defined in the integration process after implementation. However, as mentioned before, we proposed the WCSMT verification, which refers to the specification information, to reduce efforts. Since the corresponding process is not defined in the standards, we define it as the new process.

3 Calculation Framework of Worst-Case Mode Switch Time

The system based on graceful degradation consists of multiple FDs and DFs, as shown in Fig. 2(d). The mode switch processing means a series of processings, e.g. from FD against hardware failure and a selection of a DF to execute the DF.

As a calculation method of WCMST, there exists a method of worst-case response time analysis by using execution flow [10]. However, the method cannot analyze the state transition to select a DF according to the performance degradation factor. Therefore, the method determines WCSMT by addition of a FD, a FR, and a DF with maximum time. Since the FR is a common processing executed after the execution of FDs, WCMST is calculated by addition of $FD1 + FR + DF2$ or $FD1 + FR + DF3$ in Fig. 5(a). Consequently, it may show the pessimistic result because the combination between the FD and DF actually may not happen.

In this paper, we propose a calculation framework for WCMST by utilizing state transition information produced by the graceful degradation design process (see Fig. 5(b)). The framework improves the accuracy of WCMST because it evaluates only the actual combinations between FDs and FDs. However, there is a disparity about communication time from FD to FR or from FR to DF because of various function allocations (see Fig. 2(d)).

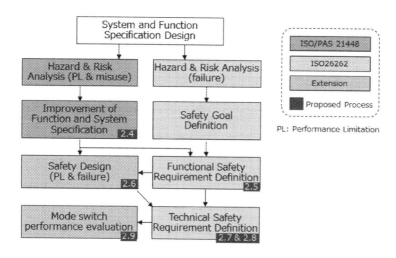

Fig. 4. Integration of Proposed Process into ISO26262 and ISO/PAS 21448

Fig. 5. Methods for worst-case mode switch time calculation

Thus, the proposed framework determines WCMST by selecting the combination between FD and DF with maximum time at each MC and by comparing with each mode switch time, which is calculated by adding the selected FD, FR, and DF. According to ISO26262, the maximum time of FD means the fault detection time interval (FDTI). The result by adding the maximum time of FR, DF, and the communication time means the fault reaction time interval (FRTI). The framework to calculate FDTI, FRTI, and WCMST is shown below.

T_{FD} means the fault detection time, T_{MP} means an execution period of FD, T_{ComFR} means the communication time from FD to FR, T_{FR} means the fault reaction time, T_{ComDF} means the communication time from FD to DF, and T_{DF} means the time until the first output of DF.

$$FDTI = T_{FD} + T_{MP} \qquad (1)$$

$$FRTI = T_{ComFR} + T_{FR} + T_{ComDF} + T_{DF} \qquad (2)$$

$$WCMST = max(FDTI + FRTI) \qquad (3)$$

Consequently, in Sect. 2.9, we can verify that the WCMST of the system satisfies FTTI.

4   Case Study

To evaluate the effectiveness of the proposed process and framework, we applied them to the AD-Lv3 prototype as a case study.

4.1   Evaluation Target

The target system architecture of AD-Lv3 for a highway is shown in Fig. 6. The system requests take-over to the driver as the fail-operational function if a critical failure occurs. The system supplies fail-operational functions for a frequently encountered part of the highway driving situations after the time-out of the request as mentioned in Sect. 1.

The target system consists of AD-ECU and degradation ECU for fail-operational purpose. The AD-ECU is connected by six camera1s and three Lidars. The degradation ECU is connected by a camera2 and five Radars. These

ECUs are connected by a redundant network bus to detect the other ECU failure. The map information inputs to AD-ECU. Each ECU can output calculated signals to integrated control ECUs via the redundant network bus. Furthermore, the AD-ECU and degradation ECU are run by different power supply devices.

Regarding sensing direction, camera1, Radar, and Lidar can monitor the surroundings of the ego vehicle by each sensor. Camera2 monitors only the front of the vehicle. The map information has lane information to the destination direction.

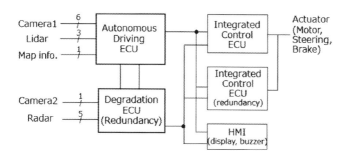

Fig. 6. System architecture of case study

The ECU architecture follows the assumption mentioned in Sect. 2.7. AD-ECU consists of three RP-MC, a PL-MC, and a CL-MC. Degradation ECU consists of a RP-MC, a PL-MC, and a CL-MC. The sensing information is input to RP-MCs via several network buses and a switch. The RP-MC processes the sensing information and sends the result to PL-MC. The PL-MC calculates the trajectory information and sends it to the integrated control ECUs via CL-MC.

The AD-ECU have functions for automated driving and passing. The degradation ECU have a function for only automated driving.

4.2   Evaluation Result on Graceful Degradation

In this section, we explain the summary of the application result of the proposed process and the evaluation result. In Sect. 2.4, we defined a DF to reduce speed for lane detection during bad weather condition. The DF conducts the automated driving based on Radar. In Sect. 2.5, we defined a DF to reduce speed according to a change of sensing range if the failure of the front camera occurs. Furthermore, we clarified the failure of a map information supply device and AD-ECU as the factors to transit to EO. As EO, we defined a DF to utilize the trajectory backup if the failure of AD-ECU occurs during passing. In Sect. 2.6, we clarified the failure of the front Radar during bad weather as the factor to transit to EO because there exists the risk on rear-end collision due to slower speed. Furthermore, we defined a DF to limit automatic passing if the side Radar failed during bad weather. In Sect. 2.7, we allocated defined DFs into MCs. In

Sect. 2.8, we found out that the failure of the network switch caused the termination of the inputs of both camera2, Radar, and map information. Consequently, we could design the AD-Lv3 based on graceful degradation according to the proposed process.

Figure 7 shows the AD-Lv3 system state machine. It consists of 2 states in SS, 2 states in NS, 3 states in LP, and 4 states in EO. Through the process, we clarify performance degradation factors, which consist of 8 factors caused by performance limitation, 36 factors caused by hardware failure, and 288 factors caused by both. Among them, 46 factors are transition events to EO. Therefore, the result showed the system can sustain 86.1% of the automated driving if a performance degradation factor occurs.

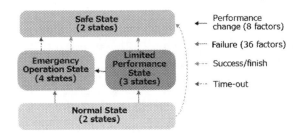

Fig. 7. Evaluation result of graceful degradation

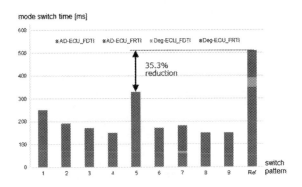

Fig. 8. Evaluation result of worst-case mode switch time

4.3   Evaluation Result on Worst-Case Mode Switch Time

We evaluated the WCMST of the designed system. In this evaluation, we calculated WCMST according to the proposed framework. We selected the FD with maximum time for each DF in 5 MCs and calculated each FRTI. Some of MCs did not transit to EO. As a result, we extract 9 combinations and calculated each mode switch time (see Fig. 8). The WCMST was 330 ms. Furthermore, we calculated WCMST according to the method based on execution flow mentioned in Sect. 3. The method showed 510 ms as WCSMT (see Ref. of Fig. 8). Therefore, the comparison result showed the proposed framework improved the calculation accuracy of WCSMT by 35.3%.

5   Conclusion

In this paper, we proposed a graceful degradation design process for an AD system and a calculation framework for WCMST. The proposed process consists of system-level, ECU-level, and microcontroller-level degradation design. The process enables to improve the automated driving continuation rate by defining degradation functions against performance limitation and hardware failure. Futhermore, we showed that the process is compliant with ISO/PAS 21448 and ISO26262. The proposed framework enables to calculate WCMST accurately by utilizing degradation design results. We applied them to an AD-Lv3 prototype and evaluated the effects as a case study. The result showed that the automated driving continuation rate of the designed system was 86.1% and the framework could improve the accuracy of WCMST by 35.3%.

As a future plan, we plan to research a method to develop a cold-standby DF by refactoring.

References

1. SAE International, J3016: Taxonomy and Definitions for Terms Related to Driving Automation Systems for On-Road Motor Vehicles (2016)
2. Shelton, C.P., Koopman, P., Nace, W.: A framework for scalable analysis and design of system-wide graceful degradation in distributed embedded systems. In: Proceedings of IEEE International Workshop on Object-Oriented Real-Time Dependable Systems (2003)
3. Reschka, A., Boehmer, J.R., Nothdurft, T., Hecker, P., Lichte, B., Maurer, M.: A surveillance and safety system based on performance criteria and functional degradation for an autonomous vehicle. In: Proceedings of IEEE Conference on Intelligent Transportation Systems (2012)
4. Nya, T.D., Stilkerich, S.C., Siemers, C.: Self-aware and self-expressive driven fault tolerance for embedded systems. In: Proceedings of IEEE Symposium on Intelligent Embedded Systems (2014)
5. Schlatow, J., et al.: Self-awareness in autonomous automotive systems. In: Proceedings of Design, Automation, and Test in Europe Conference and Exhibition (2017)
6. International Organization for Standardization, ISO 26262:2018 Road vehicles - Functional safety (2018)
7. Ishigooka, T., Honda, S., Takada, H.: Cost-effective redundancy approach for fail-operational autonomous driving system. In: Proceedings of IEEE International Symposium on Real-Time Distributed Computing (2018)
8. International Organization for Standardization, ISO/PAS 21448, Road vehicles - Safety of the intended functionality (2019)

9. Feth, P., et al.: Multi-aspect safety engineering for highly automated driving. In: Proceedings of International Conference on Computer Safety, Reliability, and Security (2018)

10. Schlatow, J., Moestl, M., Tobuschat, S., Ishigooka, T., Ernst, R.: Data-age analysis and optimization for cause-effect chains in automotive control systems. In: Proceedings of International Symposium on Industrial Embedded Systems (2018)

11. Hang, Y., Hansson, H.: Timing analysis for mode switch in component-based multi-mode systems. In: Proceedings of Euromicro Conference on Real-Time Systems (2012)

Formal Verification of Memory Preservation of x86-64 Binaries

Joshua A. Bockenek[1]($\boxtimes$), Freek Verbeek[1], Peter Lammich[2], and Binoy Ravindran[1]

[1] Bradley Department of Electrical and Computer Engineering, Virginia Tech, Blacksburg, VA 24061, USA
{jabocken,freek,binoy}@vt.edu
[2] School of Computer Science, University of Manchester, Manchester, UK
peter.lammich@manchester.ac.uk
https://ece.vt.edu/, https://www.cs.manchester.ac.uk/

Abstract. Formal verification of a binary can provide high software assurance, even when the source code is unavailable. It is, however, inherently hard due to the low level of abstraction involved; instead of verifying typed and structured source code, one has to verify machine code or reconstructed assembly. This paper presents a semi-automated methodology for formally verifying memory preservation, as well as register preservation, over disassembled binaries. The methodology is based on formal symbolic execution and Floyd-style verification. We show that the methodology is compositional on the function level, which is crucial for scalability. The methodology works for loops, recursion, and both optimized and non-optimized code. It can be used to expose preconditions required for non-exceptional behavior. We demonstrate applicability by verifying a set of functions from the HermitCore unikernel library.

Keywords: x86-64 · Assembly · Isabelle/HOL · Formal verification

1 Introduction

Building high-assurance software greatly benefits from the usage of formal verification. Typically, formal verification shows that a given piece of source code satisfies a certain property. In contrast, this paper considers formal verification of *binaries*. Binary verification can be applied to legacy software or software whose source code is unavailable, e.g., due to proprietary reasons. Moreover, it significantly reduces the trusted computing base (TCB) of the verification effort.

The drawback of binary verification is the semantical gap between a binary and its source code. The compilation process removes information such as types, control flow structure, and data structures such as arrays. Manual proofs over large sequences of assembly are so intricate and user-intensive that they are practically infeasible, and a fully automated proof methodology is theoretically impossible due to the undecidability of semantic properties over programs

© Springer Nature Switzerland AG 2019
A. Romanovsky et al. (Eds.): SAFECOMP 2019, LNCS 11698, pp. 35–49, 2019.
https://doi.org/10.1007/978-3-030-26601-1_3

(Rice's theorem [11]). An approach is required that automates binary verification as far as possible, but still allows user interaction.

This paper combines interactive theorem proving with automated generation of formal proofs. This *semi-automated* approach to binary verification eliminates the need for large and intricate proofs over assembly blocks while still allowing the user to direct the prover whenever necessary. This contrasts with fully automated methods such as SMT solvers [1,19]. The approach is tailored for a specific property called *memory preservation*. Memory preservation shows that the memory written to by a program is restrained to specified regions. This can then be used to prove the absence of common memory-related issues, such as buffer overflows or some forms of data leakage (the next section discusses memory preservation further). To achieve scalability, the approach uses function-level compositionality.

The methodology is applied to several functions from the HermitCore unikernel library [15]. HermitCore is an operating system (OS) kernel library aiming to provide real-time guarantees for high-performance computing. The functions have been compiled for the x86-64 instruction set architecture (ISA) using the GNU Compiler Collection (GCC). The functions chosen provide a variety of features, including memory operations, loops, recursion, non-trivial data structures, pointers, and subcalls.

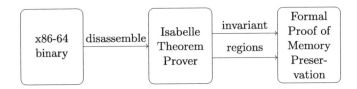

Fig. 1. Overview of methodology

Figure 1 shows an overview of the contribution's methodology. The approach disassembles a binary using an off-the-shelf disassembler, performs analysis on the binary to extract data for automation, and embeds it into a theorem prover using the symbolic execution toolchain of Roessle et al. [26], the machine model of which is based on the work of Heule et al. [9]. Within the theorem prover, two things need to be manually defined: an invariant and the set of regions that the function is allowed to write to. Defining invariants manually is traditionally a hard task, but this paper provides requirements for invariants targeted at memory preservation. Given the manually-added invariants and regions as input, a formal proof of memory preservation is generated largely automatically. The methodology is implemented in Isabelle/HOL [22] for the x86-64 ISA.

2   Memory Preservation

A program that satisfies memory preservation does not write to locations outside of pre-specified memory regions. Memory preservation is an important property for the following reasons:

Security. Various vulnerabilities occur in software whose memory usage is unbounded, such as buffer overflows or data leakage. An example of data leakage from the past few years that had a significant affect on security was the Heartbleed vulnerability, wherein invalid input caused out-of-bounds memory accesses, leaking potentially sensitive data. Memory preservation can be used as a starting point to expose such vulnerabilities.

Composition. Any verification effort over software is scalable only when it is compositional. If one targets proofs of full functional correctness over a large suite of software, that suite needs to be decomposed into separate chunks. Separation logic provides a *frame rule* that allows such decomposition [25]. This rule intuitively states that if a program can be confined to a certain part of a state, properties of this program carry over when the program is part of a bigger system. Memory preservation essentially discharges the most involved part of this frame rule when it comes to functions in a binary: it shows a function is confined to specific regions of the memory. Being able to prove memory preservation is thus a prerequisite for any larger proof effort over binaries.

Concurrency. Reasoning over concurrent programs is complicated due to potential interactions between threads. Interactions can be intended, e.g., via IPC, I/O, or interrupts. Shared memory can be a cause of *unintended* interaction between threads. By showing that the functions in two threads write to specifically allowed regions of shared memory only, unintended interactions can be removed.

2.1 Formal Definition

The formal definition of memory preservation starts with the notion of *state*. In this implementation, states are defined by a record that stores registers, flags, and 64-bit addressable byte-level memory. Moreover, a *machine model* is required. Let S denote the type of states and let A denote the type of instructions. The machine model provides a function step $:: A \times S \mapsto (S \mid \bot_E)$. This function takes as input an instruction and a state σ. It is a partial function, producing either the constant $\bot_E$ (indicating an exception) or some state σ'.

From the machine model, we manually derive a run function run_until $:: (S \mapsto \mathbb{B}) \times S \mapsto (S \mid \bot_E \mid \bot_{NT})$. This partial function takes as input a state predicate H and a state σ. Predicate H denotes the *halting condition*. Typically, the halting condition instructs the run function to stop at a certain line of the assembly, such as at a `ret` instruction. The run function iteratively fetches the current instruction via the current value of the instruction pointer and uses the machine model to execute it. Whenever an exception occurs, it stops and returns $\bot_E$. If the execution were to continue forever without an exception or reaching the halting condition (e.g. due to an infinite loop), the function returns $\bot_{NT}$. Formally, this is achieved by a standard least-fixed-point construction.

A *Hoare triple* denotes a pre- and postcondition for a certain program. Let P and Q be state predicates. In our notation, $\{P\}\ H\ \{Q\}$ denotes that, for any state σ, assuming precondition P and termination, run_until(H, σ) produces a non-exceptional state that satisfies postcondition Q. Note that this differs from standard textbook Hoare triples [10,20] as it uses a halting condition instead of an explicit program statement. Instead, the program statement is characterized by the addresses of its initial and ending instructions, defined in P and H.

Before memory preservation can be defined, some further notations and definitions need to be introduced. A *memory region* $[a, s]$ is defined by its address a (a 64-bit word) and size s in bytes (a natural number). A memory region is assumed not to overflow, i.e., the address plus the size is less than 2^{64}. To read a region of memory in the state, we use the notation $\sigma : *[a, s]$. If it is clear from context which state is meant, that state will be omitted. This function reads a list of bytes from the given address, reverses it (since we are dealing with a little-endian architecture) and converts it to a word. The following notation denotes writing a word v to address a in state σ: $\sigma(\!|a \overset{M}{=} v|\!)$. This function decomposes the given word into bytes, reverses them and then writes it into memory. Note that an explicit size is not necessary, since that information is enclosed in the type of v. Similarly, operators $\overset{R}{=}$ and $\overset{F}{=}$ write to registers and flags, respectively; := is also used for register assignment in places. Central notions concerning memory regions are separation, enclosure, and overlapping:

Definition 1. *Two regions* $r = [a, s]$ *and* $r' = [a', s']$ *are separated,* $r \bowtie r'$, *if and only if* $s = 0 \lor s' = 0 \lor a + s \le a' \lor a' + s' \le a$. *Region* $r = [a, s]$ *is enclosed by region* $r' = [a', s']$, $r \sqsubseteq r'$, *if and only if* $a \ge a' \land a + s \le a' + s'$. *Two regions overlap if they are not separate.*

Memory preservation is defined as a Hoare triple. Assume a predicate P that characterizes the initial state, e.g., sets the instruction pointer to the first instruction of a function body. Moreover, let R be a set of regions that the function is allowed to write to. Set R includes the stack frame and utilized data sections from the binary as well as any utilized heap memory. Memory preservation formulates that any byte not within any region in R has to remain unchanged. This is formalized as follows.

Definition 2. *Let* R *be a set of regions, let* P *be a precondition and let* H *denote a halting condition. A piece of assembly provides* memory preservation *if and only if, for any address* a *and byte-value* v_0:

$$(\forall r \in R \ \cdot \ r \bowtie [a, 1]) \implies \{P \land *[a, 1] = v_0\}\ H\ \{*[a, 1] = v_0\} \tag{1}$$

3 Blocks

This section describes how to prove memory preservation over blocks of assembly. A *block* is defined as a sequence of assembly instructions whose behavior can be described using only state transitions and branches. A block always terminates and has no loops.

3.1 Symbolic Execution

The main proof technique applied is *symbolic execution*, which uses rewrite rules to establish the semantics of a block. Since we do symbolic execution within Isabelle/HOL, each rewrite rule is formally proven correct. Rewrite rules essentially allow lifting the level of abstraction. For example, the next subsection defines rewrite rules for writing into memory. Instead of unfolding the write function – which contains details on byte-level little-endian memory – the write function is kept abstract: the fact that writing decomposes a value into a byte list and reverses it is invisible in the rewritten state.

An inherent difficulty caused by symbolic execution is the alias problem. Consider the following symbolic state: $\sigma(\!| a \overset{M}{=} v, a' \overset{M}{=} v' |\!)$. Two values have been written into memory, first value v to address a and then value v' to address a'. The addresses are however completely symbolic, meaning that it is unknown whether regions $[a, |v|]$ and $[a', |v'|]$ overlap or not ($|x|$ meaning the size of value x). If they do not overlap, then this is indeed the most concise symbolic representation of the current state. In that case, reading from address a will simply return value v. However, problems occur when the regions do overlap. Consider, e.g., $a = a'$ and $|v| = |v'|$. In that case, the most concise symbolic representation is actually $\sigma(\!| a \overset{M}{=} v' |\!)$. Reading from address a will then return v' instead of v. This becomes more complicated when the regions do overlap but the addresses are not equal or the sizes of the values are different, such as when writing multi-byte objects into a byte array and vice versa.

3.2 Rewriting of Memory Accesses

Symbolic execution of a block of assembly will result in a symbolic state with a series of memory writes: $\sigma(\!| a_0 \overset{M}{=} v_0, a_1 \overset{M}{=} v_1, \ldots |\!)$. In order to read from such a state, the alias problem must be solved: if it is unknown whether any of the written regions overlap, then reading from memory cannot be resolved deterministically. To solve the alias problem, rewrite rules are formulated that ensure that the symbolic state always satisfies the following form: any two regions written to memory are separate. This is an invariant over the form of the symbolic state, e.g., it prevents a state of the form $\sigma(\!| a_0 \overset{M}{=} v_0, a_0 \overset{M}{=} v_0 |\!)$. Given this invariant, reading a region $r = [a, s]$ can be achieved by looping over the written regions $r_0, r_1, \ldots$ one by one. If a region r_n is found such that $r \sqsubseteq r_n$, then a value can be read. Any region r_n such that $r \bowtie r_n$ can be ignored. It might be possible that no single written region encloses region r completely, but a set of written regions encloses it. In that case, that set of regions can be *merged* into one region. Subsequently, that new region encloses region r and can thus be used to resolve the read.

Writing to Memory. In order to preserve the region separation invariant, writing a region into memory can require region merging, defined as follows. Let r_0 be the region to be written and let r_1 be a region already in memory.

If the regions overlap, the state after having written region r_0 will contain one region that is the result of overwriting region r_1 with r_0. To define that merged region, we use list functions $\mathrm{tk}(n, x)$ and $\mathrm{dr}(n, x)$ (for taking/dropping the first n elements of list x) and list appending (@). The merged region is defined as $\mathrm{mrg}([a_1, v_1], [a_0, v_0]) \overset{\mathrm{def}}{=} [\min(a_0, a_1), r']$, where

$$r' = \mathrm{tk}(\max(0, a_0 - a_1), v_0) \ @ \ v_0 \ @$$
$$\mathrm{dr}(a_0 + |v_0| < a_1 + |v_1| \ ? \ a_0 + |v_0| - a_1 \ : \ |v_1|, v_1) \quad (2)$$

Rewrite Rule Eq. 3 shows the rewrite rule used whenever a new region is written into memory. That rule preserves the necessary invariant. The right hand side underlines the redexes in the rewritten statement (note this notation is only used for this particular rewrite rule). That is, after application of this rewrite rule, non-underlined parts will not be rewritten any further. For this rule only, we use an alternative notation for writing to memory: e.g., $\sigma (\![a_0 \overset{M}{=} v_0, a_1 \overset{M}{=} v_1]\!)$ is equivalent to $\mathrm{w}(a_1, v_1, \mathrm{w}(a_0, v_0, \sigma))$, and we also have $r_0 = [a_0, |v_0|]$ and $r_1 = [a_1, |v_1|]$.

$$\mathrm{w}(a_0, v_0, \mathrm{w}(a_1, v_1, \sigma)) \equiv \begin{cases} \mathrm{w}(a_1, v_1, \underline{\mathrm{w}(a_0, v_0, \sigma)}) & \text{if } r_0 \bowtie r_1 \\ \underline{\mathrm{w}(\mathrm{mrg}(r_1, r_0), \sigma)} & \text{otherwise} \end{cases} \quad (3)$$

In order to admit this rule to the Isabelle/HOL logic, it needs to be formally proven correct. The proof is based on two lemmas. First, writing separate blocks is commutative. Second, the merge function is correct: the produced region is the result of two sequential and overlapping memory writes.

Reading from Memory. Let $r = [a, s]$ be a region to be read in a state with a series of memory writes. Rewrite Rule Eq. 4 provides a rule for this case.

$$\sigma (\![a_1 \overset{M}{=} v_1]\!) : *[a, s] \equiv \begin{cases} \mathrm{tk}(s, \mathrm{dr}(a - a_1, v_1)) & \text{if } [a, s] \sqsubseteq [a_1, |v_1|] \\ \sigma : *[a, s] & \text{if } [a, s] \bowtie [a_1, |v_1|] \end{cases} \quad (4)$$

If an enclosing region has been found, the read can occur. A separate region can be ignored. However, the rule is incomplete: the memory might contain a written region that overlaps with r but does not enclose it. Two cases can arise. First, it can be the case that the set of overlapping regions is still not sufficient to enclose region r. In that case, no further rewriting is possible. This corresponds to a case where memory that has not been written to is read. The second case occurs when there is a set of overlapping regions enclosing region r. In that case, those regions have to be merged before Rule Eq. 4 can be applied. The proof of Rewrite Rule Eq. 4 is among other things based on correctness of the functions that (a) split a word value into a byte list, (b) reverse that list, and (c) concatenates that byte list back to a word value.

3.3   Reasoning over Memory Regions

The previous subsection showed that we need to reason over separation and enclosure of memory regions. Given assumptions on the memory layout, it needs to be automatically inferred whether two regions overlap or not. We first detail how to formulate these assumptions, and then show what steps are needed to set up automatic inference of memory region properties.

Without any assumptions, the memory model is a simple flat function from 64-bit words to bytes. Symbolic execution then places the data sections of a binary in some part of the memory and places the stack frame in some other part of the memory. Naturally, these should not overlap. We use function $\bigotimes$ to formulate such assumptions. This function takes as input a set of regions annotated with a unique ID. This ID allows reasoning over (in)equality of regions: without an ID, it is impossible to decide whether two regions of the same size are equal.

Definition 3. *Let R be a set of pairs of unique IDs and regions. Set R is separated if and only if all of its regions are separated:*

$$\bigotimes(R) \stackrel{def}{=} \forall (i_0, r_0), (i_1, r_1) \in R \; \cdot \; if \; i_0 = i_1 \; then \; r_0 = r_1 \; else \; r_0 \bowtie r_1 \quad (5)$$

Typically, set R contains large regions, such as the stack frame. The rewrite rules typically concern small regions, such as the region of a local variable within the stack frame. We thus need rules that infer properties over small regions from larger ones.

$$r_0 \bowtie r_1 \equiv r_1 \bowtie r_0 \quad (6)$$

$$r_0 \sqsubseteq r_2 \wedge r_1 \sqsubseteq r_3 \wedge r_2 \bowtie r_3 \Longrightarrow r_0 \bowtie r_1 \quad (7)$$

$$r \sqsubseteq r \quad (8)$$

$$r_0 \sqsubseteq r_1 \wedge r_1 \sqsubseteq r_0 \Longrightarrow r_0 = r_1 \quad (9)$$

$$r_0 \sqsubseteq r_1 \wedge r_1 \sqsubseteq r_2 \Longrightarrow r_0 \sqsubseteq r_2 \quad (10)$$

$$r_0 \bowtie r_1 \wedge r_0.size \neq 0 \wedge r_1.size \neq 0 \Longrightarrow r_0 \not\sqsubseteq r_1 \quad (11)$$

$$\bigotimes(R) \wedge (i_0, r_0), (i_1, r_1) \in R \wedge i_0 \neq i_1 \Longrightarrow r_0 \bowtie r_1 \quad (12)$$

Fig. 2. Rewrite rules for properties over memory regions.

Figure 2 shows such rules. These rewrite rules are able to infer, from the assumptions over larger regions, the properties separation and non-enclosure over smaller regions. However, they can *not* sufficiently infer enclosure. Often, the only way to prove enclosure is to unfold its definition. This introduces two inequalities over words (see Definition 1). Such inequalities can be solved using the Isabelle/HOL tool *unat_arith*, which is a solver for arithmetic bit-vector equations [6]. This tool is augmented with several heuristics and auxiliary lemmas to facilitate proofs of enclosure. These proofs are time-consuming and can significantly clutter the proof effort. Therefore, we introduce the concept of *parent regions*. A parent region is a member of set R, and is thus a region annotated with an ID. The parent region for each memory region occurring in an assembly block must be manually established. For example, local variables have as parent region the stack frame, whereas constants have as parent frame some data section. The following notation is used to link a memory region r_0 to a parent region r_1 with ID i: $\text{parent}(r_0, i, r_1)$. The parent regions are thus manually defined. Given that information, the proof of enclosure is done automatically, and only once. The established enclosure properties are then used in the inference based on the rules in Fig. 2.

As a concrete example, consider a two-byte array starting at address 10 and having ID 5. The region for this array would be $[10, 2]$, with ID formulation $(5, [10, 2])$. If we take the two bytes of the array as child regions, the region relations would be $\text{parent}([10, 1], 5, [10, 2])$ and $\text{parent}([11, 1], 5, [10, 2])$.

4   Loops

When using symbolic execution to analyze code, loops pose a significant problem. First, they result in significant path explosion. There exist methodologies to reduce the number of paths to execute when using loops [23,27]. However, these are not formally verified and therefore not usable within Isabelle/HOL. Second, deciding the looping condition on a symbolic state may produce nondeterminism, which can cause symbolic execution itself to loop infinitely.

We instead apply a method similar to Floyd verification [7]. This style of verification assumes that, for each loop, at least one instruction is annotated with a state predicate. In this way, blocks lie between annotated state pairs. If, for each annotated state, the succeeding annotated state satisfies its state predicate, a Hoare triple can be inferred for the program as a whole. Floyd-style verification allows breaking up a larger program with loops into smaller blocks, each of which is verifiable using symbolic execution.

A *Floyd invariant* is a function $I :: L \mapsto ((S \mapsto \mathbb{B}) \mid \bot)$. For each program location L it can optionally provide a state predicate. We use $\text{loc}(\sigma)$ to get the location of the given state (e.g., the current instruction pointer). Notation $I(\sigma)$ applies the Floyd invariant to the current state, i.e., $I(\sigma) = I(\text{loc}(\sigma)) \neq \bot \wedge I(\text{loc}(\sigma), \sigma)$.

Definition 4. *A Floyd invariant I holds if and only if, for any state σ,*

$$I(\sigma) \longrightarrow \sigma' \neq \bot_E \wedge (\sigma' = \bot_{NT} \vee I(\sigma')), \tag{13}$$

where $\sigma' = \text{run\_until}((\lambda\sigma \ \cdot \ I(\text{loc}(\sigma)) \neq \bot), \sigma)$.

If the Floyd invariant holds in the current state σ, then running to the next annotated location does not produce an exception. If it terminates, the produced state σ' satisfies the Floyd invariant.

The following theorem states that a Floyd invariant can be used to prove a property over the program as a whole:

Theorem 1. *Assume that Floyd invariant I holds, and provides an annotation for locations l_0 and l_f (the initial and final location). Let halting condition H stop at location l_f, i.e., $H(\sigma) \longrightarrow \text{loc}(\sigma) = l_f$. Then $\{I(l_0)\}\ H\ \{I(l_f)\}$.*

Intuitively, Floyd style verification allows a program to be modeled as a control flow graph (CFG). In that CFG, each arrow can be seen as an implication.

5   Composition

Compositionality is crucial for scalability. It is required for two different reasons. First, at the level of function calls, compositionality should ensure that when a function is called, a previous verification effort over that function can be reused, without opening up the function body. Second, compositionality can drastically improve scalability *within* a function body as well. Consider the following pseudocode, which sequentially executes an if-statement and some program P:

if b then x else y; P

The assembly code corresponding to this code can be verified using symbolic execution. This would first consider the case where b is true, execute x and subsequently symbolically execute program P. Then it would consider the case where b is false, execute y and then P. Program P is thus symbolically executed twice. Without compositionality, programs with if-statements may require certain parts to be executed a number of times exponentially in the number of if-statements. With compositionality, program P needs to be symbolically executed only once.

The notion of Hoare triples as defined in this paper (see Sect. 2.1) uses a halting condition. Standard composition [10, 20] does not apply to this kind of Hoare triples. Consider a run obtained by halting condition H'. It is possible to break this run into two, by first running until a halting condition H, and then until H'. This requires that H' is *stronger* than H, i.e., H' implies H. This ensures that the run first stops at H before it stops at H'.

Theorem 2. *Hoare triples are compositional with respect to stronger halting conditions:*

$$\frac{\{P\}\ H\ \{Q\} \qquad \{Q\}\ H'\ \{R\} \qquad \forall \sigma \cdot H'(\sigma) \longrightarrow H(\sigma)}{\{P\}\ H'\ \{R\}} \tag{14}$$

Consider the block of assembly associated with the pseudocode example. Let l_f denote the final location, and let l_P denote the initial location of program P. Theorem 2 can be used by instantiating H with halting at either location l_f or l_P, and H' with halting at l_f. Assuming programs x and y do not contain goto's, condition H' is actually equivalent to halting at l_P. Since H' is stronger than H, compositionality is then possible.

Generally, compositionality over function calls requires a proof that the stack pointer remains unchanged after execution of a function call. Consider a function body of function f starting in a text section at location l_0. The function is called from a different text section by `call f` at location l_{call}. This means the return address is $l_{call} + 5$ (the size of the `call` instruction is 5). After execution of the instruction `call f`, the program is at location l_0 and the stack pointer has some value rsp_0. In order to apply compositionality to function calls, the pre- and postcondition have to meet the following requirements. The precondition must imply that the return address is pushed on the stack (which has been done by `call`): $*[rsp_0, 8] = l_{call} + 5 \land \mathtt{rsp} = rsp_0$.

The postcondition must imply that after `ret`, the net effect of the function body is that the stack pointer has been incremented by 8: $\mathtt{rsp} = rsp_0 + 8 \land \mathrm{loc} = l_{call} + 5$. Note that `call` has decremented it with 8, so this implies the net effect from the point of view of the caller is that the stack pointer has been unchanged. Also, the postcondition shows that the location has been set back to right after the call.

Besides the stack pointer, modern calling conventions have other *callee-saved* registers, such as `rbp` and `r12-r15`. It is generally assumed that the net effect of a function call does not touch these registers. Consider a situation in which `rbp` contains an address, to which a value is written after a function call. In order to prove memory preservation, it must be known that `rbp` is preserved. Generally, this is easy to prove by strengthening the pre- and postcondition with a conjunct $\mathtt{rbp} = rbp_0$. The proof is generally not complicated, since these callee-saved registers are pushed onto the stack at the beginning of the functional calls, and popped at the end.

6   Case Study: HermitCore

A relatively recent trend in the field of virtualization is the usage of *unikernels*: programs designed for specific tasks that are compiled with all the kernel code necessary to run the programs on a hypervisor or even bare metal without an intermediary OS [17]. Unikernels allow an application to include only the necessary parts of the OS, increasing security by reducing the attack surface. Hermit-Core is such a unikernel [15]. It is designed for the x86-64 ISA and is written in C with some inline assembly. HermitCore is an interesting target for verification, as it aims to provide a high-speed and real-time environment for cloud software. In order to demonstrate the applicability of our methodology, we verified a subset of HermitCore's library functions. These functions contain loops, recursion, structs, unions, pointers, and function calls. Generally, both non-optimized and optimized versions have been verified. The proofs and all associated code are available at https://doi.org/10.6084/m9.figshare.7356110.v2.

Machine Model. The machine model must provide a step function that provides semantics for instructions. We have used the machine model of Roessle et al. [26], which is built upon the work of Heule et al. [9]. Heule et al. used machine learning to derive semantics by executing instructions on an actual x86-64 machine. Their semantics have been validated against the Intel

Table 1. Summary of functions analyzed

Functions	Count	SLOC	Insts[†]	Loops	Recursion	Pointer args	Globals	Subcalls	-O3
dequeue_*	3	46	159			3		3	3
buddy_*	5	67	225	1	1	1	3	3	3
task_list_*	3	43	128			3			3
vring_*	3	19	80			1			3
string.h	8	81	280	8		8			
syscall.c	23	293	857	5		19	7	17	
tasks.c	10	122	396	2		3	9	4	
spinlock.h	8	89	254	2		8	2	6	
Total	71	760	2379	18	1	46	21	33	12

[†] Non-optimized count

reference manual. The formal model is obtained by embedding these semantics into Isabelle/HOL. It has been tested against an actual x86-64 machine, increasing the model's reliability. It provides a formalization of large parts of the x86-64 ISA, including several modern instruction sets. Concurrency is not modeled.

Functions Analyzed. The selected functions (see Table 1) include functionality pertaining to a generic circular queue or ring buffer (the dequeue_* functions), the internals of HermitCore's kmalloc setup (the buddy_* functions), task management lists used by HermitCore's scheduler (task_list_*), and functions concerning virtual I/O (vring_*). We also verified standard string and memory related functions: memcpy, memcmp, memset, strlen, strcpy, strncpy, strcmp, and strncmp. This verification effort affirmed the well-known fact that some of those functions require an extra precondition, i.e., that the given string is null-terminated; failure to use null-terminated strings and/or using output buffers of too small a size can result in buffer overflows. Additional functions that were verified consist of some providing syscall support, more task- and scheduler-related functions, and functions for manipulating spinlocks.

Figures 3a and 3b show the CFGs for two of those functions, dequeue_push and buddy_large_avail. The former pushes a value onto a generic array-based queue while the latter checks for the smallest available reused memory block for a given allocation size. The former, lacking any loops, requires only pre- and post-conditions (though additional invariants may be added). In contrast, the latter function requires a loop invariant in addition to the pre- and postconditions.

Discussion on Usability. In order to apply the method to a function in a binary, three steps require user interaction: (a) defining a Floyd invariant, (b) defining set R, and (c) proving. Traditionally, defining invariants over software is a complicated matter. However, by restricting ourselves to memory preservation, invariants become significantly easier.

Section 5 provides requirements that define common parts of the invariants. For loops, one simply has to annotate each jump with a state predicate as in

$$0 : \quad \begin{aligned} &*[a, 1] = v_0 \ \wedge \ \mathbf{rsp} = rsp_0 \ \wedge \\ &\mathbf{rbp} = rbp_0 \ \wedge *[rsp_0, 8] = \mathbf{ret\_addr} \end{aligned}$$

$$\begin{vmatrix} \mathbf{rsp} := \mathbf{rsp} - 8 \\ \mathbf{rbp} := \mathbf{rsp} \end{vmatrix}$$

$$129 : \begin{aligned} &*[a, 1] = v_0 \ \wedge \ \mathbf{rsp} = rsp_0 \ \wedge \\ &\mathbf{rbp} = rbp_0 \ \wedge \ \mathbf{rdi} = deq_{\mathrm{ptr}} \ \wedge \\ &*[rsp_0, 8] = \mathbf{ret\_addr} \end{aligned}$$

$$21 : \begin{aligned} &*[a, 1] = v_0 \ \wedge \ \mathbf{rsp} = rsp_0 - 8 \ \wedge \\ &\mathbf{rbp} = rsp_0 - 8 \ \wedge \\ &*[rsp_0 - 8, 8] = rbp_0 \ \wedge \\ &*[rsp_0, 8] = \mathbf{ret\_addr} \end{aligned}$$

$$\begin{vmatrix} \cdots \end{vmatrix}$$

$$\begin{vmatrix} \mathbf{rbp} := *[\mathbf{rsp}, 8] \\ \mathbf{rsp} := \mathbf{rsp} + 16 \end{vmatrix}$$

$$\mathbf{ret\_addr} : \begin{aligned} &*[a, 1] = v_0 \ \wedge \\ &\mathbf{rsp} = rsp_0 + 8 \ \wedge \\ &\mathbf{rbp} = rbp_0 \end{aligned}$$

$$\mathbf{ret\_addr} : \begin{aligned} &*[a, 1] = v_0 \ \wedge \\ &\mathbf{rsp} = rsp_0 + 8 \ \wedge \\ &\mathbf{rbp} = rbp_0 \end{aligned}$$

(a) dequeue_push   (b) buddy_large_avail

Fig. 3. Example Floyd invariants

Fig. 3b. However, for recursion the invariant becomes more complicated. Generally, it has to be shown that both the stack and frame pointers are preserved throughout the recursion. Moreover, it has to be shown that return addresses are pushed correctly. A second interaction in defining a Floyd invariant is finding the right precondition. Such preconditions need not be derived from a reference manual or from source code annotations; instead, users can run symbolic execution until non-determinism occurs. At that point, Isabelle/HOL provides the exact condition under which exceptional behavior happens. It is then up to the user to strengthen the precondition based on that condition. This means that the proof methodology may expose implicit or undocumented preconditions.

The proof effort consists of defining parent relations and running symbolic execution. After symbolic execution, it must be proved that the resulting state satisfies the invariant. In most of the cases, those proofs could be handled by Isabelle/HOL using standard off-the-shelf tools. The exception is again recursion. The proof that the stack and frame pointers preserve their values requires interactive theorem proving with a large focus on word arithmetic.

7   Related Work

Going back to the late 80's and early 90's, Yu and Boyer [3,28] provided semantics and mechanized reasoning for a subset of instructions of the MC68020 microprocessor in the Boyer-Moore theorem prover (Nqthm) [2], a precursor to ACL2 [12]. This work also utilized symbolic execution and even covered many of the same string functions we did, such as strcpy and strcmp. Similarly, Clutterbuck and Carré performed formal verification of low-level code using SPACE-8080 [5], a verifiable subset of the Intel 8080 ISA that is analyzable and formally verifiable using the Southampton Program Analysis Development Environment (SPADE)

[4]. Another usage of SPADE for verification of assembly was in the correctness proof of fuel control code for a Rolls-Royce jet engine [24].

Decompilation into logic allows formal verification of assembly and machine code [21]. Developed in the HOL4 theorem prover, that work uses operational semantics of machine code to lift programs into a functional form, which can then be used in a Hoare logic framework for program analysis. It has been successfully used with machine models of the ARM ISA. This work builds upon decompilation to derive highly automated proofs for a specific property.

Matthews et al. [18] used the theorem prover ACL2 [12] to target a simple machine model called TINY as well as Java virtual machine (JVM) bitcode using the M5 operational model. Both of these assembly-style languages feature a stack for handling scratch variables rather than a register file as x86, ARM, and most other mainstream ISAs do. They utilize symbolic execution of code annotated with invariants on specific instructions. While they proved functional correctness, they did not show effective scalability due to the restricted models and small amount of code verified.

In contrast to the bottom-up approach presented in this paper, top-down approaches have been studied extensively. The CompCert project [16] provides a compiler that has been verified to produce assembly or machine code with the same semantics as the source, thus removing them from the TCB. A top-down approach requires verification of the original source code as well. One such verification project is AutoCorres [8], part of the seL4 verified microkernel project [13]. This tool parses C code into a shallowly-embedded monadic representation. It produces proofs of the semantic equivalence between the original code and the monadic version and can be used to prove properties via Hoare logic. Another top-down project is CakeML [14], a full-toolchain project for proof synthesis and in-logic execution. It utilizes a subset of Standard ML modeled with big-step operational semantics.

8   Conclusion

Formal verification of binaries can produce highly reliable claims over software. By eliminating trust in a compiler or in the semantics of a source language, the TCB is drastically decreased. It is, however, fundamentally a harder problem than source code verification.

This paper targets formal verification of memory usage in x86-64 binaries, showing that functions in a binary restrict themselves to certain regions of memory. It aims to automate verification as much as possible while still allowing user interaction wherever necessary. This semi-automated methodology requires setting up an invariant, which traditionally is a hard problem in itself. Requirements for memory preservation invariants are provided. For recursive functions, more involved invariants are required, plus interactive theorem proving to show preservation of the stack and frame pointers. Invariants include preconditions necessary for excluding exceptional behavior. Such preconditions are exposed by applying the methodology to a binary, instead of deriving them from documents or source code annotations.

The approach was applied to functions of HermitCore, a unikernel OS. We formally proved memory preservation for functions with loops, recursion, C structs and unions, and dynamic memory operations. Both optimized and non-optimized versions were verified.

Major additions to our framework would be handling of concurrency and related instruction variants. Additionally, proper modeling of virtual machine and hypervisor calls in logic would allow verification of a wider range of functions from the HermitCore library.

Acknowledgments. We thank the reviewers for their insightful comments, which have significantly improved the paper. This work is supported in part by ONR under grant N00014-17-1-2297 and NAVSEA/NEEC under grant N00174-16-C-0018.

References

1. Barrett, C., et al.: CVC4. In: Gopalakrishnan, G., Qadeer, S. (eds.) CAV 2011. LNCS, vol. 6806, pp. 171–177. Springer, Heidelberg (2011). https://doi.org/10.1007/978-3-642-22110-1_14
2. Boyer, R.S., Moore, J.S.: A Computational Logic. Academic Press Inc., Cambridge (1979)
3. Boyer, R.S., Yu, Y.: Automated proofs of object code for a widely used microprocessor. J. ACM **43**(1), 166–192 (1996)
4. Carré, B.A., O'Neill, I.M., Clutterbuck, D.L., Debney, C.W.: SPADE-the southampton program analysis and development environment. In: Software Engineering Environments. Peter Peregrinus, Ltd., Stevenage (1986)
5. Clutterbuck, D.L., Carré, B.A.: The verification of low-level code. Softw. Eng. J. **3**(3), 97–111 (1988). https://doi.org/10.1049/sej.1988.0012
6. Dawson, J.: Isabelle theories for machine words. Electron. Notes Theor. Comput. Sci. **250**(1), 55–70 (2009)
7. Floyd, R.W.: Assigning meanings to programs. Math. Aspects Comput. Sci. **19**(1), 19–32 (1967)
8. Greenaway, D., Andronick, J., Klein, G.: Bridging the gap: automatic verified abstraction of C. In: Beringer, L., Felty, A. (eds.) ITP 2012. LNCS, vol. 7406, pp. 99–115. Springer, Heidelberg (2012). https://doi.org/10.1007/978-3-642-32347-8_8
9. Heule, S., Schkufza, E., Sharma, R., Aiken, A.: Stratified synthesis: automatically learning the x86-64 instruction set. In: Proceedings of the 37th ACM SIGPLAN Conference on Programming Language Design and Implementation, PLDI 2016, pp. 237–250. ACM, New York, NY, USA (2016)
10. Hoare, C.A.R.: An axiomatic basis for computer programming. Commun. ACM **12**(10), 576–580 (1969)
11. Hopcroft, J.E., Motwani, R., Ullman, J.D.: Introduction to Automata Theory, Languages, and Computation. Pearson, London (2006)
12. Kaufmann, M., Manolios, P., Moore, J.S.: Computer-Aided Reasoning: An Approach. Kluwer Academic Publishers, Dordrecht (2000)
13. Klein, G., et al.: seL4: formal verification of an OS kernel. In: Proceedings of the ACM SIGOPS 22nd Symposium on Operating Systems Principles, SOSP 2009, pp. 207–220. ACM Press, New York, NY, USA (2009). https://sel4.systems/

14. Kumar, R., Myreen, M.O., Norrish, M., Owens, S.: CakeML: a verified implementation of ML. In: Proceedings of the 41st ACM SIGPLAN-SIGACT Symposium on Principles of Programming Languages, POPL 2014, pp. 179–191. ACM, New York, NY, USA (2014). https://cakeml.org/

15. Lankes, S., Pickartz, S., Breitbart, J.: HermitCore: a unikernel for extreme scale computing. In: ROSS 2016, pp. 4:1–4:8. ACM, New York, NY, USA (2016)

16. Leroy, X., Blazy, S., Kästner, D., Schommer, B., Pister, M., Ferdinand, C.: CompCert - a formally verified optimizing compiler. In: Embedded Real Time Software and Systems, 8th European Congress, ERTS 2016, SEE, HAL, Toulouse, France, January 2016. http://compcert.inria.fr/

17. Madhavapeddy, A., Scott, D.J.: Unikernels: the rise of the virtual library operating system. Commun. ACM **57**(1), 61–69 (2014)

18. Matthews, J., Moore, J.S., Ray, S., Vroon, D.: Verification condition generation via theorem proving. In: Hermann, M., Voronkov, A. (eds.) LPAR 2006. LNCS (LNAI), vol. 4246, pp. 362–376. Springer, Heidelberg (2006). https://doi.org/10.1007/11916277_25

19. de Moura, L., Bjørner, N.: Z3: an efficient SMT solver. In: Ramakrishnan, C.R., Rehof, J. (eds.) TACAS 2008. LNCS, vol. 4963, pp. 337–340. Springer, Heidelberg (2008). https://doi.org/10.1007/978-3-540-78800-3_24

20. Myreen, M.O., Gordon, M.J.C.: Hoare logic for realistically modelled machine code. In: Grumberg, O., Huth, M. (eds.) TACAS 2007. LNCS, vol. 4424, pp. 568–582. Springer, Heidelberg (2007). https://doi.org/10.1007/978-3-540-71209-1_44

21. Myreen, M.O., Gordon, M.J.C., Slind, K.: Machine-code verification for multiple architectures - an application of decompilation into logic. In: 2008 Formal Methods in Computer-Aided Design, pp. 1–8. IEEE, November 2008

22. Nipkow, T., Paulson, L.C., Wenzel, M.: Isabelle/HOL: A Proof Assistant for Higher-Order Logic. Lecture Notes in Computer Science, vol. 2283, 1st edn. Springer Science & Business Media, Heidelberg (2002). https://doi.org/10.1007/3-540-45949-9

23. Obdržálek, J., Trtík, M.: Efficient loop navigation for symbolic execution. In: Bultan, T., Hsiung, P.-A. (eds.) ATVA 2011. LNCS, vol. 6996, pp. 453–462. Springer, Heidelberg (2011). https://doi.org/10.1007/978-3-642-24372-1_34

24. O'Neill, I.M., Clutterbuck, D.L., Farrow, P.F., Summers, P.G., Dolman, W.C.: The formal verification of safety-critical assembly code. In: IFAC Symposium on Safety of Computer Control Systems 1988, SAFECOMP 1988, vol. 21, pp. 115–120, November 1988. https://doi.org/10.1016/S1474-6670(17)54540-1

25. Reynolds, J.C.: Separation logic: a logic for shared mutable data structures. In: 17th Annual IEEE Symposium on Logic in Computer Science, Proceedings, pp. 55–74. IEEE (2002)

26. Roessle, I., Verbeek, F., Ravindran, B.: Formally verified big step semantics out of x86-64 binaries. In: Proceedings of the 8th ACM SIGPLAN International Conference on Certified Programs and Proofs, CPP 2019, pp. 181–195. ACM, New York, NY, USA (2019)

27. Saxena, P., Poosankam, P., McCamant, S., Song, D.: Loop-extended symbolic execution on binary programs. In: Proceedings of the Eighteenth International Symposium on Software Testing and Analysis, ISSTA 2009, pp. 225–236. ACM, New York, NY, USA (2009)

28. Yu, Y.: Automated proofs of object code for a widely used microprocessor. Ph.D. thesis, University of Texas at Austin (1992)

Autonomous Driving

Brace Touch: A Dependable, Turbulence-Tolerant, Multi-touch Interaction Technique for Interactive Cockpits

Philippe Palanque[1,2]([✉]), Andy Cockburn[3],
Léopold Désert-Legendre[1], Carl Gutwin[4], and Yannick Deleris[5]

[1] ICS-IRIT, Université Paul Sabatier, Toulouse 3, France
palanque@irit.fr
[2] Industrial Design, Technical University of Eindhoven,
Eindhoven, The Netherlands
[3] University of Canterbury, Christchurch, New Zealand
andy@cosc.canterbury.ac.nz
[4] University of Saskatchewan, Saskatoon, Canada
gutwin@cs.usask.ca
[5] Airbus Operations, Toulouse, France
yannick.deleris@airbus.com

Abstract. A cockpit (also called a flight deck) is an interactive environment of an aircraft that enables both pilot and first officer to monitor and control the aircraft systems. Allowing the crew to control aircraft systems through display units by using a keyboard and cursor control unit is one of the main features in the new generation of cockpits based on the ARINC 661 standard. Aircraft manufacturers are now investigating the deployment of touch interactions in future cockpits and ARINC 661 standard (supplement 7) extends it for that purpose. While touch interactions have demonstrated benefits in terms of performance (from the user point of view), their dependability is an important issue that has not been addressed so far. This paper proposes an interaction technique for touch devices called Brace Touch that aims at increasing the dependability of touch interactions by providing solutions to address development, natural and operation faults.

Keywords: Human-computer interaction · Interaction techniques · Fault-tolerance · Dependability · Usability

1 Introduction

The evolution of cockpits in large civil aircraft has followed two different paths:

- Small increments/evolutions targeting identified problems or integrating new equipment (similar to existing technology) into an existing cockpit;
- Significant steps/evolutions resulting in complete re-design of the cockpit including control and displays. Examples of such evolutions include the glass cockpit (where large display units were included in the flight deck) and more recently interactive

© Springer Nature Switzerland AG 2019
A. Romanovsky et al. (Eds.): SAFECOMP 2019, LNCS 11698, pp. 53–68, 2019.
https://doi.org/10.1007/978-3-030-26601-1_4

cockpits compliant with ARINC 661 specifications [3] where interaction takes place through mouse-like input devices and keyboards.

In parallel with these evolutions, multi-touch interfaces have appeared in most environments including mobile technologies, flight entertainment systems, and consumer electronics. Such interfaces have demonstrated benefits related to the fact that the output device (screen) integrates input management (touch device) thus bridging the (usual) gap between input and output in user interfaces. These systems have also demonstrated benefits in terms of performance for triggering commands by exploiting multi-finger interactions that can reduce the number of unnecessary modes.

Changing interaction in cockpits brings a set of issues that already appeared when interactions in the cockpit evolved from "physical interactions" (by manipulating physical knobs and reading information on dials) to software controls mainly based on the ARINC 661 specification [3]. Often considered as reliable means to trigger commands, devices such as pushbuttons, rotators and safe-guarded physical buttons are now common in the flight deck. However, these devices generate significant weight load and bring maintenance issues in terms of augmentation of cockpit functions [6]. This is a key issue as these physical components are directly linked to the aircraft systems they control, resulting in the fact that evolutions (of the aforementioned systems) are likely to require modifications to the components themselves or their organization in the cockpit. This is extremely costly as tuning part of the cockpit is likely to have broad implications for the aircraft and its operation [24]. Local changes might affect performance, and ultimately require adaptation of procedures and flying crew training going far beyond the system itself. Bringing touch interactions to commercial cockpits offers potential advantages to pilots, airlines, and aircraft manufacturers. Pilots may benefit (beyond the touch advantages presented above) from their familiarity with touch interactions on personal devices. Airlines and manufacturers could benefit from reduced hardware installation complexities, easier maintenance and reduced training. Replacing hard-wired physical controls with touchscreens could therefore ease development, facilitate upgrades, reduce weight, and improve pilot interaction as argued in [8]; and this is why AEEC produced a supplement of ARINC 661 for touch [4].

Providing multi-touch interactions for the command and control of civil aircraft would be another significant evolutionary step as far as cockpits design is concerned. However, together with the benefits presented above, multi-touch interfaces bring a set of issues that are still to be solved prior to making them "certifiable" and thus deployable for command and control of (safety) critical interactive systems. These issues affect multiple properties such as *reliability*, *fault-tolerance*, and *usability*.

Our previous work [22] and [21] mostly addressed the modeling aspects of multi-touch interactions and their use for cockpit applications to deal with development faults by providing a dedicated formal description technique based on high-level Petri nets [20]. This paper builds on that previous work and focuses on the dependability aspects of multi-touch interactions from a holistic point of view, addressing development faults, natural faults, and operation faults (according to the taxonomy from [6]). To this end, we propose a new interaction technique called Brace Touch (introduced in [12]) where the empirical evaluation of its usability is demonstrated. This interaction technique allows flying crew to interact with touchscreens even under turbulence [11], which one of the main usability problems for touch interactions in cockpits, together with muscular fatigue and postures, as studied by Airbus human factors experts [8].

The remainder of this paper is organized as follows. The next section describes the underlying hardware, software, and interaction techniques for touchscreens. Section 3 identifies the dependability aspects of touch interactions. Section 4 presents the design and the principles of Brace Touch interaction together with a precise description of its behavior. Section 5 presents our proposal for addressing the dependability of Brace Touch interactions, including development, operation, and natural faults. Section 6 concludes the paper and highlights future directions.

2   Touch Interactions

This section introduces the usability and user experience (UX) aspects of touch interactions before focusing on touch device hardware, software and interaction aspects.

2.1   Usability and UX (Operations)

As presented above and argued in [36] (much before the advent of multi-touch interactions on personal and mobile devices), touch interactions provide the advantage of bridging the gap between input and output allowing users to interact without any artificial input device such as stylus or mouse. Interaction thus does not occur remotely but directly at the fingertip of the users, and early work such as [26] has demonstrated that touch screens can provide better performance for task completion. Such benefits do not come without disadvantages. First, current user interfaces are designed for interaction with mice or trackpads that provide higher levels of precisions that the so-called "fat finger". Fingers occlude small targets during selection and this reduced precision results in higher error rates on small targets. Beyond fingers, hands and arms increase occlusion on large touch screens. These issues have been at the center of recent research in human-computer interaction and solutions have identified new touch interaction techniques such as offering a fixed cursor offset [34], enlarging the target area [32], and providing on-screen widgets to facilitate selection [1].

This paper proposes a similar approach presenting the Brace Touch interaction technique designed to guarantee a reasonable level of usability even in the context of moderate or severe turbulence. In other work on compensating for vibration during touch interaction, [11] has shown that users stabilized their hand by resting on the bezels, i.e., the non-interactive part of the screen, in order to select targets with accuracy. However, as the hand is stabilized on the bezel only a small proportion of a large display can be reached. The Brace Touch interaction aims at increasing accuracy and reducing errors during turbulence while allowing interaction with the entire touchscreen.

2.2   Hardware

A touchscreen consists of a pointing device (touch sensor) combined with a display (e.g., LCD or CRT). The pointing device is responsible for capturing (X,Y) coordinates on the touch sensor and dispatching this information to the software component (exploiting a dedicated driver). There are multiple touch screen technologies but this paper focusses on the four main categories available on the market (beyond research prototypes): resistive, capacitive, surface acoustical wave (SAW) and infrared (IR). The interested reader can find a full review on touch technologies in [40].

Resistive technology consists of two conductive layers separated by an isolating layer (pierced with very small holes in a grid manner). On finger contact, the two layers get in contact at the closest location of a hole, creating a new voltage. This technology is cheap, contaminant-proof and works with any pointed object (not only a finger). However, it has poor screen clarity and does not support multi-touch. Moreover, such technology requires pressure, which may interfere with user interaction and performance.

Capacitive technology uses the user's body capacitance to detect contact on the screen. This technology is largely used on smartphones since Apple's first iPhone in 2007. It offers excellent clarity and supports multi-touch, but only detects body contact.

Infrared technologies consist of IR LEDs and photodetectors organized as a grid. The IR light is stopped by an opaque object contacting the screen. IR technology offers excellent screen clarity, supports multi-touch, and is very robust to the environment. However, such technology remains expensive.

Surface acoustic wave technology uses piezo transducers that emit and receive ultrasonic Raleigh waves along the bezels of the screen. On contact, the finger partially absorbs the wave which results in a temporary loss of amplitude in the received wave. This technology is cheap and offers excellent visual quality. However, it requires the user to press (rather strongly) on the screen (thus potentially reducing user performance) and it only supports two contact points.

This multiplicity of technologies demonstrates the maturity of the domain and the fact that diversity can be addressed at the hardware level to tolerate and possibly remove hardware faults. For instance, on the input side, it would be possible to combine a layer of capacitive technology on top of a resistive touchscreen. The main touchscreen manufacturers do not provide information about the frequency of hardware transient failures, but 10^{-5} is informally put forward by manufacturers. Such a combination would be a path towards deployment of tactile screens for Development Assurance Levels (DAL) B or C applications [13] by bringing together diversity, redundancy and segregation at the hardware level.

2.3   Software

Even though hardware can significantly vary from one touch screen to another, most programming toolkits offer the same low level events and information: a location (X,Y) on the screen, an event type *Down*, *Move*, or *Up* and a touch id to identify continuous *Move* events. This id allows identifying that the second move event received has been performed by the same finger as the first move. Apart from this common basis, particular hardware can enrich the touch information with physical data such as pressure, finger contact area, or finger orientation. All this information may be used to design touch interaction techniques (as presented in Sect. 2.4).

Many dedicated programming toolkits exist for the development of multi-touch interactive applications, including libraries from hardware platform manufacturers such as Google, Microsoft, or Apple. Such toolkits usually support the user interface guidelines defined by the manufacturer and are more or less in line with the ISO standard on touch devices [25]. The number of users and the iterative correction of defects are typical arguments put forward to argue for the reliability of this layer. However, despite some work on the use of formal methods for input device driver description [2], OS manufacturers do not provide information about the reliability means used in the development of that layer.

2.4   Touch Interaction

Touch interaction techniques are highly dependent on the low-level events produced by the hardware. As seen in the previous section, most platforms only provide touch location, the event type, and an identification number of the finger (id). These events enable designers to build temporal interactions (e.g., dwelling), spatial interactions [7], and spatio-temporal interactions such as gestures [27]. Other interactions rely on hardware capturing particular physical data such as pressure [12], finger contact area [23], or finger orientation [41]. Finally, finger identification consists in linking a touch event to a particular finger; this problem has proved difficult even though some research contributions are promising using geometrical analysis of touch points [5], using additional camera input [15], biometric data [37], or additional hardware worn on the fingers [28].

These elements provide the basic underlying language on top of which touch interaction techniques have to be built. For instance, a horizontal movement of the finger on the surface of the screen will trigger a higher level event called a *swipe* in most platforms. This *swipe* event is only triggered if the quantity of horizontal movement is large enough and if no additional fingers have been pressed during the movement. Only work from [22] has addressed the formal definition of touch inter-action techniques that are usually crafted jointly by user interface designers and developers. Interaction techniques are thus usually of low reliability and exhibit faults at operation time. Detection of development faults is only addressed by testing which cannot be exhaustive due to the very nature of interactive systems [29]. Beyond that, the inner nature of interaction techniques might be more or less fault-tolerant (as shown in Fig. 1). In case of a hardware failure of a line on the touchscreen hardware grid, the swipe in Fig. 1(a) might not be recognized even though the operator has correctly performed the gesture. In Fig. 1(b) the swipe gesture is now an upside-down V shape that could still be recognized even in the presence of several hardware touch screen lines failures. However, these more complex gestures come with a cost in terms of usability (more movements and thus more time) and their use must be the result of a thorough analysis of the usability-dependability trade-off, such as the ones presented in [17] for standard non-touch interaction techniques.

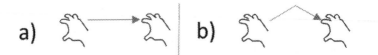

Fig. 1. Tolerance of *swipe* touch interaction techniques to hardware faults (loss of a line in the hardware grid) – (a) non tolerant (b) tolerant

3   Fault Model for Touch Interactions

As for any kind of computing systems, multi-touch interactive systems can be subject to faults at development and operation time but may also be subject to natural faults (such as bit flips due to cosmic rays). Interactive cockpits are a specific kind of command and control system and, as such, the entire taxonomy of faults presented in [6] applies. The fault model considered in the current paper does not include malicious faults because, during operation, the cockpit can be considered as a closed world and development is carefully monitored.

Our research work aims at contributing to the dependability of touch interaction by considering development, natural, and operation faults. Due to space constraints, the current paper focusses on operation faults for touch interactions but we present in this section how to address other faults.

Addressing Development Faults. We propose to address development faults by using formal description techniques and dedicated verification mechanisms. However, due to the very nature of interactive systems, specific methods are required that are able to handle:

- *Concurrency*: for instance to represent multiple concurrent interactions with multiple fingers on the touch screen;
- *Dynamic instantiation of objects*: for instance, when fingers are added and removed from the touch screen, their reference must be captured by models;
- *Quantitative time*, as most interaction techniques include temporal evolutions: for instance, the time between two touch events required to trigger a double-tap higher level event;
- *Large number of states*: for instance, current requirements for touch screen in aircraft cockpit mandate the management of up to 20 fingers on a given touch screen. Such a large number of fingers make it possible to use complex interaction such as finger clustering [21] exhibiting a very large state space.

For this reason, we propose to use a formal description techniques called ICOs [31] that covers these needs and has been used for describing in a complete and unambiguous way all the components of the previous generation of interactive cockpits [9].

Addressing Natural Faults. We consider here a similar fault model as the one presented in [16] with a focus on erroneous control (transmission of a different action from the one done by crew members – e.g., sending a *swipe* event while the user has performed a *long tap*) and inadvertent control (transmission of an action without any crew member action). These faults can be addressed by extending touch technologies with self-checking capabilities as was done with interactive cockpits [16] but this is not presented here due to space constraints. In addition, the diversity and redundancy of hardware platforms as presented above would increase tolerance to natural faults.

Addressing Operation Faults. In aircraft cockpits, operation faults typically fall in the classification of human errors either being intentional (called violation) or non-intentional (called mistakes, lapses, or slips depending on their type [35]). While such errors may have multiple sources, some of them are induced by the user interface design itself [38], but they can result from the operation environment too. For touch interactions, there is a need for safeguards against undesirable and potentially dangerous environmental conditions, such as turbulence, that might be precursors for each error type presented above. This paper proposes an interaction technique that aims at reducing operation faults triggered by turbulence.

4   Brace Touch to Improve Dependability of Touch Interactions

4.1   Principles of Brace Touch

The primary design intention of Brace Touch is to allow users to mechanically stabilize touch interactions by concurrently placing multiple fingers onto the display. Selections and other interactions are then completed by the user issuing a recognizable gesture while the other stabilizing contacts are maintained on the display. For example, Fig. 2 shows the index finger selecting an item by tapping while all of the other digits of the hand are pressed onto the display.

Fig. 2. Illustration of the brace touch interaction concept

Brace Touch uses the multi-touch capabilities of contemporary touchscreens to give users two alternative ways of completing selections. First, when the interaction environment is stable (i.e., no turbulence), users can select items by simply tapping on them with a single finger, which allows convenient touchscreen interaction in a manner similar to that used on current mobile devices. Second, during turbulence, braced selections can be made when certain selection criteria are satisfied. These selection criteria involve waiting until at least four concurrent contacts are registered on the touchscreen, then selecting the item (if any) beneath the last-placed contact when it is removed from the display. In this way, the user can place four fingers of one hand (e.g., all but the index finger) onto the display – thereby stabilizing their hand on the display– then complete a gesture on the target using their index finger (a fifth contact) to select it. Subsequent selections can be made by dragging the four initially placed contacts across the display, then gesturing again with the index finger – there is no need to lift all fingers off the display when completing a series of selections.

Our experimental validation of Brace Touch (results briefly described in Sect. 5) compared user performance with three different variants of the terminating selection gesture: double tap, dwell (a long press), and force-press. As double-tap is the most usable (better efficiency and higher satisfaction), we detail this technique in the following sections).

4.2 Hardware and Software Architecture of Brace Touch Interaction

Figure 3 shows the general software architecture to manage touch events in order to provide brace touch interaction. The architecture is mapped onto the generic ARCH architecture for interactive systems [10] (left-hand side of Fig. 3). As a result, the hardware and drivers belong to the physical interaction level, finger management and brace interaction models to the logical interaction level. We present the formal description of each element of this logical interaction level using the ICO description technique [31].

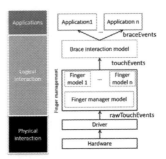

Fig. 3. High-level software architecture of brace interaction

For each user action, the hardware driver produces raw touch events with basic information (e.g., the event type and a touch id). The finger manager handles those events and manages creation and destruction of finger models. The finger model processes low-level events provided by the hardware layer and offers data consultation and update services. The brace interaction model handles interaction logic from the finger manager and produces higher-level events (brace touches) dispatched to interested applications.

4.3 Behavioral Description of Brace Touch Using ICOs

Informal Description of the ICO Formal Notation. The ICO (Interactive Cooperative Objects) notation is a formal description technique devoted to interactive systems. Using high-level Petri nets [20] for dynamic behavior description, the notation also relies on an object-oriented approach (dynamic instantiation, classification, encapsulation, inheritance and client/server relationships) to describe the structural or static aspects of systems. ICO notation objects are composed of four components: a cooperative object for the behavior description, a presentation part (i.e. Graphical Interface), and two functions (activation and rendering) describing the links between the cooperative object and the presentation part. The interested reader can find more information in [31]. ICO addresses all the issues presented in the previous sections including representation of dynamic instantiation of input devices (fingers) which is not addressed in other modelling techniques. For instance, ICO uses the capabilities of Petri nets to describe tokens' creations which are used in models to represent input devices such as fingers on a touchscreen. In the following sections, we will use the following formalism to describe ICO models: **places**, *events*, and <u>transitions</u>.

Finger Behavioral Model. The finger model handles touch information through the *Info* place (center of Fig. 4). The model provides accessors services to touch data through *getTouchInfo* which is accessible by other models to get information about a given finger. The information of the finger can be modified using the *update* service called by the low level architecture to store a new value for the finger. Finally, the *terminate* service handles finger model removal (triggered when the finger is not in contact with the touchscreen anymore).

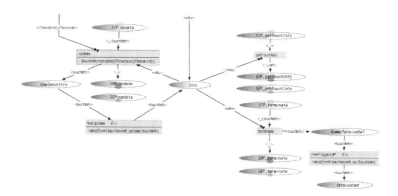

Fig. 4. ICO behavioral model of a finger using ICO notation

Finger Manager Behavioral Model. The finger manager is a model responsible for managing the set of fingers currently on the touch screen. That model received raw events from the platform and abstracted them away in meaningful information in terms of interaction. Figure 5 shows an abstract model of the behavior of the finger manager (the full ICO model cannot be presented due to space constraints). In this view, **places** are represented with ovals, <u>transitions</u> with rectangles, event transitions by rectangles with italic text, produced *events* in italic font alongside the producing transition, and conditions of transition activation under the transition name, separated by a horizontal line.

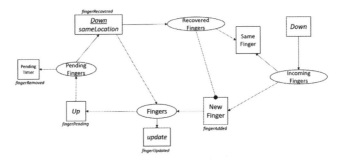

Fig. 5. Abstract behavioral model of the finger manager

In Fig. 5, place **Fingers** stores the references to the finger models (one per finger currently present on the touchscreen). As Brace interaction relies on double tap for target selection, the finger used to perform this interaction will leave (for a short period of time) the surface of the touch screen and will come back at the same location. According to the finger model, leaving the surface would require removing the finger from the pool of fingers. The Brace model thus handles this short disappearance by storing fingers in the **Pending Fingers** place. In order to disambiguate an *Up-Down* from the same finger with an *Up* and *Down* from two different fingers, we chose a temporal and geographical logic. Thus, on finger *Up*, the reference to the finger model is set in place **Pending Fingers** for a duration defined in the PendingTimer transition. If a *Down* event is received before the time has elapsed, its location is compared with the location of the finger when *Up* occurred. If the location is close enough (a parameter in the model), the same finger model is updated and set back into **Fingers** and a *fingerRecovered* event is raised (*Down/sameLocation*). A copy of the reference of that finger model is also stored in **RecoveredFingers**.

Down events correspond to the arrival of a new finger on the touchscreen. When this occurs, a new finger model is instantiated (by the finger manager) and its reference is stored in **IncomingFingers**. If the *Down* event corresponds to a finger that was in the pending state, the information stored in **IncomingFingers** is filtered with SameFinger, thus preventing the creation of a new finger model. Finally, on update, the finger model is updated and *fingerUpdated* event is raised so the information (e.g., the location on the screen) is updated in the corresponding finger model.

Figure 6 shows the finger manager model pending process using the ICO notation. PendingTimer, timed transition is set to 500 ms which corresponds to the maximum time allowed to the user to perform a double tap. Finally, the geographical disambiguation logic consists in verifying that the *Down* event received lies within 30px from the previous *Up* event location (see shapeProcessing transition performing the proximity calculation).

Brace Touch Interaction Behavioral Model. Figure 7 shows an abstract view of the Brace Touch interaction behavior in a similar way as we presented the finger manager in Fig. 5.

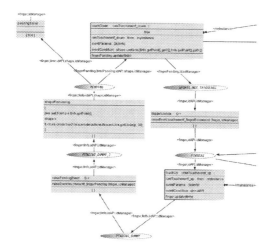

Fig. 6. Part of the finger manager behavior filtering new fingers from returning fingers

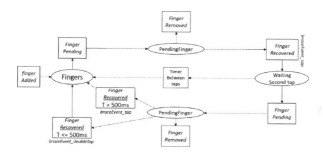

Fig. 7. Abstract model of Brace Touch interaction behavior

The Brace Touch Interaction model listens to the events produced by the Finger Manager namely *fingerAdded*, *fingerPending*, *fingerRemoved* and *fingerRecovered* events, the production of which was detailed in the previous section.

On *fingerAdded*, the reference of the created finger model is stored in place **Fingers**. According to Brace Touch design [12], a double tap is specified as two consecutive taps within 500 ms, a tap being a consecutive *Up* and *Down* with the same finger on the same location (spatial threshold of 30 pixels). Thus, on finger *Up* and *Down*, the finger manager produces respectively *fingerPending* and *fingerRecovered*, unless the finger does not touch the screen again, in which case a *fingerRemoved* event is received. On fingerRecovered, the *braceEvent_tap* is raised and the reference to the finger model is stored in **WaitingSecondTap**.

If a second tap is not initiated within the time frame specified in TimerBetweenTaps, the double tap interaction is exited and the reference to the finger model is stored back in **Fingers**. The second tap interaction has the same behavior as the first tap, apart from the validation of the double tap interaction: if the time between the first tap and the second tap is less than 500 ms, *braceEvent_doubleTap* is raised. Otherwise, the second tap is considered as a single tap following a first tap.

Due to space constraints we cannot present the ICO model of brace interaction but its main features have been highlighted. It is important to note that these models can be analyzed using knowledge from Petri nets theory, such as computing locks and traps as well as P and T invariants [18]. These verification techniques allow interaction designers to assess the correctness of a given model (absence of deadlock) and also evaluate the compatibility between models (e.g., the events produces by a model are consumed by an upper model). The formal analysis performed by the development platform called PetShop [18] supports the detection of development faults.

5   Dependability and Usability of Brace Touch

While a formal notation was presented in previous section to deal with software development faults of interaction techniques in general and Brace Touch interaction in particular, dealing with natural and operational faults is required to bring such concepts into real operation in aircraft cockpits. We have briefly mentioned diversity, redundancy and segregation in hardware technologies for touch devices as a mean to address hardware faults.

Natural faults could affect software (via bit flips, for example) but also operators (via vibration of the touch device). As for natural software faults, self-checking techniques for interactive widgets and interaction techniques as presented in [39] could support detection and removal of faults in touch interactions. However, touch interactions are more sensitive to natural faults such as turbulence that will trigger unintentional operational faults. Brace Touch interaction aims at reducing the effect of turbulence on operational faults for touch interactions.

However, as presented in [17] the introduction of dependability mechanisms might affect negatively usability of the interactive system. It was thus important to assess the impact on the overall performance of braced interaction to ensure that the technique does not slow down operation. This is demonstrated in Fig. 8: in vibrating conditions, braced interaction with selection using double-tap has a similar (though slightly slower) performance to non-braced interactions in non-vibrating conditions.

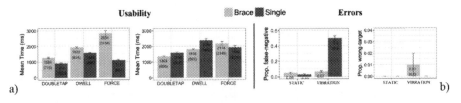

Fig. 8. Target selection times with Braced and Single-Finger selections in static (left) and vibrating (right) conditions [12].

In [12], Cockburn et al. report results of an experiment examining three different forms of braced selections in turbulent and static environments. Turbulence was simulated using a Mikrolar motion platform, with a seat and touchscreen mounted on the platform. The three bracing variants differed in the gesture used for completing a selection: doubletap, dwell (long press) and force threshold (not considered further in this paper). Participants also completed selections using traditional single-finger tap-to-select modalities, with this data serving as a baseline comparator for the braced selection methods. Additionally, in one portion of the experiment, participants were allowed to choose whether to complete selections using braced touch (placing multiple fingers on the display) or normal hand postures (using a single finger without bracing, terminated with a doubletap, dwell or force-press).

Figure 8 summarises the usability study of Brace Touch looking at performance (a) and user errors (b). Selection time results using the three bracing methods and equivalent single-finger selections in static (pink bar) and turbulent (bleu bar) settings. As expected, in static settings single-finger selections are faster than braced selections, but when vibration is present, braced selections were significantly faster and more accurate than single-finger selections. In tasks where participants were free to choose whether or not to use braced postures, 88% of double-tap users chose to use bracing when vibration was present, compared to only 19% when static. This suggests that users were aware of the benefits provided by bracing and appropriately chose to use it to overcome interaction problems stemming from vibration.

Two types of errors were analysed: false-negative selections, in which subjects tried but failed to complete a selection; and wrong-target selections, in which a target other than the intended one was selected. Figure 8(b) summarises the results of errors from the user study. The histogram highlight the strong tolerance to vibrations of Brace Touch with respect to false negatives. Value of wrong target selection (not as good as false negatives) was influenced by the tasks performed by the users which were related to aircraft operations with which they were not familiar. In [12], Cokburn et al. show that for the later tasks, wrong target selection errors with Brace Touch disappeared and that in 87.3% of selections, subjects elected to use braced selections during vibrations.

According to Avizienis et al.'s taxonomy [6], as far as touch screens are concerned, vibrations would belong to natural faults triggering non-intentional human-made faults during operation, and would correspond to slips in the human error classifications [35]. Looking at the interaction itself, the operator decides intentionally to interact with the touch screen and to use (preferably) Brace Touch interactions in cases of turbulence [12]. However, while interacting, the user might unintentionally make errors that will prevent Brace Touch interaction from being performed. For instance, in Brace, the index finger is meant to be the finger used for performing the double-tap while the other fingers are constantly touching the touch device. Vibrations might make other fingers (especially the little finger) bounce and thus trigger unintentional double-taps. We have extended the behavior of Brace Touch to detect the position of index fingers (which can be deduced from the relative position of the other fingers) and discard spurious double-taps triggered by the other fingers. Due to space constraints, we do not present the ICO model here, but the approach is the same as the one presented in Brace Interaction model.

6   Conclusion and Perspective

New interactive technologies are making their way into command and control positions of safety critical systems. This is due to the new type of work and new type of data that operators have to manipulate, but also because those technologies are now pervasive and used in everyday life. This paper presented a contribution to the dependability of touch interactions to be deployed in real life contexts such as aircraft cockpits.

We have presented a formal description technique dedicated to interactive system description that addresses the problem of development faults in interaction techniques. We used that formal description technique to model a new touch interaction technique called Brace Touch that is able to avoid operational natural faults. We also shown that Brace Touch does not jeopardize the usability of touch interactions, providing good performance, recall, and user satisfaction.

This work cannot be separated from design aspects of interactive systems that include how to present information to the operators, and more precisely, the size and the colors of objects. Previous work [14] has highlighted that vibrations affects perception and thus there is a need to address the entire interaction loop (perception, cognition, and action). This is what will be done in future studies that could lead to user interface guidelines for touch interfaces in transportation. It is important to note that previous work on model-based approaches for usability engineering [33] and interaction reconfigurations [30] provide some bases to address that problem.

References

1. Albinsson, P.A., Zhai, S.: High precision touch screen interaction. In: Proceedings of ACM CHI Conference, pp. 105–112 (2003)
2. Accot, J., Chatty, S., Maury, S., Palanque, P.: Formal transducers: models of devices and building bricks for the design of highly interactive systems. In: Harrison, M.D., Torres, J.C. (eds) Design, Specification and Verification of Interactive Systems 1997. Eurographics, pp. 143–159. Springer, Vienna (1997). https://doi.org/10.1007/978-3-7091-6878-3_10
3. ARINC 661 Cockpit Display System Interfaces to User Systems. ARINC Specification 661. Airlines Electronic Engineering Committee (AEEC) (2002)
4. ARINC 661. Cockpit display system interfaces to user systems. ARINC Specification 661, supplement 7 (April 2019). Airlines Electronic Engineering Committee (AEEC) (2019)
5. Au, O.K.C., Tai, C.L.: Multitouch finger registration and its applications. In: ACM CHI Conference, pp. 41–48 (2010)
6. Avizienis, A., Laprie, J.-C., Randell, B., Landwehr, C.: Basic concepts and taxonomy of dependable and secure computing. IEEE Trans. Dependable Secure Comput. 1(1), 11–33 (2004)
7. Bailly, G., Lecolinet, E., Guiard, Y.: Finger-count & radial-stroke shortcuts: 2 techniques for augmenting linear menus on multi-touch surfaces. In: ACM CHI Conference, pp. 591–594 (2010)
8. Barbé, J., Chatrenet, N., et al.: Physical ergonomics approach for touch screen interaction in an aircraft cockpit. In: Conference on Interaction Homme-Machine (IHM), pp. 9–16. ACM DL (2012)

9. Barboni, E., Conversy, S., Navarre, D., Palanque, P.: Model-based engineering of widgets, user applications and servers compliant with ARINC 661 specification. In: Doherty, G., Blandford, A. (eds.) DSV-IS 2006. LNCS, vol. 4323, pp. 25–38. Springer, Heidelberg (2007). https://doi.org/10.1007/978-3-540-69554-7_3
10. Bass, L., et al.: The arch model: Seeheim revisited. In: User Interface Developers' Workshop, April 1991
11. Cockburn, A., et al.: Turbulent touch: Touchscreen input for cockpit flight displays. In: Proceedings of ACM CHI Conference, pp. 6742–6753 (2017)
12. Cockburn, A., et al.: Design and evaluation of brace touch for touchscreen input stabilisation. Int. J. Hum.-Comput. Stud. **122**(21–37), 7 (2019)
13. DO-178C/ED-12C, Software Considerations in Airborne Systems and Equipment Certification, published by RTCA and EUROCAE (2012)
14. Dodd, S., Lancaster, J., Miranda, A., Grothe, S., DeMers, B., Rogers, B.: Touch screens on the flight deck: the impact of touch target size, spacing, touch technology and turbulence on pilot performance. In: Proceedings of the HFES Annual Meeting, vol. 58, no. 1, pp. 6–10 (2014)
15. Ewerling, P., Kulik, A., Froehlich, B.: Finger and hand detection for multi-touch interfaces based on maximally stable extremal regions. In: ACM TEI Conference, pp. 173–182 (2012)
16. Fayollas, C., Palanque, P., Fabre, J-C., Martinie, C., Déléris, Y.: Dealing with faults during operations: beyond classical use of formal methods. In: [19], pp. 549–575 (2017)
17. Fayollas, C., Martinie, C., Palanque, P., Deleris, Y., Fabre, J.-C., Navarre, D.: An approach for assessing the impact of dependability on usability: application to interactive cockpits. In: IEEE European Dependable Computing Conference (EDCC), pp. 198–209 (2014)
18. Fayollas, C., Martinie, C., Palanque, P., Barboni, E., Fahssi, R., Hamon, A.: Exploiting action theory as a framework for analysis and design of formal methods approaches: application to the CIRCUS integrated development environment. In: [19], pp. 465–504
19. Weyers, B., Bowen, J., Dix, A., Palanque, P. (eds.): The Handbook of Formal Methods in Human-Computer Interaction. HIS. Springer, Cham (2017). https://doi.org/10.1007/978-3-319-51838-1
20. Genrich, H.J.: Predicate/transitions nets. In: Jensen, K., Rozenberg, G. (eds) High-Levels Petri Nets: Theory and Application. Springer, Heidelberg, pp. 3–43 (1991). https://doi.org/10.1007/978-3-642-84524-6_1
21. Hamon-Keromen, A., Palanque, P., Deleris, Y., Navarre, D., Barboni, E.: A tool-supported development process for bringing touch interactions into interactive cockpits for controlling embedded critical systems. In: HCI in Aeronautics (HCI'Aero), pp. 25–36. ACM DL (2012)
22. Hamon-Keromen, A., Palanque, P., Silva, J.-L., Deleris, Y., Barboni, E.: Formal description of multi-touch interactions. In: ACM Engineering Interactive Computing Systems, pp. 207–216 (2013)
23. Harrison, C., Schwarz, J., Hudson, S.E.: TapSense: enhancing finger interaction on touch surfaces. In: Proceedings on ACM UIST Conference, pp. 627–636. ACM (2011)
24. Hutchins, E., Lauwsen, T.: Distributed cognition in an airline cockpit. In: Engeström, Y., Middleton, D. (Eds) Cognition and Communication at work. Cambridge University Press, Cambridge (1996)
25. ISO 9241-9:2010 Usability - Part 9: Requirements for non-keyboard input devices (2010)
26. Karat, J., McDonald, J., Anderson, M.: A comparison of selection techniques: touch panel, mouse, keyboard. Int. J. Man-Mach. Stud. **1**, 73–92 (1986)
27. Kin, K., Hartmann, B., Agrawala, M.: Two-handed marking menus for multitouch devices. ACM Trans. Comput.-Hum. Interact. (TOCHI) **18**(3), 16 (2011)

28. Marquardt, N., Kiemer, J., Ledo, D., Boring, S., Greenberg, S.: Designing user-, hand-, and handpart-aware tabletop interactions with the TouchID toolkit. In: Proceedings of ACM TEI, pp. 21–30 (2011)
29. Memon, A.M.: An event-flow model of GUI-based applications for testing. Softw. Test. Verif. Reliab. **17**, 137–157 (2007)
30. Navarre, D., Palanque, P., Basnyat, S.: A formal approach for user interaction reconfiguration of safety critical interactive systems. In: Harrison, M.D., Sujan, M.-A. (eds.) SAFECOMP 2008. LNCS, vol. 5219, pp. 373–386. Springer, Heidelberg (2008). https://doi.org/10.1007/978-3-540-87698-4_31
31. Navarre, D., Palanque, P., Ladry, J.F., Barboni, E.: ICOs: a model-based user interface description technique dedicated to interactive systems addressing usability, reliability and scalability. ACM Trans. Comput.-Hum. Interact. **16**(4), 18 (2009)
32. Olwal, A., Feiner, S.: Rubbing the fisheye: precise touch-screen interaction with gestures and fisheye views. In: Conference Supplement of UIST 2003, pp. 83–84 (2003)
33. Palanque, P., Barboni, E., Martinie, C., Navarre, D., Winckler, M.: A model-based approach for supporting engineering usability evaluation of interaction techniques. In: Conference on ACM Engineering Interactive Computing Systems (EICS 2011), pp. 21–30 (2011)
34. Potter, R.L., Weldon, L.J., Shneiderman, B.: Improving the accuracy of touchscreens: an experimental evaluation of three strategies. In: Proceedings of CHI 1988, pp. 27–32 (1988)
35. Reason, J.: Human Error. Cambridge University Press, Cambridge (1990)
36. Shneiderman, B.: Touchscreens now offer compelling uses. In: Sparks of Innovation in Human-Computer Interaction. Ablex, Norwood (1993)
37. Sugiura, A., Koseki, Y.: A user interface using fingerprint recognition: holding commands and data objects on fingers. In: Proceedings of ACM UIST Conference, pp. 71–79 (1998)
38. Stanton, N., et al.: Predicting design induced pilot error using HET (Human Error Template) – a new formal human error identification method for flight decks. J. Aeronaut. Sci. **110**, 107–115 (2006)
39. Tankeu-Choitat, A., Navarre, D., Palanque, P., Deleris, Y., Fabre, J.-C., Fayollas, C.: Self-checking components for dependable interactive cockpits using formal description techniques. In: IEEE Pacific Rim Dependable Computing Conference, pp. 164–173 (2011)
40. Walker, G.: A review of technologies for sensing contact location on the surface of a display. J. Soc. Inf. Disp. **20**(8), 413–440 (2012)
41. Wang, F., Cao, X., Ren, X., Irani, P.: Detecting and leveraging finger orientation for interaction with direct-touch surfaces. In: Proceedings of ACM UIST Conference, pp. 23–32 (2009)

Fitness Functions for Testing Automated and Autonomous Driving Systems

Florian Hauer[1]([⊠]), Alexander Pretschner[1], and Bernd Holzmüller[2]

[1] Technical University of Munich, Arcisstraße 21, 80333 Munich, Germany
{florian.hauer,alexander.pretschner}@tum.de
[2] ITK Engineering GmbH, Im Speyerer Tal 6, 76761 Ruelzheim, Germany
bernd.holzmueller@itk-engineering.de

Abstract. Functional specifications and real drive data are typically used to derive parameterized scenarios for scenario-based testing of driving systems. The domains of the parameters span a huge space of possible test cases, from which "good" ones have to be selected. Heuristic search, guided by fitness functions, has been proposed as a suitable technique in the past. However, the *methodological challenge of creating suitable fitness functions* has not been addressed yet. We provide templates to formulate fitness functions for testing automated and autonomous driving systems. Those templates ensure correct positioning of scenario objects in space, yield a suitable ordering of maneuvers in time, and enable the search for scenarios in which the system leaves its safe operating envelope. We show how to compose them into fitness functions for heuristic search. Collision and close-to-collision scenarios from real drive data serve as a use case to show the applicability of the presented templates.

Keywords: System verification · Automated and autonomous driving · Scenario-based testing · Search-based techniques

1 Introduction

Striving for highly automated and autonomous driving systems results in evermore complex and capable systems. Due to the complexity of these systems and the complexity and sheer number of possible scenarios, ensuring safety and functional correctness is a crucial challenge [9]. Since verification and validation by real test drives alone are practically infeasible [17], the focus shifts to virtual test drives. For virtual testing, scenario-based closed-loop testing in the form of X-in-the-Loop settings is used [16]. Such scenarios describe dynamic traffic situations to test the behavior of the automated or autonomous driving system. A whole set of such scenarios is encoded by a *parameterized scenario*. We show such a parameterized scenario for a highway pilot in Fig. 1. The ego vehicle e accelerates from standstill and approaches car c_3, which is driving at lower velocity than e. e then changes to the middle lane, while simultaneously c_1 changes also to the middle lane behind e. During this scenario, e must not violate the

© Springer Nature Switzerland AG 2019
A. Romanovsky et al. (Eds.): SAFECOMP 2019, LNCS 11698, pp. 69–84, 2019.
https://doi.org/10.1007/978-3-030-26601-1_5

safety distances, e.g. the one to c_2 (shaded area in Fig. 1). Each other car c_i, $i \in \{1, 2, 3\}$ has a parameter for its longitudinal starting position s_{0,c_i}, a starting time t_{start,c_i} for accelerating from standstill, and a desired velocity v_i it tries to reach and hold throughout the scenarios. In addition, the lane change of c_1 is triggered at a specific time, described by parameter t_{lc,c_1}. The domains of these ten parameters span a ten-dimensional space of possible test scenarios.

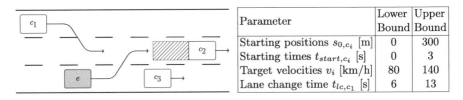

Parameter	Lower Bound	Upper Bound
Starting positions s_{0,c_i} [m]	0	300
Starting times t_{start,c_i} [s]	0	3
Target velocities v_i [km/h]	80	140
Lane change time t_{lc,c_1} [s]	6	13

Fig. 1. Parameterized highway scenario with ten parameters and their domains

Most scenarios in this space are not useful test cases, however. In some scenarios, e will not even perform a lane change; will perform it in front of c_2 instead of behind it; or c_1 performs its lane change several seconds later than e. Instead, "good" test cases need to be identified within the parameter space. In one interpretation of "good" test scenarios, a correct system *approaches* safe operating limits, and a faulty system violates them. Existing works suggest the use of search-based techniques. These were successfully applied for testing classic advanced driver assistance systems (SAE levels 1&2 [14]), e.g. a parking assistant, an adaptive cruise control, an emergency braking system, and their combination.

Those works focus on technical aspects, e.g. on how to improve the search algorithm, and assume the fitness functions to be given or created ad-hoc. This was an important, and successful, first step. Because these search-based techniques are so promising, we want to apply them to testing automated and autonomous driving systems of SAE levels 4&5 [14]. Such systems are fundamentally different, as they take over the complete driving task including decision making and executing active maneuvers in dynamic traffic scenarios. Thus, the variety of different possible parameterized scenarios is huge, which requires the definition of many different fitness functions. However, formulating fitness functions correctly is difficult, time-consuming, and requires experience. Wrongly derived fitness functions leave "good" test cases unidentified, which might even lead to wrong conclusions about the test results. It seems clear that creating fitness functions ad-hoc, as done in the past, is not sufficient. For the derivation of fitness functions at large scale, methodological guidance for test engineers is needed.

The **contribution of this paper** is the following: We provide such guidance in the form of a set of fitness function *templates* for testing automated and autonomous driving systems in dynamic traffic scenarios with heuristic search.

It is further explained how those templates can be easily combined and applied to identify "good" test cases for complex scenario types.

Section 2 explains scenario-based testing and the application of search-based techniques in this domain. The templates are described in Sect. 3, before Sect. 4 presents ways to combine them. An application is provided in Sect. 5. We discuss related work in Sect. 6 and conclude in Sect. 7.

2 Scenario-Based Testing with Search-Based Techniques

In scenario-based testing of automated and autonomous driving systems, the goal is to test the behavior of such systems in dynamic traffic situations. A multitude of different scenario types exist. Several sources of information are used for the identification of those types, e.g. requirements, safety analysis, functional specifications, traffic rules, and real (test) drives. For each scenario type, one or more parameterized scenarios are derived, each describing a set of test cases. Generalizing and adapting the formalism of [2] and [10], we define a parameterized scenario as (X, V, D), where X is the data set that describes the scenario type (e.g. lane change) and context (e.g. two-lane highway). It can be described using the OpenScenario [1] or CommonRoad [5] formats. The variables $v_i \in V$ ($i \leq n$) are parameters (e.g. velocities of traffic participants) with their domains $D_i \in D$. Assigning a value to each v_i yields a single test case. The domains in D span an infinite search space $A = D_1 \times D_2 \times \ldots \times D_n \subset \mathbb{R}^n$ of test cases.

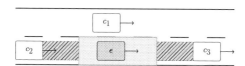

Fig. 2. Example of a simple safe operating envelope (green plain rectangle) bounded by the necessary safety distances (red shaded rectangles) and lane markings (Color figure online)

The simulated scenario describes input and environment conditions of a **test case**. The expected behavior of continuous systems is described with the help of domains and thresholds. In this context, a safe operating envelope is used (Fig. 2). Inside the envelope, the system is allowed to freely optimize its performance [9], and as long as it does not leave the envelope, it is considered safe. By that the safe operating envelope provides a description of safe system behavior. It depends on the scenario and changes over time during the scenario. Recent works, e.g. the responsibility-sensitive safety (RSS) model [15], the safety force field model [11] as well as other formal models [13] presented such envelopes. These works provide a model of safe system behavior even for scenarios, in which the system alone cannot guarantee complete safety, as other traffic participants may still cause accidents. In the spirit of limit testing, we define a **"good" test case** as follows (see [12]):

*A "good" test case can reveal potentially faulty system behavior. That
means in a "good" test scenario, a correct system approaches the limits
of the safe operating envelope, and a faulty system violates them.*

A **fitness function** $f : A \rightarrow W$ assigns every test case a **quality** value
$w \in W$, which depends on the observed behavior of the system under test in
the respective test case. It is important that a total order on the fitness values
is preserved, such that a scenario gets a better quality value than another if it is
a better test case. If the search space A and the quality function f are created
accordingly, then search-based techniques may be used to find the "good" test
cases in the following way (see Fig. 3):

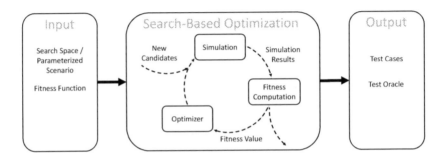

Fig. 3. Search-based techniques for scenario optimization

An initial set of scenario candidates is created either by reusing existing
scenarios, by using manually created ones by experts, or by generating them
randomly. These candidates are then executed in a simulation and the simulation results are evaluated by the fitness function, which returns a quantitative
quality measure for the respective scenario. According to these fitness values, the
optimization algorithm tries to adapt the parameter values in order to obtain
scenarios of better quality. This iteration may be continued until a maximum
number of iterations is reached, the assigned computation time is spent or the
optimizer fails to find a better solution. This means that during the optimization process, the system is usually tested in one test case per fitness function
evaluation, depending on the applied optimization technique. In the ideal case,
search-based techniques would find the global optimum, which is the best scenario. This scenario is called worst-case. In the case that the system does not
leave the safe operating envelope in the worst-case, it is considered to be safe.

In the following, templates are presented, which may be combined to fitness
functions. For this work, the search space is assumed to be given, e.g. we use a
parameterized scenario created by a domain expert.

3   Fitness Function Templates

In order to capture all potential scenarios, we present templates to aim for qualitative and quantitative test goals. Our goal is to find test cases, in which the

system violates the safe operating envelope, e.g. by coming below a distance threshold. We call this a quantitative test goal, since a quantitative value (e.g. a distance between cars) is used to assign a fitness value. We present a suitable template to search for a violation of the safe operating envelope.

However, search spaces usually contain many scenarios in which a desired system behavior, e.g. a lane change, does not take place because the necessary context to provoke it does not occur. For instance, there is no lane change if there is no car to be overtaken. In theory it might be possible to only use a quantitative test goal and search for the violation of a safe operating envelope in a search space covering all possible scenarios. However, in practice this is undesired for several reasons. Scenario types (e.g. lane change, cut-in) are human-interpretable; testing every type on its own provides information about the quality of the system behavior in those specific scenarios. Further, testing these interpretable scenario types will be required by certification authorities. Lastly, such a theoretical search space that contains all possible scenarios is high-dimensional and complex. The search for a safety violation would be difficult - or even practically infeasible - for current search-based techniques. Thus, we need to ensure that the scenario description encodes the relevant parts of the context. Those are called qualitative test goals, since the mere existence of the relevant circumstances is used to assign a fitness value.

For dynamic scenarios, two aspects are of fundamental importance: space and time. Scenario objects need to be at the correct location at a specific moment, e.g. one car should be ahead of another. Furthermore, scenario events need to take place at the right moment in time, e.g. two cars should change the lane simultaneously. Since the (dynamic) behavior of the ego vehicle is unknown a-priori, the correct timing of maneuvers and positioning of scenario objects cannot be established statically and a-priori, e.g. by setting suitable parameter domain boundaries. However, incorporating such desired qualitative test goals into fitness functions is possible. We hence present specific templates for timing and positioning to ensure that such qualitative goals are fulfilled. During optimization those templates identify the scenarios that fulfill the qualitative test goals. Among them the best scenario is searched with the template that aims at the quantitative test goal. Note that in this work, **minimization** is used for optimization purposes. In the following, we will explain the generic idea first, before transferring it to templates for automated and autonomous driving systems.

3.1   Template for Testing Against Safe Operating Envelopes

We start with a very basic, simple, and intuitive template. Even though most of the existing works in this domain do not state it explicitly, their idea is to measure a certain system behavior and identify a test case in which this system behavior exceeds a threshold. For the case of a constant threshold, a qualitative generic example is provided in Fig. 4.

The blue time series describes a system behavior and the red line a threshold that must not be violated. This means the maximum value of the blue curve must not be greater than the threshold. During an optimization process, it is desired

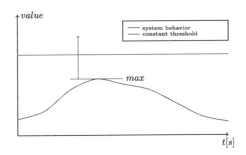

Fig. 4. Generic case of testing system behavior against a constant threshold (Color figure online)

that better and better scenarios are found, which means that the maximum of the blue curve gets closer and closer to the red line or even surpasses it. The following fitness function idea may be used to achieve the described search behavior (assuming minimization): $f_{\text{idea},1} = -\max(blue\ curve)$

Now, this idea is transferred for testing automated and autonomous driving systems in dynamic traffic scenarios. As described in Sect. 2, instead of a constant threshold, a safe operating envelope is used, e.g. as presented in recent works [11,13,15]. Those works express safety often as a safety distance in time or space, which is usually depending on velocities of and relative positions among cars and, thus, is changing over time. We use *safeDist* as a placeholder for the computation of a safety distance according to such a safe operating envelope. We stick to the example of Fig. 1, but for the sake of simplicity, only c_2 and the safety distance to it are considered on a single lane for now (see Fig. 5):

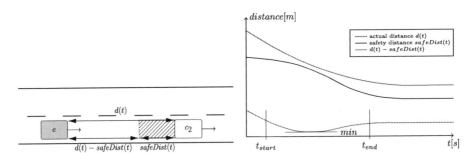

Fig. 5. Schematic depiction of a safety distance that should not be violated

The ego vehicle e is approaching another vehicle c_2, which is driving at lower velocity. Once e gets closer, it will reduce its velocity until it reaches the velocity of c_2. During this period, e must not violate the safety distance. Applying the classic idea $f_{\text{idea},1}$ as fitness function would mean that the scenario is searched, in which the distance d between e and c_2 gets smallest. However, a small d does not necessarily mean that the *safeDist* threshold is violated, since safety distances might be even smaller (relatively speaking) in scenarios with low velocities. One cannot conclude by the achieved fitness value whether the safe operating envelope has been violated or not. The dynamically changing safety distance has to be included into the template:

Template 1: $$f_{\text{template},1} = \min(d(t) - safeDist(t)) \qquad (1)$$

The difference of $d(t)$ and $safeDist(t)$ is denoted as the remaining buffer until violation of the threshold (see Fig. 5). Within the scenario, the minimum remaining buffer is used as characteristic value, since it is the most dangerous moment. By applying this template, search techniques will identify the scenario in which the minimum of the remaining buffer is smaller than the minimum remaining buffer in all other scenarios. This has the side effect that the following test oracle can be applied for this template: If the remaining buffer is greater or equal than 0 even in the worst-case scenario, the system did never enter and, thus, never violate the safety distance. It even kept an additional distance equal to the remaining buffer in the worst-case. It never left the safe operating envelope and it is considered safe. If the remaining buffer is negative, a faulty system behavior is revealed. In this case, the absolute value is the amount by which the system violated the safety distance. Using this template, an argumentation basis for the release process is provided by making the system behavior measurable. With the help of this measurement, systems can be compared with respect to their performance in the system-specific worst-case.

3.2   Templates for Ensuring Qualitative Test Goals

General Idea to Ensure Qualitative Test Goals. A specific scenario does or does not satisfy the desired qualitative test goals. The following templates can be used to ensure such goals. By combination of multiple templates (Sect. 4), multiple qualitative test goals can be fulfilled. In the case of non-fulfillment of a goal, we assign the value m as fitness value, which has to be greater than any value that corresponds to a qualitative test goal being fulfilled. If m is constant, the optimizer will perform like random selection. However, we want to apply search-based techniques to identify scenarios that satisfy the desired qualitative test goals. Thus, this m should be a gradual measurement to provide a ranking among the scenarios that do not fulfill this qualitative test goal. In order to gradually reach a "fulfilling" scenario, a measurement is used for how far a scenario is away from fulfilling the goal. Since the mere fulfillment of the qualitative test goal is sufficient, every scenario that does so is equally good and, thus, receives the same constant fitness value, e.g. 0:

$$f_{\text{idea},2} = \begin{cases} m, & \text{qualitative test goal not fulfilled} \\ 0, & \text{otherwise} \end{cases} \qquad (2)$$

Assume a time series (blue curve in Fig. 6), which serves as input for the computation of m. At a specific time t_1, a qualitative test goal should be fulfilled.

Fulfillment means that the value of the time series $value(t_1)$ at t_1 is in between the red thresholds z_{min} and z_{max}. Note that in general those thresholds do not need to be constant.

If $value(t_1)$ is outside the area described by the thresholds, m is the distance of $value(t_1)$ to the closer threshold to reach the area in between. During the optimization, $value(t_1)$ would approach the area. To avoid having one fitness function per threshold, the mean of the thresholds is chosen:

$$f_{idea,3} = \begin{cases} \left| \frac{z_{min}+z_{max}}{2} - value(t_1) \right|, & value(t_1) \text{ outside} \\ 0, & \text{otherwise} \end{cases} \quad (3)$$

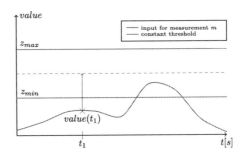

Fig. 6. Depiction of the general idea: The value of a curve at a specific moment has to be within a specific domain. (Color figure online)

Template for Correct Positioning of Scenario Objects. This general idea is now transferred to a template. It ensures that scenario objects, e.g. cars, are correctly located relative to each other at a specific moment in time during the scenario. In Fig. 7, a scenario is depicted in which the ego vehicle e and the other cars c_1, c_2 are driving on two lanes next to each other. Assume that the qualitative test goal is that e is located in between c_1 and c_2 at a specific moment t_{event}. This might be desired in the case that e should perform a lane change into the gap bounded by c_1 and c_2.

The position of the ego vehicle s_e is used to compute the measurement m. The positions of the other cars s_{c_1}, s_{c_2} serve as thresholds. Note that in contrast to above, here the thresholds are not constant. The transferred template looks as follows:

Template 2a: $\hspace{8cm}$ (4)

$$f_{template,2a} = \begin{cases} \left| \frac{s_{c_1}(t_{event})+s_{c_2}(t_{event})}{2} - s_e(t_{event}) \right|, & e \text{ not in between } c_1 \text{ and } c_2 \\ 0, & \text{otherwise} \end{cases}$$

During the optimization, the structure of the template will bring e closer and closer to the gap until it is in the gap. However, as it is the case for the introductory example in Fig. 1, there might not be a gap. Only a single other car

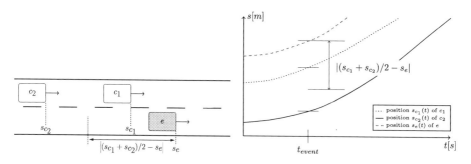

Fig. 7. Qualitative test goal: e should be located in the gap at t_{event}

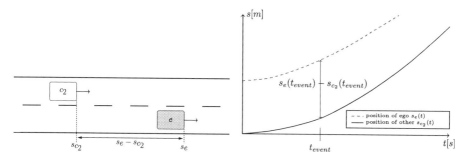

Fig. 8. Qualitative test goal: e should be located behind c_1 at t_{event}

is of interest for relative positioning. The ego vehicle should be located behind c_2 for its lane change. This is reduced to the situation of Fig. 8.

In the case that e is ahead of c_2, the distance between them is used as measurement m. Since there is only one threshold ("behind of"), there is a slight difference to template 2a. This simplifies the template to the following, where only the distance to the one threshold is used:

Template 2b: (5)

$$f_{template,2b} = \begin{cases} s_{c_2}(t_{event}) - s_e(t_{event}), & s_e(t_{event}) < s_{c_2}(t_{event}) \\ 0, & \text{otherwise} \end{cases}$$

Template for Correct Timing of Scenario Events. So far, a template for the search of safe operating violations as well as templates for correct positioning of scenario elements were discussed. In the following, a template for timing is presented. It can be used to ensure that events, e.g. the start of a maneuver, are happening at the right moments in time relatively to each other. In the example of Fig. 1, the ego vehicle and the c_1 are supposed to perform their lane changes onto the middle lane simultaneously. This means that c_1 starts its lane change during the lane change of e. This is resembled in Fig. 9.

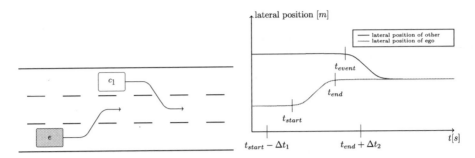

Fig. 9. Qualitative test goal: Lane changes should happen simultaneously

To allow c_1 to start its lane change even a bit before e, an offset Δt_1 can be used. In general, also an offset Δt_2 is possible, even though here it is set to 0. A $\Delta t_2 > 0$ would mean that c_1 starts lane changing after e already completed its lane change. The general idea of $f_{idea,3}$ is adjusted to yield a template for timings. However, this time the thresholds are not on the vertical axis as it is the case for the location templates, but on the horizontal one. The thresholds are the start t_{start} and the end t_{end} of the ego vehicle's lane change. In the case that the start of the other vehicle's lane change is not in between $t_{start} - \Delta t_1$ and $t_{end} + \Delta t_2$, the distance to the middle of the interval is chosen. The template for timing looks as follows:

Template 3: $\hspace{10cm}$ (6)

$$f_{template,3} = \begin{cases} \left| \frac{t_{start} - \Delta t_1 + t_{end} + \Delta t_2}{2} - t_{event} \right|, & t_{event} \text{ not in between bounds} \\ 0, & \text{otherwise} \end{cases}$$

4   Combining Templates

We have presented several templates, each addressing a specific aspect. In the following, it is described how those templates can be combined to a fitness function that can be used by search-based techniques to yield complex scenarios. There are two possibilities: Combining the set of templates to a single fitness function allows the usage of single-objective optimizers, while for multi-objective search, the fitness functions stay separated.

4.1   Combination for Single-Objective Search

The templates are nested into each other with the help of case distinctions. The innermost level in the nesting is a template that measures the behavior of the system with respect to a safe operating envelope; it aims for a quantitative test goal. The outer levels of nesting are templates for qualitative test goals (e.g. positioning and timing), which need to be fulfilled for the inner ones. Each level consists of one template returning the measurement m as described above.

Instead of returning 0 in the case that the qualitative test goal is fulfilled, the measurement m of the next inner level is returned. This structure causes the optimizer to approach the search in steps. First, scenarios are searched that are of the desired form. Among those, the best scenario is identified for testing against a safe operating envelope. To ensure the necessary total order of fitness values, offsets are added to all levels of nesting except for the most inner one. This offset needs to be greater than the maximum value of the next inner level. A simple overapproximation of the sum of the m of the next inner level plus the offset of the next inner level is sufficient.

4.2 Combination for Multi-objective Search

Most likely, there are some goals that are not dependent on each other, meaning that each of those independent goals can be fulfilled without the constraint that the others need to be fulfilled. For instance in the introductory example in Fig. 1, the goal that "e performs its lane change behind c_2" can be fulfilled even though the goal that "c_1 performs its lane change simultaneously with e" is not fulfilled. In contrast to the usage of single-objective search, independent goals can be optimized simultaneously with multi-objective search. Multi-objective search optimizes a vector x of fitness values x_i instead of a single fitness value. The concept of Pareto optimization is used. A vector x is better than another vector y if all $x_i \leq y_i$ and at least one $x_i < y_i$. Each x_i is computed by a single template f_j, which may depend on one or more $f_k, j \neq k$. The f_j that are dependent on other $f_k, j \neq k$ need to be adjusted in the following way: In the case that at least one of the f_k is not 0, which means that the qualitative test goal connected to at least one of the f_k is not fulfilled, x_j is set to a very bad, high value. Step by step, the preliminary qualitative test goals will get fulfilled before the remaining test goals are optimized.

5 Application of the Templates

Since many car manufacturers and suppliers are currently developing a highway pilot system or a comparable system, such a system is chosen for demonstration purposes. It has to cope with all possible situations on the highway and does not require the driver to take over in critical situations. Therefore, the highway pilot is considered to be an automated driving system of SAE's level 4 [14]. Many natural driving studies have been conducted to gather data for further understanding of road traffic and the driver's task (e.g. [8]). The database of the biggest one [8] got analyzed for near-collision and collision recordings on highways. The findings were grouped to 24 scenario types [18]. We used those as use cases for the presented templates. In fact, the example of Figs. 1 and 10 is one of those scenario types. The presented templates ensure that maneuvers happen at the right moment and objects are located correctly, while another template searches for violations of the safe operating envelope. Using these templates, we were able to create suitable fitness functions for all of those scenario types. Since those are the near-collision and collision scenarios, they are the most critical ones. By at least covering those 24 scenarios with the templates, we argue that the presented set of templates is sufficient for most of the critical highway traffic scenarios. The following depicts the ease of use of the templates by applying them to the most complex scenario of the 24, which is the introductory example of Figs. 1 and 10. A variety of other scenarios is contained in this one, e.g. a lane change of the ego vehicle behind another car without further surrounding cars.

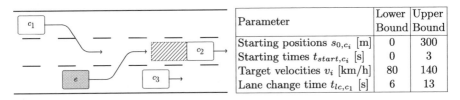

Parameter	Lower Bound	Upper Bound
Starting positions s_{0,c_i} [m]	0	300
Starting times t_{start,c_i} [s]	0	3
Target velocities v_i [km/h]	80	140
Lane change time t_{lc,c_1} [s]	6	13

Fig. 10. Most complex (close-to-)collision scenario of the reduced set of scenarios from the database analysis [18]

For this scenario, several fitness functions are needed:

- The lane change of e needs to happen, for which a constant template is used. For the given search space, a constant measurement m is not problematic, since many candidates contain a lane change of e.

$$\alpha = \begin{cases} \infty, & e \text{ does not change lanes} \\ 0, & \text{otherwise} \end{cases} \tag{7}$$

- The lane change of e needs to happen **behind** c_2, which indicates the use of the positioning template. Let the moment, when e gets past the lane markings between the starting lane and the target lane, be denoted as $t_{e,start}$.

$$\beta = \begin{cases} s_e(t_{e,start}) - s_{c_2}(t_{e,start}), & s_{c_2}(t_{e,start}) < s_e(t_{e,start}) \\ 0, & \text{otherwise} \end{cases} \tag{8}$$

- The lane change of c_1 needs to happen **behind** e. Again, the template for positioning is used. Let the moment, when c_1 gets past the lane markings between the starting lane and the target lane, be denoted as $t_{c_1,start}$.

$$\gamma = \begin{cases} s_{c_1}(t_{c_1,start}) - s_e(t_{c_1,start}), & s_e(t_{c_1,start}) < s_{c_1}(t_{c_1,start}) \\ 0, & \text{otherwise} \end{cases} \tag{9}$$

- Lane changes of e and c_1 need to be **simultaneously**, for which the timing template is used. Let the moment, when e and c_1 are fully on the target lane, be denoted as $t_{e,end}$ and $t_{c_1,end}$. If either $t_{c_1,start} + \Delta t_1 < t_{e,start}$ or $t_{e,end} < t_{c_1,end} - \Delta t_2$ is true, the lane changes are not considered to be simultaneous anymore. Δt_1 is set to 1 s to allow for an earlier start of the lane change of c_1, while Δt_2 is set to 0 s such that c_1 does not finish the lane change before e starts changing lanes.

$$\delta = \begin{cases} \left| \frac{t_{e.start} - 1 + t_{e.end} + 0}{2} - \frac{t_{c_1.start} + t_{c_1.end}}{2} \right|, & \text{not simultaneous} \\ 0, & \text{otherwise} \end{cases} \tag{10}$$

- We need to search for a **violation of the safety distance**.

$$\epsilon = \min(s_{c_2}(t) - s_e(t) - safeDist(t)) \qquad [t_{e,start}, t_{e,end}] \tag{11}$$

The combined fitness function for single-objective search does look as follows. Powers of ten are used as offsets o_i, e.g. $o_1 = 10^3$ and $o_2 = 10^4$.

$$f_{single} = \begin{cases} \alpha + o_4, & e \text{ does not change lanes} \\ \begin{cases} \beta + o_3, & s_{c_2}(t_{e,start}) < s_e(t_{e,start}) \\ \begin{cases} \gamma + o_2, & s_e(t_{c_1,start}) < s_{c_1}(t_{c_1,start}) \\ \begin{cases} \delta + o_1, & \text{not simultaneous} \\ \epsilon, & \text{otherwise} \end{cases} \end{cases} \end{cases} \end{cases} \tag{12}$$

For an application of multi-objective search, the templates need to be changed, e.g. ϵ can only be computed if all qualitative test goals underlying the other templates are fulfilled.

$$\tilde{\epsilon} = \begin{cases} \infty, & \alpha + \beta + \gamma + \delta > 0 \\ \epsilon \end{cases} \tag{13}$$

Incorporating the dependencies also in the other templates yields the final vector of fitness values. β, γ, and δ are independent of each other; they only depend on α. In contrast to a combination for single-objective search as above, they can be optimized simultaneously when combined for multi-objective search. α stays unchanged as it does not depend on other templates.

$$f_{multi} = [\alpha \quad \tilde{\beta} \quad \tilde{\gamma} \quad \tilde{\delta} \quad \tilde{\epsilon}] \tag{14}$$

The actual technical application of search-based techniques is not the focus of this work as is has been done by various existing works. However, for interested readers, we provide supplementary material online at https://mediatum.ub.tum. de/1474281. Contained are two experiments that use the presented parameterized scenario and combined fitness function as well as videos of the worst-case scenarios identified by single- and multi-objective search during the experiments.

6   Related Work

Search-based techniques have been proposed for test scenario selection. The initial research presented the idea of applying search-based techniques for the functional testing of advanced driver assistance systems by testing a parking assistant [6] and a braking assistant [7]. Their setup is close to what we describe as scenario-based testing. Recently, machine learning was introduced to improve the performance of test case generation in this domain. For instance, with learning surrogate models the optimization speed may be improved [3] and with building decision-trees the test engineer receives information about the search space during test case selection [2]. Both works apply the presented techniques on an emergency braking system. For testing a feature interaction of an adaptive cruise control and an emergency braking system, search-based techniques are improved in a way that they search for multiple faulty interactions simultaneously [4].

While all these technical improvements are important and show great results, these works assume the fitness function to be given or create them ad-hoc, e.g. to test the interaction of some specific features [4]. This is, because those works focus on the technical aspect of the search-based techniques. Neither of them addresses the methodological aspect of how fitness functions are correctly created to allow for statements about safety, e.g. by testing against a safe operating envelope as for instance provided by recent works [11,13,15]. Additionally, the evaluation systems are rather reactive driver assistance systems of SAE level 1&2 [14] or combination of such. The provided fitness functions for those systems are mostly not applicable to higher automated systems (e.g. level 4&5) with decision making and active functionality (e.g. lane changing or overtaking) in complex dynamic traffic scenarios, which require the fulfillment of qualitative test goals. This motivates the need for methodological guidance when deriving fitness functions.

7   Conclusion

We started by describing the necessity of suitable fitness functions to identify "good" test cases within huge search spaces, described by parameterized scenarios for automated and autonomous driving. A correct derivation of such suitable functions is crucial, but difficult. For the application of search-based techniques at larger scale for testing automated and autonomous driving systems, guidance for test engineers is necessary. In this work, we provide such guidance in form of templates and the means to combine them to fitness functions for complex traffic scenarios. To test against thresholds of a safe operating envelope, we presented a specific template which provides the test engineer with an automated oracle. Additional templates for relative positioning in time and space ensure that the optimizer identifies scenarios that fulfill the qualitative test goals. For combining the templates, we presented both a single and a multi-objective approach which make use of case distinctions to provide a total ordering on scenario candidates such that better scenarios are assigned to better fitness values. As an evaluation, we presented the application of the templates on the most complex (close-to-)collision highway scenario contained in the biggest natural driving study database (identified by [18]). We conclude that the presented templates provide a structured way for test engineers to formulate fitness functions to identify "good" test cases. Thus, this work adds a much needed methodological angle to the otherwise technical solutions.

The application of search-based techniques requires both a fitness function and a search space. The derivation of the search space is not discussed in this work. Similarly to the fitness function derivation, methodological guidance for the derivation of search spaces (parameterized scenarios) is of high interest. Both are difficult the creation of a suitable skeleton of a parameterized scenario and the identification of suitable parameters and their domains. Further, in addition to the methodological guidance presented in this work, an automated fitness function derivation would be very useful to support test engineers. Using a suitable scenario description as input, the described combination for single- and multi-objective techniques might be automated.

References

1. OpenScenario 0.9.1 (2017). Technical report, OpenScenario Initiative. http://www.openscenario.org. Accessed 11 Jan 2019
2. Abdessalem, R.B., Nejati, S., Briand, L., Stifter, T.: Testing vision-based control systems using learnable evolutionary algorithms. In: Proceedings of the 40th International Conference on Software Engineering (ICSE 2018). ACM (2018)
3. Abdessalem, R.B., Nejati, S., Briand, L.C., Stifter, T.: Testing advanced driver assistance systems using multi-objective search and neural networks. In: 31st IEEE/ACM International Conference on Automated Software Engineering (ASE), pp. 63–74 (2016)
4. Abdessalem, R.B., Panichella, A., Nejati, S., Briand, L.C., Stifter, T.: Testing autonomous cars for feature interaction failures using many-objective search. In: 33rd ACM/IEEE International Conference on Automated Software Engineering, pp. 143–154 (2018)
5. Althoff, M., Koschi, M., Manzinger, S.: Commonroad: composable benchmarks for motion planning on roads. In: 2017 IEEE Intelligent Vehicles Symposium (IV), pp. 719–726. IEEE (2017)
6. Bühler, O., Wegener, J.: Evolutionary functional testing of an automated parking system. In: Proceedings of the International Conference on Computer, Communication and Control Technologies (CCCT) and the 9th. International Conference on Information Systems Analysis and Synthesis (ISAS) (2003)
7. Bühler, O., Wegener, J.: Evolutionary functional testing. Comput. Oper. Res. **35**(10), 3144–3160 (2008)
8. Hankey, J.M., Perez, M.A., McClafferty, J.A.: Description of the shrp 2 naturalistic database and the crash, near-crash, and baseline data sets. Technical report, Virginia Tech Transportation Institute (2016)
9. Koopman, P., Wagner, M.: Challenges in autonomous vehicle testing and validation. SAE Int. J. Transp. Saf. **4**(1), 15–24 (2016)
10. Mullins, G.E., Stankiewicz, P.G., Gupta, S.K.: Automated generation of diverse and challenging scenarios for test and evaluation of autonomous vehicles. In: IEEE International Conference on Robotics and Automation (ICRA), pp. 1443–1450 (2017)
11. Nister, D., Lee, H.L., Ng, J., Wang, Y.: The safety force field. https://www.nvidia.com/content/dam/en-zz/Solutions/self-driving-cars/safety-force-field/the-safety-force-field.pdf. Accessed 10 May 2019
12. Pretschner, A.: Defect-based testing. In: Dependable Software Systems Engineering (2015)

13. Rizaldi, A., et al.: Formalising and monitoring traffic rules for autonomous vehicles in Isabelle/HOL. In: Polikarpova, N., Schneider, S. (eds.) IFM 2017. LNCS, vol. 10510, pp. 50–66. Springer, Cham (2017). https://doi.org/10.1007/978-3-319-66845-1_4

14. SAE: Definitions for terms related to on-road motor vehicle automated driving systems. J3016, SAE International Standard (2014)

15. Shalev-Shwartz, S., Shammah, S., Shashua, A.: On a formal model of safe and scalable self-driving cars. arXiv:1708.06374. Accessed 5 May 2019

16. Ulbrich, S., et al.: Testing and validating tactical lane change behavior planning for automated driving. In: Watzenig, D., Horn, M. (eds.) Automated Driving, pp. 451–471. Springer, Cham (2017). https://doi.org/10.1007/978-3-319-31895-0_19

17. Wachenfeld, W., Winner, H.: The release of autonomous vehicles. In: Autonomous Driving, pp. 425–449. Springer (2016)

18. Zhou, J., del Re, L.: Reduced complexity safety testing for adas & adf. IFAC-PapersOnLine **50**(1), 5985–5990 (2017)

A SysML Profile for Fault Trees—Linking Safety Models to System Design

Kester Clegg[1]([✉]), Mole Li[2], David Stamp[2], Alan Grigg[2], and John McDermid[1]

[1] University of York, York YO10 5DD, UK
{kester.clegg,john.mcdermid}@york.ac.uk
[2] Rolls-Royce (Controls) PLC, Derby, UK
{mole.li,david.stamp,alan.grigg}@rolls-royce.com

Abstract. Model Based Systems Engineering (MBSE) has encouraged the use of a single systems model in languages such as SysML that fully specify the system and which form the basis of all development effort. However, using SysML models for safety analysis has been restricted by the lack of defined modelling standards for analytical techniques like Fault Tree Analysis (FTA). In lieu of such standards, the ENCASE project (See acknowledgements.) has formulated a simple SysML profile that captures the information required to represent fault trees and which enables the linkage of failure modes to other parts of the SysML model. We describe our experience of integrating fault tree models within a SysML MBSE environment for critical systems development, and show how that can be done while keeping existing (often certified) analytical tools as part of the development process. Common definitions of the system specification improves the quality of safety analysis, and the closer alignment of system and safety models provides opportunities for greater traceability, coherence and verification.

Keywords: SysML · Fault Tree Analysis · Failure modes

1 Introduction

Systems Modelling Language (SysML)[1] is an extension of the Unified Modelling Language (UML) that focuses on systems modelling. SysML supports the specification, analysis, design, verification and validation of a broad range of systems and systems-of-systems. However, 'support' in this sense is intended to mean a well-defined specification to describe the system, so that development and analysis can be performed using tools that take their data from a single model repository. The approach is widely described as Model Based Systems Engineering (MBSE) and among its benefits is the hope it will remove most of the errors and wasted development effort caused by conflicting sources of information. However

---

[1] This paper refers to the current Object Modelling Group (OMG) SysML v1.5, not the upcoming 2.0 standard. See http://www.omgsysml.org/.

© Springer Nature Switzerland AG 2019
A. Romanovsky et al. (Eds.): SAFECOMP 2019, LNCS 11698, pp. 85–93, 2019.
https://doi.org/10.1007/978-3-030-26601-1_6

there are also benefits for safety analysis, provided that the tool chains typically used in traditional critical systems development can be brought under the single SysML model. Unfortunately support for safety analysis has lagged behind the Object Modelling Group's (OMG) SysML specification. This paper details our progress in the setting of Rolls-Royce's UltraFan engine demonstrator development to provide SysML support to Fault Tree Analysis. The profile outlined here will form part of a wider safety and reliability profile similar to that recently proposed by the OMG (see below).

1.1 Background and Previous Work

To date, SysML has focused on supporting the requirements capture and functional side of systems engineering. However for safety critical systems, non-functional forms of analysis can be essential to argue that the system meets a required safety standard. Fault logic is typically modelled using a graphical representation of logic gates that traces the fault from base event to effect and which can contain additional information, such as failure rate, dispatch information and descriptive failure modes. A typical example is shown on the right hand side of Fig. 3 and the technique is defined in standards like IEC 61025 [4].

ENCASE's initial starting point after conducting a wider review of model based approaches [6] and taking into account the choice of SysML by Rolls-Royce as the modelling language to use on UltraFan, was an early paper from the National Aeronautics and Space Administration (NASA)'s Jet Propulsion Laboratory on fault protection modelling, which captured fault logic using activity diagrams [2]. We investigated using this approach but found issues with it. For example, there is no provision for AND gate representation in Activity Diagrams and the fault logic modelling at Rolls-Royce requires this to express the redundancy provided by a dual channel FADEC (Full Authority Digital Engine Control) [5]. Secondly activity diagrams were never intended to model fault trees. Activities on Activity Diagrams become Call Behaviour Actions, which semantically seems at odds with fault logic, which is generally expressed as logic gates and failure modes. Although there are other potential diagram types none offer specific support for fault tree analysis and we decided we could best meet our needs by creating a bespoke diagram type.

In 2017 the OMG issued a Request for Proposals on how to represent fault trees in SysML as part of the Safety and Reliability Analysis Profile for UML, which will extend the SysML language with "the capability to model safety information, such as hazards and the harms they may cause, model reliability analyses, including Fault Tree Analysis (FTA) and Failure Mode and Effects Analysis (FMEA), and use structured argument notation to organize the model and specify assurance cases" [1]. As part of this, an early profile for Fault Tree Analysis (FTA) and Failure Mode and Effects Analysis (FMEA) has been developed and published [1] and is likely to form part of SysML 2.0. However, while the new profile is a step in the right direction, there were several pragmatic aspects that made it unsuitable to adopt for the development of UltraFan within Rolls-Royce. These are primarily to do with how the Failure Mode and Effects

Analysis (FMEA) results are kept and used as part of FTA in the existing tool chain, and discussions around how failure modes could be linked to functional specifications in the model. This is discussed in more detail in Sect. 2.

There is also recent work investigating the formal translation of Activity Diagrams in UML/SysML to fault trees [3]. While this is a rigorous method, that entails a one to one correspondence between the two models, at this stage in the ENCASE project a more pragmatic approach is required due to the variety of ways engineers model activities. For example there are parts of Activity Diagrams, such as Join Nodes, that are semantically ambiguous and can be used/interpreted differently by users which would make automated translation difficult. More importantly there is a different approach to modelling between the system engineers (who model how things work) and the safety analysts (who model how things fail). The primary practical concern for the safety team was that the SysML fault tree models should be capable of modelling the system fault logic as it had been done historically and exporting it in a format where it could be analyzed by their existing tools such as FaultTree+ (part of Isograph's Reliability Workbench suite[2]). Extensions to SysML such as proposed in [7] for component fault trees were rejected for this reason. It is relatively simple to model the fault logic to the point at which the base events are specified, the base event details (failure rates from the FMEA/FMECA, exposure periods, etc.) can then be extracted from the Failure Modes and Effects Summary (FMES) database (see [8]) using spreadsheet macros and exported as a workbook to be imported by FaultTree+. This gives a low risk migration strategy from the existing approach to that offered by MBSE, even though as we discuss in Sect. 2.1 changing the way fault logic is currently modelled will be necessary to maximize the benefits of MBSE.

2   A Bespoke Fault Tree Profile for SysML

Rolls-Royce (Controls, UK) currently use failure modes as human readable placeholders or descriptions within the fault tree that describe the fault logic gate below them (see right hand side of Fig. 3). Their primary purpose is to help safety analysts understand and keep track of the fault logic of the system, which can be extremely large (i.e. hundreds of pages) and complex. By associating them with specific functional behavior modelled as activities in SysML, the system engineers gain visibility of failure modes while modelling system functions and can view the associated fault logic. However, this linkage (through failure mode linked elements) also gives the future possibility of validating fault trees against a system function or associated hardware when changes to the SysML model are made. See Fig. 1 and its description below for more details.

To meet the challenges of traditional safety engineering that uses separate models from system models, and in a similar spirit to the OMG RFP mentioned earlier, we propose part of a new Model Based Safety Assurance (MBSA) profile

---

[2] https://www.isograph.com/software/reliability-workbench/fault-tree-analysis-software/.

that allows safety analysis models to link to existing system models. Our profile remains a work in progress—we are aware there are additional logic gates (such as vote gates) to add to the profile. However what we outline is sufficient to start to migrate the existing fault tree models into the SysML repository. Similar to SysML extensions in UML, the proposed Fault Tree Profile reuses a subset of UML 2.5 and provides additional extensions to aid Fault Tree analysis in UML and SysML [1].

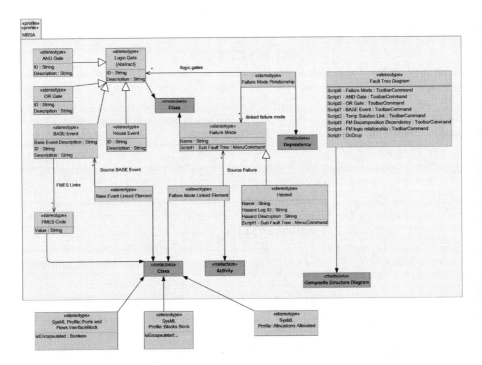

Fig. 1. Meta model of the proposed Fault Tree Profile, which will form part of a larger MBSA profile. The Fault Tree Diagram scripts are not part of the profile but serve to recreate a familiar user interface for safety analysts in PTC Integrity Modeller (PTC IM).

The meta-model of our Fault Tree profile is shown in Fig. 1.[3] In software engineering, a meta-model is a mechanism for representing a well-formed formula or the abstract syntax of a modelling language [9]. The definitions and semantics of each concept of the meta-model are introduced as follows:

---

[3] The meta-model we have developed includes a domain view meta-model as well, which provides a modelling tool and language independent view and shows meta-associations. We considered this to be out of scope for SAFECOMP but the authors are happy to give details if requested.

Logic Gate. Abstract meta-class (i.e. no concrete entity in the SysML model) and implemented as a stereotype (i.e. an applied extension) that generalises the common attributes of *AND Gate, OR Gate, Base Event* and *House Event*. As it is a general modelling concept, its *ID* tag definition specifies the unique reference for gates in the fault tree. *Description* allows users to specify textual information to assist identification.

AND & OR Gate. Concrete meta-classes that represent the two most common gates in fault trees. Implemented as the stereotyped UML: Class meta-class making *AND & OR Gates* first-class entities. As they generalize the *Logic Gate* meta-class, they inherit *ID* and *Description* tag definitions.

Base Event. Concrete meta-class that represents lowest level of a fault tree diagram. Meta-modelling mechanism similar to *AND & OR Gates*. Links to hardware components via *Base Event Linked Element* meta-class. The *Base Event* FMES code allows scripts to retrieve its failure rates, probabilities, exposure periods and dispatch information from the FMES database.

House Event. Concrete meta-class similar to a *base event* except that it serves as a Boolean flag or switch to isolate parts of the fault tree under a particular analysis (i.e. it's a "normal event" expected to happen, not a "failure").

Failure Mode. Concrete meta-class that represents a descriptive placeholder used to describe the fault logic at that point in the fault tree. The meta-modelling mechanism is similar to the logic gates.

Failure Mode Relationship. Concrete meta-class that defines the relationship between *Logic Gate* such as *AND Gate, OR Gate, Base Event, House Event* and *Failure Mode*. Implemented as a stereotyped UML: Dependency meta-class to represent *Failure Mode Relationship* as a first-class entity. Two reference-type tag definitions *Logic Gates* and *Linked Failure Mode* connect *Logic Gate* and *Failure Mode*.

Hazard. Concrete meta-class that represents the top level *Hazard* in a fault tree. We intend this class to be part of wider profile used to capture Functional Hazard Analysis (see ARP4761 [8]). It generalises *Failure Mode* and extends the tag definitions *Hazard Log ID* and *Hazard Description*.

Base Event Linked Element. Meta-class that links one or more *Base Event* to system hardware components defined in SysML Internal Block Diagrams and Block Definition Diagrams. Not implemented as a first-class entity, therefore cannot exist by itself. The stereotype applies to UML: Class (SysML Block is a stereo-typed UML: Class) in order to increase safety visibility for systems engineers. In addition, it has a reference type tag definition *Source Base Event* to connect stereotyped system hardware component and *Base Event*.

Failure Mode Linked Element. Meta-class that links one or more *Failure Mode* to abstract hardware specifications defined in SysML Internal Block Diagrams and Block Definition Diagrams, and system features and functions in SysML Activity Diagrams. The meta-modelling mechanism is similar to *Base Event Linked Element*.

FMES Code. Concrete meta-class that represents FMES Base Event codes. Linked with zero or more *Base Event* via reference tag definition *FMES Links* of *Base Event*. The Value tag is a unique identifier in the FMES database.

90 K. Clegg et al.

Fault Tree Diagram. A bespoke diagram type to model fault logic using fault trees. In order to make the current SysML modelling tool (PTC's Integrity Modeler) a user friendly interface for safety analysts accustomed to working with Isograph's FaultTree+, user defined scripts provide some UI behaviour (more details in Sect. 2.1). The extension mechanism is the same as the SysML Internal Block Diagram that extends UML Composite Structure Diagram.

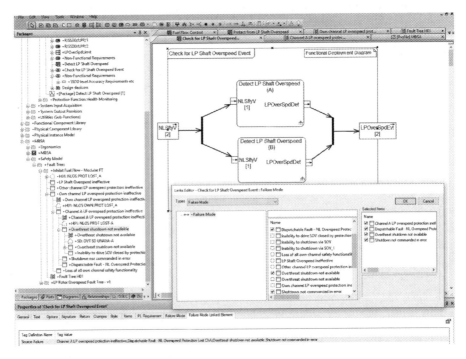

Fig. 2. Assigning failure modes (RHS dialogue box) from the fault tree level "Channel A LP overspeed protection ineffective" (LHS tree hierarchy) via a Failure Mode Linked Element on the Activity 'Check for LP Shaft Overspeed Event' (RHS top panel).

2.1 Implementation

For the UltraFan demonstrator, Rolls-Royce are using SysML as the focus of their systems specification and development. The current modelling environment is provided by PTC's Integrity Modeler. The use of scripts enable user defined toolbars and actions on a bespoke diagram type. A typical screenshot is shown in Fig. 2. This has one "level" in a branch of the fault tree defined as an AND gate, with failure modes describing the junction point above and below. Double clicking on either of the failure modes below will take the user to the next level below or create a new level (defined as a failure mode) in the tree. The hierarchical structure (i.e. the fault logic) of the fault tree is shown in the left hand panel. At the lowest level of this branch in the fault tree are the base events with their FMES codes. Scripts will be able to "walk" the fault tree hierarchy down to the base events and export this to a spreadsheet within the FMES database, where macros can combine it with information linked to the Base Event FMES codes to be imported into FaultTree+ for analysis.

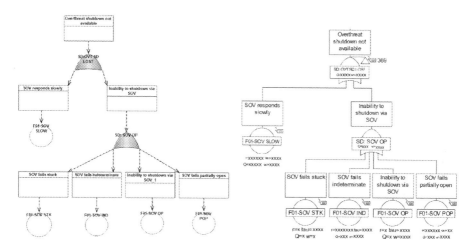

Fig. 3. Lower level of H01 fault tree showing base events with FMES identifiers. The LHS is our profile as rendered by PTC IM, the RHS shows the output from FaultTree+.

The most striking difference between our profile and the initial safety profile published by the working group for the OMG [1] is our decision not to bring the FMEA information directly into the SysML model. Instead, the base events keep their unique identifier that can allow that information to be extracted from the FMES database. The reason for this is that the FMES is quite large (>3K rows) and there has to be an explicit case made for bringing that information into the SysML model where it is less easy to keep it maintained and checked. In the case of dispatch events (these are faults that have an exposure period with respect to maintenance intervals), a case can be made for linking them to derived safety requirements kept elsewhere in the model and we will be issuing an updated profile at a later date to reflect this, but otherwise all that is needed is the FMES code. The FMES is a summary of the FMECA database (>25K rows), and it is this database that is changed and maintained with the latest failure rates. Therefore it is easiest if a new analysis is to be run to extract the summary failure rate data directly from the databases, while keeping the fault logic and knowledge of the failure modes within the SysML model. This is in keeping with our belief that the SysML model represents a knowledge repository, whereas the FMECA and FMES databases are designed to handle, import and export large amounts of data efficiently and are able to interface with a wide range of tools. Figure 3 shows the implementation of our profile in PTC Integrity Modeler and compares two fault tree structures. Removing the FMES data (which is not used by the safety analysts when modelling the fault logic - it is added by FaultTree+ by combining the failure rates of base events) gives a much cleaner interface, with greater opportunity to add explicit descriptions within the failure modes that can then be linked outwards to activities or hardware components.

2.2   Alignment of Safety and System Models

Advocates of MBSE are quick to point out the improved fidelity and efficiency of maintaining a single development model. However, as safety engineers have traditionally modelled their understanding of the system's fault logic with respect to a hazard independently of other system models, some abstract failure modes may have little obvious connection to system functions. In such cases, a realignment and reassessment of failure modes may be necessary. For example safety engineers often model a system with respect to its redundancy and mitigation against a hazard, thus an analysis for a dual channel control system might query why the mitigation provided by the redundant channel has failed in addition to the channel in control. Contrast this with the system engineer's perspective, which is to consider an engine protection feature in its abstract specification first, then to consider its implementation and finally how it is implemented on a respective channel. In MBSE, fault logic models should follow where possible the functional breakdown of the system engineers. Fault trees are often "richer" models that can include physical or external factors outside the system's functional specification but required to understand how that function could fail. To maximise benefits such as being able to cross-check models for inconsistencies, or auto-generate fault trees from parts of the model, the profile must allow failure modes to be associated with and traceable to specific parts of the SysML model.

3   Conclusions

The use of MBSE may lower development costs but it is not proven that it results in safer systems. Part of the challenge is how to transition from a tried and trusted development process to one that offers better coherence, traceability and verification potential. Our proposal here is to accept that everything can move under the SysML umbrella, but that by keeping trusted analytical tools as part of the process, the transition can be managed, remain trustworthy and begin to reap some of the benefits of MBSE. It is critical to understand at an earlier stage what will be needed to export data from models so that it can be analysed by existing tools. Losing the additional assurance of an independent model of the system's fault logic needs to be justified by demonstrating the value of validation checks between models and being able to more easily identify changes to models during development. Bringing safety and system models together to share their definition of system artifacts improves the quality of safety analysis, helps assure compliance and moves us a step closer to auto-generating parts of the fault tree model from the system design.

Acknowledgements. Development supported by Rolls-Royce PLC and funded as part of Innovate UK's ENCASE project (Enabling Novel Controls and Advanced Sensors for Engines).

References

1. Biggs, G., Juknevicius, T., Armonas, A., Post, K.: Integrating safety and reliability analysis into MBSE: overview of the new proposed OMG standard. In: INCOSE International Symposium, vol. 28, pp. 1322–1336, July 2018. https://doi.org/10.1002/j.2334-5837.2018.00551.x
2. Day, J., Murray, A., Meakin, P.: Toward a model-based approach to flight system fault protection. In: Aerospace Conference, 2012 IEEE, pp. 1–17. IEEE (2012)
3. Dickerson, C.E., Roslan, R., Ji, S.: A formal transformation method for automated fault tree generation from a UML activity model. IEEE Trans. Reliab. **67**(3), 1219–1236 (2018). https://doi.org/10.1109/TR.2018.2849013
4. IEC 61025: Fault tree analysis (FTA). Standard, International Electrotechnical Commission, Geneva, CH, August 2006
5. Li, M., Batmaz, F., Guan, L., Grigg, A., Ingham, M., Bull, P.: Model-based systems engineering with requirements variability for embedded real-time systems. In: 2015 IEEE International Model-Driven Requirements Engineering Workshop (MoDRE), pp. 1–10, August 2015. https://doi.org/10.1109/MoDRE.2015.7343874
6. Lisagor, O., Kelly, T., Niu, R.: Model-based safety assessment: review of the discipline and its challenges. In: The Proceedings of 2011 9th International Conference on Reliability, Maintainability and Safety, pp. 625–632, June 2011. https://doi.org/10.1109/ICRMS.2011.5979344
7. Nordmann, A., Munk, P.: Lessons learned from model-based safety assessment with SysML and component fault trees. In: Proceedings of the 21st ACM/IEEE International Conference on Model Driven Engineering Languages and Systems, pp. 134–143, MODELS 2018. ACM, New York (2018). https://doi.org/10.1145/3239372.3239373
8. Guidelines and methods for conducting the safety assessment process on civil airborne systems and equipment ARP4761, Standard, SAE International, Warrendale, PA, USA, 1 December 1996
9. Seidewitz, E.: What models mean. IEEE Softw. **20**(5), 26–32 (2003)

Safety and Reliability Modeling

Spectrum-Based Fault Localization in Deployed Embedded Systems with Driver Interaction Models

Ulrich Thomas Gabor[1]([✉]) [iD], Simon Dierl[1] [iD], and Olaf Spinczyk[2]

[1] Department of Computer Science, TU Dortmund, 44227 Dortmund, Germany
{ulrich.gabor,simon.dierl}@tu-dortmund.de
[2] Institute of Computer Science, Osnabrück University, 49090 Osnabrück, Germany
olaf.spinczyk@uni-osnabrueck.de

Abstract. Software faults are still a problem especially in deployed systems. We propose a new approach to monitor a deployed embedded system with another embedded system, which acts autonomously and isolated. The monitoring system generates reports containing probable fault locations, which can later be obtained without requiring expensive debugging hardware or continuous access to the monitored embedded system. For this, we assessed failure-detection oracles, transaction detectors and suspiciousness metrics and evaluated them in a practical combustion engine scenario. Especially, we propose a driver interaction model to capture correct interaction with periphery and use it as oracle. Our results show that for the repetitive behavior of an engine control unit, simple approaches perform best.

Keywords: Reliability · Fault tolerance · Software reliability · Embedded software · Software quality

1 Introduction

Despite the continuous efforts of software engineering researchers, software faults are still a problem in modern software development [19] leading to failures. They can bring down spacecrafts [27] or whole data centers[1] and with the increasing number of pervasive embedded systems in households, e.g., smart speakers, failures are becoming more in absolute numbers due to the sheer number of devices.

While debugging techniques have improved in recent years, for example due to better update mechanisms and systematic capture of crash/trace logs, regularly there is still a lot of manual effort required to deal with logs, bug reports and traces. Since manual labor is not only time-consuming, but also expensive, the vision is to automatically assess such bug-related data and pinpoint the most probable fault location for the expensive skilled developer.

---

[1] https://status.aws.amazon.com/s3-20080720.html.

A. Romanovsky et al. (Eds.): SAFECOMP 2019, LNCS 11698, pp. 97–112, 2019.
https://doi.org/10.1007/978-3-030-26601-1_7

Spectrum-Based Fault Localization (SBFL) [24] is one approach serving this purpose and is based on the fact that if a failure is observed, the faulty component of a program must have been executed and therefore should be present in information regarding this run. A program **spectrum** [24] entails execution information from a specific perspective, e.g., which components were executed. Such multiple spectra can be obtained for multiple runs together with an error vector containing if the corresponding run failed or succeeded.

The idea is to find a relation between the spectra and the error vector, such that components can be ranked for examination. The function mapping spectra and an error vector to a **suspiciousness** [15] is called **suspiciousness metric** [31]. For efficient computation, some suspiciousness metrics depend only on aggregated information. For each component an **aggregated matrix** [3] can be constructed, which lists the four counts for "component was or was not executed in a succeeding or failing run".

These definitions can be modified in granularity such that a component is not a module or file, but a called function. Another variant is that a run is actually not a full run, but a run is split into transactions and each transaction is assessed as failing or succeeding.

1.1   Motivation

Observing already deployed embedded systems can be challenging, because access to deployed systems is often restricted, for example, because the device is not accessible physically. Attaching debuggers to every deployed system may also not be an option due to regularly high costs of debuggers and it might not be possible to reach the devices at all, besides scheduling an on-site appointment.

Our motivation is to be able to assess information on another small, cheap embedded system which we will call monitor and only transmit or save an aggregated fault localization report. These reports can then be transmitted using little bandwidth or can be downloaded at the next on-site inspection.

1.2   Requirements

The proposed idea to generate fault localization reports directly in the field should fulfill multiple requirements. First, the reports should obviously assist in localizing bugs. Second, the monitoring should work autonomously, without manual intervention, at least until the reports are obtained. Third, the monitoring must operate in isolation, because a failure in the embedded device must be assessed properly and should not lead to a failure of the monitor and vice versa. As an additional bonus, it should be possible to monitor arbitrary existing software without the need to change the source code of the monitored application.

1.3   Contributions

In this paper we present a new approach, which fulfills the aforementioned requirements. We use an additional embedded system to monitor the physically isolated application-under-test. Further, we assess multiple spectrum types and suspiciousness metrics regarding their suitability for the proposed use case and evaluate them in the context of control software for a simulated combustion engine. Since the monitoring should work autonomously, we also need an oracle to determine if a failure actually occurred and for long-running systems the execution must be split into shorter so-called transactions by a transaction detector [8]. To the best of our knowledge, we are the first to consider machine-learned driver interaction models as failure-oracle in a spectrum-based software fault localization resulting in suspiciousness rankings. These models allow us to detect failures based on the modeled communication with periphery. Finally, we use the AspectC++ compiler, which provides aspect-oriented programming (AOP) features for C++ [26], to instrument the application-under-test and make it transmit information to the monitoring device without forcing the developer to modify the source code.

1.4   Paper Organization

We will list related work in Sect. 2 and our new approach performing fault localization on an deployed embedded system in Sect. 3. Section 4 will demonstrate why our approach is feasible for our specific use case and in Sect. 5 we will name threats to validity, since our use-case is quite specific. Finally, Sect. 6 will summarize our findings.

2   Related Work

Fault localization can be done using multiple approaches. One of these approaches is model-based diagnosis. Abreu et al. use observations to construct a propositional formula, but finding an assignment, i.e., a faulty component, boils down to find a minimal hitting set [2], for which even approximations require noticeable computational power. Other approaches require manual modeling of the expected behavior [14], which can be a complex and error-prone task. Model-based approaches are therefore not the best choice for our setting.

Another approach is based on coverage-based techniques, which often require to compute full or dynamic slices, showing which statements of a program modify a variable or were executed. Xiaolin et al. have combined execution coverage of statements based on test cases with execution slices in a prototype implementation called HSFal to improve suspiciousness metrics and found their approach to reduce the average cost of examined code around $2.98\% - 31.79\%$ [16]. While the idea seems reasonable to us, slices are statement-based and that will likely exceed the available memory on small systems.

The most promising approach for our setting are spectrum-based fault localization approaches, where only a subset of the observable information of an application is taken into account, therefore we used this method. This approach has already successfully been used for embedded systems by Abreu et al. [5], but they inserted detectors manually in source code, which requires human effort and knowledge of the functionality of the application. Others regularly use unit tests or metamorphic testing [32] for failure detection in case unit tests are not possible. There are also approaches which combine spectrum-based with model-based techniques [3], but they also require more computational power than is available on low-cost microprocessors.

One core-component of classical spectrum-based approaches is the choice of an appropriate suspiciousness metric, where the so-called Ochiai metric outperformed other metrics when applied in real scenarios [4,18]. Recent approaches tried to combine multiple metrics by learning a weight from previous faults and applying the weights to compute suspiciousness for new faults [33], but this again requires computational power not available in the field of embedded systems. It might be possible though to perform the learning phase before deploying the system, but we have not yet examined this. Instead we just selected multiple existing metrics and compared them.

3   Methodology

Our overall methodology is shown in Fig. 1. On the left side the system-under-test is shown, which was augmented with a tracing component, transmitting trace data to the monitoring machine. In our case we have used AspectC++ to inject the tracing seamlessly into an existing application. Although this does not have to be done with AOP, it has the advantage of injecting trace code into the application without modifying the original source code.

The monitoring machine on the right performs all of the fault localization functionality. The continuous stream of information provided by the target machine is assessed by an oracle to decide if the current transaction is succeeding or failing. At the same time the stream is analyzed by a transaction detector to check if the data belongs to a new transaction, in which case the aggregation unit is informed. All information is aggregated to save space and a report based on the obtained information can be generated.

The report should rank software components according to their suspiciousness for being responsible for a failed run. A human can then inspect the components in that order.

3.1   Methodology Variants

Our method is not concrete about the used mechanisms as oracle or transaction detector. In fact, we will evaluate multiple variants in Sect. 4. Therefore, we will introduce multiple concepts in the rest of this section, which are evaluated regarding their individual efficacy later.

3.2   Observed Entities for Spectrum Generation

Section 1 introduced the concept of "components" in different granularity. We will use the called functions of a program as "components" to be able to pinpoint faults with little human effort.

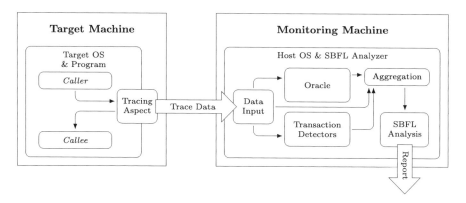

Fig. 1. High-level architecture of the analysis framework yielding a fault localization report

Additionally, we will assess the benefit of using the extension **method call sequence hit spectra** (MCSHS) [9,30] in our evaluation, where "components" are method call sequences of length z. For example, for the method hit sequence $\langle f(), g(), h() \rangle$ and $z = 2$ the following two "components" would be marked as executed $\{(f(), g()), (g(), g())\}$. With $z = 1$ the extension is disabled and only called functions without their predecessors will be used.

3.3 Transaction Detector

We have assessed the well-known timing-based transaction detector, which splits the input stream every second into separate transactions as proposed by Abreu et al. [1]. This is necessary if a system cannot easily provide separate runs, for example because it runs continuously. Since results with these transactions were already good, see Sect. 4, we have not examined other approaches.

3.4 Failure-Detection Oracle

Our idea for a failure-detecting oracle is based on the fact that one of the main purposes of an embedded system is to interact with its environment. We use this fact to learn how correct interaction with periphery looks like and use this model to decide, if an embedded system still behaves as expected or failed. We call this model **driver interaction model (DIM)**, which is a finite state machine where all states are accepting and the input symbols are communication messages to the hardware. A DIM for a fictional wireless chipset driver can be seen in Fig. 2.

We propose that either a correct implementation or the successful executions during development, e.g., supported by unit tests, can be used to learn a DIM, which can then be deployed with the monitoring system. In the unfamiliar environment our model will detect potential failures, which can be used by the developer to either fix a fault or to improve the DIM iteratively. Our approach is

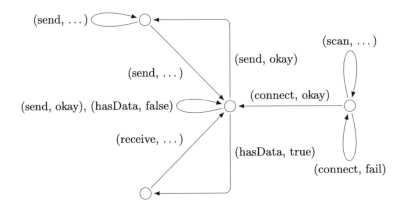

Fig. 2. A fictional DIM for a wireless chipset driver

therefore applicable in multiple scenarios, for example helping a developer implement new software, but also checking a re-implementation or software variant.

For that, once a driver interaction model was learned, it can be saved. It can then be loaded later again and augmented with new information, but it is also possible to manually modify or check the model according to a specification.

Learning driver interaction models is a CPU-and memory-intensive task and requires multiple runs as reference data, which is another reason why we propose to learn the model beforehand and deploy it on the monitoring machine. We used a variance of the k-tails algorithm [6] to merge equivalent states during learning. Regularly, two states are equivalent if their k-tails are equal, i.e., the same words of length k are accepted beginning from the two states. We relaxed this and consider states for merging if the source state's k-tail is contained in the target state's k-tail to obtain more realistic models. Since the learning data is based on sequences of method calls, each node (besides an initial node) has exactly one k-tail and merging nodes will not lead to more k-tails, otherwise the nodes would not have been merged. This observation allows to merge states during learning using a map from k-tails to already inferred nodes. Learning a new node is done by first checking if the k-tail is present in the map. If it is, the two nodes are merged; if not, a new node is created and the map updated with this newly created node.

This algorithm is used to merge similar traces. Consider the most basic example, where identical message sequences occur in two traces, e.g., *(connect, okay)* → *(send, okay)* → *(send, . . .)*. It is likely that in both traces the periphery's internal state was identical, therefore the origin states are merged.

Such a driver interaction model can be used as oracle by following transitions and in case this is not possible, a failure is detected. If the execution should continue after a failure was detected, we just try to find fitting transitions for the next events starting in the erroneous state. A reset threshold r is used and after r successful consecutive transitions, the oracle is used to detect failures again. If not specified otherwise, we used the learning parameter k also as reset threshold, as this is the first intuitive choice.

Interaction can be observed on different abstraction levels, e.g., binary communication or already decoded packages, and the data can be obtained either directly in the driver or via an external sniffer.

We also examined **software behavior graphs (SBG)** [20], a graph where nodes correspond to functions and an edge (s, t) exists, if function s calls function t. They can be learned from trace data and during fault localization encountering a missing edge can be interpreted as a failure. Since the evaluation in Sect. 4 shows that they do not perform well in our setting, we will not go into details.

3.5 Thread Separation

Since modern software is often executed in parallel and even embedded systems make use of multi-core CPUs nowadays, it is sometimes necessary or at least helpful to know which CPU or thread caused a failure. We investigated a mechanism to isolate parallel executions. Since we did not want to expect that an embedded operating system provides a thread abstraction, we configured our approach to use the CPU core id as identifier, although it is possible to use a thread id in systems where this abstraction exists.

3.6 Failure Indexing

Spectrum-based fault localization (SBFL) is guided by the idea to localize one fault, whereas in practice often multiple faults will be present simultaneously. If enough computational power is present, this is not a problem, as one fault can be fixed, and then another SBFL experiment can be run. In long-running, isolated systems, this is not that easy, therefore it is preferable to collect information regarding multiple faults at the same time, if possible. One problem is, how the observed effects can be pinpointed to one of multiple faults. One idea is to use the information which oracle detected the failure caused by a fault or how it detected the failure to distinguish different causes. This is called **failure indexing**. We will assess in the next section if this feature helps in our use case.

4 Evaluation and Application

We have implemented our approach and performed multiple experiments to determine the best choice and configuration regarding oracles/detectors and parameters presented in the last section.

4.1 Testbed

We have implemented our approach exemplarily based on the embedded operating system CyPhOS [7], running the application *EMSComponent* [25] simulating an engine control unit on a Wandboard Quad – a development board hosting an i.MX6 CPU providing the ARM Cortex-A9 instruction set and 2GB of RAM. We used the same operating system and board to deploy the monitoring system. To simulate a combustion engine, EMSBench[2] [17] was used, which was deployed on an STM32F4-Discovery development board – a low-power development board featuring an ARM Cortex-M3 CPU.

To trace the application we used AspectC++, which can be easily integrated into the CyPhOS build process. It was used to transmit information about called methods and driver interaction events to the monitoring machine. Since AspectC++ automatically numbers relevant methods sequentially (join point ID, short: JPID), we used these numbers to identify functions. Although this is not necessary for our approach, it is convenient to transmit information efficiently. We also used AspectC++ to modify the low-level GPIO driver to obtain trace data for the driver-interaction-model oracle.

Since most suspiciousness metrics are easy to compute, we included five metrics in total: Barinel [3], D^* [28], Ochiai [23], Op2 [21] and Tarantula [15], where D^* is parametrized with $* \in \mathbb{N}$.

To compute these metrics we only need the aggregated matrices as described in Sect. 1. Further, we reduced memory occupation by only storing the lower row of aggregated matrices, the one which counts the succeeding/failing transactions the component participated in, and two counters for succeeding and failing over all transactions. The upper row can be recomputed from these. Actually, storing the spectra and aggregated matrix requires some more thought to not exhaust the available memory. We have used a variation of the trie data structure [12] to be able to use method call sequences as keys for storing.

Our approach uses a domain-agnostic oracle and transaction detector. As a baseline for our experiments, we implemented domain-specific counterparts. The domain-specific oracle detects an error in CyPhOS by monitoring the crash handler. Since CyPhOS is a component-based operating system, it was possible to use calls of the function to switch between two components as an identifier for a new transaction. We will later refer to this transaction detector as "OSC".

We used our own tool [13] to inject software faults according to a well-known fault model [10,22], without the addition for more realistic faults based on software metrics. We filtered faults which were not useful, e.g., resulted in images that did not boot or modifications in dead code, resulting in 41 patches inserting faults into the application, see Fig. 2 for an explanation of the corresponding abbreviations.

4.2   Experiments

We performed multiple experiments to determine the best oracle and the best configuration for our use case. For that, we have performed the following steps:

– Generate patch files to inject software faults into our application.

---

[2] https://www.informatik.uni-augsburg.de/en/chairs/sik/research/running/emsbench/.

- Learn a driver interaction model and a software behavior graph from successful runs to determine the quality of the oracles regarding detection of
  failures triggered by the previously generated faults, and assess the impact of
  parameter k of our k-tails learning algorithm.
- Determine speed and therefore feasible configurations for continuous monitoring.
- Determine whether thread separation and which transaction detection mechanism performs best.
- Assess found configurations as a whole.

Table 1. Oracle-detected errors for the injected faults per driver interaction model
(DIM) with different k, software behavior graph (SBG) and domain-specific CPU
exception detector

Fault type	Oracle	Fault type	Oracle	Fault type	Oracle
MFC-1	2-DIM	MIES-2		MLPA-2	
MFC-2	1, 2-DIM	MIES-4		MLPA-10	1, 2-DIM
MFC-4		MIES-6	2-DIM	MLPA-26	1, 2-DIM
MFC-5		MIES-7	2-DIM	MLPA-29	2-DIM
MFC-6	1, 2-DIM	MIES-11	2-DIM	MLPA-30	2-DIM
MIA-2		MIFS-1		MRS-1	
MIA-3		MIFS-3		MRS-9	2-DIM
MIA-5		MIFS-5		MRS-10	CPU ex. & SBG
MIA-6		MIFS-7	2-DIM	MRS-15	
MIA-7		MIFS-8	2-DIM	MRS-18	2-DIM
MIEB-2	1, 2-DIM	MLOC-3	1, 2-DIM & SBG	MVIV-7	
MIEB-3	1, 2-DIM	MLOC-4	1, 2-DIM	MVIV-15	
MIEB-4	2-DIM	MLOC-5			
MIEB-7	2-DIM	MLOC-8			
MIEB-10	2-DIM				

To learn driver interaction models, we used 15 runs of the EMSComponent
for k-tails with $k = 1, \ldots, 10$, but already for $k = 3$ the resulting oracle returns
false-positives. Therefore, we only used $k = 1$ and $k = 2$, where for $k = 2$ the
oracle detected 53.7% of the errors, whereas for $k = 1$ only 19.5% were detected.
Table 1 shows detected errors caused by injected faults (see Table 2 for the fault
type acronyms) for the driver interaction model (DIM) with $k = 1$ or 2 in
comparison to the domain-specific CPU exception detector, which detected only
one error, and the software behavior graph (SBG), which detected two errors.
Since only our driver interaction model with learning parameter $k = 2$ was able
to identify a notable number of errors at all, we used this oracle for all further
experiments.

Table 2. Fault types used for software fault injection in our experiments

MFC	Missing function call
MIA	Missing if construct around statements
MIEB	Missing if construct plus statements plus else before statements
MIES	Missing if construct plus statements plus else plus statements
MIFS	Missing if construct plus statements
MLOC	Missing OR clause in branch condition
MLPA	Missing small and localized part of the algorithm
MRS	Missing return statement
MVIV	Missing variable initialization using a value

Next, we evaluated the parameter specifying the length of method call sequences with and without failure indexing and thread separation, so that trace information can be processed on another device without loosing information. The maximum baud rate of the used UART is 460800, which leads to a maximum of 57600B/s or, with our encoding, 3840 event messages per second. Table 3 shows the resulting numbers, where the processing numbers high enough to cope with the maximum baud rate are highlighted bold. As can be seen, only for a method call sequence length of $z = 1$ (see Sect. 3.2) the speed is always above the necessary computation border. Since it may be possible to improve the implementation and therefore increase the processing speed or use buffers on the monitoring device to puffer trace bursts, we did not drop sequence length of 2 altogether, but will assess it in later experiments. Although, it remains an open question if the computations can be actually improved to fulfill the real-time requirements.

Table 3. Processing speeds for different campaign configurations

Sequence length	Failure indexing	Thread separation	Avg. B/s	Min. B/s
2	Yes	Yes	11 196	5 441
2	Yes	No	7 445	3 344
2	No	Yes	20 788	10 032
2	No	No	12 813	5 777
1	Yes	Yes	**81 335**	48 819
1	Yes	No	**68 147**	39 683
1	No	Yes	**146 787**	**95 129**
1	No	No	**127 094**	**76 523**

Our overall goal is to find the best combination and configuration of techniques and parameters for our fault-localization approach. We will use the well-known EXAM metric [29] to assess the performance. The EXAM metric specifies in percent what proportion of the reported code positions have to be examined before actually encountering the faulty position. Therefore, a value of 0% is best.

We first compared the six suspiciousness metrics mentioned in the introduction, see Sect. 1, each with and without thread separation and different transaction detection approaches in Table 4. We show the average EXAM score over all faults and its standard deviation. Since multiple experiments resulted in a perfect EXAM score of 0%, we also show the number of these experiments.

One can draw at least two conclusions from these experiments. First, activating thread separation leads to worse EXAM scores in nearly all cases. Although our workload was mostly single-threaded it is still a surprise that this feature is mostly hindering. Our best guess at the moment is that activating this feature led to a high number of successful transactions on other cores which had a negative influence on the metrics. This would explain the good performance of Barinel and Tarantula metric, which become more accurate when the number of successful runs vastly exceed the number of runs of the faulty component. Since our workload was not suitable to examine this problem further, we leave this for future work. Second, the timer-based transaction detector outperformed the domain-agnostic component-based detector ("OSC"), although the influence is not as severe as that of thread separation.

Table 4. Accuracy results in EXAM metric for different analysis configurations

Thread Sep.	Trans. Detect.	#0%	Avg.	σ	#0%	Avg.	σ	#0%	Avg.	σ
		Barinel Ochiai			D^2 Op2			D^3 Tarantula		
Off	OSC	11	5.1%	8.1pp	13	4.7%	8.2pp	13	4.7%	8.2pp
		13	4.7%	8.2pp	13	4.7%	8.2pp	11	5.1%	8.1pp
Off	Timer	13	2.9%	4.1pp	**15**	**2.7%**	**4.7pp**	**15**	**2.7%**	**4.7pp**
		14	3.0%	4.7pp	14	3.0%	4.7pp	12	3.6%	4.7pp
On	OSC	1	43.2%	21.2pp	1	44.5%	18.4pp	0	43.1%	15.3pp
		1	44.5%	18.4pp	0	43.1%	14.6pp	1	43.2%	21.2pp
On	timer	13	5.6%	10.5pp	0	27.4%	8.8pp	0	27.8%	8.8pp
		0	27.8%	8.7pp	0	28.3%	8.7pp	12	6.0%	10.5pp

Since the results of Table 4 are quite clear, we configured our method without thread separation and with the timer-based transaction detector to assess some remaining questions in a last experiment. First, we analyzed whether using parameters as part of the call sequence improves or worsens the results. Second, we analyzed whether reducing the reset threshold has notable impact. Lastly, we analyzed whether increasing the sequence length, and therefore actually using the MCSHS extension, improves fault localization. We performed the last experiment despite having assessed already that our current implementation is not able to cope with the trace data on time, but it may be possible to improve the runtime of our method.

The results of our last experiments are shown in Table 5. As can be seen, none of the experiments leads to significantly better results. If we ignore function parameters and for example compare D^2 and D^3 with Table 4 it can be seen that only the standard deviation improves, whereas the number of zero percent occurrences is reduced, i.e., some faulty components are not inspected first anymore. Reducing the reset threshold to 1 actually worsens the results a bit. Regarding the MCSHS extension, if we use the averaging proposed in the corresponding paper [9], where each function is assigned a suspiciousness based on the suspiciousness values of all sequences it appeared in, the results are significantly worse than before, see the last row. If we instead use an approach where each method occurring in the sequence is examined and therefore the suspiciousness of the first occurrence of the faulty method in any sequence is significant, the results improve a little bit, see the results highlighted bold, but we might lose trace data due to missing real-time requirements, cf. Table 3. Additionally, depending on the selected examination strategy, the number of methods to check is doubled with $k = 2$. We can conclude that for our repetitive application the reset threshold is not relevant and that using the MCSHS extension, if it could cope with the trace data in real-time, would not improve the results significantly.

Table 5. Accuracy results in EXAM metric for variants of the "ideal" configuration

Mode	#0%	Avg	σ	#0%	Avg	σ	#0%	Avg	σ
	Barinel			D^2			D^3		
	Ochiai			Op2			Tarantula		
Ignore	12	2.9%	3.8 pp	13	2.7%	3.9 pp	13	2.7%	3.9 pp
Parameters	12	3.0%	4.0 pp	12	3.0%	4.0 pp	10	3.6%	4.0 pp
Reset Threshold	12	3.2%	4.2 pp	14	3.0%	4.7 pp	14	3.0%	4.7 pp
	13	3.3%	4.7 pp	14	3.0%	4.7 pp	11	3.9%	4.7 pp
Seq. Len. $z = 2$	12	3.8%	5.5 pp	14	2.7%	4.9 pp	14	2.7%	4.9 pp
Best EXAM-Score	13	2.9%	4.9 pp	**14**	**2.4%**	**4.6 pp**	11	4.1%	5.5 pp
Seq. Len. $z = 2$	9	18.8%	24.1 pp	10	17.1%	22.2 pp	10	19.2%	23.3 pp
Avg EXAM-Score	9	17.9%	23.7 pp	10	21.1%	28.0 pp	8	19.3%	24.3 pp

5   Threats to Validity

While our results are promising, we used a specific setting hindering the extension of these results to other experiments. Foremost, the repetitive work of the engine control unit is very helpful when using statistical methods. In a setting where the software or device has a wider range of functionality, our results may not hold. However, many embedded systems implement control loops and are therefore similar to our experiment. Second, the used fault model has a great impact on the results. While we used a fault model widely accepted in the fault-injection community it still may not accurately represent real faults of specific scenarios.

Another problem can be that our instrumentation to transfer trace data to another system might have an impact on the timing behavior of the system-under-test. This can lead to modified behavior or cause it to violate real-time constraints.

6 Conclusion

In this paper we have assessed spectrum-based fault localization techniques especially in the setting of deployed embedded systems, where continuous access to the systems and expensive debugging hardware is not an option. We have compared multiple known suspiciousness metrics using the EXAM score by applying them in an engine-control-unit scenario and found that regularly less than 10% of probable fault locations have to be analyzed to find the fault. Further, we showed how oracles other than unit tests can be used to decide if an execution was successful or failing, and for that case demonstrated a new form of passively learned automaton, the driver interaction model, which can be used to learn correct behavior when interacting with periphery. We have compared this oracle with others and were able to show that our approach works well in our setting.

While our driver interaction models already performed good, during qualitative examination we found that it may still be possible to improve their representativeness. In future work it may be promising to try to improve their accuracy and expressiveness by using probabilistic or extended probabilistic automata [11] instead.

In general it seems that a spectrum-based approach based on behavior-comparing oracles seems useful above-average in a setting where the application behavior is repetitive, where only limited memory is available to store (aggregated) trace data and where observable interaction with external units takes place. In this case even simple approaches already provide good results, i.e., it is often enough to analyze the single most suspiciousness component to already find the underlying fault.

Acknowledgement. We thank Erwin Schoitsch, Austrian Institute of Technology (AIT), for his valuable feedback and dedicated effort to improve this paper.

References

1. Abreu, R., Zoeteweij, P., van Gemund, A.J.C.: Program spectra analysis in embedded software: a case study. Technical report, TUD-SERG-2006-007, Software Engineering Research Group, Delft University of Technology (2006). http://arxiv.org/abs/cs/0607116
2. Abreu, R., Zoeteweij, P., van Gemund, A.J.C.: An observation-based model for fault localization. In: Proceedings of the 2008 International Workshop on Dynamic Analysis: Held in Conjunction with the ACM SIGSOFT International Symposium on Software Testing and Analysis (ISSTA 2008), WODA 2008, pp. 64–70. ACM, New York (2008). https://doi.org/10.1145/1401827.1401841

3. Abreu, R., Zoeteweij, P., van Gemund, A.J.C.: Spectrum-based multiple fault localization. In: Proceedings of the 2009 IEEE/ACM International Conference on Automated Software Engineering, ASE 2009, pp. 88–99. IEEE Computer Society, Washington, DC (2009). https://doi.org/10.1109/ASE.2009.25

4. Abreu, R., Zoeteweij, P., Gemund, A.J.V.: An evaluation of similarity coefficients for software fault localization. In: 2006 12th Pacific Rim International Symposium on Dependable Computing (PRDC 2006), pp. 39–46, December 2006. https://doi.org/10.1109/PRDC.2006.18

5. Abreu, R., Zoeteweij, P., Golsteijn, R., van Gemund, A.J.: A practical evaluation of spectrum-based fault localization. J. Syst. Softw. **82**(11), 1780–1792 (2009). https://doi.org/10.1016/j.jss.2009.06.035. sI: TAIC PART 2007 and MUTATION 2007

6. Biermann, A.W., Feldman, J.A.: On the synthesis of finite-state machines from samples of their behavior. IEEE Trans. Comput. **C−21**(6), 592–597 (1972). https://doi.org/10.1109/TC.1972.5009015

7. Borghorst, H., Spinczyk, O.: CyPhOS - a component-based cache-aware multi-core operating system. In: Schoeberl, M., Hochberger, C., Uhrig, S., Brehm, J., Pionteck, T. (eds.) ARCS 2019. Lecture Notes in Computer Science, vol. 11479, pp. 171–182. Springer, Cham (2019). https://doi.org/10.1007/978-3-030-18656-2_13

8. Casanova, P., Schmerl, B., Garlan, D., Abreu, R.: Architecture-based run-time fault diagnosis. In: Crnkovic, I., Gruhn, V., Book, M. (eds.) ECSA 2011. LNCS, vol. 6903, pp. 261–277. Springer, Heidelberg (2011). https://doi.org/10.1007/978-3-642-23798-0_29

9. Dallmeier, V., Lindig, C., Zeller, A.: Lightweight defect localization for Java. In: Black, A.P. (ed.) ECOOP 2005. LNCS, vol. 3586, pp. 528–550. Springer, Heidelberg (2005). https://doi.org/10.1007/11531142_23

10. Durães, J.A., Madeira, H.S.: Emulation of software faults: a field data study and a practical approach. IEEE Trans. Softw. Eng. **32**(11), 849–867 (2006). https://doi.org/10.1109/TSE.2006.113

11. Emam, S.S., Miller, J.: Inferring extended probabilistic finite-state automaton models from software executions. ACM Trans. Softw. Eng. Methodol. **27**(1), 4:1–4:39 (2018). https://doi.org/10.1145/3196883

12. Fredkin, E.: Trie memory. Commun. ACM **3**(9), 490–499 (1960). https://doi.org/10.1145/367390.367400

13. Gabor, U.T., Siegert, D., Spinczyk, O.: Software-fault injection in source code with Clang. In: Proceedings of the 32nd International Conference on Architecture of Computing Systems (ARCS 2019), Workshop Proceedings (2019, to appear)

14. Hooman, J., Hendriks, T.: Model-based run-time error detection. In: Giese, H. (ed.) MODELS 2007. LNCS, vol. 5002, pp. 225–236. Springer, Heidelberg (2008). https://doi.org/10.1007/978-3-540-69073-3_24

15. Jones, J.A., Harrold, M.J.: Empirical evaluation of the tarantula automatic fault-localization technique. In: Proceedings of the 20th IEEE/ACM International Conference on Automated Software Engineering, ASE 2005, pp. 273–282. ACM, New York (2005). https://doi.org/10.1145/1101908.1101949

16. Ju, X., Jiang, S., Chen, X., Wang, X., Zhang, Y., Cao, H.: HSFal: effective fault localization using hybrid spectrum of full slices and execution slices. J. Syst. Softw. **90**, 3–17 (2014). https://doi.org/10.1016/j.jss.2013.11.1109

17. Kluge, F., Ungerer, T.: EMSBench: Benchmark und Testumgebung für reaktive Systeme. Betriebssysteme und Echtzeit. I, pp. 11–20. Springer, Heidelberg (2015). https://doi.org/10.1007/978-3-662-48611-5_2

18. Le, T.D.B., Thung, F., Lo, D.: Theory and practice, do they match? A case with spectrum-based fault localization. In: 2013 IEEE International Conference on Software Maintenance, pp. 380–383, September 2013. https://doi.org/10.1109/ICSM.2013.52

19. Li, Z., Tan, L., Wang, X., Lu, S., Zhou, Y., Zhai, C.: Have things changed now? An empirical study of bug characteristics in modern open source software. In: Proceedings of the 1st Workshop on Architectural and System Support for Improving Software Dependability, ASID 2006, pp. 25 33. ACM, New York (2006). https://doi.org/10.1145/1181309.1181314

20. Liu, C., Yan, X., Yu, H., Han, J., Yu, P.S.: Mining behavior graphs for "backtrace" of noncrashing bugs. In: Proceedings of the 2005 SIAM International Conference on Data Mining, pp. 286–297. Society for Industrial and Applied Mathematics (2005). https://doi.org/10.1137/1.9781611972757.26

21. Naish, L., Lee, H.J., Ramamohanarao, K.: A model for spectra-based software diagnosis. ACM Trans. Softw. Eng. Methodol. **20**(3), 11:1–11:32 (2011). https://doi.org/10.1145/2000791.2000795

22. Natella, R., Cotroneo, D., Duraes, J.A., Madeira, H.S.: On fault representativeness of software fault injection. IEEE Trans. Softw. Eng. **39**(1), 80–96 (2013). https://doi.org/10.1109/TSE.2011.124

23. Ochiai, A.: Zoogeographical studies on the soleoid fishes found in Japan and its neighbouring regions-II. Bull. Japan. Soc. Sci. Fish **22**(9), 526–530 (1957). https://doi.org/10.2331/suisan.22.526

24. Reps, T., Ball, T., Das, M., Larus, J.: The use of program profiling for software maintenance with applications to the year 2000 problem. In: Jazayeri, M., Schauer, H. (eds.) ESEC/SIGSOFT FSE -1997. LNCS, vol. 1301, pp. 432–449. Springer, Heidelberg (1997). https://doi.org/10.1007/3-540-63531-9_29

25. Schulte-Althoff, T.: Validierung des Echtzeitverhaltens des ereignisbasierten Betriebssystems CyPhOS am Beispiel einer Motorsteuerung (2017). https://ess.cs.tu-dortmund.de/Teaching/Theses/

26. Spinczyk, O., Lohmann, D.: The design and implementation of AspectC++. Knowl. Based Syst. Spec. Issue Tech. Produce Intell. Secure Softw. **20**(7), 636–651 (2007). https://doi.org/10.1016/j.knosys.2007.05.004

27. Stephenson, A.G., et al.: Mars climate orbiter mishap investigation board phase I report, November 1999. https://llis.nasa.gov/llis_lib/pdf/1009464main1_0641-mr.pdf

28. Wong, W.E., Debroy, V., Gao, R., Li, Y.: The DStar method for effective software fault localization. IEEE Trans. Reliab. **63**(1), 290–308 (2014). https://doi.org/10.1109/TR.2013.2285319

29. Wong, W.E., Debroy, V., Xu, D.: Towards better fault localization: a crosstab-based statistical approach. IEEE Trans. Syst. Man Cybern. Part C (Appl. Rev.) **42**(3), 378–396 (2012). https://doi.org/10.1109/TSMCC.2011.2118751

30. Wong, W.E., Gao, R., Li, Y., Abreu, R., Wotawa, F.: A survey on software fault localization. IEEE Trans. Softw. Eng. **PP**(99), 1 (2016). https://doi.org/10.1109/TSE.2016.2521368

31. Xie, X., Chen, T.Y., Kuo, F.C., Xu, B.: A theoretical analysis of the risk evaluation formulas for spectrum-based fault localization. ACM Trans. Softw. Eng. Methodol. **22**(4), 31:1–31:40 (2013). https://doi.org/10.1145/2522920.2522924

32. Xie, X., Wong, W.E., Chen, T.Y., Xu, B.: Spectrum-based fault localization: Testing oracles are no longer mandatory. In: 2011 11th International Conference on Quality Software, pp. 1–10, July 2011. https://doi.org/10.1109/QSIC.2011.20
33. Xuan, J., Monperrus, M.: Learning to combine multiple ranking metrics for fault localization. In: 2014 IEEE International Conference on Software Maintenance and Evolution, pp. 191–200, September 2014. https://doi.org/10.1109/ICSME.2014.41

Forecast Horizon for Automated Safety Actions in Automated Driving Systems

Ayhan Mehmed[1,2(✉)], Moritz Antlanger[1], Wilfried Steiner[1], and Sasikumar Punnekkat[2]

[1] TTTech Auto AG, Vienna, Austria
{ayhan.mehmed, moritz.antlanger}@tttech-auto.com
wilfried.steiner@tttech.com
[2] Mälardalen University, Västerås, Sweden
sasikumar.punnekkat@mdh.se

Abstract. Future Automated Driving Systems (ADS) will ultimately take over all driving responsibilities from the driver. This will as well include the overall safety goal of avoiding hazards on the road by executing automated safety actions (ASA). It is the purpose of this paper to address the general properties of the ASA. One property of particular interest is the forecast horizon (FH) that defines how much in advance a hazard has to be identified in order to ensure the timely execution of an ASA. For the estimation of the FH, we study the fault-tolerant time interval concept defined by the ISO 26262 and extend it for the use case of fail-operational ADS. We then perform a thorough study on all parameters contributing to the FH, assign typical values for each parameter for a running example, and formalize our work by a set of equations. The set of equations are then applied to two specific driving scenarios, and based on the running example values, the FH is estimated. We conclude our work with a summary of the estimated FH for each of the specific driving scenarios at different road conditions and the recommended road speed limits. Such a scientific way of deciding optimal bounds on the FH is essential to ensure the safety of the future autonomous vehicles and can be a major requirement for clearing the regulatory needs on certification.

Keywords: Automated safety actions · Forecast horizon · Automated driving system · Specific relevant scenarios

1 Introduction

Today, major car manufacturers have their first series production vehicles with driving automation capabilities. Apart from serving as a comfort feature (automatically maneuvering the vehicle from point A to B), the Automated Driving System (ADS) is responsible for the overall vehicle safety. For example, the ADS shall reliably execute automated safety actions (ASAs) by detecting obstacles in the driving path and either safely circumvent the obstacles or reach a

© Springer Nature Switzerland AG 2019
A. Romanovsky et al. (Eds.): SAFECOMP 2019, LNCS 11698, pp. 113–127, 2019.
https://doi.org/10.1007/978-3-030-26601-1_8

safe halt before colliding with them. In case of an ADS failure, these vehicles do still require a fallback-ready driver to be alerted and ready to take immediately or in a timely manner over the fallback driving tasks. Ultimately, in the race for higher automated driving capabilities (L3, L4, and L5 ADS [8]), all driving responsibilities are to be shifted from the driver to the ADS itself - including the fallback driving tasks. As no fallback-ready driver exists, the responsibility for executing an ASA also remains in case of internal ADS failures. Thus, requiring a continuous operation after a failure - a fail-operational system design.

The currently accepted automotive standard ISO 26262 only covers functional safety, i.e., it only addresses how to engineer a system such that it safely executes its functions (including the ASA function). However, the ISO 26262 defines neither which specific ASA to implement, nor general properties of ASA. The time to execute an ASA, for instance, can vary from milliseconds up to tens of seconds depending on factors as the ASA strategy (e.g., evasive maneuver, emergency braking), the road conditions (dry, wet, snowy, icy), and others. In some cases, the time needed to execute the ASA can be higher than the time to the hazard - thus jeopardizing the overall safety of the vehicle.

A way to ensure the safety of the vehicle is to provide the required time for the ASA execution by detecting the hazard early enough in advance. We define this as the forecast horizon, that is the lower bound of a time interval that defines how much in advance an impending potential hazard has to be identified so that the execution of ASA is guaranteed. It is the purpose of this paper to define the bounds of the forecast horizon for specific automated safety actions.

While the ISO 26262 does not cover ASA, we need to consider it when extracting general properties for ASA. For example, in the forecast horizon, we need to consider the functional safety of the ASA functions: the function responsible for identifying a hazard may be faulty. Thus fault detection and fault-mitigation actions need to be factored in when calculating the forecast horizon. While, such fault detection and fault-mitigation aspects are the subject of ISO 26262 we also critically review these aspects and extend them, as ISO 26262 has been designed for achieving safe systems mainly by fail-silent system design (e.g., switching-off), while ADSs demand a fail-operational system design. Throughout the paper we follow the terminology of ISO 26262, version 2011 [3].

The paper continues with Sect. 2, that formulates in details the problem to be addressed. Next, in Sect. 3 we explore the parameters contributing to the forecast horizon and exemplify using running example values. In Sect. 4, we define the specific driving scenarios that later in Sect. 5 are used for the estimation of the forecast horizon. We conclude our work in Sect. 6.

2   Problem Statement

Ensuring the safety of fully automated vehicles is a well-recognized complex interdisciplinary challenge [5]. At present, there is no single straightforward solution for ensuring automated vehicle's safety. Instead, the consensus of cross-domain experts is to use a set of complementary safety methods that together are sufficient to ensure the safety levels required from the automotive safety standards and most importantly for public acceptance.

The problem under investigation contributes to the overall goal of automated vehicle safety by estimating the sufficient forecast horizon. The forecast horizon aims to guarantee the execution of ASA and thus ensures the vehicle reaching a safe state in case of hazardous situations. As a reference for our estimations we take a fail-operational ADS consisting of a primary ADS and a fallback ADS working in a hot-standby configuration, and a safety monitor responsible for the overall ADS safety by verifying the correctness of the primary and fallback outputs.

The first parameter contributing to the forecast horizon is the time needed to execute the ASA. It may range from milliseconds up to a second when only a small to medium amount of braking is needed to keep a safe distance to a vehicle cutting into the ego vehicle's lane. Another example is when an immediate emergency braking in the current lane is needed to avoid a crash with an unavoidable static obstacle - resulting in an ASA time of more than ten seconds in bad road conditions and at a high initial speed of the ego vehicle.

The factors influencing the ASA time are the ASA strategy and the road conditions (dry, wet, snowy, icy). The ASA strategy is influenced by the (i) the operational design domain (e.g. highway traffic jam pilot, highway pilot, urban pilot), (ii) the type of the primary ADS fault (see Fig. 7), (iii) the type of the obstacles on the road (static or dynamic), (iv) and the ego vehicle state (speed, position on the road, etc.) at the moment of fault occurrence. The combination of the above results in a vast number of possible scenarios that are difficult to enumerate exhaustively.

This makes the definition of a sufficient forecast horizon time a complex task. Indeed, a single wide forecast horizon of tens of seconds will be sufficient for all possible scenarios that may occur. However, in our work, we have not found studies addressing concepts as the forecast horizon with such a wide range. To address the complexity introduced by the numerous scenarios, we define a set of specific highway driving scenarios in Sect. 4. In Sect. 5 we then estimate the forecast horizon for the specific scenarios.

For fail-operational ADS, further parameters have to be taken into account for the estimation of the sufficient forecast horizon. In particular, we analyze a scenario where the primary (active) ADS does not detect a hazardous situation on the road, thus leading to non-initiation of an ASA. To activate an ASA, (i) the primary ADS fault has to be detected by the safety monitor, (ii) the fallback ADS has to take over, and (iii) then initiate the execution the ASA. To estimate the forecast horizon, the time needed for the actions above has to be accounted and summed with the ASA execution time (Fig. 1).

Forecast horizon			
Primary ADS fault detection time	Fallback ADS takeover time	ASA initiation time	ASA execution time

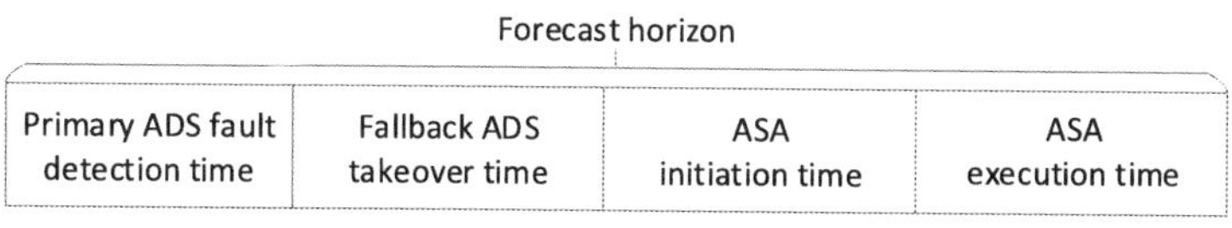

Fig. 1. Parameters influencing the forecast horizon: a high-level overview.

3   Parameters Influencing the Forecast Horizon

In this section, we investigate the parameters contributing to the forecast horizon. For each of the parameters, we define upper bounds and exemplify using realistic numbers. A basis for our estimations is the fault-tolerant time interval (FTTI) concept defined in the ISO 26262 [3]. We then (i) further break down the existing parameters in the FTTI concept and (ii) extend it to account for the time to execute the ASA - thus adapting to the fail-operational system design.

3.1   The FTTI Concept and Proposed Extension

In late 2011, the International Organization for Standardization (ISO), released the "Road vehicles - Functional safety" standard - the ISO 26262. With the aim of supporting the definition of the safety requirements for the safety mechanisms, the ISO defined the FTTI: the time-span in which a fault can be present in a system before a hazardous event occurs (Fig. 1).

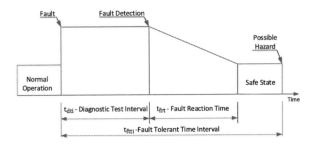

Fig. 2. Fault reaction time and fault tolerant time interval (source: [3]).

The requirement towards any safety mechanism is to bring the vehicle to a safe state in less than the FTTI (t_{ftti}). The time to bring the system to a safe state is defined by (i) the time to detect the fault, defined by the diagnostic test interval (t_{dti}), (ii) and fault reaction time (t_{fr}) that is the time-span from the detection of a fault to reaching the safe state. To ensure the prevention of the hazard and reaching a safe state, the following condition needs to be satisfied:

$$t_{dti} + t_{fr} < t_{ftti} \tag{1}$$

The ISO 26262 defines a safe state as an operating mode of an item without an unreasonable level of risk. The operating modes are defined as (i) a normal or degraded operating mode, (ii) a switched-off mode, or (iii) emergency operation. For ADS with a fallback-ready driver switching-off (fail-silent behavior) upon a failure is enough to reach a safe state. For ADS without a fallback-ready driver, a continuous operation after a failure is necessary. However, continuing with normal or degraded operation after an ADS failure, does not guarantee the safe state has been reached. For instance, detecting a fault in the primary ADS which has failed to recognize a static obstacle on the road, and reacting to the fault by switching to the fallback ADS which continues with a degraded operation, does not ensure a safe state is reached. The fallback ADS should then execute specific "actions" to avoid the obstacle and reach a safe state. A candidate to describe these "actions" in ISO 26262 terms is the emergency operation. However, this term is ambiguously defined in the ISO 26262 version 2011 [3]. Thus the FTTI concept is not fully suitable for the fail-operational ADS use case.[1]

We propose the use of the ASA, to describe the case where after the reaction to the fault (e.g., switchover) the fallback ADS should execute certain actions to reach a safe state. An extension of the ISO 26262 concept is presented in Fig. 3.

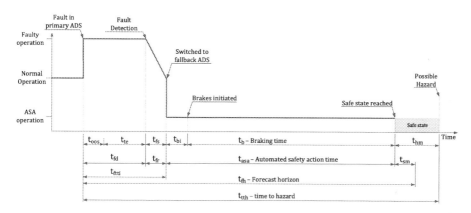

Fig. 3. Proposed extension of the FTTI concept for the use case of fail-operational ADS where to reach a safe state, an ASA is needed after reaction to a fault.

The ADS is assumed to consist of primary ADS, fallback ADS and a monitor serving as a safety mechanism. The vehicle is either in normal, faulty or in ASA operation. The primary ADS experiences a fault leading to the vehicle being in faulty operation. In order to reach a safe state:

1. The primary ADS fault should be detected by the monitor in a certain fault detection time (t_{fd}). To optimize the t_{fd}, we propose the use of the test execution out-of-sync time (t_{oos}) and the test execution time (t_{te}) instead of the diagnostic test interval (t_{dti}) in Fig. 2.
2. The fault has to be mitigated, and the vehicle should be brought to a normal operation mode in a certain fault reaction time (t_{fr}). For a fail-operational

---

[1] At the time of finalization of this paper, the 2018 version of ISO26262 was published and we note that the emergency operation term has been refined. The emergency operation time interval was introduced and extended the original FTTI concept making it suitable for fail-operational ADS. However, we have kept our original terminology since it was a parallel and independent development.

ADS, this is done by switching over to the fallback ADS. Thus the fault reaction time is equal to the fallback switch-over time (t_{fs}).

3. The fallback ADS should execute an ASA to avoid the hazard and bring the vehicle to a safe state. The time for the execution of the ASA is defined as t_{asa}. In particular, emergency braking is assumed. Thus the t_{asa} consists of the brakes initiation time (t_{bi}) and the emergency braking time (t_b).

The time to hazard (t_{tth}) defines the time from occurrence of the fault in the primary ADS to the occurrence of the hazard. In order to ensure the safe state will be reached before the occurrence of the hazard, the sum of t_{fd}, t_{fr}, and t_{asa} has to be smaller than the t_{tth} (Eq. 2).

$$t_{fd} + t_{fr} + t_{asa} < t_{tth} \tag{2}$$

Equation 2 may not always be kept, as in some cases the t_{asa} can be in the range of tens of seconds - much higher than t_{tth}. To ensure the ASA will be executed and a safe state will be reached, the fault has to be detected early in advance. The answer of "how much earlier in advance is enough?" is defined by the forecast horizon. For the estimation of the forecast horizon the t_{fd}, the t_{fr}, the t_{asa}, and the t_{sm} have to be taken into account (Eq. 3). Where the t_{sm} ensures a certain safe distance to the hazard after the completion of the ASA (see Sect. 3.5). Table 1 summarizes the parameters and the exemplified values that will be used as a running example throughout this paper.

$$t_{fh} = t_{fd} + t_{fr} + t_{asa} + t_{sm} \tag{3}$$

Table 1. Summary of the values for the parameters influencing the forecast horizon

Parameter	Value	Parameter	Value
Test execution out-of-sync time (t_{oos})	1 μs	Brakes initiation time (t_{bi})	11 ms
Test execution time (t_{te})	10 ms	Emergency braking time (t_b)	$\frac{-v_0}{2a_b}$
Fallback switch-over time (t_{fs})	10 ms	Safety Margin (t_{sm})	140 ms

The following subsections depict our studies on defining the upper bounds for these parameters.

3.2   Fault Detection Time

The fault detection time (t_{fd}) is the time span from when the fault in the primary ADS has occurred to the time when the monitor detects the fault. The assumption is that the monitoring tasks are executed in a certain time interval (diagnostic test interval (t_{dti})) that is then used to define the upper bound of the t_{fd} (Fig. 2). Hence, the lower the t_{dti} is, the lower the t_{fd} will be. For the sake of further lowering the upper bound for t_{fd}, we define the test execution time (t_{te}) and the test execution out-of-sync time (t_{oos}) is described next.

Figure 4 depicts an example where the primary ADS generates an output in certain time interval defined by t_{po}. A monitor is verifying the correctness of the primary ADS outputs by means of a predefined test criteria. The time to execute the test is defined by the t_{te}. Depending on how well the tasks of ADS outputting the signal and the monitor testing the signal are synchronized, different delays to the fault detection time are added. To account for such delays, we define the t_{oos} and consider it in t_{fd}. Based on this, the time needed to detect the fault is given by

$$t_{fd} = t_{oos} + t_{te}. \tag{4}$$

Hence Eq. 3 accordingly updated (Eq. 5).

$$t_{fh} = t_{oos} + t_{te} + t_{fr} + t_{asa} + t_{sm} \tag{5}$$

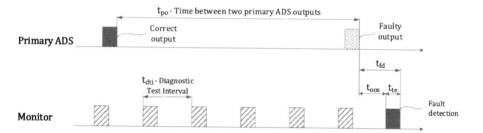

Fig. 4. Time to detect the fault.

Test Execution Out-of-Sync Time. To lower the test execution out-of-sync time (t_{oos}), we envision two approaches. The first is lowering of the diagnostic test interval - thus the lower the t_{dti}, the smaller the t_{oos} is. The second is to design an event chain based on the predefined offline tasks schedule that enables the execution of a check immediately after an ADS output is generated.

While the upper bound for the first approach is defined by the t_{dti} ($t_{oos}^{max^1} \leq t_{dti}$), the upper bound for the second is defined by "how well" the predefined schedule is executed. The "how well" is dependent on the clock synchronization accuracy of the doer (primary ADS) and the checker (the monitor) with respect to the UTC (Coordinated Universal Time). We assume that both, primary ADS and the monitor are time-aware systems, implementing the time synchronization protocol defined in IEEE 802.1AS (.1AS) standard. In recent simulation studies, the .1AS guarantees a synchronization quality of $1\,\mu s$ for time-aware systems that are up to 30 hops away from the grandmaster [2]. Hence, we bound the upper limit of the out-of sync-time of the second approach to $t_{oos}^{max^2} = 1\,\mu s$ and use it as a value for the t_{oos} in the running example.

Test Execution Time. The test execution time (t_{te}) is dependent on the algorithmic solution used for testing and the underlying hardware performance and optimization techniques. To bound the test execution time, a standard method such as worst-case execution time analysis is advisable - a topic requiring a study on its own. For the approximation of t_{te}, we assume it to be 10% of the automated driving system's end-to-end latency: i.e., from sensor acquisition of the environment to actuator response. A recently published study in [6] suggests an end-to-end latency for ADS of 100 ms or below. Hence leading to an estimated test execution time of $t_{te} = 10$ ms for the running example.

3.3   Fault Reaction Time

In a fail-operational ADS example composed of a primary and fallback ADS, a reaction to a primary ADS fault is to switch over to the fallback ADS ($t_{fr} = t_{fs}$). Hence Eq. 5 is updated to:

$$t_{fh} = t_{oos} + t_{te} + t_{fs} + t_{asa} + t_{sm} \tag{6}$$

The fallback switch-over time (t_{fs}) is the time from when the primary ADS fault is detected by the monitor, to the time when the fallback ADS has taken over control of the vehicle. Redundant pairs can generally be in cold or hot standby configuration. We consider a cold-standby redundant configuration as inapplicable for fail-operational ADS since it does not meet the real-time requirements for automated driving. Based on practical experience, a hot-standby configuration enables primary to fallback switch-over times in the range of milliseconds. To exemplify, we assume a switchover time of $t_{fs} = 10$ ms.

3.4   Automated Safety Action

In the case of emergency braking, the automated safety action time (t_{asa}) is the sum of the time to initiate the brakes (t_{bi}) and the time to brake (t_b) until a full stop is reached:

$$t_{asa} = t_{bi} + t_b \tag{7}$$

Brakes Initiation Time. The brakes initiation time (t_{bi}) is the time from when the fallback ADS outputs a braking signal to the time when the actuators start braking. We assume that future automated driving system-equipped vehicles will utilize brake-by-wire systems. Therefore we do not consider any delays caused by mechanical or hydraulically nature. For the estimation of t_{bi} we consider (i) the communication latency from the time when the fallback ADS outputs a braking signal to the time when that signal reaches the electronic control unit (ECU) responsible for the braking (t_{cl}), (ii) the ECU processing time (t_{ecup}), and (iii) the time from when the ECU outputs the control signal to the time when the brakes actually start braking (t_{ba}).

$$t_{bi} = t_{cl} + t_{ecup} + t_{ba} \tag{8}$$

To estimate the communication latency, we look in studies for real-time communication networks (FlexRay and TSN) in [7,9,10], that based on analysis and simulations conclude on a communication latency below a millisecond and latency jitter below 10 μs. Therefore, we assume a communication latency of $t_{cl} = 1$ ms for the running example.

The estimation of (ii) and (iii) is strongly depending on the underlying system hardware, hence requiring future simulation or prototype studies to be done. For the current estimation, we assume the sum of $t_{ecup} + t_{ba}$ to be roughly 10% from the ADS end-to-end latency. Based on [6], the assumed value for the sum of $t_{ecup} + t_{ba}$ is estimated to be 10 ms. Thus the estimated brakes initiation time for the running example is $t_{bi} = 11$ ms.

Time to Brake. By use of equation of motion, the time to brake (t_b) and the distance to brake $(x_{(t_b)})$ are estimated as

$$t_b = -v_0/a_b \tag{9}$$

and

$$x_{(t_b)} = -v_0^2/2a. \tag{10}$$

Where v_0 is the vehicle's initial speed. The $v(t_b)$ is the vehicle speed after execution of the braking - for emergency braking $v(t_b) = 0$ at full stop. The a_b is the acceleration: for braking $a_b < 0$. The estimations are valid under the assumption that the ego vehicle is moving in a straight line with constant deceleration. Braking curve model is not taken into account for the sake of simplicity and will be added in future studies.

Due to the non-constant speed of the vehicle, the braking time (t_b) cannot be used for the estimation of the forecast horizon (t_{fh}). Instead, one has to answer the question of "how far in advance the error needs to be predicted in order to provide the required braking distance $(x_{(t_b)})$?". For that, we define the t_b', which is the time the vehicle needs to travel the braking distance $x_{(t_b)}$ with the initial speed (v_0) being constant (Fig. 5).

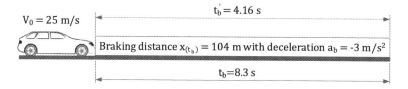

Fig. 5. Differentiation between the time to break (t_b) and the t_b'.

The relation between the t'_b and t_b can be expressed as

$$v_0 t'_b = v_0 t_b + \frac{1}{2} a_b t_b^2. \tag{11}$$

Having the time to brake equal to $t_b = {-v_0}/{a_b}$, the Eq. 11 can be further simplified to Eq. 12.

$$t'_b = \frac{-v_0}{a_b} + \frac{1}{2} \frac{a_b}{v_0} \left(\frac{-v_0}{a_b} \right)^2 = \frac{-v_0}{2 a_b} \tag{12}$$

Based on Eqs. 12, 7 for the case where the ASA is emergency braking is updated to

$$t_{asa} = t_{bi} + t'_b. \tag{13}$$

Furthermore, the forecast horizon equation in Eq. 6 can be updated to:

$$t_{fh} = t_{oos} + t_{te} + t_{fs} + t_{bi} + t'_b + t_{sm} \tag{14}$$

3.5 Safety Margin

The purpose of introducing the safety margin is to ensure there will be a reasonable safety distance (x_{sm}) between the vehicle and the potential hazard after the ASA is completed (Fig. 6). If no safety margin exists the distance (x_{hm}) left between the vehicle and the hazard after the ASA execution cannot be ensured.

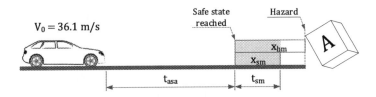

Fig. 6. Time to brake vs forecast horizon

The safety margin to be added to the forecast horizon is defined as follows:

$$t_{sm} = {x_{sm}}/{v_0}. \tag{15}$$

To exemplify the time needed to be added (t_{sm}) to the forecast horizon, we assume a safety margin of 5 meters ($x_{sm} = 5$ m) and a vehicle moving with an initial speed of 130 km/h ($v_0 = 36, 1$ m/s). Thus the assumed safety margin for the running example is equal to 138.5 ms ($t_{sm} \approx 140$ ms).

4   Complexity Reduction

In this section, we address the complexity introduced by the numerous scenarios that may occur. The approach is to decompose the general problem to specific problems. Such a decomposition can be in regards to a restriction of the automated vehicle's operational design domain (e.g., highway pilot, traffic jam pilot, etc.), the operating conditions (e.g., weather and road condition), and the vehicle state (e.g., operating mode, vehicle speed). Hence, instead of solving the general problem to finding "all relevant scenarios", we decompose the problem by defining "specific relevant scenarios". For each of the "specific relevant scenarios" we then define the corresponding safe state and specific strategy to reach it. As the research and technology in automated driving progress, we expect that more and more complex driving scenarios can be mastered.

4.1   Specific Relevant Scenarios

Figure 7 depicts an example of four specific relevant scenarios. We restrict the operational design domain to a highway driving scenario with 130 km/h speed limit (highway pilot). The vehicle state is defined as the primary ADS being in faulty operation. To generate the specific scenarios, we then introduce three parameters: (i) the type of fault, (ii) the type of the obstacle (static or dynamic), and (iii) the avoidability of the obstacle. For each of the scenarios, different road conditions and initial vehicle speeds is applied in the following sections.

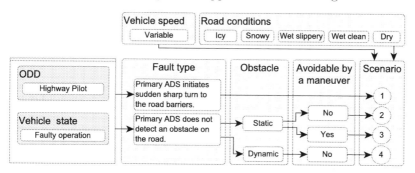

Fig. 7. Generalized scenarios for a highway ADS experiencing different faults.

In scenario 1, the primary ADS experiences a failure that causes the generation of a faulty output leading to a sudden sharp turn to the road barriers. In scenario 2, the primary ADS experiences a failure caused by reasons varying from incapability of the environment perception algorithm to low sensor performance. As a result, a static obstacle on the road is not detected. The object is not avoidable, e.g., a traffic jam on the road. Scenario 3 is similar to scenario 2, this time the obstacle is avoidable. In scenario 4 the obstacle is dynamic and not avoidable (e.g., another vehicle cutting in ego vehicle's lane).[2]

---

[2] The analyses done for scenario 3 and 4 are not described further in this paper due to page limitations. A follow-up paper will be produced to publish our work.

4.2   Safe States and Strategies for the Specific Relevant Scenarios

Figure 8, defines the safe states and corresponding strategy to reach them for scenario 1 and 2. In scenario 1, going back from incorrect to correct operation is considered a safe state. The strategy to reach the safe state is to isolate the faulty primary ADS operation by switching to the fallback ADS and continuing the dynamic driving tasks with full or degraded functionality. A safe state in scenario 2 is reached once the static obstacle is avoided. Since the obstacle is not avoidable by a maneuver, the strategy is to initiate an emergency braking until the vehicle is at a full stop.

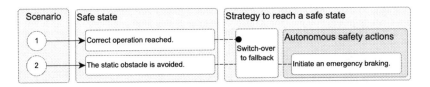

Fig. 8. Safe states for the specific scenarios and strategies to reach the safe states.

4.3   Road Conditions and Speed Limits

For scenarios that require braking, we investigate the change of the sufficient forecast horizon depending on different road conditions as dry, wet clean, wet slippery (e.g. during the first minutes of the rainfall), snowy and icy road. For this we use braking adhesion coefficients from [4] and [12]. The maximum achievable braking deceleration is estimated as $a_b = gk$ [m/s^2], where $g = 9.8 \approx 10$ m/s^2 is the gravity and k is the adhesion coefficient. Table 2 summarizes the k for different road (asphalt) conditions and the corresponding braking deceleration.[3]

Different speed limits apply depending on the road conditions. The speed limits are taken from [1] and [11] and summarized as follows: 30 km/h for icy road, 110 km/h for wet/snowy roads, and 130 km/h for dry roads.

Table 2. Adhesion coefficient at different road conditions and maximum deceleration.

Road condition	Ice	Snow	Wet slippery	Wet clean	Dry
Adhesion coefficient (k)	0.1	0.2	0.25	0.5	0.7
Braking deceleration (a_b)	1	2	2.5	5	7

---

[3] In reality, the adhesion coefficient (k) is not constant: starting at zero at time zero, during the first second is rising to the maximum stated values and then slowly declining. For simplicity, we assume a constant k and thus a constant a_b.

5   Estimation of the Forecast Horizon

In this section, we estimate the values of the forecast horizon for the specific scenarios 1 and 2. For the estimations the exemplified parameter values in Table 1 are used. The change of the forecast horizon in different road condition is investigated based on the values in Table 2.

5.1   Scenario 1

Due to the type of fault in scenario 1, no ASA is needed to reach the safe state. Instead, a simple switchover to the fallback ADS and continuing with full or degraded functionality is sufficient. The forecast horizon for this scenario ($t_{fh}^{s_1}$) is estimated via Eq. 16, resulting to a sufficient forecast horizon of $t_{fh}^{s_1} = 31$ ms. As no braking is performed, the forecast horizon is not affected by road conditions.

$$t_{fh}^{s_1} = t_{oos} + t_{te} + t_{fs} + t_{sm} \tag{16}$$

For faults that do not require an AHA, we recommend using the original FTTI concept from the ISO 26262 (Fig. 2) and Eq. 1. As long as $t_{dti} + t_{fs} < t_{ftti}$ is guaranteed, no prediction of the hazard (forecast horizon) is needed.

5.2   Scenario 2

In scenario 2, the ASA is an execution of an emergency braking until the vehicle reaches a full stop. Equation 17 estimates the $t_{fh}^{s_2}$ and Fig. 9 depicts the results.

$$t_{fh}^{s_2} = t_{oos} + t_{te} + t_{fs} + t_{bi} + t_b' + t_{sm} \tag{17}$$

For a scenario where the road is dry, the estimated forecast horizon at speed $v_0 = 130$ km/h is $t_{fh}^{s_2} = 2.75$ s assuming a constant braking deceleration $a_b = 7$ m/s^2. In case of a wet clean surface, the estimated forecast horizon at speed $v_0 = 110$ km/h is $t_{fh}^{s_2} = 3.23$ s with constant braking deceleration $a_b = 5$ m/s^2.

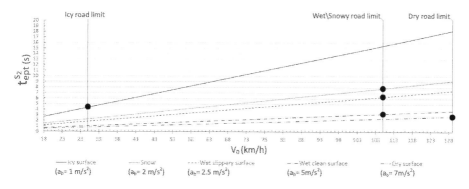

Fig. 9. Forecast horizon time for a scenario, a full stop is needed to reach a safe state.

The forecast horizon increases significantly once the road is wet and slippery at the beginning of the rainfall. The estimation is $t_{fh}^{s_2} = 6.28\,\mathrm{s}$ at initial vehicle speed $v_0 = 110\,\mathrm{km/h}$ with assumed constant deceleration $a_b = 2.5\,\mathrm{m/s^2}$. For a snowy road scenario, the estimated forecast horizon at speed $v_0 = 110\,\mathrm{km/h}$ is $t_{fh}^{s_2} = 7.81\,\mathrm{s}$ with constant braking deceleration $a_b = 2\,\mathrm{m/s^2}$. Finally, in a scenario with an icy road surface the estimated forecast horizon is $t_{fh}^{s_2} = 4.34\,\mathrm{s}$ at speed $v_0 = 30\,\mathrm{km/h}$ with constant braking deceleration $a_b = 1\,\mathrm{m/s^2}$.

6   Conclusions

Fully automated vehicles are no longer a distant future goal. Both, the academic and industrial sectors invest a vast amount of resources in meeting the market demands on the one hand and ensure the vehicle's safety on the other. Reaching an automated vehicle safety level, such that the user trust is not lost is a complex interdisciplinary challenge. In this paper, we contribute to solving this challenge by studying the sufficient forecast horizon used to ensure the vehicle will always have the time for executing the needed automated safety action (ASA). For that, we first looked into the already existing fault-tolerant time interval concept defined by ISO 26262 (version 2011 [3]) and extended it for the use case of fail-operational ADS where upon a failure an ASA execution is needed. Next, we (i) conducted a detailed study on the parameters contributing to the estimation of the forecast horizon and assigned theoretic values for these parameters, (ii) formalized our work by a set of equations, (iii) defined four specific highway driving scenarios to reduce the complexity introduced by the high number of possible scenarios, and last (iv) estimated the sufficient forecast horizon for the first two scenarios at different road conditions and the recommended road speed limits. Although the fault detection time and the fallback switch-over time may be considered as small in comparison to the rest of the parameters (e.g., the ASA time), for the vehicle's safety to be guaranteed, these parameters have to be accounted in the forecast horizon estimation.

Our studies show that in certain scenarios, such as emergency braking, demand forecast horizon values that we believe are very hard to achieve. In particular in case of an emergency braking at icy ($t_{fh}^{s_4} = 4.34\,\mathrm{s}$), wet (slippery) ($t_{fh}^{s_4} = 6.28\,\mathrm{s}$), and snowy ($t_{fh}^{s_4} = 7.81\,\mathrm{s}$) road surfaces. It is for this reason that we here open the discussion on whether different road speed limits for automated vehicles will be needed. Reducing the speed limit from $110\,\mathrm{km/h}$ to $90\,\mathrm{km/h}$ or lower at wet or snowy road conditions will significantly lower the required forecast horizon. Thus the overall goal of ensuring the automated vehicle's safety can be practically achieved.

References

1. European Mobility and Transport: Passenger cars standard speed limits in Europe, October 2018. https://ec.europa.eu/transport/road_safety/specialist/knowledge/speed/speed_limits/current_speed_limit_policies_en

2. Gutiérrez, M., et al.: Synchronization quality of IEEE 802.1 AS in large-scale industrial automation networks. In: IEEE RTAS, pp. 273–282. IEEE (2017)
3. ISO 26262–2011: Road vehicles-functional safety (2011)
4. Kiencke, U.: Realtime estimation of adhesion characteristic between tyres and road. IFAC Proc. Vol. **26**(2), 15–18 (1993)
5. Koopman, P., Wagner, M.: Autonomous vehicle safety: an interdisciplinary challenge. IEEE Intell. Transp. Syst. Mag. **9**(1), 90–96 (2017)
6. Lin, S.-C., et al.: The architectural implications of autonomous driving: constraints and acceleration. In: Proceedings of the International conference on ASPLOS, pp. 751–766. ACM (2018)
7. Meyer, P., Steinbach, T., Korf, F., Schmidt, T.C.: Extending IEEE 802.1 AVB with time-triggered scheduling: a simulation study of the coexistence of synchronous and asynchronous traffic. In: IEEE VNC, pp. 47–54. IEEE (2013)
8. SAE: SAE J3016: Taxonomy and definitions for terms related to on-road motor vehicle automated driving systems. SAE J3016, June 2018
9. Steinbach, T.: Comparing time-triggered Ethernet with FlexRay: an evaluation of competing approaches to real-time for in-vehicle networks. In: WFCS, pp. 199–202. IEEE (2010)
10. Steinbach, T.: An extension of the OMNeT++ INET framework for simulating real-time Ethernet with high accuracy. In: ICST, pp. 375–382 (2011)
11. Swedish Road Administration: Speed limits on icy roads, October 2018. https://en.wikipedia.org/wiki/Ice_road
12. WABCO: Braking deceleration and projection, October 2018. http://inform.wabco-auto.com/intl/pdf/815/00/57/8150100573-23.pdf

Digital Forensics in Industrial Control Systems

Robert Altschaffel$^{(\boxtimes)}$, Mario Hildebrandt, Stefan Kiltz, and Jana Dittmann

Otto-von-Guericke University, 39102 Magdeburg, ST, Germany
{altschaf,mhildebrandt,kiltz,jana.dittmann}@iti.cs.uni-magdeburg.de

Abstract. The increasing complexity of industrial control systems (ICS) and interconnection with other systems poses more safety- and/or security-related challenges due to a rising number of attacks and errors. The event reconstruction is the goal of the new field of ICS forensics differing from well-established Desktop-IT forensics. We identify ICS properties, implications and the impact on the forensic process.

Our primary contribution is the identifcation of ICS specific properties and their impact on the forensic process in order to foster forensic capabilities and forensic readiness in ICS. An existing model for Desktop-IT forensics is successfully adapted for use in ICS.

Keywords: Non-traditional forensic scenarios · SCADA · ICS

1 Introduction

Modern industry relies on interconnected embedded systems with growing complexity and rising threats security, and by the cyber-physical nature, to safety. Though prevention is preferred, detection and recovery from security events is vital for lessons-learned experience, which requires event reconstruction using forensics. Contrary to well established Desktop-IT forensics, ICS forensics is still a relatively new field with specific constraints (see Sect. 3). In this paper we adapt an existing forensic process model to ICS' specifics, stress the need for a new forensic data type of functional data and identify sources of forensic data. This paper is structured as follows: Sect. 2 gives an overview on Desktop-IT forensics and on ICS. Section 3 discusses the specifics of ICS and their impact on forensic processes. Section 4 discusses concepts for increased forensic capabilities and forensic readiness in ICS. A forensic process model for Desktop-IT is adapted to the ICS specifics. Section 5 provides a conclusion and future work.

2 Background

This section gives a brief overview of Desktop-IT forensics and ICS properties.

© Springer Nature Switzerland AG 2019
A. Romanovsky et al. (Eds.): SAFECOMP 2019, LNCS 11698, pp. 128–136, 2019.
https://doi.org/10.1007/978-3-030-26601-1_9

2.1   Forensics in Desktop IT

The forensic process aims at finding traces to support event reconstruction. The validity and reliability depends on the way traces are gathered, processed and analyzed. Of paramount importance is the preservation of authenticity (information about the trace origin) and integrity (information if the trace is unaltered) of the digital evidence. A range of models for the forensic process exist to aid this process. These models address both classical crime scenes [1] and digital crime scenes in Desktop IT [2]. These models are often practitioner-driven and usually break down the forensic process into distinct phases to gather and analyze the respective traces. We choose the forensic process model from [3] for further considerations as it contains the practitioner's and the computer scientist's view (see [4]), the latter often being neglected. This model includes *investigation steps* (practitioner's view), *data types* (computer scientist's view) and *methods* for data access (computer scientist's view). We discuss changes to investigation steps and data types in Sect. 4 together with an overview on its original semantics.

The forensic process is further divided into live forensics (the investigated system is still active) and post-mortem forensics (the investigated system is inactive). Live forensics allows trace access from highly volatile areas (e.g. main memory) at the risk of substantial alteration of system states - either by continued operation or by forensic tool intervention (structural impact [3]). Post-mortem forensics accesses lesser volatile mass storage, ensuring mass storage device integrity (typically with write-blocking-devices). When to switch from live forensics to post-mortem is a crucial decision in every forensic examination.

2.2   Industrial Control Systems

At a fundamental level, Industrial Control Systems (ICS) comprise actuators, sensors, processing units and the communication wiring between them. Sensors collect environment information whilst actuators manipulate the environment. The processing units in ICS are Programmable Logic Controller (PLCs) reading the sensors and driving the actuators. For communication between the various components direct connections (either analog or digital) are used. Various carrier mediums are employed and digital connections are often multiplexed using field bus systems (e.g. PROFIBUS [5]) or industrial Ethernet (e.g. PROFINET [6] or Modbus TCP [7]). The Purdue enterprise reference architecture [12] is often used to describe the control hierarchies of the components [9]:

- **Level 0 - Process** sensors and actuators involved in the basic manufacturing process, performing basic functions of the ICS
- **Level 1 - Basic Control** controllers (typically a PLC) that direct and manipulate the manufacturing process, interfacing with the Level 0 devices
- **Level 2 - Area Supervisory Control** applications and functions associated with the Cell/Area zone runtime supervision and operation (incl. operator interfaces or alarms)
- **Level 3 - Site Level** plant-wide ICS functions,

– **Level 4 - Site Business Planning and Logistics** functions and systems
(incl. basic business administration tasks) that need standard access to services provided by the enterprise network
– **Level 5 - Enterprise** centralized IT systems and functions

3   A Forensic Understanding of ICS

Forensic investigations in ICS require a deep understanding of ICS architectures,
which are described e.g. by the Purdue Model (see Subsect. 2.2). In this section
we provide the forensic perspective. The Enterprise Zone is akin to the classical
Desktop-IT domain in using standard hard- and software. For ICS forensics,
levels 0 to 2 are more important since components specific to ICS are employed.

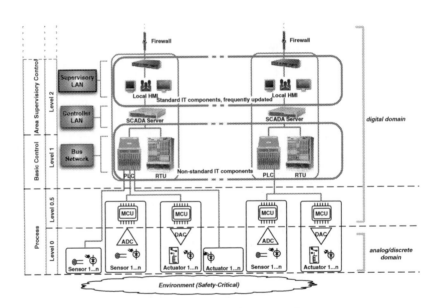

Fig. 1. Levels in Industrial Control Systems according to [9]

Figure 1 gives an overview of the structure of low level components in ICS.
Level 2 represents the SCADA (Supervisory Control And Data Acquisition) control systems as well as a local HMI (Human Machine Interface) and, possibly, a
process historian. These control systems and HMI consist of purpose-built software, which either runs on purpose-built hardware (e.g. Siemens SIMATIC or
Allen-Bradley PanelView) or on generic desktop hardware (e.g. Siemens WinCC
or Rockwell FactoryTalk View). These level 2 components contain information
about the physical process performed by the ICS, like the digital representation
of the physical measurements attained by sensors. Further, these components
usually contain information about the software process, (e.g its starting time,
file names). Level 1 describes the PLCs, which control the manufacturing process.
These hardware components are purpose-built PLCs (e.g. Siemens S7-Series or

Allan-Bradley ControlLogix-Series), running purpose-built software. While this level contains information about the physical process and about the software process, this information is harder to obtain than in classical Desktop IT (see Sect. 3.1). Level 0 consists of sensors and actuators involved in the basic manufacturing process. The Purdue model does not distinguish between components performing their task hard-wired and those that are programmable. However, there is a key difference for ICS forensics. A component which is hard-wired or does not contain any program logic offers less attack vectors, since an alteration of the performed operations would require a physical alteration (or defect) of the component. If such a physical tampering can be excluded, the firmware of the component is not of particular interest for a forensic investigation, since it is unaltered. Thus, we propose the introduction of a Level 0.5 in the computer forensic view on the Purdue model as follows:

- **Level 0 - hard-wired Process** any components directly involved in the basic manufacturing process that does not contain any program logic.
- **Level 0.5 - programmable Process** components with program logic directly involved in the basic manufacturing process.

3.1   Implications on Forensic Investigations in ICS

The architecture and properties of ICS and their components present a significant difference to the forensic process for the classical Desktop-IT domain:

- The specific low-level components on Level 0 are of low complexity, including processing power and storage capacity for event logs. Additionally, mass storage is part of the MCU (Microcontroller Unit) itself, complicating access to its contents.
- ICS are often process-critical. Shutting down an ICS can come with a high monetary cost or safety. Sometimes, redundant systems might be present, allowing forensic investigations in specific ICS part while others take over.
- In general, heterogeneous systems and components are common in ICS. This further increases the difficulty of component access.
- Some ICS might be rarely updated, leading to more legacy hard- and software in ICS and further complicating access to traces [11].
- ICS are usually geared towards safety, neglecting security. While detection for transmission errors is usually present in ICS protocols, very few of them offer any encryption. In addition, sender authenticity is often not given in ICS networks. Hence, the presence of a given communication does not necessarily warrant that it was initiated by the given sender, impacting security aspects considerations and the selection of measures to their implementation [10].
- A lack of publicly available documentation makes access to contents harder. It hampers understanding of the systems and thus complicating forensics.
- ICS come with an inherent safety implication since they control physical processes. Interfering with the physical process can harm property and health.

4   Revisiting the Forensic Process Model for ICS Forensics

Because ICS are different from classical Desktop IT we discuss what alterations of the forensic process (Sect. 2.1)) are needed for ICS.

4.1   Revising Investigation Steps for ICS

Whereas the steps of forensic investigation are applicable to ICS forensics in general, the importance of the *Strategic Preparation* is significantly increased due to the limited resources of the lower level components. [3] describes measures be taken by the operator of an IT-system, prior to an incident, which support a forensic investigation techniques by increasing the amount of available traces. Intrusion detection systems, might be the only accessible source for potential traces in ICS on level 1 or 2. Thus, a careful planning of the ICS is absolutely crucial to allow for forensic investigations within it.

Historians recording data from the ICS process are already in use at different levels of the reference architecture (see Sect. 2.2). A Historian on level 2 would have overview on the a single, physical process and would be referred to as a 'Process Historian'. It captures data required to supervise and control the physical process for a short period of time, giving an operator access to this data to make decisions based on it. A 'Plant Historian' might reside on a higher level (3 or 4), capturing data for a longer time period. This data is mostly used for analysis of the physical process or accounting. These Historians might include means to ensure authenticity and integrity of the capture data as best as possible. However, the data they collect is geared towards supervising the physical process and not so much for detecting attacks. The inclusion of various other data points might broaden the potential usage of historian data in a forensic process. This inclusion would also be part of the *Strategic Preparation*.

In the *Operational Preparation* the course of the reaction to a symptom is set. [3] describes measures to prepare for a forensic investigation after a suspected incident. This includes the decisions if an ICS should be stopped and/or investigated. ICS are tied to physical processes and the system operator might judge the continuation of the physical process (availability of the process) more important than stopping a possible exfiltration of process data (process confidentiality). Such a decision becomes more complicated, if an alteration of the physical process (process integrity) cannot be excluded and carries the risk of harm for life and property. However, some physical process simple can not be interrupted, leaving live forensics the only possible option. Ideally, the system has a sufficient redundancy to switch process control to non-compromised backup controllers and thus, enabling thorough investigation of the involved components. However, if the system is not ideally implemented, the live forensic investigation must not influence the process controls. Thus, we propose the introduction of a **Criticality Map** (Sect. 4.2).

In addition, a deep understanding of the processes and the underlying data is necessary in order to determine which traces might be important a forensic investigation. Due to the fact that non-volatile storage is not readily accessible in

ICS systems, network communication data is more important in ICS forensics, also due to the distribution of process controls over multiple components. A central source of information can be the plant historian, which usually exists already to log the process-relevant data. The data and the historian itself must be protected against attacks in order to ensure the integrity, authenticity and availability of the forensic traces.

The *Data Gathering*, i.e. acquiring and securing digital evidence [3] depends on the type of the attack. If the data logging mechanisms are sufficient, the low-level devices might not be investigated directly. However, if the readily available data implies that the low level ICS components might have been compromised, e.g. by replacing parts of their programming or firmware, a thorough investigation of the components is still necessary. Here, low-level means of accessing the data, such as debugging interfaces (e.g. JTAG) or serial programming interfaces (SPI) need to be used. This way the *Data Investigation*, i.e. the evaluation and extraction of data for further use [3], and *Data Analysis*, i.e. analysis and correlation between digital evidence [3], are significantly more complicated because the forensic technician needs to analyze machine code from lots of different proprietary architectures and systems to identify the specific impact of the attack.

The ICS forensics expert needs to have knowledge about the ICS components and processes they control to identify anomalies as potential traces of an incident. The last step of *Documentation (DO)* remains unmodified from [3].

4.2   Criticality Map

A Criticality Map contains the layout of the ICS in question as well as the possible access points for an investigator usable during data gathering (see Fig. 2).

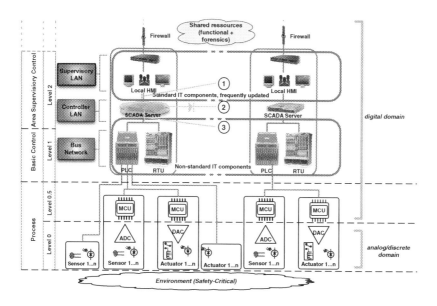

Fig. 2. An example of a Criticality Map based on [9]

A Criticality Map's main purpose is the identification of resources shared between the ICS and any measure deployed during forensic investigations. It identifies any resources where a forensic investigation is in danger to interfere with the process controls and cause Structural Impact (see Sect. 2.1). In case 3, a forensic utility triggering data requests would be attached to the communication between SCADA Server, PLC and RTU using the same communication medium. If the forensic utility would cause large data traffic, this might cause a high load on this medium, effectively undermining the availability of the ICS process. Additionally, the SCADA Server is a shared resource and diagnostic requests might cause a high load in the SCADA Server and cause interference. In case 1, a forensic utility is directly attached to the SCADA Server. The SCADA Server is the only shared resource in this case, reducing possible influence on the control process. A forensic utility not triggering any data requests (e.g. a passive data tap) would avoid resource sharing even if attached directly to the communication between SCADA Server, PLC and RTU (case 2). It would reduce access to possible forensic traces, but avoids influencing the control process (see [8] for a monitoring example). Formulating a Criticality Map should be part of the Strategic Preparation to support the Operational Preparation.

4.3   Revising Data Types for ICS

Data types [3] group different types of data by the way they are gathered or analyzed. They are not mutually exclusive. Context-dependend, the same (physical) bit of data might represent different data types. The ICS forensic data types are:

- DT_1 **hardware data** is defined as *not or only in a limited way influenced by the operating system (OS) and applications.* As such, DT_1 describes in the ICS context, data a PLC possesses about its hardware configuration.
- DT_2 **raw data** is defined as *a sequence of bits (or data streams) of components of the system not (yet) interpreted. Can contain data of all the other data types.* DT_2 can describe the physical representation of all data within a system. On a higher abstraction level, raw data will represent different data types. In ICS it describes any occurrence of digital data.
- DT_3 **details about data** is defined as *meta data added to data, either stored within this data or externally. It can be persistent or volatile.* DT_3 can be attached to various types of data. Furthermore, a clarification on the relationship between data and its meta data is required. We suggest the following alteration: *meta data added to other data, stored within the annotated chuck of data or externally.*
- DT_4 **configuration data** is defined as *can be changed by the OS or applications, modifying the system behavior, including the configuration of hardware, of the OS and applications, but not its behavior with regards to communication.* Here, another clarification is required since DT_4 in ICS describes the configuration of the specific PLCs with regards to their behavior: *can be changed by the OS or applications and which modifies system behavior, including hardware, OS and applications, but not its communication behavior.*
- DT_5 **network communication data** is defined as *data that modifies system behavior with regards to communication.*

– DT_6 **process data** is defined as *data about a running process including the status of the process, the owner of the process, its priority and memory.* This is problematic, since the word 'process' in an ICS usually describes the physical process, the ICS in question should perform. Hence, we propose: *is data about a running software process within a computing unit.*

– DT_7 **session data** is defined as *data collected by a system during a session, regardless of whether the session was initiated by a user, an application or the OS.* It relies on an unclear definition of a session. From the perspective of a forensic investigation, a session should include all processes and their communication within the same scope and time frame. In an ICS context, this describes a snapshot of the sensor readings and actor controls stored by the plant historian within a specific time frame. For production processes session data can also relate to the data gathered during the production of one specific item. Hence, we propose: *data collected by a system during a session, which consist of a number of processes with the same scope and time frame.*

– **user data** is defined as *content created, edited or consumed by the user including media.* This data type represents the data linked to the key functionality (or purpose) of a system in question. In Desktop IT, this might be handling of office files or the creation of images. In an ICS context, this would be the physical process itself. However, from an forensic point of view, the means of such file handling (or processing) are different. An executable will be analyzed in a different way and with a different scope than a media file. An executable file might also be a media file in another context, e.g. an executable be executed on a PLC and edited on a Desktop PC might be seen (and analysed) as 'media file' in one context and an 'executable' in another case. Hence, we propose the creation of two distinct data types. These two data types are linked to performing the key functionality of the system in question. One of these data types contains the media, which is created, edited, consumed or processed by the user (the ends). The other contains the applications used to perform this creating, editing or processing (the means). The media might be anything fulfilling the purpose of the system - editing office files, developing software by editing source code, displaying video files. In an ICS, this media would represent the programming of physical processes performed on a workstation (with the corresponding means being the environment used to perform this programming and the execution). The means to process this media might change over time but the nature of this media does not. We propose for the investigated system:

– DT_8 **application data** *is data representing functions needed to create, edit, consume or process content relied to the key functionality of the system.*

– DT_9 **functional data** *is data content created, edited, consumed or processed as the key functionality of the system.*

5 Conclusion

We discussed the specifics ICS forensics and adapted a forensic process model to also include the ICS components. We revised the steps of the forensic process and the types of forensic data in computer systems. The semantics of these steps and data types in the context of ICS have been discussed, leading to a better understanding of the forensic process in ICS. In due course the Purdue model was extended with an additional level in the hierarchy necessary for the different implications of hard-wired ('dumb') and programmable low-level ICS components. Further, the data types are refined to better represent the different handling of the same data in different contexts. Our findings should serve future work to increase forensic capabilities in ICS.

Acknowledgements. This document was produced with the financial assistance of the European Union. The views expressed herein can in no way be taken to reflect the official opinion of the European Union.

References

1. Inman, K., Rudin, N.: Principles and Practises of Criminalistics: The Profession of Forensic Science. CRC Press LLC, Boca Raton (2001)
2. Pollitt, M.: Applying traditional forensic taxonomy to digital forensics. In: Ray, I., Shenoi, S. (eds.) DigitalForensics 2008. ITIFIP, vol. 285, pp. 17–26. Springer, Boston, MA (2008). https://doi.org/10.1007/978-0-387-84927-0_2
3. Kiltz, S., Dittmann, J., Vielhauer, C.: Supporting forensic design - a course profile to teach forensics. In: IMF 2015. IEEE, Magdeburg (2015)
4. Peisert, S., Bishop, M., Marzullo, K.: Computer forensics in forensis. In: SADFE 2008, pp. 102–112. IEEA, Seattle (2008)
5. PROFIBUS and PROFINET International, PROFIBUS. https://www.profibus.com/technology/profibus/. Accessed 3 Feb 2019
6. PROFIBUS and PROFINET International: PROFINET. https://www.profibus.com/technology/profinet/. Accessed 3 Feb 2019
7. Modbus Organisation: Modbus. http://www.modbus.org/. Accessed 3 Feb 2019
8. ENISA: Introduction to Network Forensics. https://www.enisa.europa.eu/topics/trainings-for-cybersecurity-specialists/online-training-material/documents/introduction-to-network-forensics-ex1-toolset.pdf. Accessed 20 Feb 2019
9. Rockwell Automation: Converged Plantwide Ethernet (CPwE) Design and Implementation Guide. https://literature.rockwellautomation.com/idc/groups/literature/documents/td/enet-td001_-en-p.pdf. Accessed 3 Feb 2019
10. International Electrotechnical Commission: IEC 62443-2-1:2010 Industrial communication networks - Network and system security - Part 2-1: Establishing an industrial automation and control system security program (2010)
11. Van Vliet, P., Kechadi, M.-T., Le-Khac, N.-A.: Forensics in industrial control system: a case study. https://arxiv.org/ftp/arxiv/papers/1611/1611.01754.pdf. Accessed 3 Feb 19
12. Williams, T.J.: The Purdue enterprise reference architecture: a technical guide for CIM planning and implementation. Instrument Society of America, Research Triangle Park, NC (1992)

Security Engineering and Risk Assessment

Efficient Model-Level Reliability Analysis of Simulink Models

Kai Ding[(✉)], Andrey Morozov, and Klaus Janschek

Institute of Automation, Technische Universität Dresden, Dresden, Germany
{kai.ding,andrey.morozov,klaus.janschek}@tu-dresden.de

Abstract. Model-based software development using MATLAB Simulink is widely used in safety-critical domains. The reliability properties of the developed software have to be numerically evaluated for the precise system-level dependability analysis. Data errors occurred in RAM or CPU registers can propagate to critical outputs and cause a failure. The reliability properties can be evaluated at the assembly level, i.e. on the compiled instructions, by performing a probabilistic modeling of data errors. It is more accurate to conduct reliability assessment at the low level, however, the method scalability is questionable due to the complicated procedure, complexity of the assembly code, and considerable computation effort. Thus assembly-level evaluation is unsuitable for huge and complex Simulink models. In addition, it is more convenient for design engineers to estimate dependability properties of Simulink models and even to design reliable control systems at the model level.

In this paper, we propose a method for the reliability evaluation of Simulink models at the model level, extended with the assembly-level evaluation. More specifically, we transform the Simulink model into a stochastic dual-graph error propagation model and specify the reliability properties of individual Simulink blocks by loading the data from a database that have been obtained via the assembly-level evaluation. We verified the efficiency of the proposed method by the comparison of the reliability properties, evaluated at the assembly level and at the model level. The experimental results indicate that the reliability metrics, evaluated at the model level, are almost equivalent to the ones, evaluated at the assembly level. Most prominently, the application of the proposed model-level assessment can reduce the computation and engineering effort, and increase the method scalability.

Keywords: Model-based design · Model-level assessment · Reliability · Dependability · Stochastic analysis · Probabilistic modeling · Bit-flips · Soft errors · Silent data corruption · Embedded systems · Simulink

1 Introduction

Model-based design is increasingly used in safety-critical domains since it enables fast and cost-effective system development. MATLAB® Simulink® [12] is one

© Springer Nature Switzerland AG 2019
A. Romanovsky et al. (Eds.): SAFECOMP 2019, LNCS 11698, pp. 139–154, 2019.
https://doi.org/10.1007/978-3-030-26601-1_10

of the most well-known model-based system development modeling environments, which is very popular among control engineers. Simulink Coder^{TM} or TargetLink$^{\circledR}$ can generate highly efficient C/C++ code from Simulink models and compile it into the assembly code.

Embedded systems are susceptible to hardware faults. Single Event Upset (SEU) [16] can cause bit-flips, which are hardware transient faults, also known as soft errors, that may occur in safety-critical systems [2,10,22,23]. Electronic devices may exhibit abnormal behavior due to the occurrence of bit-flips. During the flight of the spacecraft Cassini, the NASA reports a rate of 280 soft errors per day [21]. Data errors occur when a bit-flip alters the content of a memory cell or a register storing data values. Data errors are more common than timing or control-flow errors [7,19], thus are the focus of the paper.

The current trend of software analysis is to perform verification and validation, or fault injection in the early development phase, i.e. at the Simulink model level. Design deficiencies that are found early in the development phase are less costly to correct. Verification and validation can be applied to Simulink models in the early development phase to check whether the model meets specified requirements and whether it fulfills its intended functions. Additionally, for safety analyses during model-based development, fault injection mechanisms can be applied directly to models. A simulation-based fault injection approach aimed at finding acceptable safety properties for model-based design of automotive systems is presented in [9]. Tools, like MODIFI (MODel-Implemented Fault Injection) [20] or ErrorSim [15], can inject faults in Simulink models in order to evaluate robustness against several types of hardware faults. Fault injection in model-based development facilitates the verification of software during early phases of the development life-cycle.

Regarding the evaluation of the software tolerance to data errors caused by bit-flips, an analytical method for the reliability evaluation of Simulink models at the assembly level is introduced in [5], where a formal Dual-graph Error Propagation model (DEPM) is used to capture the control flow and data flow structures of the assembly code. A probabilistic modeling of data errors occurred in RAM and in CPU is performed using the DEPM. The DEPM [6,13] allows the computation of the reliability metrics using underlying Discrete-time Markov Chain (DTMC) based on model checking techniques. However, the reliability evaluation of Simulink models at the assembly level is highly complicated due to the sophisticated procedure, complexity of the assembly code, and the considerable computation effort. Despite the fact that modern model checkers can handle models with up to 10^8 states, the computational complexity may increase exponentially as the assembly code size increases. As a result, the scalability of the assembly-level analysis is questionable. In this paper, instead of reducing the DTMC size directly at model checking level using techniques, e.g. bisimulations, we propose a new model-level assessment of Simulink models.

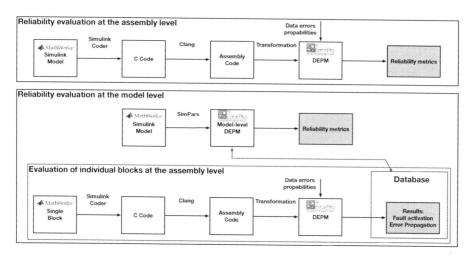

Fig. 1. Overview of the reliability evaluation of a Simulink model (i) at the assembly level (top) and (ii) at the model level (bottom).

2 Related Work

2.1 Effectiveness of Fault Injections at the Model Level

Usually, the reliability evaluation of software is performed using fault injection techniques. The concept of the *model-implemented fault injection* is defined recently in [7,20]. MODIFI is a model-level fault injection tool for dependability assessment of software developed as Simulink models. MODIFI is simulative, targeting the emulation of faults at the model level in order to analyze the effects of injected faults. The injection of bit-flips into Simulink models for robustness assessment is addressed in [18]. ErrorSim [15] allows a user to inject different types of faults and analyze error propagation to critical system parts for Simulink models.

The effectiveness of fault injection in model-based development is verified by performing a back-to-back fault injection testing [8] between two different abstraction levels using MODIFI for the Simulink model and GOOFI-2 [17] for the generated code running on the target microcontroller. The experimental results indicate that MODIFI may be used to identify most of the severe failures in an early development stage, although it is stated in [8,19] that there are target locations, e.g. internal variables of blocks, which are not accessible or considered in MODIFI, and also several hardware faults that can only be injected when using GOOFI-2 at the assembly level since MODIFI only allows the user to inject faults into signals of the Simulink models as it injects faults by adding separate blocks modeling the faults between the connected blocks of the model.

2.2   Reliability Evaluation at the Assembly Level

An analytical method for the reliability evaluation of Simulink models at the assembly level is introduced in [5]. The evaluation process is shown at the top of Fig. 1 (assembly-level assessment). In the first step, the C code is automatically generated from the Simulink model. Then the generated C code is compiled into the assembly code. In the next step, the assembly code is transformed into the DEPM for the error propagation analysis. After that, a probabilistic modeling of data errors occurred in RAM and in CPU is performed at the DEPM level. Finally, the reliability properties of the Simulink model are computed. It is stated that the modeling of data errors caused by bit-flips in RAM or CPU at the assembly level is more accurate for the reliability evaluation. The introduced analytical method numerically evaluates the system reliability. Therefore, it supports, in particular, realistic low probabilities of the error occurrence, in contrast to the experimental approaches, e.g. by Monte Carlo methods, that require a huge number of simulations in order to obtain confident results. In [4], a model-based redundancy technique to tolerate hardware faults for Simulink models, called MOdel-based REdundancy, is proposed. The authors have applied the voting pattern [3] separately to the P, I, D terms of a Simulink PID (Proportional-Integral-Derivative) controller and evaluated the reliability properties at the assembly level.

In the aforementioned two papers, the authors have evaluated the reliability properties of Simulink models at the assembly level that is compiled from the C code. The evaluation procedure is rather complicated and the scalability of the proposed method is questionable, thus the method could not be efficiently employed for the analysis of complex Simulink models. These are the motivations behind the concept of the model-level assessment.

2.3   Contributions of the Paper

In this paper, we propose an analytical approach for the reliability evaluation of Simulink models under data errors caused by bit-flips at the model level in an early development phase. We transform the Simulink model into a stochastic DEPM and specify the reliability properties loaded from a database, where we have stored reliability properties of individual Simulink blocks evaluated at the assembly level by performing a probabilistic modeling of data errors occurred in RAM and in CPU. We assess and validate the effectiveness of the proposed model-level evaluation experimentally by performing the reliability evaluations of Simulink models, conducted at the model level and at the assembly level respectively. The experimental results show that the reliability metrics, evaluated at the model level, are almost equivalent to the ones, evaluated at the assembly level, but with a better performance. Consequently, the reliability evaluation of Simulink models can be performed directly at the model level that has several attractive features:

1. First, the reliability evaluation of Simulink models under data errors can be conducted in the early development phase. It is more convenient for design

engineers to estimate the reliability properties of Simulink models and even to design reliable models.

2. Second, the evaluation procedure at the model level is significantly simpler than at the assembly level. Application of the model-level assessment helps to reduce the DEPM complexity, computation and engineering effort, improve the applicability and scalability of the method. As a consequence, model-level assessment has a higher scalability, and can be applied for the reliability evaluation of complex and huge Simulink models.

3. Third, the generated model-level DEPMs from Simulink models are much more transparent and interpretable compared to the DEPMs generated from assembly level.

4. Fourth, in the model-level assessment, we have used assembly-level assessment for individual Simulink blocks that is platform dependent, however, this assembly-level assessment is performed only once, and the evaluated reliability properties of individual block functions stored in the database can be reused at the model level for any aggregated Simulink models.

3   Reliability Assessment at the Assembly Level

An overview of the reliability evaluation of Simulink models at the assembly level is shown at the top of Fig. 1. We use this assembly-level assessment to evaluate reliability properties of individual Simulink blocks in Sect. 4.1, therefore, we give a brief method explanation here.

Simulink model: A Simulink PID controller is illustrated in Fig. 2, where Gain, Discrete-Time Integrator, and Discrete Derivative blocks are used to model the P, I, D terms. The Discrete Derivative block D is implemented as a subsystem, shown at the bottom of Fig. 2. Value e is considered always correct since the closed control loop system has the ability to handle disturbances in the input signals. The incorrect value of the output u of the PID controller is defined to be a system failure since u is a control variable sent to the plant.

Generated C code: Fig. 3a shows the *step function* of the automatically generated C code, which is invoked in each iteration to compute the output u of the PID controller and update the state variables. This *step function* consists of three constants $\{P\_Gain, I\_gainval, TSamp\_WtEt\}$, two state variables $\{I\_DSTATE, UD\_DSTATE\}$, and two temporary variables $\{rtb\_TSamp, I\}$.

Compiled assembly code: The *step function* in Fig. 3a is compiled into the assembly code with Clang. The resulting assembly code is presented in AT&T syntax in Fig. 3b. In general, each instruction consists of an operation and two operands. The first operand is the source operand and the second operand is the destination operand.

Generated DEPM: The Dual-graph Error Propagation Model (DEPM) [6,13] is a mathematical model that captures system control and data flow structures and reliability properties of system components. The compiled assembly code in Fig. 3b is transformed into the DEPM, shown in Fig. 4a, based on the following mapping rules: (i) The operations, e.g. *movsd*, are mapped into DEPM

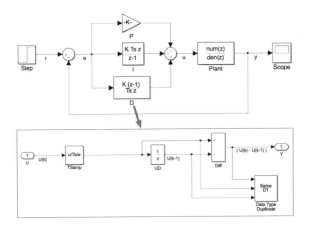

Fig. 2. An illustrative reference example: a PID (Proportional-Integral-Derivative) controller designed in Simulink.

elements. *Element* nodes represent fundamental executable parts of the system. (ii) The operands are mapped into the DEPM data storages. *Data* storages represent variables that can be read or written by *Elements*. (iii) The execution sequences of instructions are mapped into the DEPM control-flow arcs, extended with transition probabilities that are described by the *control flow command* of *elements*. iv) The relations between the operation and its operands are mapped into the DEPM data-flow arcs. *DataFlow* arcs, connect *Elements* with *Data* or vice versa.

The DEPM elements can have *data flow commands* that specify (i) the fault activations during the element execution and (ii) the error propagation from data inputs to outputs. The red arrow-shaped node *Failure* specifies the system failure: the incorrect value of the output u. We will evaluate two reliability properties (metrics) of Simulink models, (i) *mean number of failures* (N_{err}) and (ii) *probability of a failure* (P_{err}), using automatically generated DTMC models based on model checking techniques. An open-source tool OPENERRORPRO that supports the DEPM is available on GitHub [1].

Probabilistic modeling of data errors: Table 1 lists the probabilities of data errors activation in RAM and in CPU registers. The data errors activation, as well as the error propagation through the DEPM elements, can be modeled, by specifying the probabilistic *data flow commands* of the DEPM elements.

Table 1. The data errors activation probabilities in RAM, and in CPU registers [5].

Data errors location		Time interval	Data errors probability
RAM	Variable	Sample time (T_s)	p_{RAM}
CPU	mov	Execution of an instruction	$0.8 \times p_{CPU}$
	add, sub		p_{CPU}
	mul, div		$1.5 \times p_{CPU}$

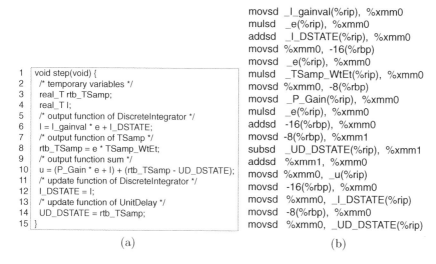

```
1    void step(void) {
2      /* temporary variables */
3      real_T rtb_TSamp;
4      real_T I;
5      /* output function of DiscreteIntegrator */
6      I = I_gainval * e + I_DSTATE;
7      /* output function of TSamp */
8      rtb_TSamp = e * TSamp_WtEt;
9      /* output function sum */
10     u = (P_Gain * e + I) + (rtb_TSamp - UD_DSTATE);
11     /* update function of DiscreteIntegrator */
12     I_DSTATE = I;
13     /* update function of UnitDelay */
14     UD_DSTATE = rtb_TSamp;
15   }
```

```
movsd   _I_gainval(%rip), %xmm0
mulsd   _e(%rip), %xmm0
addsd   _I_DSTATE(%rip), %xmm0
movsd   %xmm0, -16(%rbp)
movsd   _e(%rip), %xmm0
mulsd   _TSamp_WtEt(%rip), %xmm0
movsd   %xmm0, -8(%rbp)
movsd   _P_Gain(%rip), %xmm0
mulsd   _e(%rip), %xmm0
addsd   -16(%rbp), %xmm0
movsd   -8(%rbp), %xmm1
subsd   _UD_DSTATE(%rip), %xmm1
addsd   %xmm1, %xmm0
movsd   %xmm0, _u(%rip)
movsd   -16(%rbp), %xmm0
movsd   %xmm0, _I_DSTATE(%rip)
movsd   -8(%rbp), %xmm0
movsd   %xmm0, _UD_DSTATE(%rip)
```

(a)   (b)

Fig. 3. (a) The automatically generated model step function of the Simulink PID controller in Fig. 2, (b) the compiled assembly code from (a).

Data errors in RAM variables: Bit-flips may occur in the RAM cells, storing data values. It is assumed that the probability of data errors in a single variable during the sample time, i.e. each iteration, is independent and defined as p_{RAM} (see Table 1). An additional DEPM element *FI* is generated (see Fig. 4a), and connected with all five variables of the *step function*. After the occurrence of data errors, the variable value is altered to an erroneous (incorrect) value. Thus, in this specific example, each data storage in the generated DEPM has two states: ok (correct) or error (incorrect). The *data flow commands* of the element *FI* model the independent error occurrence for each RAM variable. For instance, in the modeling of data errors in the variable P_Gain, the *data flow commands* of the DEPM element *FI* are defined, as follows: (i) (P_Gain=ok) -> $(1-p_{RAM})$:(P_Gain'=ok) + p_{RAM}:(P_Gain'=error); (ii) (P_Gain=error) -> 1.0:(P_Gain'=error); The first command represents the data errors activation with the probability p_{RAM} in the variable P_Gain in RAM. In each iteration, the data errors can be activated in the variable P_Gain with probability p_{RAM}. The second command denotes the error propagation with probability 1, i.e. if the value of P_Gain is incorrect, already affected by a data error in a previous iteration, then the P_Gain value will stay incorrect in the following iterations.

Since only data errors in RAM are modeled, the other DEPM instruction elements, e.g. *mov1*, *add1*, can not activate data errors. However, data errors may propagate through these elements. If any data input is incorrect, then all data outputs are incorrect. For instance, the *data flow commands* of the element *add1* are specified, as follows: (i) (I_DSTATE=ok)&(xmm0=ok) -> 1.0:(xmm0'=ok); (ii) (I_DSTATE=error)|(xmm0=error) -> 1.0:(xmm0'=error);

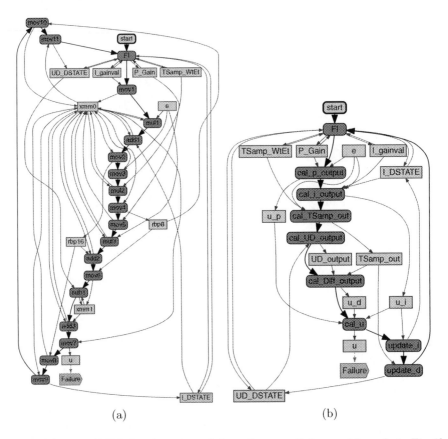

(a)   (b)

Fig. 4. (a) The DEPM that is generated from the compiled assembly code in Fig. 3b, (b) the model-level DEPM is generated directly from the Simulink model in Fig. 2.

Data errors in CPU: In the probabilistic modeling of data errors in CPU, data errors in the destination registers are modeled, where the computed values are stored, during the execution of each assembly instruction. It is assumed that the data errors probabilities during instructions execution time are related to their computation complexities, listed in Table 1. The justification is given in [5]. For instance, the *data flow commands* of the third instruction element *add1* in the DEPM are specified, as follows: (i) $(I\_DSTATE=ok)\&(xmm0=ok)$ $\rightarrow$ $(1-p_{CPU}):(xmm0'=ok)$ + $p_{CPU}:(xmm0'=error)$; (ii) $(I\_DSTATE=error)$ $|$ $(xmm0=error)$ $\rightarrow$ $1.0:(xmm0'=error)$; The first command specifies the data errors activation in the destination register with the probability p_{CPU}. The second command specifies the error propagation from the erroneous input data to the output data.

4   Reliability Assessment at the Model Level

It is impossible (insufficient) to evaluate the reliability metrics of a Simulink model under data errors occurred in RAM and CPU only at the Simulink level, since the RAM and CPU registers are not accessible at the Simulink model level.

In this paper, we propose an analytical method for the reliability evaluation of Simulink models under data errors at the model level, extended with the assembly-level evaluation. The process of the reliability assessment of Simulink models at the model level is shown at the bottom of Fig. 1. In the database, we have stored the reliability results, i.e. fault activation and error propagation probabilities, of each individual block functions, that have been evaluated at the assembly level. We then transform a Simulink model directly into a model-level DEPM automatically, considering the interconnections, execution sequence of blocks, and signal/data transfer among them. Thus the size and complexity of the model-level DEPM are significantly smaller than the assembly-level DEPM (see Fig. 4). Then in the generated model-level DEPM, we perform the probabilistic modeling of data errors, by loading the stored reliability results of each individual block from the database. As we can see, the reliability evaluation of individual blocks at the assembly level is the foundation of the model-level assessment, but this process is performed only once. The evaluated reliability metrics of individual blocks, stored in a database, can be reused at the model level for any aggregated Simulink models. The evaluated reliability metrics are heavily dependent on the tools, e.g. code generation, hardware platform, and settings. However, the proposed analytical method itself is tool-independent.

4.1   Reliability Evaluation of Individual Simulink Blocks Functions at the Assembly Level

We use the assembly-level assessment, discussed in Sect. 3, to evaluate reliability properties of individual Simulink blocks. We generate the C code (Fig. 5b) from the illustrative Discrete-Time Integrator block (Fig. 5a). The model *step function* consists of an *output function* and an *update function*. The compiled assembly code of the *output function* is shown in Fig. 5c. We then generate the DEPM automatically from the compiled assembly code, as shown in Fig. 5d. The incorrect value of the output u_i is defined to be a failure.

Data errors in RAM: In the *output function* of the Discrete-Time Integrator block, I_DSTATE and $I\_gainval$ are the variables stored in RAM (see Fig. 5). We set the value of I_DSTATE and $I\_gainval$ in the DEPM to be correct, then we compute that the probability of the failure is 0. In the same way, we set both values to be erroneous, then the computed failure probability is 1. Thus, the computed reliability properties of the *output function* of the Integrator block are specified: (i) (I_DSTATE=ok)&(I_gainval=ok) -> 1.0:(u_i'=ok); (ii) (I_DSTATE=error)|(I_gainval=error) -> 1.0:(u_i'=error); and stored into the database in Fig. 6a.

Data errors in CPU: In this case, the value of I_DSTATE and $I\_gainval$ are initialized to correct. In the DEPM (Fig. 5d), we specify the *data*

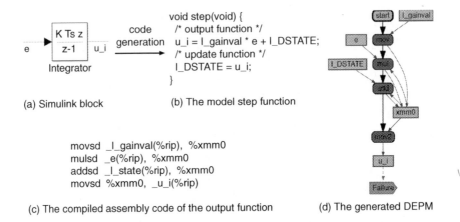

Fig. 5. The generated DEPM from the compiled assembly code of the Integrator block.

flow commands of each instruction element according to the probabilities in Table 1. For instance, we specify the *data flow commands* of the *add* instruction element: (i) (I_DSTATE=ok)&(xmm0=ok) -> (1-p_{CPU}):(xmm0'=ok) + p_{CPU}:(xmm0'=error); (ii) (I_DSTATE=error)|(xmm0=error) -> 1.0: (xmm0'=error); The first command shows the data errors activation in the destination register with probability p_{CPU}. The second command represents the error propagation from the erroneous input data to the output data. Then in the generated PRISM model [11], using parametric model checking we can compute the probability of an erroneous value in u_i: $-0.96p_{CPU}^4 + 4p_{CPU}^3 - 6.14p_{CPU}^2 + 4.1p_{CPU}$. For the simplicity and transparency of the method explanation, we assume that $p_{CPU} = 1e-4$. We store this computed probability of an erroneous output value into the database in Fig. 6b.

4.2 Generated Model-Level DEPM from the Simulink Model

A Simulink model (block diagram) consists of a set of blocks, interconnected by lines. A block represents an elementary dynamic system, comprising a set of inputs, states, and outputs. Blocks with states must store previous values of the states to compute its current state. At each step of execution, Simulink (i) computes the outputs of blocks in a sorted order, then (ii) updates the states of blocks in a sorted order. Thus, the *output functions* and the *update functions* of blocks are the fundamental executable units of a Simulink model.

A tool, SimPars [14], can help us to accomplish the transformation from a Simulink model into a model-level (top-level) DEPM automatically. The Simulink API provides full access to the model, blocks, ports, and lines. The transformation method consists of two main steps: (i) control flow analysis, (ii) data flow analysis. For control flow analysis, we instrument the model and gather the execution order of the blocks functions. The data flow analysis is realized as an algorithm that traces the lines that define signal flows between the output/input ports of blocks.

Gain block:
Output function:
1) P_Gain=ok -> 1.0:(u_p'=ok);
2) P_Gain=error -> 1.0:(u_p'=error);

Discrete-Time Integrator:
Output function:
1) (I_DSTATE=ok)&(I_gainval=ok) -> 1.0:(u_i'=ok);
2) (I_DSTATE=error)|(I_gainval=error) -> 1.0:(u_i'=error);
Update function:
1) (u_i=ok) -> 1.0:(I_DSTATE'=ok);
2) (u_i=error) -> 1.0:(I_DSTATE'=error);

Sum block (three inputs):
Output function:
1) (i1=ok)&(i2=ok)&(i3=ok) -> 1.0:(u'=ok);
2) (i1=error)|(i2=error)|(i3=error) -> 1.0:(u'=error);

...

Functions of blocks	Probabilities
Output function of a Gain block	3.09970e-4
Output function of a Discrete-Time Integrator block	4.09939e-4
Output function of a Sum block (three inputs)	3.59952e-4
Update function of a Discrete-Time Integrator block	1.59994e-4
...	...

(a) Error propagation properties of block functions   (b) Probabilities of an incorrect value in the output variable

Fig. 6. In the database, we have stored the reliability properties of Simulink blocks functions, evaluated at the assembly level by a probabilistic modeling of data errors (a) in RAM, and (b) in CPU ($p_{CPU} = 1e - 4$).

Figure 4b shows the automatically generated model-level DEPM from the Simulink PID controller model in Fig. 2. At the Simulink level, this transformation considers the functions executions of blocks and the input/output signals of blocks. Thereby the generated DEPM can be employed for the data error propagations analysis.

4.3   Probabilistic Modeling of Data Errors at the Model Level

Data errors in RAM: In the model-level DEPM (Fig. 4b), (i) we perform the probabilistic modeling of data errors activations in RAM variables by specifying the *data flow commands* of the element *FI*. (ii) The error propagation through the system can be specified with the *data flow commands* of other DEPM elements, by loading the (corresponding) evaluated properties from the database in Fig. 6a. For instance, we load the reliability properties of the *output function* of a Discrete-Time Integrator block from the database to specify the *data flow commands* of the element *cal_i_output* in the model-level DEPM (Fig. 4b), as follows: (i) `(I_DSTATE=ok)&(I_gainval=ok) -> 1.0:(u_i'=ok);` (ii) `(I_DSTATE=error)|(I_gainval=error) -> 1.0:(u_i'=error);`

Data errors in CPU: In the model-level DEPM, we can specify the *data flow commands* of elements, by loading the evaluated properties from the database in Fig. 6b. For instance, we specify the *data flow commands* of the element *cal_i_output*: (i) `(I_DSTATE=ok)&(I_gainval=ok) -> (1-4.09939e-4):(u_i'=ok) + 4.09939e-4:(u_i'=error);` (ii) `(I_DSTATE=error) | (I_gainval=error) -> (u_i'=error);` The first *data flow command* indicates the probability of an erroneous value in the output variable *i_output* is $4.09939e^{-4}$ during the execution of *cal_i_output*. The second one represents the error propagation.

5   Experimental Results

In order to verify the efficiency of the proposed model-level reliability evaluation, we conduct experiments by performing the reliability evaluation of Simulink models both at the assembly level and at the model level on the benchmark set of seven case studies, listed in Table 2. The first four case studies are the four implementations of a PID controller, discussed in [5]. The fifth to seventh case studies are the applications of *voting patterns* to the *P*, *I*, *D* terms of a PID controller, introduced in [4]. For instance, the first case study, shown in Fig. 2, has six blocks and eight blocks functions. The compiled assembly code of the first case study has 18 instructions.

Table 2. The benchmark set.

Case study ID	Assembly level	Model level	
	# of instructions	# of blocks	# of blocks functions
1	18	6	8
2	20	8	10
3	22	1	4
4	28	1	4
5	31	10	11
6	41	10	13
7	40	14	17

Figure 7 shows the comparison of the evaluated reliability properties of Simulink models obtained at the assembly level and at the model level. Figure 7a and b show that in the probabilistic modeling of data errors in RAM, the reliability metrics, *probability of a failure* and *mean number of failures*, evaluated at the model level are exactly equal to the reliability properties evaluated at the assembly level. In the probabilistic modeling of data errors in RAM, occurrences of data errors are modeled using the DEPM element *FI*, and data errors propagate through the system. Although the generated model-level DEPM has a smaller size, it describes the correct execution of the Simulink model and considers the error propagation of data errors. Concerning data errors in CPU, the results shown in Fig. 7c and d reveal that the reliability properties evaluated at the model level are equal or slightly overestimated with respect to the reliability properties evaluated at the assembly level. Thus the model-level assessment is conservative. The conservative margin is less than 17%, and 9% on average. In the probabilistic modeling of data errors in CPU, data errors might be activated during each instruction execution, thus reliability metrics depend on the number, complexity of the instructions, the internal structural, and behavioral properties of the algorithm. In the model-level assessment, we analyze the compiled assembly code of individual blocks and load the evaluated properties for the analysis of

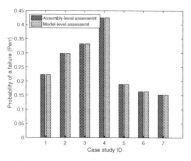

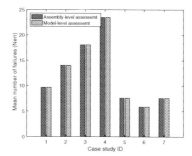

(a) P_{err} in the probabilistic modeling of data errors in RAM.

(b) N_{err} in the probabilistic modeling of data errors in RAM.

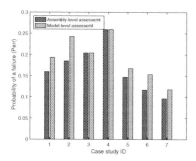

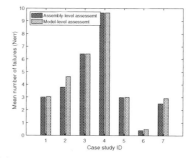

(c) P_{err} in the probabilistic modeling of data errors in CPU.

(d) N_{err} in the probabilistic modeling of data errors in CPU.

Fig. 7. The reliability metrics of Simulink models evaluated at the assembly level and at the model level.

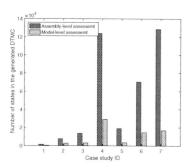

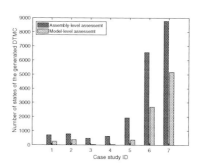

(a) The DTMC size in the probabilistic modeling of data errors in RAM.

(b) The DTMC size in the probabilistic modeling of data errors in CPU.

Fig. 8. The comparison of the resulting underlying DTMC size at the assembly level and at the model level.

the Simulink model. Whereas, in the assembly-level assessment, we analyze the complete compiled assembly code from the Simulink model, where the structure of the assembly code is optimized. The downside of the model-level analysis is that it can be more pessimistic, i.e. loss of accuracy, as the relation among the extended functional blocks is more abstract.

We also compare the sizes of the generated DTMCs, representing the computational complexity. The plots in Fig. 8 show clearly that the generated DTMCs for the model-level assessment are significantly smaller than the DTMCs for the assembly-level assessment. The size has shrunk by maximum up to 95% (case study 3, 4 in Fig. 8b), and 73% on average. Results of run time are not shown since run time depends heavily on the PC configurations. In our observations, run time is proportional to the DTMC size. For instance, the run time of the fourth case study with the assembly-level assessment is 1.881 s, and with the model-level assessment is 0.422 s.

6   Conclusion

In this paper, we have proposed the method for the evaluation of Simulink models under data errors occurred in RAM and in CPU registers at the model level in the early development phase. More specifically, first, we store the reliability properties of each individual block that have been evaluated by the probabilistic modeling of data errors at the assembly level, in a database. Then we transform the Simulink model into a model-level DEPM, considering the block functions (output and update functions) execution sequence, and data flows of signals. At the model-level DEPM, we specify the probabilistic *data flow commands* of Simulink block functions, loading from the database.

The effectiveness of the proposed approach has been assessed and verified experimentally by performing the reliability evaluation both at the assembly level and at the model level respectively. The experimental results have indicated that the evaluated reliability properties at the Simulink model level are almost equivalent to the ones evaluated at the assembly level. We have also compared the sizes of the underlying DTMCs. The generated DTMCs for the model-level assessment are significantly smaller than the DTMCs for the assembly-level assessment.

Acknowledgements. This work is supported by the German Research Foundation (DFG) under project No. JA 1559/5-1.

References

1. Open errorpro on the github. https://mbsa-tud.github.io/OpenErrorPro/
2. Ayatolahi, F., Sangchoolie, B., Johansson, R., Karlsson, J.: A study of the impact of single bit-flip and double bit-flip errors on program execution. In: Bitsch, F., Guiochet, J., Kaâniche, M. (eds.) SAFECOMP 2013. LNCS, vol. 8153, pp. 265–276. Springer, Heidelberg (2013). https://doi.org/10.1007/978-3-642-40793-2_24

3. Ding, K., Morozov, A., Janschek, K.: Classification of hierarchical fault-tolerant design patterns. In: 2017 IEEE 15th International Conference Dependable, Autonomic and Secure Computing (DASC). IEEE (2017)
4. Ding, K., Morozov, A., Janschek, K.: MORE: MOdel-based REdundancy for Simulink. In: Gallina, B., Skavhaug, A., Bitsch, F. (eds.) SAFECOMP 2018. LNCS, vol. 11093, pp. 250–264. Springer, Cham (2018). https://doi.org/10.1007/978-3-319-99130-6_17
5. Ding, K., Morozov, A., Janschek, K.: Reliability evaluation of functionally equivalent simulink implementations of a PID controller under silent data corruption. In: 2018 IEEE 29th International Symposium on Software Reliability Engineering (ISSRE). IEEE (2018)
6. Ding, K., Mutzke, T., Morozov, A., Janschek, K.: Automatic transformation of uml system models for model-based error propagation analysis of mechatronic systems
7. Eriksson, H.: D 5.1 - simulating hardware-related faults at model level. Technical report
8. Folkesson, P., Ayatolahi, F., Sangchoolie, B., Vinter, J., Islam, M., Karlsson, J.: Back-to-back fault injection testing in model-based development. In: Koornneef, F., van Gulijk, C. (eds.) SAFECOMP 2015. LNCS, vol. 9337, pp. 135–148. Springer, Cham (2015). https://doi.org/10.1007/978-3-319-24255-2_11
9. Juez, G., Amparan, E., Lattarulo, R., Ruíz, A., Pérez, J., Espinoza, H.: Early safety assessment of automotive systems using sabotage simulation-based fault injection framework. In: Tonetta, S., Schoitsch, E., Bitsch, F. (eds.) SAFECOMP 2017. LNCS, vol. 10488, pp. 255–269. Springer, Cham (2017). https://doi.org/10.1007/978-3-319-66266-4_17
10. Koopman, P.: A case study of toyota unintended acceleration and software safety. Presentation (2014)
11. Kwiatkowska, M., Norman, G., Parker, D.: PRISM 4.0: verification of probabilistic real-time systems. In: Gopalakrishnan, G., Qadeer, S. (eds.) CAV 2011. LNCS, vol. 6806, pp. 585–591. Springer, Heidelberg (2011). https://doi.org/10.1007/978-3-642-22110-1_47
12. MATLAB: version 9.6 (R2019a). The MathWorks Inc., Natick, Massachusetts
13. Morozov, A., Janschek, K.: Probabilistic error propagation model for mechatronic systems. Mechatronics **24**(8), 1189–1202 (2014)
14. Morozov, A., Janschek, K., Krüger, T., Schiele, A.: Stochastic error propagation analysis of model-driven space robotic software implemented in simulink. In: Proceedings of the 3rd Workshop on Model-Driven Robot Software Engineering. ACM (2016)
15. Saraoğlu, M., Morozov, A., Söylemez, M.T., Janschek, K.: ErrorSim: a tool for error propagation analysis of simulink models. In: Tonetta, S., Schoitsch, E., Bitsch, F. (eds.) SAFECOMP 2017. LNCS, vol. 10488, pp. 245–254. Springer, Cham (2017). https://doi.org/10.1007/978-3-319-66266-4_16
16. Schroeder, B., Pinheiro, E., Weber, W.D.: Dram errors in the wild: a large-scale field. In: ACM SIGMETRICS Performance Evaluation Review, vol. 37. ACM (2009)
17. Skarin, D., Barbosa, R., Karlsson, J.: Goofi-2: a tool for experimental dependability assessment. In: 2010 IEEE/IFIP International Conference on Dependable Systems and Networks (DSN), pp. 557–562. IEEE (2010)
18. Svenningsson, R.: Model-implemented fault injection for robustness assessment
19. Svenningsson, R., Eriksson, H., Vinter, J., Törngren, M.: Model-implemented fault injection for hardware fault simulation. In: 2010 Workshop on Model-Driven Engineering, Verification, and Validation (MoDeVVa), pp. 31–36. IEEE (2010)

20. Svenningsson, R., Vinter, J., Eriksson, H., Törngren, M.: MODIFI: A MODel-Implemented Fault Injection Tool. In: Schoitsch, E. (ed.) SAFECOMP 2010. LNCS, vol. 6351, pp. 210–222. Springer, Heidelberg (2010). https://doi.org/10.1007/978-3-642-15651-9_16
21. Swift, G.M., Guertin, S.M.: In-flight observations of multiple-bit upset in drams. IEEE Trans. Nucl. Sci. **47**(6), 2386–2391 (2000)
22. Verzola, I., Lagny, A.E., Biswas, J.: A predictive approach to failure estimation and identification for space systems operations. In: SpaceOps 2014 Conference (2014)
23. Vinter, J., Johansson, A., Folkesson, P., Karlsson, J.: On the design of robust integrators for fail-bounded control systems. In: Proceedings of 2003 International Conference on Dependable Systems and Networks, pp. 415–424, June 2003

Increasing Trust in Data-Driven Model Validation

A Framework for Probabilistic Augmentation of Images and Meta-data Generation Using Application Scope Characteristics

Lisa Jöckel[(✉)] and Michael Kläs[(✉)]

Fraunhofer Institute for Experimental Software Engineering IESE,
Fraunhofer-Platz 1, 67663 Kaiserslautern, Germany
{lisa.joeckel,michael.klaes}@iese.fraunhofer.de

Abstract. In recent years, interest in autonomous systems has increased. To observe their environment and interact with it, such systems need to process sensor data including camera images. State-of-the-art methods for object recognition and image segmentation rely on complex data-driven models such as convolutional neural networks. Although no final answer exists yet on how to perform safety evaluation of systems containing such models, such evaluation should comprise at least validation with realistic input data, including settings with suboptimal data quality. Because many test datasets still lack a sufficient number of representative quality deficits, we consider augmenting existing data with quality deficits as necessary. For this purpose, a novel tool framework is presented and illustrated using traffic sign recognition as a use case. The extendable approach distinguishes between augmentation at the object, context, and sensor levels. To provide realistic augmentation and meta-data for existing image datasets, known context information and conditional probabilities are processed. First applications on the GTSRB dataset show promising results. The augmentation of datasets facilitates a more rigorous investigation of how various quality deficits affect the accuracy of a model in its target application scope.

Keywords: Safety · Traffic sign recognition · Data augmentation · Data quality · Application scope characteristics · Uncertainty · Convolutional Neural Networks

1 Motivation

In recent years, interest in autonomous systems – particularly, but not limited to, autonomous driving – has increased [2]. Such systems work in an open context, which cannot be exhaustively specified upfront. They need to sense their environment in order to adapt their behavior. A self-driving car needs to detect pedestrians crossing the street or a temporary stop sign and react appropriately. Cameras are still the sensor of choice here, providing the key input for detecting and recognizing objects through, e.g., deep

A. Romanovsky et al. (Eds.): SAFECOMP 2019, LNCS 11698, pp. 155–164, 2019.
https://doi.org/10.1007/978-3-030-26601-1_11

convolutional neural networks (CNNs) [3]. Ciresan et al. [4], e.g., achieved a classification accuracy of 99.46% on GTSRB, a German traffic sign benchmark dataset [1].

However, especially when we consider safety-related functionality of autonomous systems such as detection of a stop sign, we need to ask how much we can rely on accuracy statements obtained from processing existing test datasets.

Like any data-driven model used for image recognition, CNNs face the problem that their intended input-output relationship cannot be completely specified [5]; i.e., the model needs to learn this relationship on a comparatively small and probably not representative sample of input-output examples. This strongly limits traditional verification, making sound statistical validation on test data even more essential. Statistical conclusions on how a data-driven model performs in its target application scope can only be drawn, however, if the test dataset is representative for the target scope.

Today, we can commonly not assume that available test datasets are representative for the intended target application scope of a tested model. Our experience shows that most datasets are artificially clean, i.e., they omit or at least underrepresent many of the quality deficits that arise in real-world settings [6]. However, it does not appear reasonable to make statements about the real-world performance of a data-driven model if it was not tested on data reflecting the real world. For example, a model for traffic sign recognition should also be tested on images with heavy rain or backlight conditions, a dirty camera lens, or snow-covered traffic signs if such deficits can occur in its target application scope. A related challenge is that even if representative test data is available, most critical edge cases might be too rare to be included in sufficient numbers in a reasonably sized dataset. Examples are pedestrians on a rural road at night or the combination of a defective headlight and oncoming traffic with high beam.

Besides intensifying the collection of real data, there are two ways to deal with these problems: creating artificial images using simulation environments [7] or augmenting existing images with quality deficits. The first approach suffers from the 'reality gap'. Attempts to narrow this gap train specialized GANs [8] and apply them to artificially generated images to make them look more realistic. Even though success has been reported for restricted settings, such as grasping tasks of a stationary robot [7], we are not aware of successful applications in more complex environments such as road traffic.

Our contribution is a framework and a tool instantiation for augmenting image data with realistic quality issues and corresponding meta-data. The framework provides guidance for the identification of possible quality deficits, the design of a context model for deriving conditional probabilities for the occurrence of possible deficits, and the layering of various kinds of potentially interacting augmentations. Extending existing work, the framework allows (1) enriching datasets with quality deficits reflecting their natural distribution in the target application scope and (2) applying several deficits to the same image without causing artificial overlay issues.

The remainder of this paper is structured as follows. Section 2 provides an overview of related work in the area of quality-related augmentation of images. Section 3 outlines and illustrates nine steps for building an augmentation-tooling instance for a given data-driven component and three steps for applying it to a given image dataset. Section 4 concludes the paper by discussing limitations and future work.

2   Related Work

Image augmentation is a commonly used preprocessing technique to improve the performance of data-driven models and make them more robust by increasing the count and variety of data points available during model training [9]. In the context of model validation, augmentation has been applied less frequently to date.

Three kinds of augmentation can be distinguished: (1) those mainly used to increase the number and variety of data points, such as image rotations and shifts; (2) those used to intentionally decrease the quality of the image, making the task harder for the model; and (3) those specifically designed to fool a given data-driven model by generating adversarial examples [10]. Because this work focuses on the validation of data-driven models, we consider neither the first kind, which is mainly relevant for model training, nor the third kind, which is an important but security-related topic.

Quality-related augmentations can be distinguished with respect to the degree of realism they intend to provide: (a) Simple artificial augmentations do not intend to emulate concrete, real quality deficits but are added to images, e.g., in the form of various kinds of random noise [6, 11, 12]. (b) Artificially appearing augmentations capture specific aspects of a real quality deficit, e.g., emulating snow by reducing the saturation of an image [13]. (c) Near-photorealistic augmentations use, e.g., available depth information to adjust haze on a pixel basis [14]. There are also approaches that utilize style transfer and GANs [15, 16]. Because our aim is to use augmentations to make a given test dataset more realistic and to investigate the effects of specific quality deficits, this work focuses on near-photorealistic augmentations. However, we decided against the use of GANs because the quality of their results still appears to be unstable.

A review in the context of street scenes and traffic sign recognition showed that besides work on specific deficits such as haze and fog, snow, rain, shadows, and defocus [14, 17], a number of frameworks exist that include augmentations for several quality deficits. Cheng et al. address, e.g., haze, fog, and snow [13] and Temel et al. examined the robustness of traffic sign recognition under challenging conditions [18].

However, most reviewed papers on quality-related augmentation, including the identified frameworks, deal with quality deficits on an individual basis; i.e., they apply only a single deficit to a given image or ignore possible interactions when applying multiple deficits. One exception from this observation is an approach that combines augmentations on a LAB color space [19]. Moreover, the reviewed papers do not consider probabilistic dependencies between meta-data characterizing the context of an image and the applied augmentations. This means that they neither allow generating a realistic distribution of deficits, such as would occur in the target application scope, nor do they consider correlations between various kinds of deficits (including the extreme of mutual exclusivity).

3   Conceptual Augmentation Framework

This section introduces a general augmentation framework for data-driven components processing image data. Moreover, it illustrates how to instantiate it using the example of a tool that supports the augmentation of traffic sign images in an existing dataset.

The overall process consists of two major stages. The first stage (P1-P9) comprises all the steps for building the specific augmentation-tooling instance for a given data-driven component and its target application scope. The second stage (A1-3) comprises all the steps required to apply an augmentation-tooling instance to an image dataset.

P1 - Understand the Data-Driven Component and Its Target Application Scope. Building an augmentation-tooling instance requires an understanding of the investigated data-driven component, including its potential input data and the scope in which it is intended to be applied.

Our example considers a traffic sign recognition component with an image of the detected traffic sign as its main input and data from other vehicle sensors as optional additional information sources (e.g., outside temperature sensor, velocity signal, GPS signal, rain sensor, brightness sensor, online weather broadcast).

Furthermore, we defined its target application scope as passenger vehicles using public roads in Germany, independent of the time of year or the time of day.

P2 - Identify Quality Deficits (QD) Affecting the Data-Driven Component. Considering realistic conditions in the target application scope, there are situations that reduce the quality of the data. In order to build a framework that augments data with quality deficits, relevant quality issues occurring in the target application scope have to be identified and described, considering existing literature and domain expert opinion. The findings should be consolidated in a list and grouped according to sensor, context, and object. If necessary, quality deficits can be prioritize with respect to their occurrence probability and expected impact on the outcome quality of the data-driven component.

For traffic sign recognition, we identified quality deficits concerning either the context of the sign, the sign itself (object), or the built-in camera as the sensor. Specifically, these deficits include: for **context** – light, darkness, weather condition (rain, snow, haze, heat shimmer), shadows, occlusion; for **object** – physical damage (bent, broken, holes), graffiti and stickers, faded colors, dirty sign, wet sign, snow on sign; and for **sensor** – placement, particles on lens (dirt, snow, rain drops, steam), lens and sensor limitations (e.g., resolution, noise, glare effects, backlight, motion blur), camera calibration (e.g., defocus, color temperature), camera processing (e.g. compression errors).

P3 - Identify Scope Characteristics Influencing the Occurrence or Intensity of QD. In order to identify relevant scope characteristics, we go through the list of identified quality deficits, consider when and why they occur, and look at the characteristics of the target application scope influencing their occurrence or intensity.

As relevant scope characteristics that influence quality issues in recognizing traffic signs we identified factors related to geographical position, weather, time, lighting conditions, and vehicle velocity (see white boxes in Fig. 1). As the augmentation addresses traffic sign recognition – not traffic sign detection – factors influencing the detection or relevance of the detected traffic sign such as the placement or reflective surfaces causing wrongly detected mirror images are not considered.

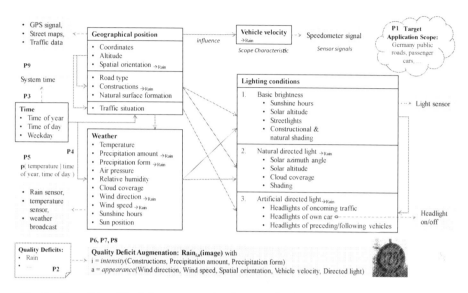

Fig. 1. Steps P1 to P9 of the augmentation framework with a focus on the context model.

P4 - Define a Causal Model with Dependencies Between Scope Characteristics.

In order to model dependencies between scope characteristics, we arrange them into an acyclic graph, where the directed relations mean 'influences'. In a refinement, missing scope characteristics that influence other relevant scope characteristics are added.

For our example application, a graph is presented in Fig. 1. Time, e.g., influences various other scope characteristics, such as weather or traffic situation, directly; others, such as lighting conditions, do so indirectly through other characteristics. From the geographical position, we can determine road type (e.g., motorway, farm road, street in town), constructions (e.g., tunnels, street canyons), natural surface formations (e.g., forest, hills, rocks) that can cause shading, and traffic situation based on the current time.

P5 - Derive Conditional Probabilities to Quantify Identified Dependencies.

Scope characteristics follow a probability distribution $p(SC_{V=u}|TAS)$ regarding their natural occurrence in the target application scope TAS, with $SC_{V=u}$ being the scope characteristic with value $V = u$. Because different characteristics can be interdependent, we also need to consider conditional probabilities. Example: How likely is it that the temperature will be higher than 30 °C when we are in location (x, y) with x being the latitude and y the longitude on day 143 of the year at 3 p.m.?

Several public data sources exist that can be used to calculate these probabilities (e.g., historic weather data from DWD [20] or maps from OpenStreetMap [21]). If no empirical data is available, reasonable expert-based approximations need to be applied, e.g., for the velocity of a car based on its geographical position or the likelihood and amount of dirt on a traffic sign.

P6 - Identify Existing Augmentation Techniques Available for QD. In the next step, we need an overview of existing work on image augmentation for the quality deficits identified as relevant. We must understand how the quality deficit manifests in an image and what needs to be considered when changing the image in order to augment a specific quality deficit.

For example, dirt on a sign can occur in different colors and degrees. It affects only the pixels of the object (i.e., the traffic sign) and needs to be applied as a randomized semitransparent pattern influencing also the reflection property of the affected areas.

P7 - Define the Order of Applying Augmentations. In many cases, there is a certain order to consider when applying augmentation. For instance, object augmentations (e.g., dirt) should be applied first, then context (e.g., darkness), and finally sensor (e.g., steamed-up). This way, consequences from having a particular quality issue can be incorporated into the augmentation of other quality issues; e.g., dirt on a traffic sign reduces its reflective effect when illuminated at night by headlights and the brightness of the fog on a camera lens decreases with the general reduction of brightness at night.

In Fig. 2, the interaction with different intensities of the quality deficits darkness, dirt on sign, and steamed-up lens is displayed, considering previous influences.

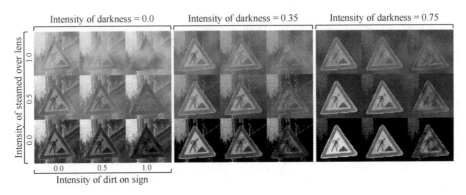

Fig. 2. Combination of darkness, dirt on sign, and steamed-up lens at different intensity levels.

P8 - Implement the Augmentations for the Quality Deficits. During implementation, we need to consider how scope characteristics determine the *intensity* of the quality deficit and influence the *appearance* of the augmentation. Characteristics of quality deficits might determine colors, specific proportions of the image, shapes, etc.

In our example, we illustrate this for the quality deficit rain in Fig. 1. The appearance of the augmentation is defined by the direction and velocity of the wind relative to the driving direction and the velocity of the car, causing a slant in the raindrops (cf. also Fig. 3). Another example is that the location of a traffic sign in the forest rather than in the city will influence the color of the dirt accumulated on it, making it greenish.

Without aug.	Gaussian noise	Poisson noise	Salt & pepper	FGSM	Fog	Haze	Snow

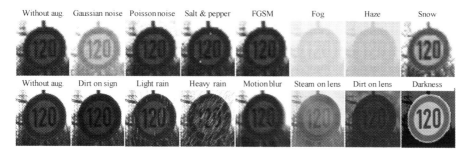

Without aug.	Dirt on sign	Light rain	Heavy rain	Motion blur	Steam on lens	Dirt on lens	Darkness

Fig. 3. Example traffic sign with augmentations from the nn-dependability kit [13] in the first row, and augmentations from our framework in the second row.

Figure 3 contrasts augmentations targeting a high degree of realism, like the ones implemented in our tooling, and artificially appearing augmentations commonly applied.

P9 - Derive Conditional Probabilities to Quantify Further Sensor Outputs. Finally, we need to specify how scope characteristics determine the output of previously identified sensors, including typical inaccuracies of sensor signals.

In our example, sensor data that might be simulated as part of the meta-data output of the framework is illustrated by gray shaded boxes in Fig. 1. Dotted lines indicate the scope characteristics used to simulate the respective sensor signal. For example, the value of the temperature sensor can be obtained by distorting the actual value with a Gaussian error term considering the standard error provided by the specification of the temperature sensor. The same is true for the GPS signal, which uses a Gaussian distribution with an approximated standard error of 8 m.

A1 - Randomly Sample a Context Vector. Realistic context information is generated by taking a sample for $p(SC_{V=u}|TAS)$, the probability of a scope characteristic taking the value u in the target application scope *TAS* considering the dependencies in the context model between different scope characteristics.

Considering Fig. 1, an approach may start by sampling a time based on available statistics on when people are driving by car, then sampling a possible location based on traffic data for each point in Germany at the given time using OpenStreetMap, next sampling specific weather conditions based on location and time, etc.

A2 - Determine Augmentation(s) to Apply and Their Parameter Values. In order to determine realistic accuracy of a data-driven model, data with quality deficits is created, where the intensity values of each quality deficit follow a probability distribution of their natural occurrence $p(QD_{I=x}|TAS)$, where $QD_{I=x}$ is a quality deficit with intensity $I = x$ in the target application scope *TAS*. If specific quality deficits are already present at a representative rate in the dataset to be augmented, they can be excluded from the augmentation.

Most quality deficits have certain demands on the environment in order to be present with a given intensity. Therefore, quality deficits that occur under the given scope characteristics are selected for every quality deficit $QD_1, \ldots, QD_n$:

$$p(QD_{i,I=x_i}|SC_{1,V=u_1}, \ldots, SC_{m,V=u_m} \& TAS), 1 \leq i \leq n. \tag{1}$$

For example, the likelihood and intensity value for the rain augmentation directly depends on the value of the context factor precipitation amount.

A3 - Apply Augmentations and Generate Meta-data. In this step, an image is first randomly drawn from the available dataset containing image data. Each image is only selected once. Next, all augmentations are applied to the image with the previously determined intensity and appearance parameter values. Then the values for relevant further data sources, e.g., rain sensor, brightness sensor, GPS signal of the vehicle, are determined. Finally, the augmented image is stored along with the generated meta-data. Such data can then be used to improve model training or analyze uncertainty [22].

4   Conclusion

This paper presented a framework for image augmentation and explained how to apply it to (UC1) introduce realistic quality deficits to existing image datasets considering the typical distribution of deficits and resulting coincidences in the target application scope. It can also be applied to (UC2) sample realistic context characteristics in which a given selection of quality deficits may occur. Besides the augmented image, meta-data comprising context information and additional sensor data (e.g., from a rain sensor) is generated. A layer concept applying quality deficits in a given order from object via context to sensor-related issues allows passing relevant information to subsequent augmentations, preventing interference between multiple augmentations on the same image.

   A preliminary evaluation showed that a tool prototype based on the framework in the context of traffic sign recognition provided visually authentic results on the GTSRB dataset. Although our approach allows combining quality deficits with various intensities and appearances considering the context of the image, several topics remain open to be addressed in the future.

   At the technical level, the challenge of automatically deriving an object mask that identifies all pixels related to the traffic sign has not been finally solved, even though image segmentation using an adapted GrabCut algorithm provides promising results. Application UC2 is also not implemented yet. As future work, we plan to address UC2 by considering the context model as a Bayesian network and inferring the unobserved scope characteristics with stochastic MCMC simulation.

   The parameters of the augmentations still need to be calibrated and validated on empirical data (e.g., which intensity value best represents 4 mm of rainfall). We also need to further investigate how well the augmented data represents the intended target application scope. This includes evaluating the coverage of relevant quality deficits and the realism of the generated images, investing the impact of the augmentations on the accuracy of data-driven component outcomes, and finally comparing the impact of the augmented quality deficits with the impact of their natural counterparts.

Acknowledgments. Parts of this work have been funded by the German Federal Ministry of Education and Research (BMBF) under grant number 01IS16043E (CrESt).

References

1. German Traffic Sign Benchmarks. http://benchmark.ini.rub.de/?section=gtsrb. Accessed 19 Feb 2019
2. CrESt Project Website. https://crest.in.tum.de/. Accessed 19 Feb 2019
3. Krizhevsky, A., Sutskever, I., Hinton G.E.: ImageNet classification with deep convolutional neural networks. In: Advances in Neural Information Processing Systems (NIPS), vol. 25, pp. 1097–1105 (2012)
4. Ciresan, D., Meier, U., Schmidhuber, J.: Multi-column deep neural networks for image classification. In: Staff, I. (ed.) 2012 IEEE Conference on Computer Vision and Pattern Recognition, pp. 3642–3649. IEEE (2012)
5. Kläs, M.: Towards identifying and managing sources of uncertainty in AI and machine learning models - an overview. arxiv.org/pdf/1811.11669v1 (2018)
6. Dodge, S., Karam, L.: Understanding how image quality affects deep neural networks. arxiv.org/pdf/1604.04004v2 (2016)
7. Shrivastava, A., Pfister, T., Tuzel, O., et al.: Learning from simulated and unsupervised images through adversarial training. In: Conference on Computer Vision and Pattern Recognition (CVPR), Honolulu, Hawaii, pp. 2242–2251 (2017)
8. Goodfellow, I., Pouget-Abadie, J., Mirza, M., et al.: Generative adversarial nets. In: Advances in Neural Information Processing Systems (NIPS), vol. 27 (2014)
9. Wong, S.C., Gatt, A., Stamatescu, V., et al.: Understanding data augmentation for classification: when to warp? In: International Conference on Digital Image Computing: Techniques and Applications (DICTA) (2016)
10. Goodfellow, I.J., Shlens, J., Szegedy, C.: Explaining and Harnessing Adversarial Examples. arxiv.org/pdf/1412.6572v3 (2014)
11. Carlson, A., Skinner, K.A., Vasudevan, R., et al.: Modeling camera effects to improve visual learning from synthetic data. arxiv.org/pdf/1803.07721v6 (2018)
12. Karahan, S., Yildirum, M.K., Kirtac, K., et al.: How image degradations affect deep cnn-based face recognition? In: International Conference of the Biometrics Special Interest Group (BIOSIG), Darmstadt, Germany (2016)
13. Cheng, C.-H., Huang, C.-H., Nührenberg, G.: nn-dependability-kit: engineering neural networks for safety-critical Systems. arxiv.org/pdf/1811.06746v1 (2018)
14. Pezzementi, Z., Tabor, T., Yim, S., et al.: Putting image manipulations in context: robustness testing for safe perception. In: International Symposium on Safety, Security, and Rescue Robotics (SSRR) (2018)
15. Luan, F., Paris, S., Shechtman, E., et al.: Deep photo style transfer. arxiv.org/pdf/1703.07511v3 (2017)
16. Liu, M.-Y., Breuel, T., Kautz, J.: Unsupervised image-to-image translation networks. arxiv.org/abs/1703.00848v6 (2018)
17. UjjwalSaxena Automold - Road Augmentation Library. http://github.com/UjjwalSaxena/Automold–Road-Augmentation-Library. Accessed 26 Feb 2019
18. Temel, D., Kwon, G., Prabhushankar, M., et al.: CURE-TSR: challenging unreal and real environments for traffic sign recognition. arxiv.org/abs/1712.02463v2 (2018)

19. Harisubramanyabalaji, S.P., ur Réhman, S., Nyberg, M., Gustavsson, J.: Improving image classification robustness using predictive data augmentation. In: Gallina, B., Skavhaug, A., Schoitsch, E., Bitsch, F. (eds.) SAFECOMP 2018. LNCS, vol. 11094, pp. 548–561. Springer, Cham (2018). https://doi.org/10.1007/978-3-319-99229-7_49
20. Climate Data Center. https://cdc.dwd.de/portal/. Accessed 19 Feb 2019
21. OpenStreetMap. https://www.openstreetmap.de/. Accessed 19 Feb 2019
22. Kläs, M., Sembach, L.: Uncertainty wrappers for data-driven models – increase the transparency of AI/ML-based models through enrichment with dependable situation-aware uncertainty estimates. In: Workshop on Artificial Intelligence Safety Engineering (WAISE), Turku, Finland (2019)

A Pattern for Arguing the Assurance of Machine Learning in Medical Diagnosis Systems

Chiara Picardi[✉], Richard Hawkins, Colin Paterson, and Ibrahim Habli

Assuring Autonomy International Programme, The University of York, York, UK
{Chiara.Picardi,Richard.Hawkins,Colin.Paterson,Ibrahim.Habli}@york.ac.uk

Abstract. Machine Learning offers the potential to revolutionise healthcare with recent work showing that machine-learned algorithms can achieve or exceed expert human performance. The adoption of such systems in the medical domain should not happen, however, unless sufficient assurance can be demonstrated. In this paper we consider the implicit assurance argument for state-of-the-art systems that uses machine-learnt models for clinical diagnosis, e.g. retinal disease diagnosis. Based upon an assessment of this implicit argument we identify a number of additional assurance considerations that would need to be addressed in order to create a compelling assurance case. We present an assurance case pattern that we have developed to explicitly address these assurance considerations. This pattern may also have the potential to be applied to a wide class of critical domains where ML is used in the decision making process.

Keywords: Machine Learning · Assurance · Assurance cases · Clinical diagnosis

1 Introduction

Machine Learning (ML) offers the potential to create health care applications that can perform as well as, or better than, human clinicians for certain tasks [16]. This could help address major societal challenges, including the shortage of clinicians to meet the demands of an ageing population and the inadequate access to health care services in poor parts of the world [28]. For example, the prevalence of sight-threatening diseases has not been matched by the availability of ophthalmologists with the clinical expertise to interpret eye scans and make the appropriate referral decisions [3]. ML has the potential to address this shortage and augment, and in certain cases improve, existing clinical practices by giving clinicians more time to care for patients [25].

However, clinical diagnosis is a critical activity, the failure of which could compromise the safety and quality of the overall care process. As such, the introduction of clinical diagnosis technologies for augmenting or replacing human

© Springer Nature Switzerland AG 2019
A. Romanovsky et al. (Eds.): SAFECOMP 2019, LNCS 11698, pp. 165–179, 2019.
https://doi.org/10.1007/978-3-030-26601-1_12

expertise has to undergo the necessary rigorous evaluation of the system in its intended context and the assurance of the processes by which the system is developed, evaluated and maintained [23]. For ML-based systems, this includes performance characteristics, e.g. hit and false alarm rates, and the appraisal of the quality and appropriateness of the data and processes by which the system is trained and tested.

Because of their critical nature, clinical diagnosis systems require assurance. Assurance is defined as justified confidence in a property of interest [12], often the property of interest is safety. The assurance of a system is typically communicated in the form of an assurance case, capturing *"a reasoned and compelling argument, supported by a body of evidence, that a system, service or organisation will operate as intended for a defined application in a defined environment"* [1].

This paper proposes an assurance argument pattern that provides a structured, clear and reusable basis for justifying, as part of an assurance case, the use of Machine Learnt models (MLM) in clinical diagnosis systems. This includes reasoning about the performance of the models and the means by which they are trained and tested. The argument pattern can be used to support the development of holistic assurance cases, potentially utilising further evidence for clinical effectiveness and patient safety from randomised control trials and pilot clinical deployments. The generation of a compelling assurance case will both guide development of MLM, as well as facilitating the necessary dialogue between ML developers, clinical users and independent assessors (e.g. regulators).

The rest of the paper is organised as follows. In Sect. 2, we motivate the need for an assurance argument pattern by focusing on a significant machine-learnt system for retinal diagnosis and referral [5]. We construct an explicit assurance argument for this system and examine the assurance factors that have to be demonstrated prior to the adoption of such a system. In Sect. 3, we propose an assurance argument pattern that addresses the assurance factors highlighted in the previous section. This considers, in an integrated manner, the performance of the MLM and the means by which these models are trained and tested. In Sect. 4 we discuss the argument pattern and consider its applicability in the wider domain, e.g. for non-healthcare industries, noting that generalisability would require a similarly detailed analysis in other domains. This is identified in Sect. 5 as one of the areas for future work.

2   Motivating Case Study

The pattern introduced in this paper arose through the consideration of the implicit assurance arguments for three major deep learning models covering the following clinical areas:

- Retinal disease diagnosis and referral [5];
- Optimal treatment strategies for sepsis in intensive care [15];
- Arrhythmia detection and classification [11].

In this paper, we focus on the first study by Fauw and colleagues [5], because of the significance and richness of the published results. The study describes a system able to examine three-dimensional Optical Coherence Tomography (OCT) scans and make referral recommendations on a range of sight-threatening retinal diseases. Figure 1 shows how the system is composed of two parts represented by two different deep neural networks: segmentation and classification.

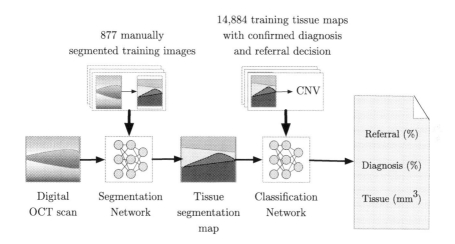

Fig. 1. Automated retinal disease diagnosis and referral system (Adapted from [5]).

The segmentation network, which is trained using 877 images manually segmented by trained ophthalmologists, takes as input OCT scans and creates a detailed device-independent tissue-segmentation map (used for identifying clinical features in scans for diagnosis). The map created is then given as input to the classification network in order to provide one of the four referral suggestions in addition to the presence or absence of multiple retinal pathologies. The classification network is trained using 14884 tissue maps labelled by four retina specialists and four optometrists with the diagnosis and the referral decision. The two neural networks represent the two MLM of the system. In this section we report our interpretation of the implicit assurance argument contained in the published study and discuss the additional assurance considerations needed to support a potential deployment of the technology.

2.1   Understanding the Implicit Assurance Argument

We represent here the assurance argument structures for the segmentation and classification neural networks which we have extracted from the information in the published study. This implicit argument has been represented explicitly using the Goal Structuring Notation (GSN) [1]. GSN is a graphical notation for explicitly capturing the different elements of an argument (claims, evidence and contextual information) and the relationships between these elements. GSN is a generic argument structuring language that is widely used in the safety-critical domain [26].

Fig. 2. GSN graphical notation

Figure 2 shows the graphical elements that we use in this paper. In GSN, the claims of the argument are documented as *Goals* and the evidence is cited in *Solutions*. Additional information, in the form of *Contexts*, are also provided. The notation includes two types of links that can be used to document the relationships between elements: *SupportedBy* (represented as lines with solid arrowheads) indicates inferential or evidential relationships; *InContextOf* (represented as lines with hollow arrowheads) declares contextual relationships. The additional elements shown in Fig. 2 are provided to support patterns and are introduced in Sect. 3. The reader is advised to consult the publicly available GSN standard [1] for a more detailed description of the notation.

The assurance arguments for the neural networks are shown in Figs. 3 and 4 (abstracted from the detailed assurance arguments in [19]). The main claim is that the neural network achieves or exceeds the intended performance (i.e. in tissue-segmentation, diagnosis and referral). This claim is supported by the performance results reported in the study. In addition to this claim and supporting evidence, the study provides a number of items of contextual information:

– description of the clinical setting (Moorfields Eye Hospital which is the largest eye hospital in Europe and North America);
– description of the neural networks used;
– description of the benchmark against which the performance of the neural networks is judged, including the profiles of the clinical experts;
– description of the data used.

The data is divided into three different sets: training, validation and test sets. The training set is used to find the best model; the validation set is used to choose the hyperparameters of the model in order to avoid overfitting; and the test set is used to verify the model with data never seen before. The type of the data, and the amount included in each set, are described as context to the main claim.

It is important to highlight that the arguments reported above represent our interpretation of the implicit argument contained within the published study, which required several review iterations of the results, including the rich supplementary material. We could characterise the structure of the implicit arguments

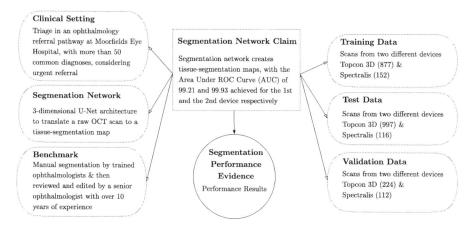

Fig. 3. Segmentation neural network assurance argument

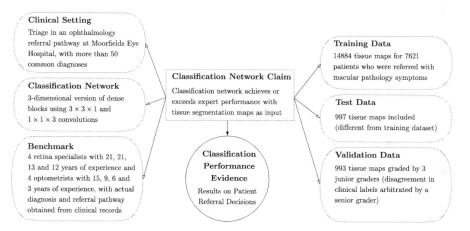

Fig. 4. Classification neural network assurance argument

for the neural networks as being of the form depicted in Fig. 5. That is, the performance claim is directly supported by evidence. Importantly, this evidential relationship is established with clear links to the machine learnt network, the clinical context, the data used and the benchmark against which the acceptability of the performance is judged.

2.2 Review of the Implicit Assurance Argument

Having identified the implicit argument shown in Fig. 5, we evaluated this argument from the point of view of an assessor who is seeking to make a decision on whether to permit the use of the system as part of real clinical diagnosis. In doing so we identified a number of additional assurance considerations that would need to be addressed in order for use of the system to be approved. It is important

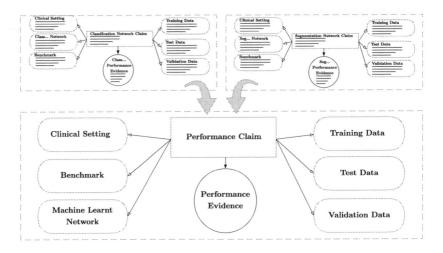

Fig. 5. The structure of the implicit assurance arguments for the ML networks

to note that the issues we identify are not deficiencies in the published study as they are beyond the scope of the reported results. However, they do represent requirements for a potential assured deployment of the system. The assurance considerations we identified are summarised below. They were identified by performing a systematic review of the argument structure in Fig. 5, following the *staged argument review process* in [1, 14], by considering the sufficiency of each of the elements in turn with respect to the confidence they provide.

1. **Clinical Setting:** In order to assure the learnt model, the context in which that model will be used must be fully and clearly understood. If the model is used in a manner for which it was not developed then there is little confidence that the model will perform as required. The clinical setting is described in the published paper, but there is no evidence to support the sufficiency of this description with respect to how the model will be used in practice. In addition, the impact of possible changes or variations in the clinical setting is not clearly considered. For example, is the model still assured if used in a hospital other than Moorfields? Is there anything in particular about this setting that is significant from an assurance perspective? An assurance case for the neural network would need to justify the validity of the clinical setting description.

2. **Benchmark:** If a judgement is to be made on the safety of the network in clinical diagnosis, then a target against which the performance of the network can be judged must be defined. The benchmark is identified in the case study as the gold standard obtained from clinical records of the final diagnosis and optimal referral pathways determined by experts. The profile of the experts involved in the diagnosis are described. The published study does not make clear how the experts were chosen: how was it decided how many years of experience are enough? What specialty is considered appropriate for the

benchmark? An assurance case would need to explain why the benchmark is considered sufficient to indicate that the output of the model is acceptable.

3. **Machine Learnt Model:** Whilst the problem domain restricts the choice of the MLM which may be employed, the number of model types and variants which can be used to tackle a problem is still typically large. Selecting a model type and variant has a significant impact on model performance and is typically performed with reference to previous domain experience. The choice of model should also be undertaken with respect to a wider set of requirements, such as the need for explainability, or with consideration of the operating environment. An argument should therefore be constructed to explain the choice of model with reference to the system level requirements. In the case study the model form is clearly shown, i.e. a convolutional network, and the performance demonstrated with respect to the classification and segmentation tasks. If an assurance case were to be created for this network, the wider impact of this choice, and explicit justification for the decisions made would be required.

4. **Training and Validation Data:** The data collected for the training of MLM is a key assurance consideration as the knowledge encoded within the model is derived directly from this data. The data should be sufficient to represent all relevant aspects of the clinical setting. An assurance argument will need to consider both the relevance and completeness of the data used for training the model. The case study gives specific details on the setting in which data was gathered, i.e. 32 clinic sites serving an urban, mixed socioeconomic and ethnicity population centered around London, but does not supply explicit justification for the relevance or coverage that this data provides.

5. **Test Data:** Whilst every effort is made to ensure that the training and validation data captures the features present in the clinical setting, evidence is required to verify that the model will continue to perform as expected when deployed for real world diagnosis. To provide such assurances requires the test data to be both representative of the clinical setting and independent of the training data and learning process. The size of the test data set is provided in the case study, however, details of independence are implicit. To form a compelling assurance case a justification of the decisions concerning the collection of test data should be presented.

6. **ML Process:** The development strategy has a profound impact on the performance of the MLM and as such an argument should be made about the choices which underpin the design strategy. Typically this will concern the validation strategies used to evaluate model performance, the hyperparameters used to control the training process and the methods employed to select and tune these hyperparameters. In the case study the authors give details of the process undertaken (e.g. the segmentation network was trained five times with different order of inputs and random initialised weights) with reference to previous work which demonstrated the effectiveness of such approaches. Further explicit justification of decisions taken during the development process are required for a more compelling case (discussed in Sect. 3).

Importantly, it is how issues such as those described above are addressed that would be of most interest to an independent assessor e.g. representing a regulatory authority; the performance evidence alone would not be considered to provide sufficient confidence, particularly when the assurance case is extended to cover safety. This is analogous to how conventional safety-related software requires an understanding of the implementation of the software in addition to black-box testing. In forming this view we have been fortunate to be able to interact with a number of assessors from the medical domain including representatives from NHS Digital. It would also be necessary to show how the MLM provides other desired features such as explainability or robustness. In the next section we propose an argument pattern that explicitly addresses these issues.

3   Making an Explicit and Compelling Assurance Argument for ML Decision Making

Figures 6 and 7 show a pattern that documents a reusable assurance argument structure that can be instantiated to create arguments for MLMs. The argument pattern is represented using the pattern language of GSN [1]. Figure 2 showed the *to be developed* and *to be instantiated* symbols that can be used to create abstract argument structures that can then be re-used as approapriate. *To be developed* attached to an element indicates that the element must be further developed as appropriate for the target system (through provision of specific argument and evidence). *To be instantiated* attached to an element indicates that some part of the element's content is a variable that requires instantiation. Variables are declared as part of the argument structure using curled braces, such as {MLM} in Fig. 6. These variables can be substituted for references to specific instances relevant to the system of application (for example a reference to the actual MLM that has been created).

The pattern extends the argument extracted from the published study in Fig. 5 such that the additional assurance considerations identified in Sect. 2.2 can be addressed. In particular, the pattern makes use of Assurance Claim Points (ACPs) [13], indicated by the black squares in the pattern. These ACPs represent points in the argument at which further assurance is required through the provision of a more detailed assurance argument focusing specifically on how confidence can be demonstrated (referred to as a confidence argument [13]). It should be noted that although the argument could be made without using ACPs we feel that it is more clear and effective to do so. The advantages of separating confidence and risk arguments within an assurance case are discussed in detail in [13]. It should be noted that the undeveloped claims in Figs. 6 and 7 will require further development when instantiated for a specific application; all claims must eventually be supported by evidence.

The pattern in Fig. 6 retains the performance claim, supported by performance evidence, and is made in the context of the defined operating environment, the performance benchmark, and the MLM. We have used 'operating environment' rather than 'clinical setting' as this represents the more general case for

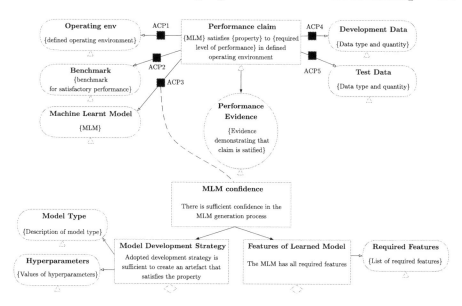

Fig. 6. Assurance argument pattern for machine learning in medical diagnosis

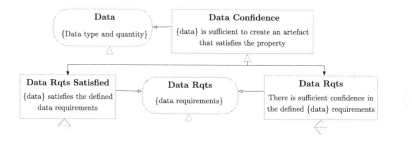

Fig. 7. Data confidence argument pattern for ACP4 and ACP5

the context that defines where and how MLM may be used. The data, that had previously been split into training, test and validation, has now been split into just development data and test data. This represents the fact that there are multiple ways in which development data may be used. Whether separate validation data is selected (as in the published study) depends upon the chosen validation strategy. This representation therefore provides a more general case. Each of the items of context has an associated ACP (ACP1 to ACP5).

As can be seen in Fig. 6 the pattern includes the structure for the confidence argument for ACP3 to demonstrate that there is sufficient confidence in the process used to generate the MLM. This is done through consideration of the development strategy adopted, including the choice of the model type and the respective hyperparameters, and the required features such as explainability or robustness that the learned model possesses. A pattern is also presented for the arguments at ACPs 4 and 5 to demonstrate confidence in the data. This pattern is shown in Fig. 7. It can be seen that, althought the particular details of the argument will be different (as discussed later), the same general approach can be taken to argue about both the development and the test data. Therefore a standard pattern can be created for these data types.

The argument pattern presented in Figs. 6 and 7 has been constructed to explicitly address the six assurance considerations identified in Sect. 2.2. Here we explain how the argument pattern addresses each:

Considerations 1 and 2 are addressed at ACP1 and ACP2 respectively, where arguments will be provided to justify that the operating environment and benchmark are correctly defined for the application of the MLM as part of the diagnosis system. The sufficiency of the environmental definition and the benchmark that is used cannot be assessed through consideration of the MLM alone. The sufficiency of both can only be assessed within the broader context of the diagnosis and referral pathway. As such these issues would be addressed as part of the broader assurance case for the diagnosis system of which this argument forms a part [10]. Further discussion of this is beyond the scope of this paper.

Consideration 3 concerning the machine learnt model is addressed at ACP3 through focusing on confidence in the machine learnt model. The structure of this argument is shown in Fig. 6. Selecting a suitable model type will typically be undertaken with reference to the category of problem being addressed by machine learning (e.g. classification or regression), type and quantity of development data available [2, 21] and in light of personal experience. The choice of model also affects a number of criteria which may impact assurance claims such as the explainability [6] or the ability of the model to be transferred between operating contexts [18]. In addition, features of the artefact produced may influence assurance arguments. Where this is the case, it should be made explicit. Reusing convolutional layers in a neural network may improve performance and training times for example, but introduce the risk of 'backdoors' [9].

Consideration 4 concerning the development data is addressed at ACP4 using the data confidence argument pattern shown in Fig. 7. It is important for the argument to consider firstly, what the requirements on the training data are. These requirements should reflect the property of interest (e.g. correct diagnosis), and the defined operating environment in which that must be achieved. Two characteristic which are of particular interest are relevance and completeness. In order to construct an argument concerning the relevance of data used in training, one should be able to demonstrate that the data is representative of the intended operational environment. In practice, collecting this data may be difficult due to safety, security or financial concerns. In such cases, it may be necessary to synthesise data sets [20] or reuse data from similar domains [22]. Even when data can be collected directly from the operating environment it is unlikely to be complete due to the complexity of most real world environments. Indeed defining completeness in many environments is a difficult task. Consider the task of photographing an injury from a single patient for use in a classification task. The lighting and position of the camera with respect to the patient will lead to a large number of possible images. A clear argument therefore needs to be presented about how the data is captured and how much data is required to adequately characterise the features of interest with the operational environment. In addition, rare cases may be known to exist but difficult to gather in practice thus leaving holes in the data set. Finally, labelling of images is a non-trivial task and experts may differ in the diagnosis offered for a given patient. In such cases, the process of labelling should be clearly stated as part of the data preparation task with conflicts and resolutions clearly stated. The supplementary information in [5] provides a detailed case of how such a task could be rigorously performed.

Consideration 5 concerning the test data is addressed at ACP5, again using the data confidence argument pattern. The central challenge of machine learning is to ensure that the trained model performs well on new, previously unseen, inputs (this is known as generalisation [8]). It is vital therefore that the test set is both representative of the operating environment and independent of the training process. It is common in machine learning to have a single data collection process and set aside a portion (usually 20%) of the data for testing. Whilst this may be suitable in some contexts, it may be more appropriate to have a collection team designated to collect testing data since the collection process itself may introduce bias into the data sets (i.e. similar to the independence requirement between the development and verification teams in the aerospace guidance DO178C [7]). Humans are very good at spotting patterns and unusual features in a data set and, if the developers have sight of the test set, the temptation to engineer features of the training set to improve training may invalidate the assumed test set independence. For the case study for example, it may be possible to collect scans from a different hospital which uses the same hardware. It is also common in traditional software engineering for the test team to check edge cases; similar tactics may be employed in the testing of MLM with rare, or complex, cases over represented in the test set.

Consideration 6 concerning the ML process is also addressed as part of ACP3 when focusing on the development strategy. Having selected a suitable artefact type, the machine learning strategy tunes parameters of the artefact to optimise an error function. The aim of the function is to quantify the performance of the artefact. In order to make such an assessment, the development team must choose a validation strategy during training. Typically this involves strategies such as cross-validation which allow the developer to reason about the artefacts ability to generalise to unseen data. This ability to generalise is important in all but the most simple domains and as such the validation strategy should be provided as part of the assurance evidence. The model training process itself is controlled through the selection of hyperparameters which, in turn, control the performance of the artefact produced. The choice of hyperparameters should, therefore, be explicitly stated to support any assurance argument. Hyperparameters such as early stopping [8] or dropout [24], for example, may be used to control overfitting of the model to training data. Once initial values for the hyperparamters are selected, these are tuned by repeatedly training the models and updating the hyperparamters through the analysis of model performance.

In this section we have presented a pattern that we have developed for arguing the assurance of MLM, based on our review of machine-learnt models for clinical diagnosis. In the next section, we discuss the benefits and implications of using such a pattern to help assure similar systems.

4   Discussion

The assurance argument pattern presented in the previous section is intended to be used to guide developers of MLM for use in clinical diagnosis systems. It identifies how to create a compelling assurance case for the MLM that is sufficient to support a decision regarding approval to deploy the models as part of a diagnosis system. The argument pattern identifies the nature of the claims that must be made about the MLM, but also importantly helps to identify where evidence is required (testing, analysis, validation, review etc.) to support those claims. As such, practitioners who make use of the pattern will be guided towards performing a particular set of assurance activities that are required to make an assurance case for their system. In this way, the pattern should help to improve processes and practices for the utilisation of ML in clinical diagnosis.

ML is often seen as essentially an optimisation problem [27]. One thing that this paper has particularly highlighted is the fact that when ML is being used in critical applications such as clinical diagnosis, although optimisation of the learnt model remains important, other aspects of the ML process and associated contextual assumptions take on a much more critical role. It should be noted that many of these additional considerations highlighted in this paper are things that ML developers are already addressing to some extent (see the excellent supplementary information in [5]), however there has been little consideration, in the ML community, for their role in a justification for the system.

It is important to emphasise that this paper has considered only the machine learnt aspects of a larger overall system that deals with the entire retinal disease diagnosis function. The arguments discussed in this paper would therefore form part of a larger assurance case that considered the safety of the entire system. One approach to decomposing a system such as this is to consider the system as an agent characterised by a need to sense the environment of operation (Sensing), to understand the information that is sensed by interpreting it in the context of the system and to create a useful model of the real-world (Understanding), to make decisions based upon that model (Deciding), and to perform actions that implement that decision (Acting). Each of these elements, as well as the interactions between them, must be considered as part of the system assurance case along with an understanding of the requirements of the system as a whole. The neural networks considered in this paper would form part of the Understanding and Deciding elements of the overall system (e.g. tissue segmentation, classification and referral for retinal disease). In other work we are investigating the form of the holistic assurance argument, but the details of this are outside of the scope of this paper.

Although this paper has focused on medical diagnosis, it is likely that the principles that have been extracted from studying these systems and that have been captured in the argument pattern are more broadly applicable, both to other medical applications, but potentially more broadly to other types of critical system that make use of MLM. Demonstrating this will require further case studies in other domains, however our experience shows that the techniques and processes applied in developing MLM for medical diagnosis are the same techniques that are often used for developing models for other domains, e.g. object detection and classification in autonomous driving [4]. The nature of the requirements and operational context will of course be unique to the application, and may bring unique challenges that must be addressed, but we hope that the general approach reported here will still be valid. This is one of our ongoing areas of research.

5   Conclusions and Future Work

Machine learning promises to revolutionise the way many tasks are performed and recent years has seen a growth in the application of ML to domains where failure would compromise the safety of critical processes. One such area is medical diagnosis where the benefits offered could address major societal challenges. However, the adoption of ML will require a change in the way machine learnt models are developed. Where ML, and the models generated by ML processes, are intended for use in these critical domains, there is a need for explicit assurance.

In this paper, we presented a reusable assurance case pattern that can be used to create arguments for machine learnt models in medical diagnosis systems and, as such, informs ML development teams of the key issues to be considered. The pattern reflects current ML practice as applied in medical diagnosis systems, and addresses identified assurance considerations. This includes the explicit justification of choices made during the development process including the nature of the data used. As part of our overall validation of the approach, we have presented our work to a wide clinical safety audience [17] and have received positive feedback on the utility of our approach. We believe that the pattern may also be applicable in a wide range of critical application contexts that make use of MLMs, however demonstrating this will require a similarly detailed analysis of multiple case studies to be conducted across a number of different domains. The focus of our future work will be to carry out such an evaluation, and to update and improve the pattern based upon this experience.

Acknowledgements. This work is funded by the Assuring Autonomy International Programme https://www.york.ac.uk/assuring-autonomy.

References

1. Assurance Case Working Group [ACWG]: Goal Structuring Notation Community Standard version 2 (2018). https://scsc.uk/r141B:1?t=1. Accessed 13 Nov 2018

2. Azure-Taxonomy: How to choose algorithms for Azure Machine Learning Studio (2019). https://docs.microsoft.com/en-us/azure/machine-learning/studio/algorithm-choice. Accessed Feb 2019
3. Bourne, R.R., et al.: Magnitude, temporal trends, and projections of the global prevalence of blindness and distance and near vision impairment: a systematic review and meta-analysis. Lancet Glob. Health **5**(9), e888–e897 (2017)
4. Burton, S., Gauerhof, L., Heinzemann, C.: Making the case for safety of machine learning in highly automated driving. In: Tonetta, S., Schoitsch, E., Bitsch, F. (eds.) SAFECOMP 2017. LNCS, vol. 10489, pp. 5–16. Springer, Cham (2017). https://doi.org/10.1007/978-3-319-66284-8_1
5. De Fauw, J., et al.: Clinically applicable deep learning for diagnosis and referral in retinal disease. Nat. Med. **24**(9), 1342 (2018)
6. Došilović, F.K., Brčić, M., Hlupić, N.: Explainable artificial intelligence: a survey. In: 41st International Convention on Information and Communication Technology, Electronics and Microelectronics (MIPRO), pp. 210–215. IEEE (2018)
7. EUROCAE WG-12, RTCA SC-205: Software Considerations in Airborne Systems and Equipment Certification. EUROCAE and RTCA (2012)
8. Goodfellow, I., Bengio, Y., Courville, A.: Deep Learning. MIT press, Cambridge (2016)
9. Gu, T., Dolan-Gavitt, B., Garg, S.: BadNets: Identifying Vulnerabilities in the Machine Learning Model Supply Chain. arXiv:1708.06733 (2017)
10. Habli, I., White, S., Sujan, M., Harrison, S., Ugarte, M.: What is the safety case for health IT? a study of assurance practices in England. Saf. Sci. **110**, 324–335 (2018)
11. Hannun, A.Y., et al.: Cardiologist-level arrhythmia detection and classification in ambulatory electrocardiograms using a deep neural network. Nat. Med. **25**(1), 65 (2019)
12. Hawkins, R., Habli, I., Kelly, T., McDermid, J.: Assurance cases and prescriptive software safety certification: a comparative study. Saf. Sci. **59**, 55–71 (2013)
13. Hawkins, R., Kelly, T., Knight, J., Graydon, P.: A new approach to creating clear safety arguments. In: Dale, C., Anderson, T. (eds) Advances in Systems Safety, pp. 3–23. Springer, London (2011). https://doi.org/10.1007/978-0-85729-133-2_1
14. Kelly, T.: Reviewing assurance arguments-a step-by-step approach. In: Workshop on Assurance Cases for Security-the Metrics Challenge, Dependable Systems and Networks (DSN) (2007)
15. Komorowski, M., Celi, L.A., Badawi, O., Gordon, A.C., Faisal, A.A.: The artificial intelligence clinician learns optimal treatment strategies for sepsis in intensive care. Nat. Med. **24**(11), 1716 (2018)
16. Maddox, T.M., Rumsfeld, J.S., Payne, P.R.: Questions for artificial intelligence in health care. JAMA **321**(1), 31–32 (2018)
17. NHS Digital: Digital Health Safety Conference (2019). https://digital.nhs.uk/news-and-events/events/2019-events/digital-health-safety-conference-2019. Accessed 30 May 2019
18. Pan, S.J., Yang, Q., et al.: A survey on transfer learning. IEEE Trans. Knowl. Data Eng. **22**(10), 1345–1359 (2010)
19. Picardi, C., Habli, I.: Perspectives on assurance case development for retinal disease diagnosis using deep learning. In: Riano, D., Wilk, S., ten Teije, A. (eds) Artificial Intelligence in Medicine. AIME 2019. LNCS, vol. 11526. Springer, Cham (2019). https://doi.org/10.1007/978-3-030-21642-9_46

20. Ros, G., Sellart, L., Materzynska, J., Vazquez, D., Lopez, A.M.: The SYNTHIA dataset: a large collection of synthetic images for semantic segmentation of urban scenes. In: Proceedings of the IEEE Conference on Computer Vision and Pattern Recognition, pp. 3234–3243 (2016)
21. scikit-Taxonomy: scikit - Choosing the right estimator (2019). https://scikit-learn. org/stable/tutorial/machine_learning_map/index.html. Accessed Feb 2019
22. Shneier, M., et al.: Repository of sensor data for autonomous driving research. In: Unmanned Ground Vehicle Technology, vol. 5083, pp. 390–396. International Society for Optics and Photonics (2003)
23. Shortliffe, E.H., Sepúlveda, M.J.: Clinical decision support in the era of artificial intelligence. JAMA **320**(21), 2199–2200 (2018)
24. Srivastava, N., Hinton, G., Krizhevsky, A., Sutskever, I., Salakhutdinov, R.: Dropout: a simple way to prevent neural networks from overfitting. J. Mach. Learn. Res. **15**(1), 1929–1958 (2014)
25. Topol, E.: The Topol Review: Preparing the healthcare workforce to deliver the digital future (2019). https://topol.hee.nhs.uk/. Accessed 27 Feb 2019
26. University of York: Goal Structuring Notation, November 2014. https://impact. ref.ac.uk/casestudies/CaseStudy.aspx?Id=43445. Accessed 03 Jan 2019
27. Wagstaff, K.: Machine Learning that Matters. arXiv preprint arXiv:1206.4656 (2012)
28. World Health Organisation (WHO): Health workforce (2019). https://www.who. int/gho/health_workforce/en. Accessed 27 Feb 2019

Safety Argumentation

BACRank: Ranking Building Automation and Control System Components by Business Continuity Impact

Herson Esquivel-Vargas[1]([✉]), Marco Caselli[2], Erik Tews[1], Doina Bucur[1], and Andreas Peter[1]

[1] University of Twente, Enschede, The Netherlands
{h.esquivelvargas,e.tews,d.bucur,a.peter}@utwente.nl
[2] Siemens AG, Munich, Germany
marco.caselli@siemens.com

Abstract. Organizations increasingly depend on Building Automation and Control Systems (BACSs) to support their daily tasks and to comply with laws and regulations. However, BACSs are prone to disruptions caused by failures or active attacks. Given the role BACSs play in critical locations such as airports and hospitals, a comprehensive impact assessment methodology is required that estimates the effect of unavailable components in the system. In this paper, we present the foundations of the first impact assessment methodology for BACSs focused on business continuity. At the core of our methodology, we introduce a novel graph centrality measure called BACRank. We quantify the contribution of BACS components to different business activities. Moreover, we take functional dependencies among components into account to estimate indirect consequences throughout the infrastructure. We show the practical applicability of our approach on a real BACS deployed at a 5-story building hosting 375 employees on an international university campus. The experimental evaluation confirms that the proposed methodology successfully prioritizes the most relevant components of the system with respect to the business continuity perspective.

1 Introduction

Operational Technology (OT), and specifically Building Automation and Control Systems (BACSs), are steadily increasing in number and complexity [18]. Many organizations depend on BACSs to comply with laws and regulations required to operate [3–5]. Thus, the dependability of BACSs is crucial for their daily operation. However, complex systems with extended uptimes are prone to occasional outages due to failures or active attacks.

Unavailable BACS components have direct consequences on the services they are part of, and indirect consequences that can spread throughout neighboring components that rely on them to execute their functions. Knowing the impact of unavailable BACS components help organizations to better prepare and react upon those undesired events. From the *preventive* perspective, they can compute

© Springer Nature Switzerland AG 2019
A. Romanovsky et al. (Eds.): SAFECOMP 2019, LNCS 11698, pp. 183–199, 2019.
https://doi.org/10.1007/978-3-030-26601-1_13

incident probabilities and obtain risk estimations (Risk = Impact × Probability). Risks are then used as an input to establish contingency plans and to decide on improvement strategies. On the other hand, the increasing interest in monitoring tools for BACSs might lead to an overwhelming number of alerts that must be managed by building administrators [11,12]. In this regard, from the *reactive* perspective, the impact measurement can be used to prioritize failure and security alerts, which helps to efficiently allocate resources to solve the problems.

Measuring the impact of unavailable IT components is a well understood problem [13]. It is not clear, however, how to implement impact assessments for OT systems like BACSs, that extend beyond the *cyber* domain to the *physical* world. From the security perspective, the situation degenerates considering that most of the reported attacks on OT systems target their availability [1]. Although in principle, BACSs could be assessed using business continuity methodologies, the peculiarities of BACSs must be taken into consideration to develop a comprehensive impact assessment in this domain.

1.1 Related Work

Impact assessments focus on diverse target goals ranging from environmental to economical impact, physical damage, and business continuity, just to mention a few examples [6,8,13,17,20]. ISO 27031 describes a consolidated methodology to perform impact assessments in the IT domain focused on business continuity [13]. The analyzed assets are typically devices such as PCs, switches, and servers. Those assets are linked to one or more pre-scored business activities in order to assign them the highest score among the related activities. The outcome is a ranking of IT assets prioritized with respect to the relevance of the business activities they participate in.

OT, on the other hand, lacks the maturity level of standardized methodologies for impact assessments. To fill this gap, a number of academic works have been proposed, mostly for Industrial Control Systems (ICSs) [6,8,20]. These works are based on the observation of cause-and-effect relations between data points representing sensors and actuators. The observations are taken from simulated environments where changes are induced to log the corresponding effects. Knowing the limits of the physical process (e.g., what is the threshold before the power plant explodes?), data points with the higher potential to reach those limits are prioritized.

The only work that is focused on BACSs prioritizes component categories rather than individual assets [23]. They automatically analyze work orders describing building's routine and maintenance operations. Based on the information recorded in the work orders, such as location, problem description, and priority, they rank equipment categories like "fans", "valves", "pumps", etc.

The approach presented in this paper aims to adapt previous works to the context of BACSs and to solve practical limitations that hinder their implementation in real BACSs. Our impact assessment is focused on *business continuity* as it is commonly done for IT systems. Nonetheless, our assets are not physical devices since we consider this approach too coarse grained. Neither are individual data points, as in the ICS prototypes, since such fine grained analysis might suffer from scalability problems in real-life systems. We chose *software modules* as a middle ground generic abstraction that provides a suitable granularity level. Instead of measuring the propagation effect via cause-and-effect experiments, unlikely to be allowed in real BACS deployments, we use *functional dependencies* among the software modules. Finally, although many software modules could be clustered by functional similarity, we acknowledge that the role they play for different business activities makes a crucial difference. Thus, we reference and prioritize software modules individually.

1.2   Contribution

We present the first impact assessment methodology for BACSs focused on business continuity. We adapt and integrate standard business continuity methodologies from the IT domain, and combine them with software analysis techniques. From the IT domain, we follow the standard procedures used to score business activities. After mapping software modules with business activities, we use the activities' score to derive the related modules' score. From the software engineering domain, we implement a module dependency analysis that aims to estimate the propagation effect of unavailable modules.

Our impact assessment methodology models BACS software modules as vertices in a graph data structure where the edges represent functional dependencies among modules. A quantitative measurement of a node's relevance in a graph is called a node's *centrality* and it is computed by means of graph centrality measures [25]. Our impact assessment methodology formally defines the requirements such centrality measure must satisfy in order to quantify the software modules' impact. Additionally, we implement an instance of such centrality measure and we call it *BACRank*. BACRank scores software modules in a dependency graph according to their relevance from the business continuity perspective. Our notion of "relevant" includes those software modules that are: (1) needed by core business processes; and (2) needed by other relevant modules.

Finally, we evaluate BACRank in a real-world BACS deployed at a 5-story office building hosting 375 employees on an international university campus. The underlying BACS graph is comprised of 160 software modules and 412 module dependencies. Such evaluation confirms that BACRank prioritizes relevant software modules according to the defined relevance notion.

2   Building Automation and Control Systems

Modern buildings provide more than a physical space to their occupants. Environmental conditions are controlled by heating, cooling, and ventilation systems. Indoor transportation of goods and people is done through escalators, elevators, and travelators. Other services like CCTV, alarms, and physical access control are also common. Control engineers implement those services and many more in *Building Automation and Control Systems* (BACSs). BACSs offer functionality that brings comfort and convenience to the users while unified control and energy efficiency engage building managers.

In BACSs, IT networking infrastructure is used to interconnect all the subsystems in a building [19]. We distinguish three levels in the typical BACS architecture as shown in Fig. 1. The *management* level provides monitoring and control functions to building administrators. The *automation* level is comprised of embedded systems called BACS controllers that implement the logic behind the building services. BACS controllers receive inputs from the environment through sensors, execute the appropriate logic, and send outputs back to the environment using actuators. Both sensors and actuators are the elements found in the *field* level. Dashed lines around field level components denote that software modules at the automation level are linking them. Building services are comprised of one or more—possibly interacting—software modules.

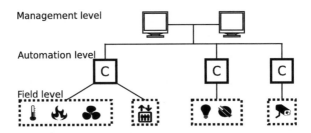

Fig. 1. Three-layer architecture of IT networks supporting BACSs.

Organizations typically have specific needs from their BACS. Deciding which building services are to be implemented depends on the organization's purpose. For example, the building services required in a hospital are quite different from the services required in an office building. Thus, let us start with a brief discussion on the role that BACSs play in organizations.

Organizations Requirements. All organizations have a goal to pursue. Nontrivial goals require a divide-and-conquer approach that splits the task at hand into smaller activities. The attainment of the organization's goal depends on the success of the individual activities. In what follows, we refer to those activities as *business processes*.

Business processes make use of diverse resources like people, supplies, and assets. Buildings are one of those resources, and fostering business processes became the main task of BACSs. BACSs, just as other technological projects like software systems, are the answer to specific business process needs. While some of those needs are nice-to-have features (perhaps comfort oriented), others constitute necessities that must be fulfilled [3–5]. In what follows we will refer to the former type of building services as *supporting services* and to the latter as *enabling services*.

Building Services Dependability. Building services, and particularly enabling services, must be dependable. Dependability involves, among others, concepts such as privacy of the data, message integrity, and in general the availability of the system, meaning that it behaves as it was designed and provides timely responses [15,21].

Previous research has identified *availability* as the most important feature in diverse OT systems such as smart-grids and Industrial Control Systems (ICS) [9,16,24]. This conclusion seems to match the trend of real-life attacks on OT systems, typically oriented towards Denial-of-Service [1]. ISO standard 27031 also recognizes the role that OT systems play in business continuity by adding an annex on "High availability embedded systems" [13]. Although an impact assessment could be tailored to any of the aforementioned dependability factors, we focus on the availability of building services, their underlying software modules, and the supported business processes.

3   System Model and Information Requirements

We consider mature organizations and critical buildings whose dependence on BACSs is crucial for their daily operations. Such organizations have undergone— or are willing to apply—business continuity methodologies like those proposed in ISO standards 22301 and 27031. Although an ISO certification is not required, critical buildings such as hospitals and airports are typically demanded to implement business continuity methodologies like those described in the standards [10,22].

On the technical side, our approach is independent of the BACS protocol in use and the underlying communication methods. We consider standard BACSs comprised of sensors and actuators connected to BACS controllers, which contain the logic behind the smart building, as in Fig. 1.

To implement a comprehensive BACS impact assessment focused on business continuity, technical and business aspects must be taken into consideration. First, it is required to make explicit the relation between BACS services and business activities. We propose to do so by considering their physical overlap in the building. Two views of the building layout are needed: one segregated by business processes and the other segregated by the area of influence of the building services. We put the two views of the building layout on top of each other to unveil the mapping. Moreover, we need to quantify the support of building services on the related business processes. The quantification can be expressed as a percentage where 100% means that the service in question is an *enabling service*, whereas lower values characterize *supporting services* (see Sect. 2).

The second aspect is to know which business activities are critical for the organization, so we can map such criticality status to the corresponding BACS services. Business activity priorities can be found in business continuity plans, where the activity scores are calculated by means of a procedure called Business Impact Analysis (BIA). The main purpose of the BIA is to score each business process based on questionnaires answered by process managers. The idea is to estimate the impact of a business process halted during different time ranges (e.g., 0–2 h, 2–8 h, etc.), considering diverse impacts like customer service, legal, financial, and reputation. The managers assign a severity level to each impact of the processes they are in charge of. Finally, the average level score is computed for all processes to determine their relevance with respect to the organization's goal. For further details on the BIA, we refer the reader to the ISO standards 22301 and 27031 [13,14]. In summary, the BIA lists all business processes, their relevance scores according to the business perspective, and a calendar that specifies their execution period.

Finally, the third aspect lies on the technical side. It is important to know *when* the building services are actually needed since they might not be relevant out of their duty periods (e.g., the heating service during summer). Furthermore, it is crucial to understand *how* the building services are implemented to find possible design flaws that could lead to availability issues (e.g., single points of failure). To obtain this information, we assume access to the BACS design documentation to identify (1) all building services, (2) their duty cycles, (3) the underlying software modules, and (4) the functional dependencies among modules. Since some dependencies might be stronger than others, a quantification is needed in this regard. We propose a percentage value as a simple mechanism to denote the dependence strength, where 100% means that the dependent module cannot operate without the other.

Table 1 summarizes the information requirements. While most of the information is typically already available in mature and critical organizations, we emphasize three components where an expert's judgment is required: (1) the building services' support on business processes; (2) the software modules' dependency strength; and (3) the building services calendar. It is worth noting that, if needed, an individual module's calendar can be derived from the calendar of the building service it belongs to.

Table 1. Information requirements summary. Expert-based information shown in *italics*.

Business Information	BACS Technical Information
Business continuity plan	Engineering design
↳ BIA	↳ Building services list
↳ Business process list	↳ *Calendar*
↳ Score	↳ Software modules
↳ Calendar	↳ Dependencies
	↳ *Strength*
Building layout	Building layout
↳ Segregated by business processes	↳ Segregated by building services
↳ *Building services support on the overlapping business processes* ↲	

The parameters described in this section provide the basic input that allows us to account for the impact, in terms of availability, of business processes supported by building services comprised of software modules. Those parameters are not only highly meaningful for the purpose of an impact assessment, but are typically already present in critical organizations. Thus, reducing the effort of implementing the methodology proposed in this paper. We do not discard, however, that other business or technical aspects could be included to complement or replace some elements in the proposed list, while the core principles of our methodology prevail.

4   Impact Assessment Methodology

We abstract the BACS as a directed graph data structure where software modules are represented by vertices and their functional dependencies are the edges. The edge direction denotes the way information flows and its weight represents the dependency strength. Formally, the BACS is defined as a graph $G(V, E)$ where V is a nonempty set of vertices (or nodes) and E is a set of edges. Each edge has exactly two vertices in V as endpoints since self-dependencies (i.e., loops) are implicit for all modules. An edge $e \in E$ is represented as $e_{u,v}$ where u and v denote the origin and the destination of the edge, respectively. Edge weights are represented as a function $\omega \colon E \to [0, 1]$ that assigns each edge $e \in E$ a weight $\omega(e)$. The set of edges with destination $m \in V$ is defined as $\Gamma^-(m)$ and the set of vertex origins in $\Gamma^-(m)$ is $N^-(m)$. Analogously, the set of edges with origin m is defined as $\Gamma^+(m)$ and the set of vertex destinations in $\Gamma^+(m)$ is $N^+(m)$.

We aim to measure the impact of BACS software modules based on their relevance to the availability of business processes and their functional dependencies with other modules. The identification of important vertices in a graph is done by means of graph centrality metrics. Therefore, our impact assessment methodology can be modeled as a graph centrality measure.

We propose a graph centrality measure comprised of two parts. First, a set up procedure that assigns vertices an initial score based on the BIA score of the related business processes and the module's support to those business processes. Second, a graph centrality measure that contemplates the propagation effect of unavailable modules. Module's rank positions are based on their final impact scores. The next sections detail both parts.

4.1   Initial Score

Notation. The set of business processes running in the building is defined as $P = \{p_1, ..., p_n\}$. The set of building services offered is defined as $S = \{s_1, ..., s_m\}$. The BIA score assigned to each business process is defined as a function $\beta \colon P \to [0, 1]$, where $\beta(p_i)$ for any $p_i \in P$ is proportional to p_i's relevance for the organization. Given an arbitrary $s_i \in S$ and $p_j \in P$, the estimated support s_i provides to p_j is defined as a function $\gamma \colon S \times P \to [0, 1]$, where higher values denote stronger support. Since building services are comprised of one or more software modules, we can formally state that $s_j \subseteq V$ for any $s_j \in S$. For an arbitrary module $m \in V$ that is part of service $s_j \in S$, the support m provides to an arbitrary $p_k \in P$ is given by $\gamma(s_j, p_k)$. Finally, we define a *time* function that takes two inputs: (1) the object whose calendar is going to be inspected (either a business process or a software module); and (2) the current time t. The output is binary and indicates whether the object given as first input is running/needed or not at time t, denoted by a 1 or a 0, respectively.

Initial Score. The initial score given to each software module in the graph, labels vertices with a numerical value that summarizes three important aspects: (1) the relevance of the related business processes represented by function β; (2) the module's support to each business process represented by function γ; and (3) the time in which both, the business process is running *and* the software module is needed (according to its building service calendar).

To determine the influence that module $m \in V$ has over each business process, we multiply $\beta(p_i) \cdot \gamma(s_j, p_i)$ for all $p_i \in P$, given that m is part of $s_j \in S$. Computing the initial score for module m at time t, denoted $\delta(m, t)$, consists of taking the maximum influence found among active business processes, given that module m is also active at time t. Formally,

$$\delta(m, t) = \begin{cases} \max_{1 \leq i \leq n}(\beta(p_i) \cdot \gamma(s_j, p_i)) & \text{if time}(p_i, t) = \text{time}(m, t) = 1, \\ 0 & \text{otherwise.} \end{cases}$$

4.2   Graph Centrality Measure

We propose to estimate the propagation effect of unavailable modules by means of a graph centrality measure. Before describing the requirements for such centrality measure we introduce some definitions.

Definition (Module *equivalence*). Two modules $m_1, m_2 \in V$ are *equivalent* *(at time t)* (denoted as $m_1 \equiv m_2$) if all of the following properties hold:

$$N^+(m_1) = N^+(m_2) \tag{1}$$

$$N^-(m_1) = N^-(m_2) \tag{2}$$

$$\forall e_{m_1, n} \in \Gamma^+(m_1), e_{m_2, n} \in \Gamma^+(m_2) : \omega(e_{m_1, n}) = \omega(e_{m_2, n}) \tag{3}$$

$$\forall e_{n, m_1} \in \Gamma^-(m_1), e_{n, m_2} \in \Gamma^-(m_2) : \omega(e_{n, m_1}) = \omega(e_{n, m_2}) \tag{4}$$

$$\delta(m_1, t) = \delta(m_2, t) \tag{5}$$

Definition (Module *equivalence with exception*). Two modules $m_1, m_2 \in V$ are called *equivalent with exception* if at least one of the above equivalence properties is violated. In this case, we explicitly mention the exception and denote this as $m_1 \equiv_e m_2$ (exception).

In what follows we define three basic requirements that a centrality measure $\Delta(m, t)$ for module m at time t, must satisfy to quantify the impact of BACS software modules.

1. *For any two active modules one of which, ceteris paribus, has higher initial score, must score higher.*

The aim of the first requirement is to ensure that the impact score difference of two modules with identical topological features in the graph is determined by their initial score. Formally described in Eq. 6, for all active modules m_1, m_2:

$$m_1 \equiv_e m_2 \ (\delta(m_1, t) > \delta(m_2, t)) \Rightarrow \Delta(m_1, t) > \Delta(m_2, t) \quad (6)$$

2. *For any two active modules one of which, ceteris paribus, sends information to an active module with higher impact score than its counterpart, must score higher.*

The goal of the second requirement is to acknowledge that feedback plays an important role in software module dependency graphs. Unlike web centrality measures, where the feedback contribution comes from a node's incoming edges [7], software modules in our setting get their contribution from the modules they send information to. The rationale being that the receiving modules depend on that input to execute their functions. Formally described in Eq. 7, for all active modules m_1, m_2:

$$m_1 \equiv_e m_2 \ (\exists n_1 \in N^+(m_1), n_2 \in N^+(m_2) : N^+(m_1) \backslash \{n_1\} = N^+(m_2) \backslash \{n_2\} \wedge$$
$$w(e_{m_1,n_1}) = w(e_{m_2,n_2}) \wedge \Delta(n_1, t) > \Delta(n_2, t)) \Rightarrow \Delta(m_1, t) > \Delta(m_2, t) \quad (7)$$

3. *For any two active modules one of which, ceteris paribus, sends information to an active module with stronger dependency than its counterpart, must score higher.*

The purpose of the third requirement is to emphasize that the link strength regulates the fraction of the impact score to be transferred from the destination vertex to the source vertex. Formally described in Eq. 8, for all active modules m_1, m_2:

$$m_1 \equiv_e m_2 \ (\exists! n' \in N^+(m_1) = N^+(m_2) : w(e_{m_1,n'}) > w(e_{m_2,n'})) \Rightarrow$$
$$\Delta(m_1, t) > \Delta(m_2, t) \quad (8)$$

4.3   BACRank

Taking into account the requirements stated before, we define a new graph centrality measure called BACRank. The BACRank score of vertex m at time t, is computed as its initial score $\delta(m, t)$ plus a contribution from the vertices m points to. From those vertices, m will get a percentage of their BACRank score determined by the strength of the link, represented by $w(e_{m,n})$. This mechanism boosts the scores of vertices that are highly important from the technical and business process availability standpoint. The algorithm is defined as

$$\mathrm{BACRank}(m, t; i) = \begin{cases} \delta(m, t), \text{ at iteration } i = 0, \\ \delta(m, t) + \sum_{n \in N^+(m)} \mathrm{BACRank}(n, t; i - 1) \cdot w(e_{m,n}), \text{ for } i > 0. \end{cases}$$

To keep BACRank scores bounded, all scores are normalized in the range $[0, 1]$ after every iteration. The algorithm is said to converge if for all vertices the score difference in two consecutive iterations is less than a small value ε. An empirical convergence proof is provided in Sect. 5 as shown in Fig. 4. The final score, simply denoted as $\text{BACRank}(m, t)$ by leaving out the iteration count i, is then iteratively computed until iteration i such that the difference between $\text{BACRank}(m, t; i)$ and $\text{BACRank}(m, t; i - 1)$ is smaller than ε.

Figure 2 shows a simple BACRank execution example. At iteration 0, in Fig. 2a, the BACRank score of software modules x and y is their corresponding initial score δ, in this example setting equals 0.35 and 0.50, respectively. At iteration 1, in Fig. 2b, module x has increased its BACRank score by 0.10, which is the result of taking 20% (edge weight) of module y's score at iteration 0. Module y remains with the same score since it does not have any outgoing edges. Convergence is already reached at iteration 2 (Fig. 2c) because the BACRank values did not change with respect to the previous iteration.

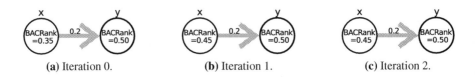

(a) Iteration 0.   (b) Iteration 1.   (c) Iteration 2.

Fig. 2. Simple execution example of the BACRank algorithm.

In what follows, we formally prove the requirements from Sect. 4.2. For the sake of brevity, in the proofs we refer to BACRank simply as BR.

Proof of requirement 1. Let m_1, m_2 be two active modules such that:

$$m_1 \equiv_e m_2 \ (\delta(m_1, t) > \delta(m_2, t)) \tag{9}$$

Then the following holds for any iteration $i > 0$:

$$\text{BR}(m_1, t; i) > \delta(m_2, t) + \sum_{n \in N^+(m_1)} \text{BR}(n, t; i) \cdot \omega(e_{m_1, n}) \qquad \text{(by (9))}$$

$$= \delta(m_2, t) + \sum_{n \in N^+(m_2)} \text{BR}(n, t; i) \cdot \omega(e_{m_1, n}) \qquad \text{(by equiv. prop. (1))}$$

$$= \delta(m_2, t) + \sum_{n \in N^+(m_2)} \text{BR}(n, t; i) \cdot \omega(e_{m_2, n}) = \text{BR}(m_2, t; i) \qquad \text{(by equiv. prop. (3))}$$

Proof of requirement 2. Let m_1, m_2 be two active modules such that:

$$m_1 \equiv_e m_2 \ (\exists n_1 \in N^+(m_1), n_2 \in N^+(m_2) : N^+(m_1) \setminus \{n_1\} = N^+(m_2) \setminus \{n_2\} \wedge$$
$$\omega(e_{m_1, n_1}) = \omega(e_{m_2, n_2}) \wedge \text{BR}(n_1, t; i) > \text{BR}(n_2, t; i)) \tag{10}$$

Then the following holds for any iteration $i > 0$:

$$\mathrm{BR}(m_1, t; i) > \delta(m_1, t) + \sum_{n \in N^+(m_1) \backslash \{n_1\}} \mathrm{BR}(n, t; i) \cdot \omega(e_{m_1, n}) + \mathrm{BR}(n_2, t; i) \cdot \omega(e_{m_2, n_2}) \qquad \text{(by (10))}$$

$$= \delta(m_1, t) + \sum_{n \in N^+(m_2)} \mathrm{BR}(n, t; i) \cdot \omega(e_{m_2, n}) \qquad \text{(by (10) and equiv. prop. (3))}$$

$$= \delta(m_2, t) + \sum_{n \in N^+(m_2)} \mathrm{BR}(n, t; i) \cdot \omega(e_{m_2, n}) = \mathrm{BR}(m_2, t; i) \qquad \text{(by equiv. prop. (5))}$$

Proof of requirement 3. Let m_1, m_2 be two active modules such that:

$$m_1 \equiv_e m_2 \; (\exists! n' \in N^+(m_1) = N^+(m_2) : \omega(e_{m_1, n'}) > \omega(e_{m_2, n'})) \qquad (11)$$

Then the following holds for any iteration $i > 0$:

$$\mathrm{BR}(m_1, t; i) > \delta(m_1, t) + \sum_{n \in N^+(m_1) \backslash \{n'\}} \mathrm{BR}(n, t; i) \cdot \omega(e_{m_1, n}) + \mathrm{BR}(n', t; i) \cdot \omega(e_{m_2, n'}) \qquad \text{(by (11))}$$

$$= \delta(m_1, t) + \sum_{n \in N^+(m_2)} \mathrm{BR}(n, t; i) \cdot \omega(e_{m_2, n}) \qquad \text{(by equiv. prop. (1))}$$

$$= \delta(m_2, t) + \sum_{n \in N^+(m_2)} \mathrm{BR}(n, t; i) \cdot \omega(e_{m_2, n}) = \mathrm{BR}(m_2, t; i) \qquad \text{(by equiv. prop. (5))}$$

5   Experimental Evaluation

Environment Description. We executed BACRank on the BACS of a 5-story office building on an international university campus, hosting about 375 employees in 252 rooms. The local building manager provided assistance with the required technical information. We identified 12 business processes that take place in this building, some of them running only at specific periods of the year. The BIA revealed the corresponding scores as presented in Table 2.

The core BACS is implemented using the BACnet protocol [2]. The BACnet system controls the heating, ventilation, cooling, and lighting services. Other building services, such as physical access control, are implemented with different protocols and tools we did not have access to. We consider here only the building services implemented in BACnet.

The BACnet system is comprised of 160 software modules running in 5 multi-purpose controllers (BACnet profile B-BC) and 28 application-specific controllers (BACnet profile B-ASC). Figure 3 shows the software modules dependency graph where 22 vertices are isolated and the remaining 138 are connected in the main subgraph. Vertex colors indicate the device they run in. Red modules are part of the heating controller, whereas blue modules are part of the cooling controller. The lighting system is controlled by the yellow modules. Green modules run in a controller in charge of multiple services (ventilation, heating, and cooling) throughout the building. Purple modules also implement multiple services but in one specific location of the building. Finally, each gray module represents one application-specific controller running exactly one software module (thermostats).

Results. We used weekly time resolution in our experiments based on the activity of the business processes and software modules analyzed. This implies that a new ranking has to be computed every week of the year to take into account business processes that start or stop execution, and software modules that might or not be needed (e.g., due to changes in climate conditions). For each week, BACRank is executed a number of iterations until the scores' convergence is reached. Figure 4 shows the quick convergence of BACRank on the real BACS graph. After the tenth iteration, on average, the difference between two consecutive scores (ϵ) is smaller than 0.0006. After 60 iterations $\epsilon = 0$. To run our evaluation we defined an $\epsilon < 10^{-6}$, which implies that 20 iterations are needed.

Table 2. Business Processes (BPs) and their corresponding BIA scores.

№	Business Process	Score	№	Business Process	Score
1	Research	.63	7	Introduction week	.60
2	Application/admission	.27	8	Administrative support	.47
3	Accounting	.60	9	Education advisory	.53
4	Technical support	.43	10	Marketing & communication	.43
5	Courses and others (periodic)	.73	11	Catering	1.0
6	Trainings and others (non-periodic)	.70	12	Student associations	.50

Fig. 3. Real software modules dependency graph. (Color figure online)

Figure 5a illustrates the 52 rankings obtained throughout the year, where each colored line represents a software module (following the same color scheme used in Fig. 3). The vertical axis represents the ranking position where top ranked modules start at position 1. Modules with identical scores in Fig. 5a are randomly assigned a slot next to their analogous. Figure 5b on the other hand, shows the actual BACRank score for each module. The impression of having fewer lines in Fig. 5b than in Fig. 5a is due to multiple overlapping lines (i.e., modules with identical score).

BACRank successfully identifies software modules that are part of relevant business processes, and are required by other relevant modules in the infrastructure. Throughout the experiments, module "Multi-purpose Substation" (vertex A in Fig. 3) was considered the most important because, among others, it supports the most important business process according to the BIA (BP_{11}) *and* it provides information required by 19 other important modules in 7 different devices. Vertex A is depicted as an horizontal green line at the top of Fig. 5a and b.

At the bottom of the ranking there is a set of approximately 30 modules consistently low ranked. Some of them, starting from the last one—"AirExtraction"—and ascending with "Electricitymeter Experiments", "CoolSection [sect. numbers 1–4]_Log", are shown in Fig. 3 as Z, Y, X, W, V, and U, respectively. There are two aspects that justify their poor scoring performance. First, a vertex with out-degree of 0 is likely to be low ranked because an important source of BACRank score comes from other vertices that depend on the module in question. Second, if no other modules depend on it, its BACRank score comes exclusively from the *initial score* which is, in turn, based on the related business processes and the module's support to them. If there are no related business processes, as in the case of safety oriented modules; or the module's participation in the business processes is marginal, then the module in question will get a low BACRank score.

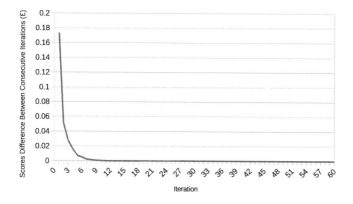

Fig. 4. BACRank scores convergence.

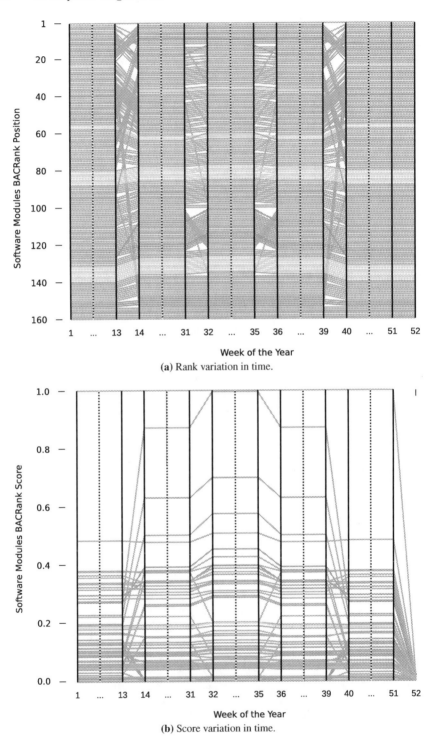

(a) Rank variation in time.

(b) Score variation in time.

Fig. 5. Software modules impact variation in time. Plots only legible in color. (Color figure online)

Time-*independent* software modules are typically ranked in similar positions throughout the year. Figure 5a shows that lighting and thermostat modules (yellow and gray lines) are good examples of time-independent modules. Their minor shifts up and down respond mostly to score variations in other modules rather than their own scores.

Time-*dependent* modules, on the other hand, are visible in Fig. 5a between weeks 14 and 39 of the year. This represents roughly the period between April and September, that is warmer than the range between October and March, taking into account the geographical location of the building. Figure 5a shows that most cooling modules increase their rank in this period whereas some heating modules suffer a substantial decrease (blue vs. red lines). Heating modules that remain similar or even increase their rank in the April–September period are benefited from neighboring cooling modules that got their rank increased. For example, heating modules "Radiatorgroup South" and "Radiatorgroup North" in positions 15 and 16 in Weeks 1–13, climbed to positions 9 and 10 in Weeks 14–39. These two modules are labeled as B and C in Fig. 3, which shows their proximity to cooling modules. Exactly 4 cooling modules—D, E, F, G—depend on B and C.

Weeks 32–35 of the year (August) are part of the organization's summer break in which some of the business processes stop execution. Student-related processes (BP_5 and BP_{12}) do not run in this period, and therefore, the related software modules lower their ranking positions. Module "AHU WestLectRoom", for example, decreases its rank from position 13 in week 31 to position 34 in week 32. The main reason for its descend is its support to the halted BP_5. This module is labeled with the letter H in Fig. 3.

In weeks 40–51 all software modules rank in the same order they ranked at the start of the year, due to identical conditions in terms of business processes running and software modules needed. Week 40 marks the start of the winter period in which cooling modules decrease their relevance in favor of heating modules as shown in Fig. 5a and b.

Finally, in week 52 the organization is closed and no business processes are running in this building. As explained before, Fig. 5a will simply assign an arbitrary order to equally ranked modules, whereas Fig. 5b shows that all the modules get a score of 0 which means that from the business continuity viewpoint all modules are "equally unimportant".

6   Conclusion

We have presented the first BACS impact assessment methodology that is focused on business continuity. Our approach takes into account business and technical aspects from diverse information sources. The proposed methodology scores BACS software modules considering their support to the related business processes and their relevance to other neighboring modules.

Since software modules constitute a dependency graph, our methodology to score modules is modeled as a graph centrality measure. We formally defined the general requirements that such centrality measure must satisfy to give scores that reflect the modules' relevance in the BACS infrastructure. Finally, we developed one instance of such centrality measure, which we called *BACRank*. We formally proved that BACRank satisfies the defined general requirements and evaluated it in a real BACS. The evaluation showed that BACRank successfully prioritizes the most relevant software modules with respect to the business continuity perspective.

Our comprehensive scoring methodology provides valuable insights about the BACS infrastructure typically overlooked by building administrators. Module dependencies, for example, might organically grow as the BACS evolves to the point in which administrators are no longer fully aware of the role they play and their overall impact in case of failures or active attacks.

Acknowledgments. This work is partially funded by the Costa Rica Institute of Technology. The authors would like to thank Henk Hobbelink and Lisseth Galán-Calderón for their help throughout this project.

References

1. Al-Mhiqani, M., et al.: Cyber-security incidents: a review cases in cyber-physical systems. IJACSA **9**(1), 499–508 (2018). https://doi.org/10.14569/IJACSA.2018.090169
2. ANSI/ASHRAE STANDARD 135–2016: A data communication protocol for building automation and control networks (2016)
3. ANSI/ASHRAE STANDARD 188–2018: Legionellosis: Risk management for building water systems (2018)
4. ANSI/ASHRAE STANDARD 62.1-2016: Ventilation for acceptable indoor air quality (2016)
5. ANSI/ASHRAE STANDARD 62.2-2016: Ventilation and acceptable indoor air quality in residential buildings (2016)
6. Béla, G., István, K., Piroska, H.: A system dynamics approach for assessing the impact of cyber attacks on critical infrastructures. IJCIP **10**, 3–17 (2015). https://doi.org/10.1016/j.ijcip.2015.04.001
7. Brin, S., Page, L.: The anatomy of a large-scale hypertextual web search engine. Comput. Netw. ISDN Syst. **30**(1–7), 107–117 (1998). https://doi.org/10.1016/S0169-7552(98)00110-X
8. Cárdenas, A., Amin, S., Lin, Z., Huang, Y., Huang, C., Sastry, S.: Attacks against process control systems: risk assessment, detection, and response. In: ASIACCS 2011. ACM (2011). https://doi.org/10.1145/1966913.1966959
9. Cheminod, M., Durante, L., Valenzano, A.: Review of security issues in industrial networks. IEEE Trans. Ind. Inform. **9**(1), 277–293 (2013). https://doi.org/10.1109/TII.2012.2198666
10. Corzine, S.: Operational and Business Continuity Planning for Prolonged Airport Disruptions, vol. 93. Transportation Research Board (2013). https://doi.org/10.17226/22531
11. Esquivel-Vargas, H., Caselli, M., Peter, A.: Automatic deployment of specification-based intrusion detection in the BACnet protocol. In: CPS-SPC 2017, pp. 25–36. ACM (2017). https://doi.org/10.1145/3140241.3140244

12. Fauri, D., Kapsalakis, M., dos Santos, D.R., Costante, E., den Hartog, J., Etalle, S.: Leveraging semantics for actionable intrusion detection in building automation systems. In: Luiijf, E., Žutautaitė, I., Hämmerli, B.M. (eds.) CRITIS 2018. LNCS, vol. 11260, pp. 113–125. Springer, Cham (2019). https://doi.org/10.1007/978-3-030-05849-4_9

13. ISO, BS: 27031: 2011. Information technology -Security techniques- Guidelines for information and communication technology readiness for business continuity. BSI (2011)

14. ISO, BS: 22301: 2012. Societal security. Business continuity management systems. Requirements. BSI (2012)

15. Krammer, L., Kastner, W., Sauter, T.: A generic dependability layer for building automation networks. In: WFCS 2016, pp. 1–4. IEEE (2016). https://doi.org/10.1109/WFCS.2016.7496536

16. Krotofil, M., Cárdenas, A.A.: Resilience of process control systems to cyber-physical attacks. In: Riis Nielson, H., Gollmann, D. (eds.) NordSec 2013. LNCS, vol. 8208, pp. 166–182. Springer, Heidelberg (2013). https://doi.org/10.1007/978-3-642-41488-6_12

17. Li, X., Zhou, C., Tian, Y., Xiong, N., Qin, Y.: Asset-based dynamic impact assessment of cyberattacks for risk analysis in industrial control systems. IEEE Trans. Ind. Inform. **14**(2), 608–618 (2018). https://doi.org/10.1109/TII.2017.2740571

18. Market Research Future: Building automation system market research report - global forecast to 2022 (2019)

19. Merz, H., Hansemann, T., Hübner, C.: Building Automation. Springer, Heidelberg (2009). https://doi.org/10.1007/978-3-540-88829-1

20. Orojloo, H., Azgomi, M.A.: A method for evaluating the consequence propagation of security attacks in cyber-physical systems. Future Gener. Comput. Syst. **67**, 57–71 (2017). https://doi.org/10.1016/j.future.2016.07.016

21. Shirey, R.: Internet Security Glossary, Version 2. RFC 4949, IETF (2007). https://tools.ietf.org/html/rfc4949

22. World Health Organization and Pan American Health Organization: Hospital safety index: Guide for evaluators (2nd edition) (2015)

23. Yang, C., Shen, W., Chen, Q., Gunay, B.: A practical solution for HVAC prognostics: failure mode and effects analysis in building maintenance. J. Build. Eng. **15**, 26–32 (2018). https://doi.org/10.1016/j.jobe.2017.10.013

24. Zeng, W., Zhang, Y., Chow, M.: Resilient distributed energy management subject to unexpected misbehaving generation units. IEEE Trans. Ind. Inform. **13**(1), 208–216 (2017). https://doi.org/10.1109/TII.2015.2496228

25. Zimmermann, T., Nagappan, N.: Predicting defects using network analysis on dependency graphs. In: ICSE 2008, pp. 531–540. ACM (2008). https://doi.org/10.1145/1368088.1368161

Model-Based Run-Time Synthesis of Architectural Configurations for Adaptive MILS Systems

Alessandro Cimatti[1], Rance DeLong[2], Ivan Stojic[1(✉)], and Stefano Tonetta[1]

[1] FBK-irst, Trento, Italy
{cimatti,stojic,tonettas}@fbk.eu
[2] The Open Group, Reading, Berkshire, UK
r.delong@opengroup.org

Abstract. In order to be resilient, a system must be adaptable. Trustworthy adaptation requires that a system can be dynamically reconfigured at run-time without compromising the robustness and integrity of the system. Adaptive MILS extends MILS, a successful paradigm for rigorously developed and assured composable static systems, with reconfiguration mechanisms and a framework within which those mechanisms may be safely and securely employed for adaptation.

In this paper, we address the problem of synthesizing at run-time reconfigurations that are trustworthy taking into account the entwining of information flows and reconfigurations. The approach is based on a new extension of the Architecture Analysis & Design Language (AADL), already used for specifying MILS policy architectures, which is now enhanced to specify the configuration state space in terms of parameters, the possible reconfigurations, monitoring properties and the related alarms. Supporting tools have been developed for the run-time synthesis of new architectural configurations that preserve safety and security properties formalized in terms of invariants and information flow.

Keywords: Safety and security · MILS · Reconfiguration ·
Adaptive systems · Model-based systems engineering ·
Formal specification

1 Introduction

MILS comprises an approach to design, a deployment platform, a set of tools for the specification, verification, configuration, and assurance of systems requiring high dependability. It originated in a seminal work, and subsequent refinements, by Rushby [3,22,23], and advanced through subsequent and ongoing research efforts world wide. The approach was named MILS and gained wider recognition due to the *MILS Initiative*, an activity within the Real Time and Embedded Systems Forum of The Open Group that cultivated a nascent ecosystem of supporting products and services. The name MILS was originally an acronym for Multiple Independent Levels of Security, which somewhat inaccurately and incompletely portrayed its essence and potential. Today "MILS" is used simply as a proper name for the concepts and technologies that manifest the general approach. An overarching objective throughout the evolution of MILS has

© Springer Nature Switzerland AG 2019
A. Romanovsky et al. (Eds.): SAFECOMP 2019, LNCS 11698, pp. 200–215, 2019.
https://doi.org/10.1007/978-3-030-26601-1_14

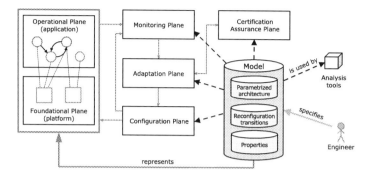

Fig. 1. Role of the system model in the CITADEL framework

been the ability to provide demonstrable assurance of safety, security, or other essential properties, necessitating design-time rigor, analysability, and runtime robustness. Ongoing research is enabling greater MILS capabilities for broader applicability while keeping to the overarching objective.

In the CITADEL Project (http://citadel-project.org/), MILS is being extended to dynamically reconfigurable systems within a framework that provides analysable and assurable adaptation. The CITADEL approach includes languages to support the design and implementation of adaptive MILS systems, via creation of a system model that describes the operational system architecture, the binding with the platform resources, and the system properties that should be guaranteed by such architecture. In addition to being used in the design and verification phases, the system model is also used in the run-time adaptation of the adaptive MILS system, where it supports the operation of the *CITADEL Framework*, which implements the higher-level adaptation control subsystem of an adaptive MILS system and consists of six *planes* (see Fig. 1). The Foundational Plane provides and controls access to the platform resources, including processors, memories, network devices, etc. It is a composition of MILS *foundational components* based on a separation kernel. The Operational Plane consists of the components of the running application as represented in the system model, deployed on the resources provided by the Foundational Plane. The Monitoring Plane monitors the components in the Operational Plane and the resources in the Foundational Plane and generates alarms when it detects faulty or suspicious behaviour. The Adaptation Plane performs reasoning about adaptive reconfigurations of the Foundational and Operational Planes. The Configuration Plane takes as input the model of the current and next configurations, based upon which it reconfigures the MILS platform to achieve the new configuration. The Certification Assurance Plane constructs and maintains the system assurance case and a database of supporting evidence.

In CITADEL, we have defined an extension [11] of SLIM (System-Level Integrated Modeling language) [26], which is supported by the COMPASS tool [6] and in turn extends AADL (Architecture Analysis & Design Language) [13], a language standardized by SAE [24]. The CITADEL extension is twofold.

First, the architecture is parametrized by a set of indexes and indexed sets of parameters to represent a possibly infinite set of architectural configurations. Each parameter assignment corresponds to a configuration, i.e. a static "normal" architecture. Second, formulas over the parameters describe the possible initial configurations and reconfigurations, including addition and removal of components and connections. Since the number of components is parametrized, formulas are in first-order logic with quantifiers over the component indexes. Due to this complexity, the formal verification of these Dynamic Parametrized Architectures (DPAs) is quite challenging [10].

The main contribution of this paper is to describe a method to decide at runtime the next configuration preserving some invariant properties. The DPA is first instantiated in the current configuration and the quantifiers in the formulas are removed by instantiating them on a finite number of terms. These terms represent the components in the next configuration which is bounded by the current one since the reconfiguration can add (or remove) a bounded number of components at a time. The resulting quantifier-free encoding is passed to an SMT (Satisfiability Modulo Theory) solver to search for the new configuration. The method has been implemented and evaluated on a number of DPAs.

Paper structure: first in Sect. 2 we overview the related work, then Sect. 3 introduces the modeling and specification language on a running example, Sect. 4 describes the new synthesis method, Sect. 5 reports the experimental evaluation, and Sect. 6 draws the conclusions and future directions.

2   Related Work

There is an abundant literature on dynamic architectures (see surveys [7,18]). While standard architecture languages may consider changing the composition of a static number of components [1,5], dynamic architectures are characterized by the ability to create/remove components and connections. There are also other approaches to dynamic changes in the coordination or topology of components such as pi-calculus [9,17,20] and graph grammars [15,19,21,28,29]. Parametrized systems are finally related to product lines where parameters are one of the methods to model variability [27].

Differently from the above approaches, we follow a more symbolic approach to the specification of components, their compositions and evolution, on the lines of works such as [4,8,16,25]. In these approaches, first-order or second-order formulas are used to specify the possible configurations and their evolution, making them suitable for formal analysis. Such approaches permit a declarative representation of the architecture evolution, which compared to operational specifications is more suitable to describe how the architecture may evolve nondeterministically, and to have run-time reasoning to decide the actual reconfigurations. Moreover, the formal logic-based framework is suitable to rigorously define the analysis problems and approach them formally, such as by model checking [10], and to synthesize the next configuration while preserving some properties, which to the best of our knowledge was not considered before.

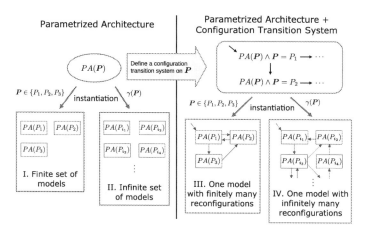

Fig. 2. High-level picture of the language and its semantics

The analysis of how information can flow from one component to another is addressed in many contexts such as program analysis, process modeling, access control, and flow latency analysis. The novel challenge addressed in this paper arises from the complexity of the adaptive system architectures, for which design and verification is an open problem. We propose a very rich system specification and we provide verification techniques for simple information-flow properties formalized as reachability problems. We consider a transitive notion of information flow that can be mapped to reachability properties. More complex information-flow properties extensively studied in the literature on security are related to the notion of *non-interference*. In the seminal work of Goguen and Meseguer [14], the simple information flow property is extended to make sure that components at different levels of security do not interfere. The non-interference on dynamic parametrized architectures has not been dealt with previously.

3   The CITADEL Language for Dynamic Parametrized Architectures

In AADL/SLIM, the system is specified by specifying component interfaces, their implementations and connections. The interfaces are specified by defining *component types* with input and output ports, and the implementations may be defined compositely by defining subcomponents and their connections. Even if the behavior of the system is dynamic, the system architecture is static.

The proposed language extends AADL/SLIM with parameters to configure the architecture and with transitions to change such configurations. Figure 2 gives a high-level picture of the extensions and the semantics. A *parametrized architecture* (PA) represents a (possibly infinite) set of "normal" architectures. The parameters P control the number of components, ports and connections, and their activation. Therefore, a configuration of the architecture can be defined by

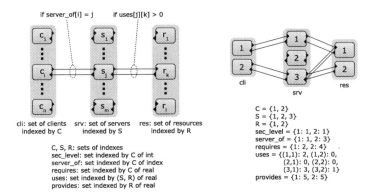

Fig. 3. The example model; left: parametrized architecture, right: architecture instance

an assignment of values to the parameters. Given an assignment to P, we obtain the corresponding static architecture. Given a constraint on the parameters, we instead consider a finite (case I. in Fig. 2) or infinite (case II.) set of architectures. In these cases, the parameters are considered frozen, i.e., they do not change with the dynamic evolution of the system.

In order to include the possibility of changing configuration, the language is further extended with configuration transitions, allowing the definition of a *configuration transition system* (CTS) over parameters P. The defined transition system represents the possible evolutions of the dynamic architecture. The dynamic evolution of the system in this case interleaves with architectural reconfigurations. Again, we can constrain the parameters P to consider a finite (case III.) or infinite (case IV.) set of architectures. In the finite case, the model can be converted into a model with reconfiguration of a static number of components.

3.1   A Dynamic Client-Server Model Example

In this section, we describe the running example of a dynamic architecture in the extended version of the AADL/SLIM language. The system represents a network of software components: clients, servers, and back-end systems which provide computational resources. The number of components in each of the categories is arbitrary, and clients and servers can be dynamically added and removed.

Clients require some amount of computational resources that are provided by the back-end systems. A client does not access the back-end systems directly, but instead connects to one of the servers, which in turn accesses any number of the back-end systems and uses their resources in order to satisfy the client requirement. We constrain the resource use in the system by the following two constraints. First, the amount of resources used by a server must be equal to the total amount required by the clients connected to it (i.e., servers do not unnecessarily use resources). Second, the total amount of resources on a back-end system used by the servers connected to it is less than the amount of resources provided by the back-end system (i.e., back-end systems are not overloaded).

Clients can be associated with a security level. The required security property is that there is no flow of information from clients with a higher security level to clients with a lower one. Such flow may happen if the two clients access the same server (in this scenario information may flow from the client with a higher security level to the server, and then to a client with a lower security level), or if the servers accessed by the two clients use the same back-end system (an example of this scenario is shown in Fig. 5). The servers and back-end systems are not assigned a security level and they are allowed to receive information from all components.

Figure 3 (left) shows a diagram of the PA which models the space of possible configurations of the described system. The parameters are listed below the diagram, and include three sets of indexes C, S, and R, which respectively serve as index sets of the sets of clients, servers and back-end systems (for each c in C, there is a client cli[c] in the system, and similarly for servers and back-end systems). The rest of the parameters

```
subject Client
  features
    pin: in event port; pout: out event port;
end Client;
subject implementation Client.Imp
  parameters sec_level: int;
  assumptions sec_level > 0;
  properties SecurityLevel => "sec_level";
end Client.Imp;
[...]
system implementation System.Imp
  parameters
    C: set of index; S: set of index; R: set of index;
    server_of: set indexed by C of index;
    sec_level: set indexed by C of int;
    requires: set indexed by C of real;
    uses: set indexed by (S,R) of real;
    provides: set indexed by R of real;
  assumptions
    [...]
    forall(r in R,
           sum(s in S, uses[s][r]) <= provides[r]);
  subcomponents
    cli: set indexed by C of subject Client.Imp
        where forall(c in C,
                     cli[c].sec_level = sec_level[c]);
    srv: set indexed by S of subject Server.Imp;
    res: set indexed by R of system Resource.Imp;
  connections
    port cli[c].pout -> srv[s].cli_pin if server_of[c] = s
        for c in C, s in S;
    [...]
end System.Imp;
CTS NetworkCTS
  architecture System.Imp;
  initial C = {1, 2} and S = {1, 2, 3} and [...];
  transitions
    add_server[s]:
      step(next(S) = add(S, {s})
           and forall(r in R, next(uses[s][r]) = 0.0))
      for s not in S;
    remove_server[u]:
      step(next(S) = remove(S, {u}) and
           forall(c in C, next(server_of[c]) = case
                                   server_of[c] = u: *;
                                   otherwise: server_of[c];
                          end) and
           forall(s in S, forall(r in R,
             next(uses[s][r]) = case
               exists(c in C, server_of[c] = u and
                              next(server_of[c]) = s): *;
               otherwise: uses[s][r];
             end)))
      for u in S; [...]
end NetworkCTS;
```

Fig. 4. Example of a dynamic architecture in the CITADEL modeling language

are in sets of parameters indexed with the above index sets. For each client with index c, there are three associated parameters: security level sec_level[c], index server_of[c] of the server to which the client is connected, and the amount requires[c] of resources required by the client. uses[s][r] is a parameter which specifies how much resources from the back-end system res[r] are used by the server srv[s], and provides[r] is the amount of resources provided by the back-end system res[r]. The clients connect to the specified servers, while the servers connect to all back-end systems from which they use resources. Figure 3 (right) shows an assignment to the parameters and the corresponding instance.

Figure 4 shows a partial listing of the above model in the extended CITADEL language. Client components are defined by specifying their interface ports, parameters, assumptions that specify the allowed values of the parameters, and properties (in this case the `SecurityLevel` property). The required security property is implicitly defined by the specified security levels. Servers and back-end systems are defined similarly (not shown in the listing).

The PA is specified in the block **system implementation** `System.Imp`. Its parameters are listed in the block **parameters**. The block **assumptions** contains constraints on the values of the parameters, such as that each index `server_of[c]` must be present in the set `S` (not shown in the listing) and constraints which encode the resource use property (only the part which specifies that back-end systems should not be overloaded is shown). Next, the block **subcomponents** defines the components present in the system, and the block **connections** defines the connections of the components. The connections are defined by iterating over the sets of indices using the keyword **for** and by conditionally including the connections using the keyword **if**. For example, the shown connection specification defines, for every pair of indexes $c \in C$ and $s \in S$, that there is a connection from `cli[c]` to `srv[s]` if and only if `server_of[c]` $= s$ (note that the syntax `<element> if <condition>` is not intended to have the semantics of a logical implication; it is used to include the `<element>` in the model if and only if the `<condition>` evaluates to true).

The CTS is specified in the block **CTS** `NetworkCTS`. At the top the related PA `System.Imp` is referenced, and the initial architecture is defined by specifying an assignment of values to the parameters. Reconfiguration transition specifications are defined in the block **transitions**. A transition specification contains (1) an optional label which is indexed by free variables used in the transition (the free variables must be of a non-set type), (2) a constraint on the **next** values of parameters, (3) an optional guard formula which is specified using keyword **when** and which must evaluate to true for the transition to be enabled, and (4) constraints on the free variables. The transition `add_server[s]` specifies an addition of a server by adding the index `s` to the set `S`. The transition `remove_server[u]` specifies a removal of the server, reconnection to other servers of all clients that were connected to the removed server, and reallocation of resources to servers to which those clients are connected in the next configuration. The `*` is a non-deterministic term: the semantics are that the next value of `server_of[c]` is non-deterministically set to some index value.

4 Run-Time Synthesis of Architectural Configurations

In this section, we give the formal definition of the problem and the solution based on SMT [2]. We give a simplified logic-based definition of the DPA to keep the paper self-contained and presentation easier to follow. Thus, we do not consider aspects such as the hierarchy of components, multiple types of components and index sets, connection ports, component behaviors. The actual language and tool support these features. The details can be found in the project deliverables [11,12]. Note that this subset is much richer and more expressive than the one used to enable model checking in [10].

4.1   System of Parameters and Symbolic Formulas

An *index set* is a finite set of integers. A set S is indexed by an index set I by specifying a bijective mapping from I to S (we write $S = \{s_i\}_{i \in I}$). For example, $I = \{1, 2, 3\}$ is an index set and $S = \{s_1, s_2, s_3\}$ is a set indexed by I.

Definition 1. *A* system of parameters P *is a pair* $(I, \mathcal{V})$ *where I is an index set parameter and $\mathcal{V}$ is finite set of sets of parameters. Each $V \in \mathcal{V}$ is associated with* $\mathtt{sort}_V \in \{\mathtt{bool}, \mathtt{int}, \mathtt{real}\}$ *and* $\mathtt{arity}_V \in \mathbb{N}_0$, *and is indexed by* $I^{\mathtt{arity}_V}$.

In practice, once we have defined the set of indexes I, an indexed set $V \in \mathcal{V}$ with arity k is a set of parameters $\{v_{i_1 \ldots i_k} \mid i_1, \ldots, i_k \in I\}$. We write $V(i_1, \ldots, i_k)$ for $v_{i_1 \ldots i_k}$. For example, if $\mathcal{V} = \{V\}$, $\mathtt{sort}_V = \mathtt{int}$ and $\mathtt{arity}_V = 2$, then, for $I = \{1, 2\}$, V is the set of integer parameters $\{v_{11}, v_{12}, v_{21}, v_{22}\}$.

Definition 2. *An* assignment μ *to a system of parameters* $P = (I, \mathcal{V})$ *maps each parameter to its domain, thus:*

- $\mu(I)$ *is a finite subset of* $\mathbb{Z}$;
- *For* $V \in \mathcal{V}$ *and* $v \in V$, $\mu(v) \in \mathbb{Z}$ *if* $\mathtt{sort}_V = \mathtt{int}$, $\mu(v) \in \mathbb{R}$ *if* $\mathtt{sort}_V = \mathtt{real}$, *and* $\mu(v) \in \mathbb{B} = \{\top, \bot\}$ *if* $\mathtt{sort}_V = \mathtt{bool}$.

Formulas used to define invariants and other constraints in the DPA are first-order formulas in a signature derived from the parameter system.

Definition 3. *Given a system of parameters* $P = (I, \mathcal{V})$, *the induced (many-sort) first-order signature* Σ_P *consists of a set symbol I (technically a constant), a functional symbol for every parameter V in $\mathcal{V}$ with arity* $\mathtt{arity}_V$ *and sort* $\mathtt{sort}_V$ *and the symbols of the theory of integers, reals, and sets.* Σ*-terms and* Σ*-formulas and their evaluation (under an assignment μ)* $[\![\cdot]\!]_\mu$ *are defined in the standard way. The only restriction is that quantifiers can only occur in the form* $\forall i \in I.\beta$ *or* $\exists i \in I.\beta$.

For example, supposing $\mathcal{V} = \{V\}$, $\mathtt{arity}_V = 2$, and $\mathtt{sort}_V = \mathtt{real}$, then $\exists i \in I.(V(1, i) < V(2, i))$ is a Σ_P-formula and $V(1, i)$ is a Σ_P-term.

4.2   Dynamic Parametrized Architectures

Definition 4. *An architectural* configuration *is a pair* (V, E), *where V is a set of* components *and $E \subseteq V \times V$ is a set of* connections *between components.*

For example, if $V = \{v_0, v_1, v_2\}$ and $E = \{(v_0, v_1), (v_1, v_2), (v_2, v_0)\}$, the architectural configuration represents a simple ring of 3 components.

A parametrized architecture represents a set of possible architectural configurations.

Definition 5. *A* parametrized architecture *is a tuple* $A = (P, id, \psi, \phi, \chi)$ *where*

- P *is a system of parameters;*

- id is a labeling function assigning to any integer i, an identifier $id(i)$;
- $\psi(x)$ is a Σ_P-formula (components guard) over a free variable x;
- $\phi(x, y)$ is a Σ_P-formula (connections guard) over free variables x, y;
- χ is a Σ_P-formula (parameters assumption) without free variables.

Given an assignment μ to the system of parameters $P = (I, V)$, the instantiated architectural configuration defined by the assignment μ is given by $\mu(A) := (V_\mu, E_\mu)$ where

- $V_\mu = \{id(i) \mid \mu \models i \in I, \mu \models \psi(i/x), \mu \models \chi\}$.
- $E_\mu = \{(id(i), id(j)) \mid \mu \models i \in I, \mu \models j \in I, \mu \models \phi(i/x, j/y), \mu \models \chi\}$.

Example: for $P = (I, V)$, $V = \{Succ, Last\}$, $Succ$ is a set of integer parameters, with $\text{arity}_{Succ} = 1$, $Last$ is a singleton containing one integer parameter ($\text{arity}_{Last} = 0$), $\psi(x) := \top$, $\phi(x, y) := y = Succ(x)$, $\chi := 0 \in I \wedge Last \in I \wedge \forall i.(i \in I \rightarrow (0 \le i \le Last \wedge Succ(i) \in I))$. By assigning $\mu(I) = \{0, 1, 2\}$, $\mu(Last) = 2$, $\mu(Succ(x)) := (x < Last\,?\,x+1:0)$, we get the configuration in the previous example.

Definition 6. A dynamic parametrized architecture is a tuple $S = (A, \iota, \kappa, \tau)$, where

- $A = (P, id, \psi, \phi, \chi)$ is a parametrized architecture;
- ι is a Σ_P-formula, specifying the set of initial assignments;
- κ is a Σ_P-formula, specifying the invariant;
- τ specifies the reconfiguration transitions and is in the form

$$\bigvee_j I' = \alpha_j(i_1, \ldots, i_{k_j}) \wedge \gamma_j(i_1, \ldots, i_{k_j})$$

where $\alpha_j(i_1, \ldots, i_{k_j})$ is a $\Sigma_P \cup \Sigma'_P$-term, $\gamma_j(i_1, \ldots, i_{k_j})$ a $\Sigma_P \cup \Sigma'_P$-formula, Σ'_P contains the primed version of symbols in Σ_P, and $i_1, \ldots, i_{k_j}$ are implicitly existentially quantified free variables.

The dynamic parametrized architecture defines a dynamically changing architecture as a transition system over architectural configurations obtained by instantiation from A. The set of initial configurations is given by

$$\{\mu(A) : \mu \text{ is an assignment to } P \text{ such that } \mu \models \iota \text{ and } \mu \models \kappa \wedge \chi\}.$$

A configuration $\mu'(A)$ is directly reachable from a configuration $\mu(A)$ iff $\mu \cup \mu' \models \tau$ and $\mu' \models \kappa \wedge \chi$, where $\mu \cup \mu'$ assigns values to P as μ and to P' as μ'.

Example: consider the parametrized architecture from the previous example, with $\iota := Last = 0$; $\kappa := \top$ and $\tau(i) := \tau_1(i) \vee \tau_2(i)$, where $\tau_1(i) := I' = I \cup \{i\} \wedge i > Last \wedge Last' = i \wedge Succ'(Last) = i \wedge Succ'(i) = 0 \wedge \forall j.((j \in I \wedge j < Last) \rightarrow Succ'(j) = Succ(j))$ and $\tau_2(i) := I' = I \setminus \{i\} \wedge i \in I \wedge 0 < i < Last \wedge Last' = Last \wedge \forall j.(((j \in I \wedge Succ(j) = i) \rightarrow Succ'(j) = Succ(i)) \wedge ((j \in I \wedge Succ(j) \neq i) \rightarrow Succ'(j) = Succ(j)))$. This defines the set of initial

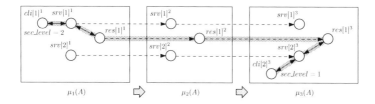

Fig. 5. Example graph of maximal information flow $G(\mu_1, \mu_2, \mu_3)$

architectures which contains only the single architecture with one component and self-loop connection. The first transition adds a new index i, which becomes the new last index and the successor is updated to maintain a ring topology. The second transition removes an index different from 0 and $Last$, again maintaining a ring topology.

4.3 Run-Time Information Flow Verification Problem

Given a system of parameters P, a parametrized architecture $A(P)$, a DPA $S(A)$, and a sequence of assignments to parameters $\mu_1, \ldots, \mu_n$. We denote the k-th configuration $\mu_k(A)$ with (V_k, E_k). We define the graph of maximal information flow as $G(\mu_1, \ldots, \mu_n) = (V, E)$ with

$$V = \bigcup_{k=1}^{n} \{v^k \mid v \in V_k\}$$

$$E = \bigcup_{k=1}^{n} \{(v^k, w^k) \mid (v, w) \in E_k\} \cup \bigcup_{k=1}^{n-1} \{(v^k, v^{k+1}) \mid v \in V_k \cap V_{k+1}\}.$$

Example graph of maximal information flow is shown in Fig. 5. Reconfigurations are shown by gray arrows, edges corresponding to connections within a configuration (the first union in the definition of E) by solid arrows, and edges between instances of the same component in adjacent configurations (the second union) by dashed arrows. An identifier v^k in V is a copy of the component identifier v from V_k and represents the instance of the component v in the configuration $\mu_k(A)$. Every path in $G(\mu_1, \ldots, \mu_n)$ represents a possible flow of information from a component to another one through a sequence of communications (between two connected components in the current configuration) and reconfigurations (the component keeps the information if it is not removed).

Given a labeling $sec : \mathbb{Z} \to \mathbb{N}_0$ that assigns to every component identifier a security level, we want to ensure that there is never a path in G from a component $id(i)$ to a component $id(j)$ if $0 < sec(j) < sec(i)$ ($sec = 0$ represents no level).

Definition 7. *Given a sequence of configurations $\mu_1, \ldots, \mu_n$ and a labeling function $sec : \mathbb{Z} \to \mathbb{N}_0$, the reconfiguration synthesis problem is the problem of finding a next configuration μ_{n+1} such that μ_{n+1} is directly reachable from μ_n and such that, in the graph of maximal information flow $G(\mu_1, \ldots, \mu_{n+1})$, there is no path from a component $id(i)$ to a component $id(j)$ if $0 < sec(j) < sec(i)$.*

4.4   Encoding into SMT

The idea of the solution that we propose is to keep track of the highest level of information that a component can have, given the history of configurations, and then encode the problem into SMT. The key of the approach is to exploit the restrictions on the set updates in the reconfiguration to instantiate the quantifiers on a finite set of symbolic terms. This way, we can obtain a quantifier-free formula that can be solved by an SMT solver.

We define maximal taint of a vertex $v \in V$ as the element of $\mathbb{N}_0$:

$$taint_n(v) = \max\{sec(w) : \text{there is a path from } w \text{ to } v \text{ in } G(\mu_1, \ldots, \mu_n)\}.$$

The following formula (1) encodes the reconfiguration synthesis problem. Any satisfying assignment will correspond to a next configuration solving the problem. The formula assigns the current parameters to the value given by μ_n and constrains the next configuration to be directly reachable from μ_n (the first row in (1)). It then encodes the propagation of information from the current to the next configuration and within the next configuration (second to fourth row). The encoded propagation of information to a component considers only its immediate predecessors in the graph of maximal information flow and the component itself (so that a newly added component is tainted by its own security level)—in Fig. 5, the considered information sources for $srv[2]^3$ are $srv[2]^2$, $res[1]^3$, $cli[2]^3$ and the component $srv[2]^3$ itself. The formula (1) finally ensures that the security level is not violated by such propagation (last row).

$$
\begin{aligned}
Enc := \; & \mu_n \wedge \tau \wedge \kappa' \wedge \chi' \wedge \\
& \forall i \in I'(((\psi'(i) \wedge i \in I \wedge \psi(i)) \to t_{n+1}(i) \geq taint_n(i)) \wedge \\
& \quad \forall j \in I'((\psi'(i) \wedge \psi'(j) \wedge \phi'(j,i)) \to t_{n+1}(i) \geq t_{n+1}(j)) \wedge \quad (1) \\
& \quad (\psi'(i) \to t_{n+1}(i) \geq sec(i))) \wedge \\
& \forall i \in I'((\psi'(i) \wedge sec(i) > 0) \to t_{n+1}(i) \leq sec(i))
\end{aligned}
$$

The formula uses an extra function t_{n+1} that represents the tainting of vertices in the next configuration. A satisfying assignment to the formula, besides the next configuration, determines also its tainting, i.e., $taint_{n+1}(v)$ is exactly the value assigned to $t_{n+1}(v)$ for components v such that $sec(v) > 0$.

Theorem 1. *Given a satisfying assignment μ of Enc, let μ_{n+1} be the restriction of μ to the symbols in $\mathbf{P'}$. Then μ_{n+1} represents a configuration directly reachable from μ_n such that there is no path in $G(\mu_1, \ldots, \mu_{n+1})$ violating the information flow property and $\mu(t_{n+1}(v)) = taint_{n+1}(v)$ for all v such that $sec(v) > 0$.*

All proofs can be found in the extended version of the paper which is available at https://es.fbk.eu/people/stojic/papers/safecomp19/.

4.5   Finding a Model of the Synthesis Encoding

The logic used in the specification of the formulas of a DPA is in general undecidable, due to the quantification over sets. However, the synthesis encoding starts from a concrete configuration and thus we can decide the satisfiability for this special case, as described below. Since the I' can be obtained from I with a finite number of additions/removals of indexes, we can define a finite number of symbolic terms over which the quantifiers over I' can be instantiated.

From the transition formula τ, we compute the finite set $pe_{I'}(\tau)$ of possible elements (terms) of I' by syntactically examining the transition formula. $pe_{I'}$ is defined recursively on the formula:

$$
pe_{I'}(\beta) := \begin{cases}
pe_{I'}(\beta_1) \cup pe_{I'}(\beta_2) & \text{if } \beta = \beta_1 \vee \beta_2, \\
pe_{I'}(\beta_1) \cup pe_{I'}(\beta_2) & \text{if } \beta = \beta_1 \wedge \beta_2, \\
pe_{I'}(\alpha) & \text{if } \beta = I' = \alpha, \\
\emptyset & \text{if } \beta \text{ is a predicate not containing } I', \\
pe_{I'}(I_1) \cup pe_{I'}(I_2) & \text{if } \beta = I_1 \cup I_2, \\
pe_{I'}(I_1) & \text{if } \beta = I_1 \setminus I_2, \\
I & \text{if } \beta = I.
\end{cases}
$$

Suppose the current assignment μ_n assigns I to $\{i_1, \dots, i_n\}$. If τ is $I' = (I \cup \{t_1, t_2\}) \setminus \{t_3\}$, the possible elements are $pe_{I'}(\tau) = \{i_1, \dots, i_n, t_1, t_2\}$.

For a concrete example, suppose that, for the running example model of Fig. 3, in the current assignment we have $\mathsf{S} = \{1, 2, 3\}$. The transitions which modify the set of indexes S are $\texttt{add\_server}$ and $\texttt{remove\_server}$ (these transitions are shown in Fig. 4). By inspecting the transitions, it is easy to compute the set of possible terms which may appear in $\texttt{next}(\mathsf{S})$ as $\{1, 2, 3, s\}$, where s is the term which appears in the transition $\texttt{add\_server}$.

In the following, let us assume that $pe_{I'}(\tau)$ is $\{t'_1, \dots, t'_m\}$. The value of I' is then encoded using m fresh Boolean variables $\{b_{t'_1}, \dots, b_{t'_m}\}$ (where $b_{t'} = \top$ if and only if $t' \in I'$). The formula Enc is transformed by eliminating quantifiers and operators involving sets using the terms $t'_1, \dots, t'_m$ and the Boolean variables $b_{t'_1}, \dots, b_{t'_m}$. This is done by the transformation QE defined by the following steps: (1) replace all occurences of the set of indexes I with the constant set $\mu_n(I)$; (2) apply the formula transformation $R(\beta)$ defined by recursion on β:

$$
R(\beta) := \begin{cases}
R(\beta_1) \vee R(\beta_2) & \text{if } \beta = \beta_1 \vee \beta_2 \\
R(\beta_1) \wedge R(\beta_2) & \text{if } \beta = \beta_1 \wedge \beta_2 \\
\bigwedge_{t \in pe_{I'}(\tau)} (b_t \leftrightarrow R(t \in \alpha)) & \text{if } \beta = I' = \alpha \\
R(t \in \alpha_1) \vee R(t \in \alpha_2) & \text{if } \beta = t \in \alpha_1 \cup \alpha_2 \\
R(t \in \alpha_1) \wedge \neg R(t \in \alpha_2) & \text{if } \beta = t \in \alpha_1 \setminus \alpha_2 \\
\bigvee_{t \in pe_{I'}(\tau)} (b_t \wedge R(t_1 = t)) & \text{if } \beta = t_1 \in I' \\
\bigvee_{j \in J} R(t = j) & \text{if } \beta = t \in J \text{ for constant set } J \\
\bowtie (R(t_1), \dots, R(t_n)) & \text{if } \beta = R(\bowtie(t_1, \dots, t_n)) \text{ for predicate } \bowtie \\
\star (R(t_1), \dots, R(t_n)) & \text{if } \beta = R(\star(t_1, \dots, t_n)) \text{ for function } \star \\
\bigvee_{t \in pe_{I'}(\tau)} (b_t \wedge R(\beta_1[t/i])) & \text{if } \beta = \exists i \in I'.\beta_1 \\
\bigwedge_{t \in pe_{I'}(\tau)} (b_t \to R(\beta_1[t/i])) & \text{if } \beta = \forall i \in I'.\beta_1 \\
\bigvee_{j \in J} \beta_1[j/i] & \text{if } \beta = \exists i \in J.\beta_1 \text{ for constant set } J \\
\bigwedge_{j \in J} \beta_1[j/i] & \text{if } \beta = \forall i \in J.\beta_1 \text{ for constant set } J
\end{cases}
$$

For example, for the assignment in which $S = \{1, 2, 3\}$, the subformula **next**(S) = **remove**$(S, \{u\})$ $(S' = S \setminus \{u\}$ in the abstract representation) of the transition `remove_server` is first transformed to $S' = \{1, 2, 3\} \setminus \{u\}$, then by case 3 in the definition of R to $\bigwedge_{t \in \{1,2,3,s\}} (b_t \leftrightarrow R(t \in \{1, 2, 3\} \setminus \{u\}))$, then by case 5 to $\bigwedge_{t \in \{1,2,3,s\}} (b_t \leftrightarrow R(t \in \{1, 2, 3\}) \wedge \neg R(t \in \{u\}))$, and finally by two applications of case 7 to $\bigwedge_{t \in \{1,2,3,s\}} (b_t \leftrightarrow (t = 1 \vee t = 2 \vee t = 3) \wedge \neg(t = u))$, which is equivalent to $(b_1 \leftrightarrow 1 \neq u) \wedge (b_2 \leftrightarrow 2 \neq u) \wedge (b_3 \leftrightarrow 3 \neq u) \wedge (b_s \leftrightarrow (s = 1 \vee s = 2 \vee s = 3) \wedge (s \neq u))$.

Theorem 2. *Enc and QE(Enc) are equivalent.*

5   Experimental Evaluation

We have tested a prototype implementation—based on the COMPASS toolset and written in Python—of the synthesis method to evaluate its scalability. The testing was done on a machine with an Intel Core i7-8550U CPU (clock up to 4 GHz) with 16 GB of memory and running Debian 9.8 (64-bit). The prototype implementation and scripts to automatically generate the models and run the tests can be found at https://es.fbk.eu/people/stojic/papers/safecomp19/.

Models and Experiments. We tested several models: the running example model described in Sect. 3 and the models *ring*, *sequence* and *converging* (in *unsafe* and *safe* variants), which are described in [10]. The *unsafe* variants contain reachable architectural configurations in which the information flow property is violated (these configurations are correctly avoided by the synthesis method), while in the case of the *safe* variants the information flow property is satisfied for all reachable configurations. For each model and each tested number of components, we instantiated a configuration with that many components and we measured the time taken by the synthesis method for that initial instance.

Results. Figure 6 shows the size of the SMT formula $QE(Enc)$ resulting from the encoding described in Sect. 4, plotted against the number of components in the initial instance. The running example (rex in Fig. 6) formula size is significantly larger than for the other examples because it contains several quantified constraints. The running time, shown in Fig. 7, shows that the method scales beyond small examples, being able to handle models of practically relevant sizes. For the tested models, about 95% of the synthesis time is spent in generating the SMT formula and instantiating the resulting model with the Python scripts, while the rest is spent in the SMT solver.

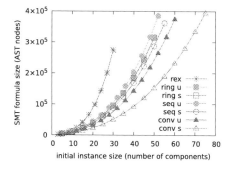

Fig. 6. Formula size

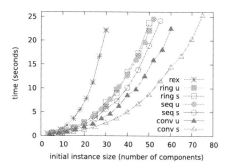

Fig. 7. Synthesis time

6   Conclusions

In order to support the model-based approach to design, verification and adaptation of MILS systems developed in project CITADEL, we propose a method for run-time synthesis of architectural configurations that preserves required system invariants and an information flow property. We describe the context and motivation behind the proposed method, overview the modeling language that is used to define dynamic architectures and their properties, and formally describe the proposed synthesis method. The method is based on the instantiation (for the current architectural configuration) of the possible reconfiguration transitions, the required invariants, and of the information flow property. This enables the removal of quantifiers and operations involving sets, and encoding in SMT of the resulting quantifier-free formulas. We perform an experimental evaluation, showing the scalability of the approach to practically relevant model sizes.

As future work, we aim to extend the method for the analysis of information flows to use different back-end solvers and to verify more general information flow properties, involving components which enforce local information flow policies.

Acknowledgement. This work was supported by the CITADEL Project, funded by the Horizon 2020 Programme of the European Union (grant agreement no. 700665).

References

1. Allen, R., Douence, R., Garlan, D.: Specifying and analyzing dynamic software architectures. In: Astesiano, E. (ed.) FASE 1998. LNCS, vol. 1382, pp. 21–37. Springer, Heidelberg (1998). https://doi.org/10.1007/BFb0053581
2. Barrett, C.W., Sebastiani, R., Seshia, S.A., Tinelli, C.: Satisfiability modulo theories. In: Handbook of Satisfiability, pp. 825–885. IOS Press (2009)
3. Boettcher, C., DeLong, R., Rushby, J., Sifre, W.: The MILS component integration approach to secure information sharing. In: DASC (2008)
4. Bozga, M., Jaber, M., Maris, N., Sifakis, J.: Modeling dynamic architectures using Dy-BIP. In: Gschwind, T., De Paoli, F., Gruhn, V., Book, M. (eds.) SC 2012. LNCS, vol. 7306, pp. 1–16. Springer, Heidelberg (2012). https://doi.org/10.1007/978-3-642-30564-1_1

5. Bozzano, M., Cimatti, A., Katoen, J., Nguyen, V.Y., Noll, T., Roveri, M.: Safety, dependability and performance analysis of extended AADL models. Comput. J. **54**(5), 754–775 (2011)

6. Bozzano, M., Cimatti, A., Katoen, J.-P., Nguyen, V.Y., Noll, T., Roveri, M.: The COMPASS approach: correctness, modelling and performability of aerospace systems. In: Buth, B., Rabe, G., Seyfarth, T. (eds.) SAFECOMP 2009. LNCS, vol. 5775, pp. 173–186. Springer, Heidelberg (2009). https://doi.org/10.1007/978-3-642-04468-7_15

7. Bradbury, J.S., Cordy, J.R., Dingel, J., Wermelinger, M.: A survey of self-management in dynamic software architecture specifications. In: WOSS, pp. 28–33 (2004)

8. Bruni, R., Melgratti, H.C., Montanari, U.: Behaviour, interaction and dynamics. In: Specification, Algebra, and Software - Essays Dedicated to Kokichi Futatsugi, pp. 382–401 (2014)

9. Canal, C., Pimentel, E., Troya, J.M.: Specification and refinement of dynamic software architectures. In: Donohoe, P. (ed.) Software Architecture. ITIFIP, vol. 12, pp. 107–125. Springer, Boston, MA (1999). https://doi.org/10.1007/978-0-387-35563-4_7

10. Cimatti, A., Stojic, I., Tonetta, S.: Formal specification and verification of dynamic parametrized architectures. In: Havelund, K., Peleska, J., Roscoe, B., de Vink, E. (eds.) FM 2018. LNCS, vol. 10951, pp. 625–644. Springer, Cham (2018). https://doi.org/10.1007/978-3-319-95582-7_37

11. CITADEL Modeling and Specification Languages. Technical report D3.1, Version 2.3, CITADEL Project, August 2018

12. CITADEL Configuration and Reconfiguration Synthesis. Technical report D3.4, Version 1.0, CITADEL Project, November 2018

13. Feiler, P.H., Gluch, D.P.: Model-Based Engineering with AADL: An Introduction to the SAE Architecture Analysis & Design Language. SEI Series in Software Engineering. Addison-Wesley, Boston (2012)

14. Goguen, J.A., Meseguer, J.: Security policies and security models. In: IEEE Symposium on Security and Privacy, pp. 11–20 (1982)

15. Hirsch, D., Inverardi, P., Montanari, U.: Reconfiguration of software architecture styles with name mobility. In: Porto, A., Roman, G.-C. (eds.) COORDINATION 2000. LNCS, vol. 1906, pp. 148–163. Springer, Heidelberg (2000). https://doi.org/10.1007/3-540-45263-X_10

16. Konnov, I.V., Kotek, T., Wang, Q., Veith, H., Bliudze, S., Sifakis, J.: Parameterized systems in BIP: design and model checking. In: CONCUR (2016)

17. Magee, J., Kramer, J.: Dynamic structure in software architectures. In: SIGSOFT, pp. 3–14 (1996)

18. Medvidovic, N., Taylor, R.N.: A classification and comparison framework for software architecture description languages. IEEE Trans. Softw. Eng. **26**(1), 70–93 (2000)

19. Métayer, D.L.: Describing software architecture styles using graph grammars. IEEE Trans. Softw. Eng. **24**(7), 521–533 (1998)

20. Milner, R., Parrow, J., Walker, D.: A calculus of mobile processes I and II. Inf. Comput. **100**(1), 1–77 (1992)

21. Rozenberg, G. (ed.): Handbook of Graph Grammars and Computing by Graph Transformations. Volume 1: Foundations. World Scientific, Singapore (1997)

22. Rushby, J.: The design and verification of secure systems. In: ACM Operating Systems Review, pp. 12–21 (1981)

23. Rushby, J.: Separation and integration in MILS (the MILS constitution). Technical report, Menlo Park, CA, February 2008
24. Architecture Analysis & Design Language (AADL) (rev. B): SAE Standard AS5506B, International Society of Automotive Engineers, September 2012
25. Sifakis, J., Bensalem, S., Bliudze, S., Bozga, M.: A theory agenda for component-based design. In: De Nicola, R., Hennicker, R. (eds.) Software, Services, and Systems. LNCS, vol. 8950, pp. 409–439. Springer, Cham (2015). https://doi.org/10.1007/978-3-319-15545-6_24
26. SLIM 3.0 - Syntax and Semantics. Technical Note D1–2, Issue 4.7, COMPASS Project, June 2016
27. Webber, D., Gomaa, H.: Modeling variability in software product lines with the variation point model. Sci. Comput. Program. **53**(3), 305–331 (2004)
28. Wermelinger, M., Fiadeiro, J.L.: Algebraic software architecture reconfiguration. In: Nierstrasz, O., Lemoine, M. (eds.) ESEC/SIGSOFT FSE -1999. LNCS, vol. 1687, pp. 393–409. Springer, Heidelberg (1999). https://doi.org/10.1007/3-540-48166-4_24
29. Xu, H., Zeng, G., Chen, B.: Description and verification of dynamic software architectures for distributed systems. JSW **5**(7), 721–728 (2010)

Dynamic Risk Assessment Enabling Automated Interventions for Medical Cyber-Physical Systems

Fábio L. Leite Jr.[1,2(✉)] 🆔, Daniel Schneider[3], and Rasmus Adler[3]

[1] Department of Software Engineering: Dependability,
University of Kaiserslautern, Kaiserslautern, Germany
[2] Center for Strategic Health Technologies – NUTES Paraíba
State University (UEPB), Campina Grande, PB, Brazil
fabioleite@cct.uepb.edu.br
[3] Fraunhofer IESE, Kaiserslautern, Germany
{daniel.schneider,rasmus.adler}@iese.fraunhofer.de

Abstract. As in many embedded systems domains, in modern healthcare we experience increasing adoption of (medical) cyber-physical systems of systems. In hospitals, for instance, different types of medical systems are integrated dynamically to render higher-level services in cooperation. One important task is the realization of smart alarms as well as, in a second step, the realization of automated interventions, such as the administration of specific drugs. A fundamental correlated problem is insufficient risk awareness, which are caused by fluctuating context conditions, insufficient context awareness, and a lack of reasoning capabilities to deduce the current risk. A potential solution to this problem is to make systems context- and risk-aware by introducing a runtime risk assessment approach. In this paper, we introduce such an approach for a wider identification of relevant risk parameters and risk assessment model building based on Bayesian Networks (BN). This model considers not only changes in the actual health status of the patient but also the changing capabilities to detect and react according to this status. This includes changing capabilities due to adding or removing different types of sensors (e.g. heart rate sensors) and replacing sensors of the same type but with other integrity level. In addition, we present an evaluation of the approach based on a simulated clinical environment for patient-controlled analgesia.

Keywords: Medical systems · Cyber-physical systems ·
Runtime safety assurance · Dynamic risk management · Risk assessment ·
Bayesian network

1 Introduction

In modern healthcare environments, we are witnessing increasing adoption of medical cyber-physical systems. There is huge potential for new kinds of applications and services aimed at increasing safety, quality of care, and efficiency while saving costs at the same time. Already today, the medical device industry and hospitals are

© Springer Nature Switzerland AG 2019
A. Romanovsky et al. (Eds.): SAFECOMP 2019, LNCS 11698, pp. 216–231, 2019.
https://doi.org/10.1007/978-3-030-26601-1_15

increasingly adopting such systems in order to deal with the flood of alarm in the wards. Despite the advances regarding alarm precision, such systems still exhibit too many false positives and false negatives. These limitations have posed challenges for the adoption of automated supervision. Even bigger challenges are faced in systems capable of automated intervention (i.e., not just calling for a human operator, but directly implementing an action) such as administering specific drugs or managing permissions for the patient to choose administration of a bolus (e.g., patient-controlled analgesia). Thus, unfortunately, several accidents still occur every year in healthcare environments due to the limitation of system alarms or the limited hospital resources to provide care [9–11].

A fundamental problem leading to the increased numbers of false positives and false negatives is the fact that alarms (as well as other triggers) are typically based on fixed thresholds of one or a few monitored parameters. Given the very volatile nature of the relevant context conditions (e.g., the patient's condition, which is characterized by a potentially complex interplay of different vital signs), fixed thresholds are a weak means for assessing the current risk.

To tackle this problem, we aim to improve the context awareness of systems and equip them with the capability to dynamically calculate the risk of the current situation. In this paper, we introduce a corresponding runtime risk assessment approach based on an executable risk model. The risk model is specified as a Bayesian Network (BN) according to a methodology that is likewise presented in this paper. The methodology utilizes a metamodel to enhance the identification of relevant risk parameters according to domain-specific information, system dynamicity, and safety engineering tasks. Moreover, we specify an adaptive risk management model capable of dealing with system configuration changes at runtime. Therefore, we define adaptive risk models so that risk monitors can properly respond to the system and context changes.

We evaluated the results of the presented approach in a simulated environment and found that the results outperformed the critical situation detection capabilities of current approaches and increased treatment availability for the patients. The results are promising and motivate further research in dynamic risk assessment and control for medical scenarios. Ultimately, we hope that it will be possible to enable the adoption of automated supervision and, at some later point in time, automated intervention, enhancing safety and comfort for the patients while saving money, which could then be spent in other places.

2   Related Work

According to [6, 17], dynamic risk management (DRA) is a risk assessment method that updates the estimated risk according to runtime updates of the processes related to the system functions. There is a wide area of application in the literature for various domains such as avionics [6], unmanned underwater vehicles [15], automotive [16], and nuclear power plants [17]. Compared with "static" quantitative risk assessment techniques, DRA is capable of dealing with runtime changes provided by novel dynamic systems of systems and cyber-physical systems.

Medical cyber-physical systems (MCPS) are life-critical, context-aware, networked sets of independent medical devices that dynamically cooperate to enable new functions at runtime. Several works have proposed solutions for risk assessment of the current situation that focus on the patient status. Arney et al. [1] propose a fail-safe device coordination protocol to avoid overdosage during PCA treatment based on the SpO2 monitoring. Stevens et al. [14] developed a smart alarm solution to improve alarm management for post coronary artery bypass graft (post-CABG) surgery patients. The authors provide patient status analysis by combining different data such as arterial line, electrocardiogram, pulse oximeter, and historical data. Jiang et al. [5] present an evolutionary sepsis screening system to speed up detection and improve the positive effect of the treatment. These approaches show advances for patient modeling and fuzzy models to predict the patient's situation based on vital signs; however, dynamicity and effective automated actuation demand models built on the foundations of risk assessment as a solid basis for situation analysis and risk control.

Identification and understanding of the manifold situations for patient-controlled analgesia requires reasoning about sensor uncertainties, treatment complexity, and system dynamicity. According to Zio [18] Bayes theorem provides a common framework to describe the uncertainties in the assessment stands on probability theory, and particularly on the subjectivistic (Bayesian) theory of probability, as the adequate framework within which expert opinions can be combined with statistical data to provide quantitative measures of risk. Furthermore, Bayesian networks have been adopted by the connected health domain as the main model for dealing with reasoning about uncertainty and probabilistic risk detection [2, 5, 14, 15, 17].

3   Running Example

Patient-controlled analgesia (PCA) enables self-administration of predetermined doses of analgesics (in most cases an opioid). It is widely used in hospitals as it enhances the patient's comfort regarding postoperative pain relief. However, PCA has been associated with accidents such as severe respiratory depression (or even distress) caused by opioid overdoses. Therefore, several works and health associations [9, 10] have urged healthcare professionals to consider the potential safety value of proper monitoring of oxygenation and ventilation in patients receiving IV opioids (e.g., sufentanil, piritramid, morphine, remifentanil, fentanyl) during the postoperative period.

The ASTM F2761-2010 standard [4] defines the safety interlock function as an abstract specification of a closed-loop scenario to avoid overdosage by the detection of respiratory depression signs, and stopping the infusion pump if a pre-defined threshold is reached. In this paper, we consider a refinement of the functionality proposed by [1, 12], where an Integrated Clinical Environment (ICE) controls the infusion, allowing the operation of the infusion pump via an expiring token that needs to be sent to the pump at specific intervals. Accordingly, the patient requiring a dose presses a button on a handheld device connected to the infusion pump, which, in turn and supervised by the ICE, only infuses the opioid if it has a valid token. Hence, the overall behavior permits bolus doses to be given only when it is considered safe for the patient and stops the infusion as soon as any respiratory depression is identified.

In our previous work [8], we evaluated the challenges posed by such dynamicity for these scenarios through the architecture of cooperative medical cyber-physical systems. Overall, the ICE monitors a patient's vital signs data through different classes of system configurations such as: (1) only a pulse oximeter as the sensor; (2) only a respiration sensor (capnography/capnometry); or (3) both medical devices as sensors. Each device provides its own set of corresponding services with their own integrity level; therefore, the same configuration class can provide different integrity levels in its instantiations at runtime.

In order to cope with such dynamic and critical environments, we established an approach for DRA based on continuous risk monitoring to support the activation of appropriate countermeasures (adaptation requirements and/or direct actuation) to deal with system or context changes [7]. If the current risk level is considered as minor or negligible, the patient is allowed to have infusion (Fig. 1). "EnableBolus" function allows the infusion pump to release an opioid dose to the patient when he/she requires it. In case the risk is deemed as serious, the system stops the bolus infusion and raises an alarm for the caregivers, showing the patient status and requiring a configuration with higher guarantees. For this situation, we defined a special check for verifying if any adaptation was made by the caregivers (bottom right of the Fig. 1). Finally, if the risk is considered higher than critical, the system stops any infusion and raises critical alerts to the caregivers.

The remaining challenge for DRA faced in this work is defining a how to derive a more comprehensive risk assessment approach that considers a wider range of relevant aspects, dealing with multidisciplinary concerns, and including the context and system dynamicity aforementioned. Therefore, the main aim of this paper in the next sections is presenting such DRA approach for specifying the function "Assess the risk" in the Fig. 1.

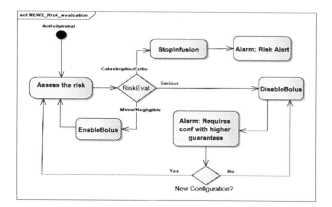

Fig. 1. Runtime risk management presented in [7]

4   Derivation of the Risk Assessment Model

In this paper, we present essential support for implementing the risk assessment and evaluation in the sketched DRM approach. Our support comprises two building blocks:

(1) **Risk parameter elicitation** - we provide a metamodel for identifying all relevant parameters for calculating the risk at runtime. In this work, we use the tree-based structure of Bayesian Networks for implementing the risk metrics. In a BN-based calculation approach, each parameter becomes a node in the BN. The challenge is then to build an overall BN based on these nodes. The metamodel provides crucial input for coping with this challenge as it shows the risk parameters and the relationship between them.

(2) **Risk model building** - we provide guidelines for deriving qualitative aspects for a BN-based risk metric from the identified risk parameters as well as define quantitative aspects such as conditional probability tables specification, discretization and defuzzification techniques.

In the following, we will explain each of these two building blocks in more detail.

4.1   Risk Parameter Elicitation

The elicitation of the risk parameters comprises dealing with multidisciplinary and (sometimes) conflicting concerns from different stakeholders. Based on our experience in dealing with people from diverse educational backgrounds, we derived a meta-model for the identification and classification of a wider range of relevant risk parameters to enhance completeness w.r.t concerns such as risk assessment, domain-specific data, system-specific data, and reliability data. In this section, we will explain the elicitation process using the risk meta-model applied for the case study.

Figure 2 depicts the meta-model for eliciting the risk parameters. The model expresses the relationships (using the UML class diagram language) between the concepts, which are concisely organized into four abstraction layers. At the top of the figure, we placed the main abstraction layer called "Risk Assessment", which contains all the other layers in the lower part of the figure: "System in its Usage Context", "System Functional Realization", and "Functional Safety Analysis".

The overall "Risk Assessment" model shall identify all aspects that contribute to risk due to an application service failure. First, we can distinguish between two aspects: (1) the system (of systems) itself and its likelihood to fail in certain ways; (2) its context, which gives us possible traces from a failure to harm. This differentiation is reflected in the top layer in Fig. 3. In the next layer, "System in Context", we focus on the second aspect and have a black-box view on the system (of systems). We only consider the user-perceivable part of the system (of systems): some systems actuate depending on some monitored parameters, that is, the application service that the system of systems realizes by orchestrating the available systems.

The layer "System in its Usage Context" presents relevant elements that may affect risk. We considered plenty of infusion scenarios and abstracted the concrete aspects that we learned from discussions with experts regarding these general classes. There might be more classes or some classes could be refined in order to enhance support for risk parameter identification. However, the evaluations showed that our metamodel is a good starting point and contributes to completeness if safety and domain experts reason about these aspects in isolation. In this sense, we carefully examined all MCPS use case scenarios defined by the ASTM standard combined with the use cases found in the literature in order to identify a common set of relevant information for deriving risk metrics. Regarding system-related elements, we structured the system interactions from/to the environment through the monitoring and actuation parameters defined by the treatment. The former defines a set of information that needs to be sensed by monitoring medical devices such as pulse oximeter, respiration monitor, and monitor multi-parameters. The latter refers to parameters controlled by delivery medical devices that change the patient (or the context) somehow; examples include infusion pump, pacemaker, ventilators, etc. Furthermore, at this layer we need to identify all parameters related to the caregivers responsible for the treatment and their related procedures. Moreover, the metamodel requires the definition of additional treatment details concerning the patient's healing, such as any additional medication or procedure that might affect the opioid effect. Finally, we further catalog risk parameters relate to the patient's history, data such as weight, age, or any potential apnea history.

The next layer, "Functional Realization", totally abstracts from the context and takes a white-box view on the system of systems, but a black-box view on the single systems. At this level, it is possible to evaluate the nominal performance, for instance, assuring if specified collaboration of systems is safe, or specifying how the system can safely change to another configuration.

As can be seen in Fig. 3, we assume that both monitoring and actuation parameters are given by provided services deployed in the medical devices. The system configuration therefore aggregates provided and required services that cooperate to accomplish a specific high-level function (application service) such as safety interlock. Finally, we have the SystemOfSytems entity, which encompasses a set of systems in a composable structure for performing the respective application services. We also assume that all context-related information regarding treatment details and patient data shall be provided by information systems supporting this infrastructure.

The last layer, "Functional Safety Analysis", addresses potential deviations from the nominal behavior. Single systems might fail and, following propagation via direct and indirect usage of the service, this may cause an application service failure. In the ideal case, the single systems already exhibit some guarantees with respect to their potential failures so that this information can be used to model some uncertainty about the correctness of the behavior at runtime. We specified a basic set of safety guarantees (e.g., service provision, timing, and value deviations guarantees) exhibited by the system services defined by the common literature [3]. We assume that such guarantees shall be specified through formal languages such as ConSerts [13], which shows reliability data defined at runtime through machine-readable certificates. Each service hence has an uncertainty model for its behavior; for example, pulse oximeters show different degradation levels while measuring blood saturation, as their accuracy varies according to the measurement technique used and/or the system implementation details.

At the end of this phase, the safety engineers shall have all the relevant input data for building the risk metric. The next section details how to build risk assessment models considering system complexity and dynamicity.

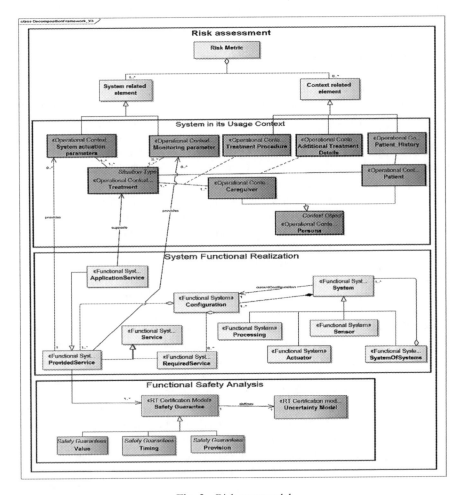

Fig. 2. Risk metamodel

4.2   Risk Model Building

A key problem for defining a risk metric for respiratory depression during PCA is that no clear rules are available that state exactly when an opioid infusion should be provided. Anesthetization experts can estimate the risk based on several parameters, but it is challenging to formalize their expert knowledge. Despite the evolution of pharmacokinetics models for vital signs, these are not sufficient yet to precisely predict all the drug effects for each single patient. After evaluating several models, we concluded that Bayesian Networks (BN) are the best fit for our task, as they provide an inherent framework for modeling expert knowledge, dealing with uncertainty, and deriving probabilistic distributions. Therefore, we make two assumptions: that (1) an infusion is always possible, and (2) the risk metric must evaluate the risk of whether the next infusion might cause overdosage. Based on the risk level, countermeasures can be defined and implemented in the system. In this subsection, we will derive a risk metric example from the metamodel previously presented - First, we will identify relevant risk parameters (qualitative aspect) for building a BN-based risk metric and then we will define the quantitative aspects of such a risk metric.

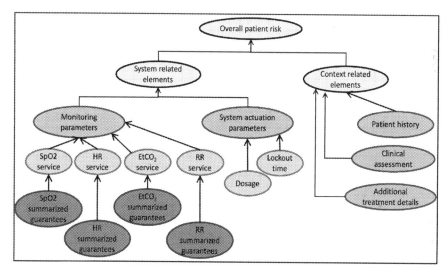

Fig. 3. Risk metric for the most complete configuration class (3) with pulse oximetry and respiration monitor

Qualitative Aspects. Initially, the previously identified information nodes are arranged in a tree structure in order to form concise data groups reflecting all the concerns of the treatment. This corresponds to the organization in the presented metamodel. In Fig. 3, we present a logical (tree structure) view of the risk metric for assessing the risk of severe respiratory depression for patient-controlled analgesia in post-operatory treatment. At the top of the figure, we have three gray nodes representing the top-level risk assessment layer elements, namely the *Overall patient risk, System-related elements*, and *Context-related elements* nodes. The root node represents the final step of the risk aggregation function. The *System-related elements* data node refers to data automatically provided by sensors and actuators; thus, this node organization includes the *Monitoring vital signs* node and the *System actuation* parameters (in Fig. 3, these are shown in blue from the "System in its Usage Context" layer). The *Monitoring vital signs* data node aggregates all relevant monitored vital signs for the treatment. In the case of PCA, the recommended data are SpO2, heart rate, respiration rate, and EtCO2.

These nodes correspond to the values of the services provided by the devices (in Fig. 3, they are highlighted in green as the elements of the "System Functional Realization" layer). Each provided service has its value adjusted by the *Guarantees* nodes (the green nodes in Fig. 3) from the "Functional Safety Layer". On the right side of Fig. 3, the *Context-related elements* node aggregates all the elements relevant to the treatment that can affect the risk of respiratory depression. The subtree encompasses nodes from the "System in its Usage Context" layer, which are further refined according to their lower layers' elements from the metamodel. Thus, all the information is structured in a tree and provides the foundation for building the Bayesian network and gathering expert knowledge for implementing the quantitative aspects of the risk metric.

Adaptation Model and Quantitative Aspects. It is necessary to identify the potential risk metric variations according to the different configuration classes. We identified all configuration classes found in the relevant standards, in the state of the art, and those recommended by anthologists. These configuration classes were presented in Sect. 3 and require different node structuring and weights for the risk function. In Fig. 3, the nodes are colored according to importance. The darker the node color, the more relevant it is for risk calculation. Thus, the *System-related elements* node is more relevant than the *Context-related elements* node due to its higher confidence from the monitors defined by the domain experts. This fact can also be observed for the subsequent nodes: Children of the *Context-related elements* node are colored with the same color as the parent node and represent its lower relevance for the overall risk. Vice versa, children of the *System-related elements* node have their relevance highlighted in dark gray colors. We particularly emphasize the dark color of the *Monitoring vital signs* node representing the most relevant nodes in the risk metric. For configuration class (2), the risk metric exhibits lower relevance of the *System-related elements* data node and higher confidence for the *Context-related elements* node. This fact is due to the confidence of the configuration class, which uses only respiration monitors as sensors, which are reliable enough for treatment but less reliable than configuration (3). For configuration class (1), the derived risk metric considers the same relevance degree for both the *System-related elements* and the *Context-related elements* data nodes. This was deemed by domain experts to be a less reliable configuration class for PCA. Hence, we consider the system's dynamicity, which varies depending on a particular adaptation, as a fundamental part of the risk assessment and the corresponding risk metrics.

In Fig. 4, we depict how the transition model should work for the identified system configurations for the case study, given the defined configuration classes and risk metrics. The blue arrows indicate how the system adaptations can activate the respective system configuration class and the corresponding risk metric. For instance, if a running configuration is monitoring the patient with pulse oximeter and capnometer (Risk Metric 3) and someone disconnects the pulse oximeter, the system monitor needs to identify that there has been an adaptation and instantiate the proper risk metric, in this case Risk Metric 2. Thereupon, the risk shall be assessed based on the particularities (defined by CPTs, defuzzification approach, etc.) of the risk metric.

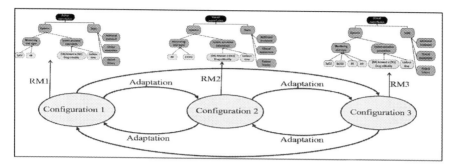

Fig. 4. The management of the Risk Metric (RM) for the adaptation model of the case study.

It is also important to note that the risk metric is defined to calculate the risk based on BN predictive algorithms (quantitative aspect). Hence, we defined with domain experts a quantification strategy for discretizing the continuous values, deriving the Conditional Probability Tables, and defuzzifying the risk values in order to obtain an estimated probability value that can be used to proceed with the runtime risk evaluation.

Discretization of Continuous Values. We abstracted and derived the conditional probabilities from the existing published literature; the experience of four medical and clinical experts from the Westpfalz-Klinikum GmbH (major regional hospital in Kaiserslautern, Germany) and from the Center for Strategic Technologies in Health (NUTES); standards (ISO 14971, IEC 62304, ISO 9001:2015 Risk Management, ASTM F2761-2010); and hospital procedures. For example, the most common class of system configurations for PCA in wards uses pulse oximetry to monitor patients. So if the patient has a blood saturation of 94%, the risk of respiratory depression is low; however, the risk increases when the patient receives additional oxygen supplementation and/or other related treatment [9]. Hence, the groups of observational nodes are divided according to the discretization strategy:

- Sensor value nodes – represent realistic vital signs readings from medical devices. Given experimental observation and simulation results, we implemented a normal distribution function that formalizes the distortion degrees according to the guarantees of the provided service. The mean is the sensor value read by the device/service and the standard deviation represents the distortion of the sensor. The lower the guarantees, the higher the standard deviation.
- System actuation parameters – these were classified according to data ranges. However, these parameters strongly impact on the risk metric due to the correlation with the severity and probability of respiratory depression (for example, type and dosage of infused drugs).
- Context nodes – context observational nodes were defined according to their data values. Domain experts defined ranges for groups of values and classified their relevance based on scale of risk, e.g., oxygen supplementation level.

Conditional Probability Tables (CPTs). CPTs are the specifications of each variable state's conditional probability, given the state of the parent variables. For the monitoring of vital signs, we defined a risk-based classification comprising negligible, minor, serious, critical, and catastrophic. For context node CPTs, we aggregate the risk using only three categories: negligible, minor, and serious, because of their lower impact on the risk. The root node *Overall risk function* also classifies the situational risk into five class scales, where each state is defined with a part of the probability space.

Defuzzification of the Root Node. Defuzzification is the process of converting a fuzzified output into a single crisp value with respect to a fuzzy set. The defuzzified value in an FLC (Fuzzy Logic Controller) represents the action to be taken in controlling the process. Hence, we selected the weighted average method for defuzzifying the values from the top node and applied a runtime evaluation algorithm based on the assessment of the final crisp value. Thus, the defuzzified value is defined as:

$$x^* = \frac{\sum \mu(x).x}{\sum \mu(x)} \tag{1}$$

Where $\sum$ denotes the algebraic summation of the valued states and x is the element with maximum membership function. We also adjust the maximum membership function x according to the system configuration; the risk thus tends to increase faster for less reliable configurations.

5   Evaluation

We evaluated our risk assessment approach with respect to the availability of treatment and the risk of overdosage. In this sense, we defined the following evaluation questions:

- **Can we enhance the runtime risk assessment for PCA?** Fixed thresholds approaches struggle to identify critical scenarios that are not beyond the thresholds yet. Our assumption is that the proposed approach will improve the identification of critical situations due to more complete risk metrics.
- **Can we improve the availability of PCA treatment regarding conservative approaches?** Improving the availability of PCA treatment will enhance the patient's experience and decrease the average pain level during the treatment. Therefore, we identified scenarios where current approaches conservatively forbid infusion and the proposed approach allow it.

The main aim of the evaluation was to evaluate simulated situations as proof-of-concept in order to answer these questions through the analysis of common scenarios provided by domain experts.

5.1   Evaluation Design

In order to answer the evaluation questions, we implemented a simulation environment for risk assessment of medical cyber-physical systems regarding the described use case and several scenarios. This environment comprises two systems. The first is an MCPS simulation implemented with OpenICE[1], which defines an integration architecture for healthcare IT ecosystems through a distributed system platform for connecting network nodes with each other. It deals with several technical issues such as node discovery, external interface definition, data publishing, proprietary protocol translation, and so on. The second system in the simulation environment is an ICE supervisor, which was responsible for monitoring the MCPS regarding the dynamic risk assessment model presented in Sect. 4. The ICE monitor implements risk assessment through a SMILE[2] Bayesian inference engine for Java. The risk metric management module identifies the current active configuration and enables the proper risk metric (presented in the Sect. 3). This system was responsible for raising risk alarms for caregivers and simulating actuation on the infusion pump that should be taken as a result of the risk evaluation procedure.

5.2   Results and Discussion

The oxygen supplementation scenario represents a common situation during PCA treatment according to domain experts and the literature. In [9, 11], the authors argue that patients treated by PCA with oxygen supplementation should be monitored by capnometry due to its efficacy in detecting respiratory depression for this kind of procedures, although several hospitals only use pulse oximeter for monitoring. Figure 5 presents the simulated results for a scenario where a patient was under PCA treatment with oxygen supplementation through an instance of configuration class (1) and the ICE Monitor recommended changing to an instance of configuration class (3), which provides higher safety guarantees regarding the procedure.

Note that in Fig. 5, the risk assessment throughout the time of the treatment is shown, as well as the situational partitioning according to the approach presented in Sect. 4. The risk is represented as the probability of the patient getting an overdose given bolus doses in the normalized range of 0% to 100%. For the situation partitioning for this procedure, the values for Negligible risk range between 0% and 27%, for Minor risk between 27% and 45%, and values higher than 45% are deemed as Serious risk. Ranges for Critical and Catastrophic risk were delimited but not used for this simulation scenario. If the risk reaches the Serious range, the ICE Monitor recommends some actions depending on the situation, such as raising risk alerts requiring caregivers to give attention to the patient and/or changing the system configuration and disabling bolus doses.

We can observe the behavior of the risk according to the SpO2 (on the right side) and EtCO2 (on the left side) data variations presented in Fig. 6. Observe the risk started at 42%, but this is still lower than 45%, the limit of the Serious range. Such value

---

[1]   https://www.openice.info/.

[2]   https://www.bayesfusion.com/.

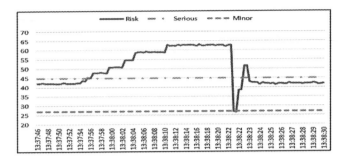

Fig. 5. Risk assessment for patient-controlled analgesia with oxygen supplementation

characterizes a careful situation, though it still allows the patient to get bolus doses. After that, the situation changed and the SpO2 decreased. This led to the risk reaching the Serious range, at time stamp 13:37:56, where the ICE Monitor triggered a risk alert requiring patient attention and a system configuration with higher guarantees and forbidding bolus doses. Note in the Fig. 6 that SpO2 reached the Alert range as 91% at time stamp 13:37:56, but did not reach the critical limit of 85% to raise a device alarm. Hence, the proposed risk model detects a hazardous situation before the concrete situation reaches a Critical state, thereby enhancing the patient's safety. As can be seen in Fig. 6, SpO2 would have only reached Serious state values later on.

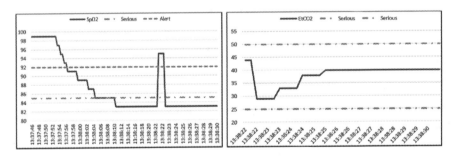

Fig. 6. Vital signs (SpO2 and EtCO2) values for the simulated scenario.

After that SpO2 reaches the Serious range above 85%, the patient received some treatment due to the opioid effects on respiration, but SpO2 stabilized at 85%. Further on, the caregiver reconfigured the system to configuration C and started to monitor the capnometry values (EtCO2 and RR), which are more reliable for this situation. In Fig. 5, we can see a sharp depression in the risk value, which stabilized around 42% at time stamp 13:38:23. This means that the risk range was Minor and the patient was allowed to have bolus doses, since the patient's EtCO2 measures remained within the acceptable range, as can be seen in Fig. 6. Hence, the ICE Monitor enables patients to get opioid bolus doses for situations where this should not be allowed considering conservative operation. In several hospitals, the patient could have the PCA treatment suspended and higher surveillance might be required in the ward. The ICE Monitor therefore improves the patient's comfort due to its monitoring ability, which allows the treatment to continue in situations where it would not be allowed traditionally.

6   Conclusion and Future Work

This article presented a novel approach for deriving dynamic and probabilistic risk assessment models for runtime monitoring of cooperative medical cyber-physical systems. A key contribution of this work is the reusable metamodel and the guidelines for a more comprehensive identification of risk parameters. As a second contribution, we derived a method for guiding safety engineers in the construction of a BBN risk model that is capable of adapting the risk metric for system changes at runtime. A case study on the implementation of safety interlocks for patient-controlled analgesia in post-operatory pain relief treatment was used as a proof of concept by means of a simulated scenario.

The evaluation section shows the breakthrough of a more comprehensive risk model for enabling automated actuation for cooperative MCPS. Throughout a wider range of relevant risk parameters, we could enhance the risk assessment and then obtain a more accurate identification of the situational status. In the simulated example scenario, the safety monitor was able to identify a critical situation before the fixed thresholds monitoring. Moreover, we managed to improve the patient's comfort by enabling opioid doses for situations in which traditional approaches conservatively forbid this.

Furthermore, the evaluation results show how the developed models could enable an adaptive risk model for dealing with system changes at runtime. We simulated a caregiver's intervention during the treatment given an increasing risk situation. In that case, the caregiver actuated on the patient to ease the effects of the opioids and changed the system configuration class in order to enhance the awareness level. Concurrently, the system also adapted its risk metric to enable proper assessment given the new configuration.

It is also worth noting that the presented approach, which promotes more comprehensive elicitation of risk parameters, can positively impact on the implementation of risk metrics independent of the technology used to realize it. In this work, we implemented the risk metric using Bayesian Networks due to the vast literature background providing examples and use cases for BN-based risk metrics. The advantage of BN is its ability to deal with uncertainty and knowledge modeling from the experts. However, we also examined other technologies for implementing risk metrics, such as Dempster-Shafer theory knowledge modeling as well as approaches based on machine learning.

Future Work. Regarding future work, we are currently proceeding with validation tasks for other treatments and validation scenarios. We need to analyze our risk model in scenarios provided by hospitals in order to assure the completeness of the model. We envision that the publication of our risk metamodel will motivate healthcare practitioners to create datasets to support statistical tests of ICE monitors. Furthermore, our approach is limited to a predefined set of configuration classes at design time. Whenever a new configuration class shows up, we need to design a new risk metric and update the adaptation models. We believe that as soon as a larger amount of historical patient data is available, we will be able to adjust our approach in terms of considering machine learning techniques so that the risk monitor can dynamically derive a new risk metric at runtime given a new configuration class.

Acknowledgments. The ongoing research that led to this paper is being funded by the Brazilian National Research Council (CNPq) under grant CSF 201715/2014-7 in cooperation with Fraunhofer IESE and TU Kaiserslautern. We would also like to thank Sonnhild Namingha for proofreading.

References

1. Arney, D., et al.: Toward patient safety in closed-loop medical device systems. In: Proceedings of the 1st ACM/IEEE International Conference on Cyber-Physical Systems - ICCPS 2010, p. 139. ACM Press, New York (2010)
2. Brito, M., Griffiths, G.: A Bayesian approach for predicting risk of autonomous underwater vehicle loss during their missions. Reliab. Eng. Syst. Saf. **146**, 55–67 (2016)
3. Fenelon, P., et al.: Towards integrated safety analysis and design. ACM SIGAPP Appl. Comput. Rev. **2**(1), 21–32 (1994)
4. Goldman, J.M.: Medical devices and medical systems - essential safety requirements for equipment comprising the patient-centric integrated clinical environment (ICE) - Part 1: general requirements and conceptual model (2009)
5. Jiang, Y., et al.: A self-adaptively evolutionary screening approach for sepsis patient. In: Proceedings - IEEE Symposium on Computer-Based Medical Systems, August 2016, pp. 60–65 (2016)
6. Kurd, Z., Kelly, T., McDermid, J., Calinescu, R., Kwiatkowska, M.: Establishing a framework for dynamic risk management in 'intelligent' aero-engine control. In: Buth, B., Rabe, G., Seyfarth, T. (eds.) SAFECOMP 2009. LNCS, vol. 5775, pp. 326–341. Springer, Heidelberg (2009). https://doi.org/10.1007/978-3-642-04468-7_26
7. Leite, F.L., Schneider, D., Adler, R.: Dynamic risk management for cooperative autonomous medical cyber-physical systems. In: Gallina, B., Skavhaug, A., Schoitsch, E., Bitsch, F. (eds.) SAFECOMP 2018. LNCS, vol. 11094, pp. 126–138. Springer, Cham (2018). https://doi.org/10.1007/978-3-319-99229-7_12
8. Leite, F.L., Adler, R., Feth, P.: Safety assurance for autonomous and collaborative medical cyber-physical systems. In: Tonetta, S., Schoitsch, E., Bitsch, F. (eds.) SAFECOMP 2017. LNCS, vol. 10489, pp. 237–248. Springer, Cham (2017). https://doi.org/10.1007/978-3-319-66284-8_20
9. Lynn, L.A., Curry, J.P.: Patterns of unexpected in-hospital deaths: a root cause analysis. Patient Saf. Surg. **5**(1), 3 (2011)
10. Maddox, R.R., et al.: Continuous respiratory monitoring and a "smart" infusion system improve safety of patient-controlled analgesia in the postoperative period. Agency for Healthcare Research and Quality (US), Rockville, MD, USA (2008)
11. McCarter, T., et al.: Capnography monitoring enhances safety of postoperative patient-controlled analgesia. Am. Heal. drug benefits. **1**(5), 28–35 (2008)
12. Pajic, M., et al.: Model-driven safety analysis of closed-loop medical systems. IEEE Trans. Ind. inform. **10**(1), 3–16 (2012)

13. Schneider, D., Trapp, M.: Conditional safety certification of open adaptive systems. ACM Trans. Auton. Adapt. Syst. **8**(2), 1–20 (2013)
14. Stevens, N., et al.: Smart alarms: multivariate medical alarm integration for post CABG surgery patients. In: Proceedings of the 2nd ACM SIGHIT symposium on International health informatics - IHI 2012, p. 533. ACM Press, New York (2012)
15. Thieme, C.A., Utne, I.B.: A risk model for autonomous marine systems and operation focusing on human–autonomy collaboration. Proc. Inst. Mech. Eng. Part O J. Risk Reliab. **231**(4), 446–464 (2017)
16. Wardziński, A.: Safety assurance strategies for autonomous vehicles. In: Harrison, M.D., Sujan, M.-A. (eds.) SAFECOMP 2008. LNCS, vol. 5219, pp. 277–290. Springer, Heidelberg (2008). https://doi.org/10.1007/978-3-540-87698-4_24
17. Zeng, Z., Zio, E.: Dynamic risk assessment based on statistical failure data and condition-monitoring degradation data. IEEE Trans. Reliab. **67**(2), 609–622 (2018)
18. Zio, E.: The future of risk assessment. Reliab. Eng. Syst. Saf. **177**(March), 176–190 (2018)

Verification and Validation of Autonomous Systems

Practical Experience Report: Engineering Safe Deep Neural Networks for Automated Driving Systems

Jelena Frtunikj[(✉)]

BMW Group, Landshuter Strasse 26, Unterschleißheim, Germany
jelena.frtunikj@bmw.de

Abstract. Deep Neural Networks (DNNs) are one of many supervised machine learning approaches. These data-driven deep learning algorithms are revolutionizing the modern society in domains such as image processing, medicine and automotive. In the field of computer vision, DNNs are outperforming the traditional approaches that use hand-crafted feature extractors. As a result, researchers and developers in the automotive industry are using DNNs for the perception tasks of automated driving. Compared to traditional rule-based approaches, DNNs raise new safety challenges that have to be solved. There are four major building blocks in the development pipeline of DNNs: (1) functionality definition, (2) data set specification, selection and preparation, (3) development and evaluation, and (4) deployment and monitoring. This paper gives an overview of the safety challenges along the whole development pipeline of DNN, proposes potential solutions that are necessary to create safe DNNs and shows first experimental results of DNN performing object detection.

Keywords: Safety · Automated driving · Deep neural networks · Uncertainty

1 Introduction

Deep learning (DL) is a data-driven machine learning technique that enables computers to learn a task by using a considerable amount of data and not by being explicitly programmed. Deep Neural Networks are becoming more widespread particularly in computer vision applications due to their powerful performance compared to traditional computer vision techniques such as edge or corner detection. This makes the usage of DNN more attractive also in safety-related tasks such as perception of an automated driving agent. However, before a DNN executing safety-related tasks finds its way into series production cars, it has to undergo strict assessment concerning safety. In traditional rule-based programmed software systems established safety engineering processes and practices are successfully applied, whereas data-driven based deep learning algorithms raise new and sometimes obscure safety challenges.

In automotive, two standards handle safety: ISO 26262 Road vehicles – Functional safety [8] and ISO/PRF PAS 21448 Road vehicles - Safety of the intended functionality (SOTIF) [9]. The ISO 26262 addresses possible hazards caused by malfunctioning behavior of electrical/electronic safety-related systems whereas SOTIF

A. Romanovsky et al. (Eds.): SAFECOMP 2019, LNCS 11698, pp. 235–244, 2019.
https://doi.org/10.1007/978-3-030-26601-1_16

addresses possible hazards caused by the intended functionality of the product function or by reasonably foreseeable misuse by the user. Intended functionality means that the product function is operating as specified including limits of nominal performance. Both standards have been defined without explicitly considering specifics of DL algorithms such data set collection and requirements on that, defining safety-related evaluation metrics, handling uncertainty etc. As a result, this leads to a challenging issue today for car manufacturers and suppliers who are determined to incorporate DL for automated driving.

In this paper, we (1) identify the safety challenges (with no claim to be exhaustive) for achieving safety of DNN along the complete development pipeline of DNNs, (2) propose potential solutions based on the state of the art w.r.t. those challenges, and (3) show first experimental results of DNN performing object detection. We target a pragmatic approach that focuses on producing safety artifacts along the development chain of DNNs. This paper does not provide a ready-made solution, but proposes potential solutions that can be used as a starting guidance.

The paper builds upon on [5] and is structured as follows: Sect. 2 provides brief background information on deep neural networks. Section 3 presents concrete safety-related challenges along the development chain of DNNs, proposes potential solutions and shows first experimental results. Section 4 summarizes and concludes this paper.

2   Deep Neural Network Background

Artificial Neural Networks (ANNs) are algorithms that mimic the biological structure of the brain. The basic structure of an ANN is a "neuron" and "neurons" have discrete layers and connections to other "neurons". Each neuron calculates a weighted sum of its inputs and applies a nonlinear activation function on this sum. Neurons are grouped in layers, which share a common set of inputs and outputs and each layer of the network learns a specific feature e.g., curves or edges in image recognition. Deep neural networks are created when multiple layers are used instead of one. In the case of a 2D/3D object detection perception task, the input of the networks are commonly images, lidar point clouds or radar detections. The outputs of an object detection DNN are commonly rectangles (called bounding boxes) that contain the objects and a label of the objects class (e.g., car, pedestrian) and its attributes.

There are four major building blocks in the development pipeline of deep learning networks: (1) functionality definition, (2) data set specification, selection and preparation, (3) development and evaluation, and (4) deployment and monitoring. Along that pipeline, DNN specific artifacts are generated in addition to the ones that are generated during traditional rule/model-based development.

Functionality definition deals with the specification of requirements w.r.t. different DNN aspects like: definition of operational design domain (ODD), definition of data set attributes which are important for the DNN task, diverse safety requirements which are interpreted with DNN specific measurable KPIs (e.g. robustness w.r.t. sensor failures or synchronization of sensors, etc.). Data specification, selection and preparation focuses on specifying the data set requirements and collecting data for training and evaluation of neural networks. This includes topics such as completeness of data set, labelling specification, labelling quality etc. In the development and evaluation phase, the DNN network architecture and the SW architecture including the DNN is developed, and the DNN training and evaluation is performed. During training the weights of the DNN are determined. This is done by minimizing the loss function of the network over a given set of training data and back-propagating the respective error terms through the network. After training the performance of the trained network is evaluated on an "unseen" test set. At the end a trained model is pruned and optimized for a deployment on specific target hardware. In the inference phase the deployed DNN performs predictions on new data at runtime, e.g. detects object in an autonomous vehicle.

Below we give an overview of the safety-related challenges in each step of the development pipeline of DNN and provide potential safety engineering solutions.

3 Safety Engineering Along the Development Pipeline of DNN

3.1 Functionality Definition

When developing particular functionality, usually diverse requirements are defined: functionality requirements, inputs & outputs of the function, software safety requirements, memory and time constraints etc. However, when using a DNN to realize particular functionality, additional aspects need to be defined. Some examples include: definition of operational design domain (ODD), definition of data set and labeling attributes that are required for the DNN task, diverse safety requirements which are interpreted with measurable KPIs (e.g. robustness w.r.t. sensor failures, synchronization of sensors or adversarial attacks, performance w.r.t. safety goals, generalizability of the DNN to unseen data within the ODD) etc. All these requirements need to be addressed in the subsequent steps in the DNN development pipeline.

3.2 Data Set Specification, Selection and Preparation

A DNN in general is only able to do what it has been taught i.e. trained for. In other words, if a training data set only contains labelled cars, a deep neural network trained on that set would not be able to recognize pedestrians. Since the variance of traffic scenes, situations and scenarios [15] in the real world is near to infinity, it is impossible to ensure a complete coverage of all scenes through a single data set, regardless of its size. Thus, two questions arise: (1) how to specify, select and collect the complete data set to be labelled such that all needed scenarios including corner cases (e.g. crossings, traffic accidents, broken infrastructure) are covered and the trained model achieves its maximum possible performance and generalization ability for its intended usage; (2) how much data is required. In addition to the challenge of defining the diversity and the amount of data, it is also important that the data have the same distribution as the ODD. Furthermore, the data set should include a measure of negative data for the purpose of allowing the DL module to reduce false alarms.

The answer to the questions above is challenging task and one idea is to use the situation analysis of the Hazard Identification and Risk Assessment (HARA) of

ISO 26262 as possible input for identifying the requirements for the collection of relevant data. The goal of the situation analysis and hazard identification is to identify the potential unintended behaviours of the item (e.g. the automated driving function) that could lead to a hazardous event. Parameters that are considered for the situation analysis and hazard identification include specific vehicle usage scenarios (e.g. high-speed driving, urban driving, parking), environmental conditions etc. A structured and systematic approach defining the parameters for describing a scene, situation and scenario is offered by the Pegasus project[1]. Concerning the amount of data required per scene or situation, a metric derived from the defined operation time and the exposure (E) parameters of each hazardous situation in the HARA can be used. The metric can be also relativized w.r.t. the severity (S) assigned to the specific hazard.

In general, a minimal set of quality metrics is required. Those are important for quantifying the sufficiency of the data set. Such metrics might include: coverage, relevance w.r.t. safety goals and requirements, equivalence classes (negative/positive) etc.

Scenes and scenarios that are needed for training but rarely happen during a recording in the real world could be compensated through generation and usage of synthetic (Fig. 1) and augmented data. These include, but are not limited to, corner case traffic scenes, hazardous weather conditions (e.g. sunset, dusk, heavy rain, fog), traffic rule violations (e.g. wrong-way driving, red light running), animal hazards. There are on-going projects [1] focusing on generating synthetic sets for autonomous driving. However, this raises another question i.e. the quality and influence of synthetic data on the DNN. Poibrenski et al. [13] introduced a methodology for training with synthetic data. By using a set of well-designed and bounded experiments, a better judgment of the "behaviour" of synthetic data is performed.

Fig. 1. Synthetic image data: (left) dusk in on a rainy day; (right) child on a skateboard crossing on a red light. (Color figure online)

In addition, an expert should carefully define the labeling specification for the data set to ensure that the labeling characteristics are defined sufficiently and can efficiently relate to the target functionality. Moreover, a quality control processes should be in place to ensure that the data is properly labeled and errors caused by the labeling process

---

[1] https://www.pegasusprojekt.de/en/

is minimized. Typical labeling errors in the case of an object detection would be: wrong classification of objects, overseen objects, bounding boxes of wrong size, etc.

The data set should be continuously improved as new scenes or scenarios are discovered, reducing the unknown space. A method to detect missing data in the data set is via measuring epistemic uncertainty. Epistemic uncertainty captures model's lack of knowledge and indicates the limitation of the detection model due to lack of training data. High epistemic uncertainty points to a trained DNN that is more likely to make inaccurate predictions and when this occurs in safety critical applications, the model should not be trusted. An approach for calculating epistemic uncertainty has been proposed by Gal [6]. Gal showed that by performing the network forward passes several times with dropout during the test time for single data sample, one can calculate the model's posterior distribution, and thus obtain the epistemic uncertainty. High epistemic uncertainty for a sample, indicates that further data has to be collected (see Fig. 2 for example result of an object detection uncertainty experiment performed).

Fig. 2. 2D object detection uncertainty experiment. Image sample taken from the VOC2007 [18] test set. Only top 2 classification uncertainties shown here. The construction pylon that does not exist in the training data set is misclassified and shows high uncertainty. The car shows also a high uncertainty which may be due to the color contrast in the image. (Legend: classification uncertainty - green, misclassification rate - blue, object detections from non-altered model – red) (Color figure online)

3.3   Development and Evaluation

DNN Development. Having defined the functionality of the DNN by means of: (1) the specific functional and non-functional DNN KPIs to be reached (Sect. 3.1) and (2) the data set (Sect. 3.2), the DNN network architecture and the SW architecture including the DNN has to be developed and the DNN has to be trained and evaluated.

Multi-modal DNN architectures [2, 11] for object detection have been introduced in order to achieve more reliable and robust performance. These DNN architectures fuse intermediate layer features coming from different sensor modalities like multiple cameras, radars and LIDARs. The goal of multi-modal learning is to achieve higher reliability and robustness using the redundant information provided by multi-modal data. To deal with degraded data or failures of different sensor inputs, Kim et al. [10] introduce novel multi-modal fusion architecture. They propose an architecture where a feature-level gated information fusion (GIF) network is introduced. The GIF network combines the features of each modality such that only information relevant to the task is aggregated and it controls the amount of information flow incoming through gating mechanism.

Robustness against degraded data quality or complete failures of sensors can also be learned i.e. by training with a data set containing various types of degraded examples, hoping that the architecture learns to use only reliable features for multi-modal fusion. Degraded examples can be either collected from real situations or created by using special data augmentation e.g. corrupting the data by blanking, noise addition, occlusions, severe change in lighting. For example, Zachary et al. [16] apply several simple image mutations to test the robustness of different person detection DNNs. The mutations include: (1) procedural perturbations like blurring and randomized changes like additive noise, or removing image data, (2) "contextual mutators" that make use of environment geometry information to perform depth-based simulation of haze and defocus effects and compare these to the simple mutations. Despite testing DNNs w.r.t. defined mutators, as mentioned earlier one could train DNNs to learn to deal with such data. Zendel et al. [17] provide list of mutators to which a vision system is potentially exposed.

The software architecture incorporating a DNN should be able to handle or mitigate an unexpected behavior of the DNN. For instance, plausibilization methods can check the DNN model output for consistency (e.g. checking for implausible positions or sizes of the detected 3D objects). Another idea is to use the monitor/actuator architecture pattern [12]. When applying this pattern, it is practicable to define rule-based algorithms that guard the system against erroneous behavior of the DNN. In this case, the "actuator" DL based module performs the primary functions and a paired "monitor" module performs an acceptance test or other behavioral validation. If the actuator misbehaves, the monitor (non-DL based algorithm) shuts the entire function down in a safe state, resulting in a fail-safe system. The monitor module must be simpler and more transparent than the DL based function so that there can be confidence in its correctness as the safety of the system depends on the monitor.

The DNN development phase covers also the training of the network. In the training phase, the weights of the network are determined. This is done by minimizing the loss function of the network over a given set of training data and back-propagating the respective error terms through the network via the corresponding gradient (e.g. stochastic gradient descent). The choice of the loss function could have impact on the performance of the resulting network and thus restrictions in the choice of possible loss functions may need to be specified. It is important to note that the safety requirements (e.g. criticality of particular error types, etc.) are not necessarily being taken into account when designing the loss function, and so the trained model should be tested against those safety requirements. Possible solutions to ensure safe functioning could be the insertion of measurable safety requirements into the loss function e.g. by using additional terms in the loss function to compensate for safety related fitting goals [6]. Other hyperparameters like types of layers, regularization terms, learning rate etc. are also specified during training. The choices of the hyperparameters and the reasonable behind it need to be tracked, as they have impact on the resulting functional and non-functional properties of the DNN.

DNN Evaluation. The quality of the DNN is indicated by its KPI performance evaluation on an "unseen" test data set. The performance is usually measured by means such as intersection over union, mean average precision (mAP) [14], false positive/ negative rate, etc. By evaluating a variety of different DNN architectures and models, w.r.t. relevant KPIs defined in the first step (i.e. functionality definition) a system designer can choose the best DNN for the task. If the defined KPI performance cannot be reached, the training and potentially the model and the data set should be adapted. This is possible via e.g. expanding the data set, changing the network architecture, changing the model via the network hyper parameters (layer type, learning rate, batch normalization, regularization, etc.). Given the nature of DL, the primary method is the extension of the training data set while respecting the relevant statistical distributions.

An experimental evaluation of the robustness of an 3D object detection network w.r.t. modality failures is shown in Table 1.

Table 1. Sensor failure evaluation for easy, medium, hard difficulty classes of 3D multi-modal object detection (excerpt from the experiment results): mAP drops when the camera has a failure.

Object detection mAP	Easy[a]	Medium	Hard
All sensors error free	89.99	87.92	80.09
Camera failure	89.38	79.40	78.83

[a]Difficulty classes - easy, medium, hard. Example easy definition - minimum bounding box height 30 image pixels, no occlusion i.e. fully visible, maximal object truncation of 15%.

100% mAP is not always possible and, in a safety-related application, not all failures have the same impact. An example is a speed limit classification task where misclassifying a speed limit of e.g. 30 km/h as 50 km/h may not have a negative safety impact. Hence, instead of measuring a single mAP and its included false/true positives and false negatives, the evaluation of the network could be adapted to application-specific metrics depending on the safety requirements. Ideas of useful object detection mAP are: (1) Environment mAP – mAP can be measured depending on certain environment conditions e.g. day/dusk/night, rainy/sunny. These metrics are useful, when the DL based application is used under specific environmental conditions. The item definition of ISO 26262 or the system description of SOTIF can be used for defining the relevant environment mAP.; (2) Distance mAP - mAP can be measured depending on the distance of other objects to be detected (Fig. 3 for distance mAP experiments performed of 3D object detection). One can imagine that from a safety perspective a higher mAP may be required for objects closer to the ego-vehicle (i.e. "our" car); (3) Perspective mAP - mAP can be measured depending on the function requirements and field of view of the sensors. For example, separate mAP can be measured for the different areas of the ego vehicle i.e. front, back and side since in those areas different sensors are used.

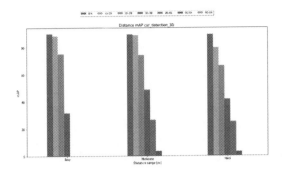

Fig. 3. Distance mAP for easy, medium, hard difficulty classes of 3D multi-modal object detection: mAP decreases as the distance between ego vehicle object and other objects increases.

Moreover, traceability between the KPIs and the data samples may be useful to identify the scenes or scenarios that the DNN cannot handle well enough.

3.4 Deployment and Monitoring

In the inference phase the deployed DNN is used to perform predictions on new data samples at runtime, e.g. to detect objects. An important aspect here is to be able to monitor and detect unseen situations and deal with unseen critical situation. This means an online monitor is required for detecting unseen situations i.e. distributional shift (ODD). One approach to detect those situations is by measuring the epistemic uncertainty as already stated above. However, timing might be an issue since the same sample has to be passed through the network forward path several times. Another solution is proposed by Cheng et al. [3]. Neuron activation patterns monitor is generated by feeding the training data to the network and storing the neuron activation patterns in an abstract form. At inference, a classification decision over an input sample is provided by examining if the activation pattern (measured by Hamming distance) is similar to one of the patterns obtained for the training set. If the monitor does not contain any similar pattern, it raises a warning that the decision is not based on the training data. Since the proposed solution uses only activation pattern of the neurons in the last layer, the applicability of the approach for complex DNN architectures is to be investigated. Runtime monitoring may result in certain measures to ensure the ongoing safety of the deployed system. Possible measures may include: development of a new safety mechanism or improving an existing safety mechanism, updating the ODD etc.

3.5 Safety Artefacts

Artefacts generated in all DNN development steps (Sects. 3.1, 3.2, 3.3 and 3.4) play a central role when building the safety argument for the safety case. When developing DNN one has to re-consider which other artefacts are needed apart from the ones that are generated during traditional rule-based development. To do so, one could consider the complete DNN development pipeline. Along that pipeline, one could identify the following artifacts w.r.t. functionality definition: DNN requirements specification

(specification of ODD, technical safety requirements etc.), KPI specification, etc. Regarding the data set possible safety artefact may include: data set KPIs, data set splitting specification, labeling specification, labeling quality report, etc. In the third step one should consider artefact like e.g. network graphs, hyper parameters of training, (trained) weight values, test & validation KPI evaluation reports, etc. During the deployment and monitoring safety artefacts like distributional shift (ODD) monitoring reports can be considered.

4 Summary and Further Work

DL algorithms are powerful and their attractiveness is gradually driving their adoption to complex tasks. Until now, most of the DNN research focused on improvements in capability and performance. However, when executing safety-related tasks, a malfunction of a DNN can lead to a system failure. The paper provided an overview of safety challenges along the DNN development pipeline, offered solution ideas, and discussed state of the art solutions. We expect the paper to awaken the interest of our industry and research peers in engineering safety for DNN and machine learning in general. In future, we expect to devote ourselves to developing a common problem understanding and solution together with our partners.

References

1. Abu Alhaija, H., et al.: Augmented Reality Meets Computer Vision: Efficient Data Generation for Urban Driving Scenes. arXiv preprint: arXiv:1708.01566 (2017)
2. Chen, X., et al.: Multi-view 3D object detection network for autonomous driving. In: IEEE Conference on Computer Vision and Pattern Recognition (2017)
3. Cheng, C., et al.: Runtime Monitoring Neuron Activation Patterns (2018)
4. Eifel, A., et al.: Multimodal deep learning for robust RGB-D object recognition. In: IEEE International Conference on Intelligent Robots and Systems (2015)
5. Frtunikj, J., Fuerst, S.: Engineering safe machine learning for automated driving systems. In: Safety-Critical Systems Symposium 2019 (2019)
6. Gal, Y.: Uncertainty in deep learning, Ph.D. dissertation, University of Cambridge (2016)
7. Girshick, R.: Fast R-CNN. In: IEEE International Conference on Computer Vision (2015)
8. ISO 26262 Road vehicles: Functional Safety (2018)
9. ISO/PRF PAS 21448 Road vehicles: Safety of the intended functionality (2018)
10. Kim, J., et al.: Robust deep multi-modal learning based on gated information fusion network. In: Computer Vision and Pattern Recognition (2018)
11. Ku, J., et al.: Joint 3D Proposal Generation and Object Detection from View Aggregation. arXiv preprint: arXiv:1712.02294 (2017)
12. Koopman, P., Wagner, M.: Challenges in autonomous vehicle testing and validation. SAE Int. J. Transp. Saf. 4(1), 15–24 (2016)
13. Poibrenski, A., Sprenger, J., Müller, C.: Towards a methodology for training with synthetic data on the example of pedestrian detection in a frame-by-frame semantic segmentation task. In: First Workshop on Software Engineering for AI in Autonomous Systems (2018)
14. Tang, S., Yuan, Y.: Object Detection based on Convolutional Neural Network (2015)

15. Ulbrich, S., Menzel, T., Reschka, A., et al.: Defining and substantiating the terms scene, situation, and scenario for automated driving. In: IEEE 18th International Conference on Intelligent Transportation Systems (2015)
16. Zachary, P., et al.: Putting Image Manipulations in Context: Robustness Testing for Safe Perception (2018)
17. Zendel, O., et al.: How good is my test data? introducing safety analysis for computer vision. Int. J. Comput. Vis. **125**(1–3), 95–109 (2017)
18. Everingham, M., et al.: The PASCAL Visual Object Classes Challenge 2007 Results (2007)

Autonomous Vehicles Meet the Physical World: RSS, Variability, Uncertainty, and Proving Safety

Philip Koopman[1,2](✉), Beth Osyk[1,2], and Jack Weast[1,2]

[1] Edge Case Research, Pittsburgh, PA, USA
koopman@cmu.edu, bosyk@ecr.guru, jack.weast@intel.com
[2] Intel, Chandler, AZ, USA

Abstract. The Responsibility-Sensitive Safety (RSS) model offers provable safety for vehicle behaviors such as minimum safe following distance. However, handling worst-case variability and uncertainty may significantly lower vehicle permissiveness, and in some situations safety cannot be guaranteed. Digging deeper into Newtonian mechanics, we identify complications that result from considering vehicle status, road geometry and environmental parameters. An especially challenging situation occurs if these parameters change during the course of a collision avoidance maneuver such as hard braking. As part of our analysis, we expand the original RSS following distance equation to account for edge cases involving potential collisions mid-way through a braking process.

Keywords: Autonomous vehicle safety · RSS · Operational design domain

1 Introduction

The Responsibility-Sensitive Safety (RSS) model proposes a way to prove the safety of self-driving vehicles [12]. The RSS approach is currently deployed in Intel/Mobileye's test fleet of fully automated vehicles. Application areas of RSS include both fully autonomous vehicles and driver assistance systems. This paper reports results of an ongoing joint project to externally validate and further improve RSS.

A salient feature of RSS is the use of Newtonian mechanics to specify behavioral constraints such as determining safe following distance to avoid collisions even when other vehicles make extreme maneuvers such as hard braking. Employing RSS as safety checking logic requires not only knowledge of the physics of the situation, but also correct measurements to feed into the RSS equations.

We consider an example of applying RSS rules to a longitudinal following distance scenario involving the vehicle under consideration (often called the *ego vehicle*) as a follower behind a lead vehicle. To put RSS into practice, the ego vehicle requires at least some knowledge of the physical parameters fed into the physics equations, including ego vehicle and lead vehicle status, road geometry, and operational environment. However, proving guaranteed safety via that approach is complicated by variability and uncertainty.

A. Romanovsky et al. (Eds.): SAFECOMP 2019, LNCS 11698, pp. 245–253, 2019.
https://doi.org/10.1007/978-3-030-26601-1_17

This paper identifies the implications for these issues in applying RSS to real vehicles. Additionally, it proposes a new following distance equation to encompass edge cases that were out of scope for the original RSS analysis.

A significant finding is that variability and uncertainty in the operational conditions introduce significant challenges for ensuring safety while maintaining acceptable permissiveness. (The permissiveness of a system is how free it is to operate without violating safety constraints [6].) Variability is especially problematic because of the large potential dynamic range of driving conditions [9]. For example, the difference between safe following distance on an icy hill compared to flat dry pavement means that a one-size-fits-all worst case approach to safe following distance is unlikely to result in a vehicle people will actually want to use. This paper seeks to identify the issues that must be resolved to use the RSS equations in a way that provides provable safety to the maximum degree practicable. Designing approaches that can use this foundation to address the challenges of variability and uncertainty is left as future work.

2 Related Work

Advanced Driver Assistance Systems (ADAS) have made large strides in improving automotive safety, especially in mitigating the risk of rear end collisions. Autonomous Emergency Braking (AEB) can now fully stop a vehicle in many lower-speed situations [1]. Beyond AEB, vehicles may offer driver assistance technologies including a safe distance warning [1]. Technologies have differing availability depending on speed and manufacturer [7]. Test protocols generally select a few speed combinations representative of urban and highway driving [7] in controlled conditions. Moreover, it is typical for current ADAS systems to used fixed rules of thumb (e.g., the two-second following rule as used by [5]) for establishing operational safety envelopes that while potentially improving safety on average can either be to conservative or too optimistic. This paper takes a broader approach that considers the specifics of the vehicles involved and environmental conditions. We are not aware of other work that considers expanding physics-based safety analysis such as RSS to consider environmental conditions and vehicle performance characteristics.

Work on characterizing and dealing with perception uncertainty in the context of safety critical systems is still developing. [3] provides a model of factors that influence development and operational uncertainty.

Safe state analysis is a theme for autonomous vehicle path planning. Path planning algorithms may consider the safety of the current state and reachable states in order to plan a path, including making predictions about potentially occluded obstacles [10]. Such approaches tend to suffer from probabilistic limitations on their ability to provide deterministic safety, whereas the RSS approach to safety aspires to provide a deterministic model for safety.

We base our analysis on an initial RSS paper [12], and are aware of a follow up paper [13]. Interest in the performance aspect of RSS continues to grow, with a model and analysis of traffic throughput presented in [Mattas19] comparing RSS to human drivers under various values for the RSS parameters. We are not aware of other published analyses of RSS equations for correctness and completeness.

3   RSS Overview

3.1   The RSS Following Distance Equation

In an RSS leader/follower scenario, the follower vehicle is presumed to be responsible for ensuring a safe longitudinal distance, so we assume that the ego vehicle is the follower. For this situation, RSS uses a safety principle of: "keep a safe distance from the car in front of you, so that if it will brake abruptly you will be able to stop in time." [12] Fig. 1 shows a notional vehicle geometry:

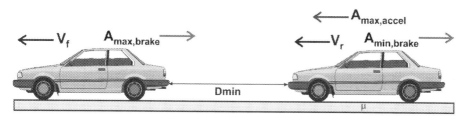

Fig. 1. Reference vehicle geometry for leader/follower.

This yields a minimum following distance (id., Lemma 2):

$$d'_{min} = MAX\left\{0, \left(v_r\rho + \frac{1}{2}a_{max,accel}\rho^2 + \frac{\left(v_r + \rho a_{max,accel}\right)^2}{2a_{min,brake}} - \frac{v_f^2}{2a_{max,brake}}\right)\right\} \quad (1)$$

Where in our case the ego vehicle is the following ("rear") vehicle, and:

- d'_{min} is the minimum following distance between the two vehicles for RSS
- v_f is the longitudinal velocity of the lead ("front") vehicle
- v_r is the longitudinal velocity of the following ("rear") vehicle
- ρ is the response time delay before the ego (rear) vehicle starts braking
- $a_{max,brake}$ is the maximum braking capability of the front vehicle
- $a_{max,accel}$ is the maximum acceleration of the ego (rear) vehicle
- $a_{min,brake}$ is the minimum braking capability of the ego (rear) vehicle

The d'_{min} equation considers a leading vehicle, going at initial speed v_f, which executes a panic stop at maximum possible braking force $a_{max,brake}$. The ego following vehicle traveling at v_r is initially no closer than distance d'_{min}. In the worst case, the ego vehicle is accelerating at $a_{max,accel}$ when the lead vehicle starts braking. There is a response time ρ during which the ego vehicle is still accelerating. Then the ego vehicle detects the lead vehicle braking and reacts by panic braking with deceleration of at least $a_{min,brake}$. RSS considers the worst case scenario to be a highly capable lead vehicle with high $a_{max,brake}$ followed by an ego vehicle that brakes at an initially lower braking capability of at least $a_{min,brake}$. A poorly braking follower requires additional distance to accommodate its inability to stop quickly.

While a derivation based on comparative stopping distances confirmed the equation, analysis using Ptolemy II [11] revealed edge cases beyond the scope of the analysis in [12]. (Additional RSS braking profile information is provided by [13].) Specifically, Eq. 1 does not detect situations in which the two vehicle positions overlap in space during – but not at the end of – the braking response scenario.

As a thought experiment, consider an ego vehicle with good brakes that has matched speeds with a leader of significantly worse braking ability. Equation 1 is derived assuming the minimum vehicle separation occurs at the final rest positions. If the rear vehicle has superior braking, it could mathematically be "ahead" of the lead vehicle at some time during braking, yet still have a final rest position "behind" the lead vehicle due to shorter stopping distance. In reality, this is a crash. Thus, an additional constraint is that the rear vehicle must remain behind the lead vehicle at all points in time.

A related scenario is a rear vehicle approaching with high relative velocity and superior braking. The rear vehicle might collide during the interval in which both vehicles are braking, while still having a computed stopping point behind the lead vehicle.

To address these situations, we break the analysis up into two parts based on the situation at the time of a collision if following distance is violated: (1) impact during response time ρ and (2) impact after ρ but before or simultaneous with the rear vehicle stopping. (Impact is no longer possible after the rear vehicle stops for this scenario.)

Accounting for situation (1) requires computing the distance change during the response time ρ. There are two cases. The first is when the front vehicle stops before ρ, and the second is when the front vehicle stops at or after ρ.

Situation (2) has two parts. First, compute the distance change during ρ:

$$d''_{min} = (v_r - v_f)\rho + \frac{(a_{max,accel} + a_{max,brake})\rho^2}{2} \tag{2}$$

Next, solve for the distance between the two vehicles after ρ as a function of time:

$$d'''_{min} = (v_r + a_{max,accel}\rho)t_r - \frac{a_{min,brake}t_r^2}{2} - \left((v_f - a_{max,brake}\rho)t_f - \frac{a_{max,brake}t_f^2}{2} \right) \tag{3}$$

This is a parametric equation involving the time after the response time for both vehicles: t_r ant t_f. The minimum distance will occur at time $t_r = t_f = t$ when both vehicles have equal speed (with the value of t then substituted into Eq. 3 for evaluation):

$$t = \frac{(v_{r0} - v_{f0}) + (a_{max,accel} + a_{max,brake})\rho}{(a_{min,brake} - a_{max,brake})} \tag{4}$$

The special case minimum following distance is the sum of d'_{min} and d''_{min}, and only holds when the rear vehicle is faster than the front vehicle at the end of the response time *and* the rear vehicle can brake better than the front vehicle:

$$d_{min} = \begin{cases} MAX\left[d'_{min},\ \left(d''_{min} + d'''_{min}\right)\right]; special\ case \\ d'_{min} \qquad\qquad\quad ; otherwise(Original\ RSS) \end{cases} \tag{5}$$

Because $a_{max,accel}$ is likely to be of secondary importance for small ρ, we focus the balance of our discussion on braking. However, similar issues apply to acceleration.

3.2   Coefficient of Friction

Implicit in the RSS equations is that the maximum frictional force exerted by the vehicle on the ground limits braking ability ([14] pg. 119):

$$F_{friction} = \mu * F_{normal} \tag{6}$$

where:

- $F_{friction}$ is the force of friction exerted by the tires against the roadway
- μ is the coefficient of friction, which can vary for each tire
- F_{normal} is the force with which the vehicle presses itself onto the road surface

The friction coefficient is a property of both the tires and the road surface. It is important to note that μ can be above 1.0 for some materials ([14] pg. 119), so a rigorous proof cannot assume limited μ without placing constraints upon installed tires.

3.3   The Normal Force and Road Slope

The normal force on each tire is a property of the vehicle weight, weight distribution, the effects of suspension, the slope of the road, and so on. The normal force is the weight of the vehicle multiplied by the cosine of the road slope, shown by Fig. 2:

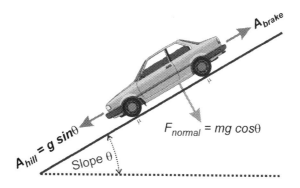

Fig. 2. Vehicle forces on an inclined roadway.

In this situation, braking ability is potentially limited by the reduced normal force. Moreover, gravity is pulling the vehicle down the hill, acting against and further reducing the net braking force ([14] pg. 102). If μ is low, the net force can result in the vehicle sliding down the hill (either forwards or backwards) if the brakes cannot overcome the gravitational downhill force vector. Transverse road slope (camber) can similarly reduce F_{normal}, but at least does not affect vehicle speed directly.

3.4 Road Curvature

An additional limitation to braking capability is that the centripetal force exerted by a vehicle to make turns must be provided by $F_{friction}$ ([14] pg. 128). The net vehicle acceleration (both radial and linear) is a result of a force vector applied by the tire contact patches to the road surface. It follows that any force used to curve the vehicle trajectory steals available force from the ability to stop the vehicle by requiring a force vector that is at off-axis from the vehicle's direction of travel. That means that if the ego vehicle is in a tight turn it will have trouble braking effectively. Lane positioning and racing line techniques [8] add additional complexity.

A banked curve complicates analysis even further, involving potential increases or decreases to F_{normal} depending upon whether the bank (superelevation) is tilted toward or away from the center of the curve.

4 Uncertainty and Variability

While Newtonian Mechanics provides us the tools to determine following distance in principle, even a simplified equation setup for a vehicle's maximum stopping distance on a downhill corkscrew turn is worthy of a college Physics final exam. But in the real world we don't actually know the precise values of all the variables in the equations.

An important issue with proving safety in a cyber-physical system is that there is inherent uncertainty in sensor measurements. That uncertainty includes both issues of accuracy (how close the measurement is to the actual value being measured) and precision (what the distribution of errors in the measurement is across multiple measurements). Uncertainty can additionally be characterized as aleatory uncertainty (e.g., sensor noise that causes non-zero precision), and epistemic uncertainty (e.g., inaccurate measurements and incorrect modeling of the environment) [2]. Both types of uncertainty impair the ability to formally prove safety for a real-world system.

The mere existence of a probability distribution for aleatory uncertainty impairs the ability to create a perfect proof. In principle any series of data points might, with some probability, be wildly inaccurate. Data filtering and statistical techniques might improve the situation, but in the end there is always some non-zero (if infinitesimal) probability that a string of outlier data samples will cause a mishap. Over-sampling to drive that uncertainty below life-critical confidence thresholds (e.g., failure rate of 10^{-9}/hr) could be impracticable due to the fast time constants required for vehicle control.

For epistemic uncertainty, a significant problem is providing a completely accurate model of the environment and the vehicle. Moreover, even if limitations on sensors and potential correlated sensor failures are mitigated through the use of high-definition maps, variability of operational environments is a significant issue.

Uncertainty cannot be completely eliminated in the real world, so the question is how to account for it within the RSS model while keeping the system practical and affordable. In support of that, we consider sources of uncertainty and variability.

4.1 Other Vehicle Parameters

Ensuring that the ego vehicle avoids colliding with other vehicles requires understanding the state of those other vehicles. Knowing where they are and where they are going requires other vehicle pose and kinematic information: {position, orientation, speed, acceleration, curvature} in addition to a prediction of how that information is going to change in the near future (e.g., path plan). That information will be imperfect.

In the absence of perfect information, RSS simply assumes that distance is known and that the lead vehicle will immediately execute a panic braking maneuver at $a_{max,brake}$. While in an ideal world all vehicles have a predetermined and consistent $a_{max,brake}$, in the current world not all vehicles are thus equipped. However, even if new vehicles are standardized, braking capability can increase further due to factors such as after-market brake upgrades, after-market tire upgrades, low tire pressure, after-market aerodynamic modifications, and even driver leg strength. While a vehicle might be equipped with a feature that intentionally limits maximum deceleration, too strict a limit would extend stopping distance and increase collision rates in other situations such as single car crashes.

If the ego vehicle wants to optimize following distance based on the actual lead vehicle capabilities, it will need a way to determine what those are. Most vehicles are not designed to brake above 1 g, but it is likely this limit is not universal on public roads.

4.2 Ego Vehicle Parameters

While knowing the exact state of the lead vehicle is difficult, it is also important to appreciate that knowing the state of the ego vehicle is also difficult. Many of the parameters that affect the lead vehicle also affect the ego vehicle, although the concern in this case is more about unexpectedly reduced braking ability. Some factors that might reduce braking capability below expectations include:

- Transient equipment degradation: brake fade due to overheating, brake wetness (e.g., due to puddle splash), cold tire temperature, etc.
- Equipment condition: brake wear, brake actuator damage, low tire tread depth, high tire pressure, etc.
- System interactions: interactions between braking system and electronic stability control, effect of anti-lock braking features, etc.

4.3 Environmental Parameters

Successfully executing an aggressive braking maneuver involves not only the vehicle, but also the environment. While environmental conditions in a road segment might be reasonably well known via a local weather service (which becomes safety critical as soon as it is relied upon for this purpose), average values might differ substantially from the instantaneous environmental conditions relevant to a braking maneuver. After all, it is not the average road conditions over a kilometer of road that matter, but rather the specific road conditions that apply to paths of the set of tire contact patches of each vehicle during the course of a panic stop maneuver. Relevant factors that could result in a faster-than-expected lead vehicle braking maneuver combined with a slower-than-expected ego vehicle braking maneuver due to differences on the roadway include:

- Road surface friction: road surface, temperature, wetness, iciness, texture (e.g., milled ridges that increase traction; bumps that cause loss of tire contact), etc.
- Road geometry: slope, banking, camber, curvature as previously discussed
- Other conditions: hydroplaning, mudslides, flooding, high winds pushing against a high profile vehicle body, road debris, potholes, road buckling, etc.

While the two vehicles will traverse the same stretch of roadway for some braking time, their contact patches are not necessarily going to follow exactly the same paths. Localized tire track road conditions can result in different stopping ability even if we attempt to measure some average value of μ. Consider, for example, a lead vehicle that brakes hard in snowy weather on a cleared tire path while the following ego vehicle gets caught slightly laterally displaced from the tracks with its tires on ice.

4.4   Potential Assumption-Violating Actions

Even if we know the values for all the variables, there are assumptions made by the RSS longitudinal safety guarantees and stated scope limitations that might be violated by real world situations. Examples include:

- Lead vehicle does not violate the assumed maximum braking deceleration limit (e.g., due to impact with a large boulder that suddenly falls onto the road).
- Roadway μ does not unexpectedly change (e.g., flash ice-over).
- Ego vehicle does not fall below minimum expected braking capability (e.g., due to brake fade, puddle splashes onto brake rotor).
- There are no significant equipment failures (e.g., catastrophic brake failure of ego vehicle during a panic braking event).
- There are no unusual vehicle maneuvers (e.g., cut-in scenarios in which a vehicle suddenly appears too close; cut-out scenarios in which the lead vehicle swerves to reveal a much slower, too-close new lead vehicle [4]).

5   Conclusion

An examination of RSS has validated the following distance equation for common situations and augmented that formula to handle a class of edge cases for potential collisions that can happen during a braking event. A significant potential impediment to practical adoption of RSS is providing sufficient permissiveness while ensuring safety in extreme conditions such as icy roads and encountering clusters of outlier sensor data.

To arrive at a practicable balance between safety and permissiveness, further engagement with government and industry standards organizations is recommended.

Acknowledgment. This research was supported by Intel.

References

1. ADAC Vehicle Testing, Comparative Test of Advanced Emergency Braking Systems (2013)
2. Chen, D., Östberg, K., Becker, M., Sivencrona, H., Warg, F.: Design of a knowledge-base strategy for capability-aware treatment of uncertainties of automated driving systems. In: Gallina, B., Skavhaug, A., Schoitsch, E., Bitsch, F. (eds.) SAFECOMP 2018. LNCS, vol. 11094, pp. 446–457. Springer, Cham (2018). https://doi.org/10.1007/978-3-319-99229-7_38
3. Czarnecki, K., Salay, R.: Towards a framework to manage perceptual uncertainty for safe automated driving. In: Gallina, B., Skavhaug, A., Schoitsch, E., Bitsch, F. (eds.) SAFECOMP 2018. LNCS, vol. 11094, pp. 439–445. Springer, Cham (2018). https://doi.org/10.1007/978-3-319-99229-7_37
4. European New Car Assessment Programme (Euro NCAP), "Test Protocol – AEB Systems", Version 2.0, March 2017
5. Fairclough, S., May, A., Carter, C.: The effect of time headway feedback on following behaviour. Accid. Anal. Prev. **29**(3), 387–397 (1997)
6. Guiochet, J., Powell, D., Baudin, É., Blanquart, J.-P.: Online safety monitoring using safety modes. In: Workshop on Technical Challenges for Dependable Robots in Human Environments, PASADENA, United States, pp. 1–13, May 2008
7. Hulshof, W., Knight, I., Edwards, A., Avery, M., Grover, C.: Autonomous emergency braking test results. In: Proceedings of the 23rd International Technical Conference on the Enhanced Safety of Vehicles (ESV) (2013)
8. Kapania, N., Subosits, J., Gerdes, J.C.: A sequential two-step algorithm for fast generation of vehicle racing trajectories. J. Dyn. Syst. Meas. Control, V **138**, Paper 091005, September 2016
9. Koopman, P., Fratrik, F.: How many operational design domains, objects, and events? In: SafeAI 2019, AAAI, 27 January 2019
10. Orzechowski, P., Meyer, A., Lauer, M.: Tackling occlusions & limited sensor range with set-based safety verification. In: 2018 21st International Conference on Intelligent Transportation Systems (ITSC), November 2018. https://arxiv.org/abs/1506.06579
11. Ptolemy Project: heterogeneous modeling and design. https://ptolemy.berkeley.edu/ptolemyII/index.htm. Accessed 5 May 2019
12. Shalev-Shwartz, S., Shammah, S., Shashua, A.: On a formal model of safe and scalable self-driving cars. Mobileye 2017. https://arxiv.org/abs/1708.06374. v6 updated 27 Oct 2018
13. Shalev-Shwartz, S., Shammah, S., Shashua, A.: Vision zero: can roadway accidents be eliminated without compromising traffic throughput? In: Mobileye 2018. https://export.arxiv.org/abs/1901.05022
14. Walker: Halliday/Resnick: Fundamentals of Physics, 8th edn., vol. 1. Wiley (2008)

Automated Evidence Analysis of Safety Arguments Using Digital Dependability Identities

Jan Reich[1]([✉]), Marc Zeller[2], and Daniel Schneider[1]

[1] Fraunhofer IESE, Kaiserslautern, Germany
{jan.reich,daniel.schneider}@iese.fraunhofer.de
[2] Siemens AG, Munich, Germany
marc.zeller@siemens.com

Abstract. Creating a sound argumentation of why a system is sufficiently safe is a major part of the assurance process. Today, compiling a safety case and maintaining its validity after changes are time-consuming manual work performed by safety experts based on their experience and knowledge. This work is further complicated when supplier components need to be integrated where important details might not be known. By using the concept provided by *Digital Dependability Identities (DDI)*, we present an approach to automatically check evidence validity for safety requirements through leveraging from formal traceability between safety argument and evidence models being both parts of the DDI. This approach reduces the effort for creating and maintaining the system-level safety argument by (a) performing automated evidence analysis for safety requirements, (b) supporting a model-based multi-tier safety engineering process and (c) eliminating the human error source by relying on DDI scripts to encode safety engineering activities. We illustrate our approach using a case study from the railway domain, which focuses on the safety assurance of a train control system (ETCS).

1 Introduction

The growing complexity of safety-critical systems in many application domains such as the automotive, avionics, or railway poses new challenges for system development. Along with the growing system complexity, also the need for safety assurance and its associated effort is drastically increasing. Safety assurance is a mandatory part in order to pass certification and to satisfy the high-quality demands imposed by the market. Consequently, without safety assurance, market introduction and success of a product is in jeopardy. In different application domains, safety standards such as ISO 26262 [3] in the automotive domain or CENELEC EN 50129 [2] for railway signaling equipment define the safety assurance process. The goal of this process is to identify all failures that cause hazardous situations and to demonstrate that their occurrence probabilities are sufficiently low and that the system's residual risk is thus acceptable. Typical

© Springer Nature Switzerland AG 2019
A. Romanovsky et al. (Eds.): SAFECOMP 2019, LNCS 11698, pp. 254–268, 2019.
https://doi.org/10.1007/978-3-030-26601-1_18

activities in this process are the identification and assessment of hazards, conducting safety analyses (e.g. using FTA) and eventually the creation of a sound safety argument as to why the system is sufficiently safe. The safety argument clearly has a central role as it communicates the relationship between safety requirements and its supporting evidence [5]. The argumentation is often part of a safety case (depending on the domain) and its creation can generally be considered a major task of the overall assurance process.

Compiling a safety case is typically very laborious and, as of today, is purely manual work performed by safety experts based on their experience and knowledge about the applied safety standard and the system under consideration. There is a lack of guidance, general tool-support and, not surprisingly, there is no automation available to support the argumentation and the linking of evidence to create the rationale for why a system is sufficiently safe.

By using the concepts provided by *Digital Dependability Identities (DDIs)* [10], we present an approach to automatically check the sufficiency of evidence for safety requirements by automating parts of the assurance process. Particularly, by means of the presented approach, the effort of compiling a sound safety case is reduced by automating the creation of the safety argumentation about the development process and the product itself. Likewise, the effort for the reassessment of a safety-critical system after performing a modification can be decreased. The presented approach further supports different engineering scenarios in the context of a multi-tier engineering process, i.e. the synthesis of modular safety-related specifications of a component (in form of a DDI) by a supplier as well as semi-automated support for the integration of different DDIs (of supplier components) by an OEM. We illustrate our approach using a case study from the railway domain, which focuses on the safety assurance of a train control system, i.e. the *European Train Control System (ETCS)*, as a running example.

The rest of the paper is organized as follows: In Sect. 2, we introduce the railway case study which is used as a running example. Afterward, we outline the concept of DDIs for safety engineering and show how it is embedded in a distributed development process. In Sect. 4, we present our approach to automate the creation of a safety argumentation about both processes and product. The state-of-the-art is briefly summarized in Sect. 5. Sect. 6 concludes the paper.

2   ETCS Running Example

2.1   ETCS System Description

The *European Train Control System (ETCS)* provides standardized train control in Europe and facilitates cross-border train operation. ETCS consists of onboard and trackside subsystems. Moreover, the ETCS subsystems may be produced by different vendors (suppliers) and must be integrated by a railway operator. Both subsystems must fulfill the safety requirements defined in Subset-091 of the ERTMS/ETCS specification [11]. However, functions such as the emergency brake service consist partly of on-board as well as parts of trackside functionalities. Thus, a proper analysis of the emergency brake function must span over both sub-systems. Consequently, the safety case of an ETCS system needed for certification w.r.t. CENELEC EN 50129 [2] requires the synthesis of a sound safety argument by the system integrator using the information provided by the different subsystem suppliers.

2.2   ETCS Safety Case

This section describes an exemplary safety case related to the ETCS trackside system. The goal of a safety case is to demonstrate in a structured argument with evidence that a system's residual safety risk has been reduced to an acceptable level. In many application domains, there are already standards in place providing a set of processes or concrete safety requirements to be executed and satisfied, depending on the required integrity. Thus, safety standards such as CENELEC EN 50129 provide a basis to structure the high-level safety argument. Figure 1 shows those parts of an exemplary ETCS safety case relevant for the paper, documented in the Goal Structuring Notation (GSN) [6]. The refinement of the top-level Goal G1 is on the one hand driven by adherence to railway safety standards as well as to the ETCS system safety specification. On the other hand, it is driven by the system decomposition into trackside and onboard subsystems, of which the trackside system will be the focus of this paper (see Fig. 1). Thereby, the root safety goal is refined into process and product argument parts.

The process-related requirements typically directly originate from safety standards implying required process execution rigor according to the Safety Integrity Level (SIL). As (at least some) trackside functions are determined highly safety-critical, they have to be developed demonstrating SIL 4 integrity (G2). In Fig. 1, G4, G7, G8 and G9 exemplify such normative requirements, of which the automated validity analysis of G9 will be elaborated in Sect. 4.3.

As rigorous process execution is only an indirect and therefore not definitive measure of safety, it has to be complemented by product-related safety requirements constraining failure rates with respect to system-level hazardous events to an acceptable level (G3 in Fig. 1). The acceptable failure rate thresholds for the hazards of the ETCS system are defined in the ETCS specification Subset-091 [11].

It is important to note that different parts of the safety case are created and assessed by different stakeholders. While the overall system part of the safety argument is the responsibility of the ETCS system integrator, G1, G2 and G3 represent the development interface with the Trackside system supplier, i.e. their further decomposition and the provision of evidence is the supplier's responsibility. This enables the supplier to be flexible regarding the choice of safety analysis techniques to demonstrate that the target failure rate has been achieved by the supplied system. For providing the required evidence to support satisfaction of trackside system goals G3, G5 and G6, Component Fault Trees (CFTs) [4] have been created. Therefore, G5 and G6 can be verified by performing a quantitative Fault Tree Analysis (FTA) of the top events representing the hazards *Erroneous*

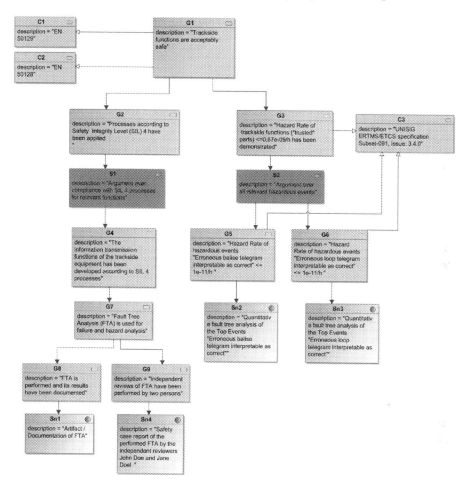

Fig. 1. Exemplary ETCS safety case

balise telegram interpretable as correct and *Erroneous loop telegram interpretable as correct*. In addition, G4 and its sub goals as the related process requirements make sure that the CFT creation and maintenance processes yield an adequate CFT model so that the CFT analysis results can be trusted. Typically, the evidence for adequate safety process adherence is found in process handbooks, review sheets or configuration management tools.

3   Distributed Safety Engineering with DDIs

This section describes the general concept of Digital Dependability Identities and how they can be used to perform continuous safety engineering processes in different integrator-supplier scenarios.

3.1 Digital Dependability Identities (DDIs)

A fundamental problem of current dependability engineering processes hampering effective assurance lies in the fact that safety argument models are not formally related to the evidence models supporting the claim. Concrete examples for such evidence are hazard and safety analysis models or dependability process execution documentation. As all those artifacts refer to the same system and therefore are naturally interrelated with each other, we claim this should also be the case for the system's model-based reflection: The Digital Dependability Identity (DDI) [10]. By establishing this kind of traceability, DDIs represent an integrated set of dependability data models (=What is the evidence data?) that are generated by engineers and are reasoned upon in dependability arguments (=How is the evidence data supporting the claim?). A DDI (see Fig. 2) is, therefore, an evolution of classical modular dependability assurance models, in that several separately defined dependability aspect models are now formally integrated allowing for comprehensive dependability reasoning. DDIs are produced during design, certified when the component or system is released, and then continuously maintained over the lifetime of a component or system. DDIs are used for dependable integration of components into systems during development.

A DDI contains information that uniquely describes the dependability characteristics of a system or component. DDIs are formed as modular assurance cases, are composable and can be synthesized to create more complex DDIs from the DDIs of constituent systems and system components. The DDI of a system contains (a) claims about the dependability guarantees given by a system to other systems (b) supporting evidence for the claims in the form of various models and analyses and (c) demands from other connected systems being necessary to support the claims.

The starting point for all dependability assurance activities is the description and planning of the functionality that the system shall render for its stakeholders, which may be either direct system users, companies or even the society. An essential property of a function is that it is executed on multiple independently developed subsystems leading to a required distribution of dependability

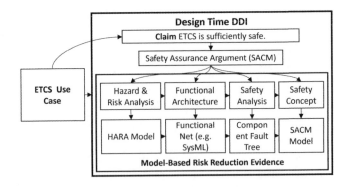

Fig. 2. Digital Dependability Identity @ Design Time

assurance over multiple system manufacturers. For example, the ETCS function is executed on the train's onboard system and the trackside system. Enabling cooperative function execution while still allowing decoupled development is only possible by making development interfaces explicit for both functional and quality aspects. Concretely, structural and behavioral aspects of the intended system function need to be made explicit along with assured constraints regarding their quality bounds.

DDIs are concerned with the comprehensive and transparent assurance of dependability claims. Thus, each assurance activity and each artifact contained in a DDI is motivated by a root dependability claim that defines sufficient risk reduction regarding a dependability property such as safety, security, availability or reliability. The definition of acceptable risk reduction is typically derived from domain-specific risk management standards targeting different risk causes such as functional safety (e.g. CENELEC EN 50129). These standards contain requirements for assessing and reducing risks to an acceptable level.

Having a dependability claim to be assured for the system function, the next step is the systematic planning of risk management activities. These activities create necessary evidence for supporting the system engineers' reasoning that the dependability claim holds for the developed system. For both risk management planning and dependability assessment purposes, an explicit argument is indispensable inductively relating the created evidence to the top-level claim through several step-wise layers of argumentation. Note that, while the performed activities and produced artifacts vary depending on the kind of risk that is being managed, the general need for argumentation supported by evidence is mandatory for all risks. DDIs deal with dependability risks, thus the currently supported design time DDI assurance activities and evidence focus on well-established dependability methods such as hazard and risk analysis, safety and security analyses, safety design concepts, validation, and verification. These activities proved sufficient over the last decades in demonstrating the dependability of embedded systems. In addition, the reliance on model-based approaches compensated for the increasing complexity of systems in the past.

Figure 2 illustrates the concept of continuous traceability between a SACM safety argument and safety-related evidence models stemming from hazard and risk analysis, functional architecture, safety analysis, and safety design concept. SACM stands for *Structured Assurance Case Metamodel* and was standardized by the OMG on the basis of GSN. [7]. It provides the assurance case backbone for creating the required traceability. Apart from relating evidence models formally to the assurance argument, a unique contribution of DDIs is the concretization of semantics specifically for safety assurance evidence. Based on this added product semantic, safety engineering activities in form of *DDI scripts* can be executed on the DDI data contents automatically. The DDI meta-model formalizing the described traceability and evidence semantics is the *Open Dependability Exchange (ODE)*[1] meta-model. Although we describe DDI usage in this paper for safety assurance activities, the concept is general enough to equally apply

---

[1] see http://www.deis-project.eu/ and https://github.com/DEIS-Project-EU/.

it to other dependability properties such as security, reliability or availability. More details on the DDI framework, its technical realization and usage benefits can be found on the DEIS project website's dissemination section [1].

3.2   Generic Safety Engineering Process Integrator/Supplier

In order to be able to identify engineering tasks that are supported by partial or full automation, it is required to anticipate a certain development process in which the engineering tasks are embedded. Figure 3 shows an abstract development process that is representative of domains such as railway or automotive. There is an integrator company (e.g. the OEM or the railway operator) that is building a system by integrating a set of components that are provided by supplier companies. This process involves four steps, in which the DDI concept together with (semi-)automated engineering support lead to improvement.

Step 1 – DDI Synthesis @ Integrator. Step 1 involves the synthesis of component specifications that the supplier company must adhere to. One particular challenge of synthesizing this specification is to collect all relevant information that is needed by the supplier in order to develop the component in isolation. This is not only necessary for information about required functionality, but also for safety requirements. In this scenario, DDIs can be seen as a container, where all this information can be captured in an integrated and structured way. Thus, engineering tool support for this step should focus on helping the engineer to collect the relevant information required by the DDI for the specific tasks the supplier should carry out. Such specific tasks could be for instance to demonstrate the adequate satisfaction of interface safety requirements or to check the compatibility of the supplier component interface with the interface definition provided by the integrator.

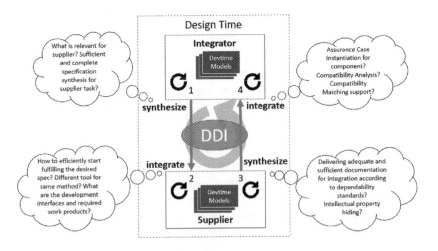

Fig. 3. Generic distributed engineering process of safety-critical systems

Step 2 – DDI Integration @ Supplier. Step 2 represents the integration of the specification DDI into the development process of the supplier company. This could mean for example that model stubs are automatically generated based on the development interface extracted from the imported DDI. Such a development interface typically consists of functional or technical data-flow interfaces or safety requirements allocated to those data-flow interfaces. This could also be placeholders for assurance evidence artifacts that are to be instantiated by the supplier and connected to the actually created evidence in shape of safety analysis, verification, validation or architectural models.

Step 3 – DDI Synthesis @ Supplier. After the DDI has been integrated in a (semi-)automated way, the supplier performs the actual development work until it is time to deliver the component back to the integrator. In this instance, delivery means not only the physical component but also the safety-related documentation that is required to build a sound safety case for the integrated system (typically according to one of the commonly known standards). Step 3 is concerned with synthesizing a DDI containing all relevant information that is needed so that the integrator can properly perform the integration task. From the supplier perspective, all *relevant* information means explicitly not all *existent* information and, therefore, engineering support for the supplier should focus on identifying and collecting the minimal set of information to be delivered. Although this paper focuses on the integrator perspective, the presented DDI approach could in principle also be used by the supplier to automatically check component safety requirement validity through checking traceability from requirements to software/hardware design to code and their respective validation activities such as tests.

Step 4 – DDI Integration @ Integrator. Step 4 deals with the integration of a component DDI into the overall system. This engineering task typically involves performing compatibility and structural analyses as well as behavioral compatibility matching with other components. This task needs to be performed for both functional and safety aspects. Thus, the component safety case has to be integrated into the system safety case in order to demonstrate confidence in the high-level safety assurance claims. Engineering support should focus on the (semi-)automated generation, integration and verification of safety case fragments, i.e. (semi-)automated assessment of claim satisfaction in system safety cases. Thereby, it is necessary to assess whether the provided argumentation and evidence yields sufficient confidence in the validity of system-level assurance claims. In order to assess the adequacy of evidence and argumentation with partial or full automation, we make use of the aforementioned formal interrelation of safety case models and product models provided by a DDI. This approach enables assessing how changes in any of the DDI product models propagate up to the safety case and indicating to the dependability engineer the impact of changes on the validity of claims. As safety cases and the models representing the evidence for supporting the claims tend to be quite large in the real world, partially automated change impact analysis gives valuable information to the engineer, which parts of the existing safety artifacts need to be reassessed.

4   DDI-Based Evidence Analysis in a Railway Case Study

This section first describes the ETCS System DDI (Sect. 4.1) and afterward exemplifies the DDI engineering approach for two concrete safety engineering activities related to the verification of product-related (Sect. 4.2) and process-related (Sect. 4.3) safety requirements.

4.1   ETCS System DDI

In the ETCS use case, we utilize DDIs to represent the information provided in the safety assurance process of the ETCS system, in particular, to turn the integration of the trackside subsystem safety assurance artifacts more efficient.

A high-level overview of a DDI and its contents for the ETCS example is depicted in Fig. 4. The ETCS DDI's backbone is the system-level safety argument expressed in SACM. As described in Sect. 2.2, the concrete safety argument contains a process-related part motivated by safety requirements from CENELEC EN 50129 and a product-related part mostly driven by the ETCS specification. In hierarchical system (of system) structures, the refinement of the system-level safety argument results in safety requirements to be satisfied by the subsystems, in the ETCS case by the trackside and onboard subsystems. Note that the principal structure of the trackside system DDI (lower part of Fig. 4) is almost equal to the ETCS DDI, with the exception that the root (=the safety guarantees to be given) of the trackside safety case are the interface safety requirements posed by the ETCS integrator. From that point on, a safety argument needs to be provided by the trackside system manufacturer within the context of the trackside system. This safety argument is supported by evidence artifacts synthesized from various kinds of models such as failure logic, architecture or process models. The most notable innovation introduced by DDIs is that the source models for evidence are formally linked to the argument bits supported by them and organized within an all-embracing container. This characteristic together with the possibility to automatically match demanded and satisfied requirements in different DDIs (see the "Trackside System Safety Requirements" *demanded* by the ETCS system and *satisfied* by the trackside system) enable efficient safety-related collaboration across multi-tier supply chains and semi-automated change management through explicitly defined exchange interfaces. After the DDIs of all subsystems have been integrated into the ETCS system DDI by using DDI scripts, the last step in the assurance process is the provision of integration-level evidence that is typically based on analyses of the integrated system's architecture and failure logic as well as the verification and validation of safety goals and that any assumptions posed during the development process still hold in the final product.

4.2   Automated Evidence Analysis of Product Safety Argument

In this Section, we want to show how to automatically analyze evidence completeness for the following ETCS product safety requirement across the supply chain with the DDI framework (see Figs. 1 and 5).

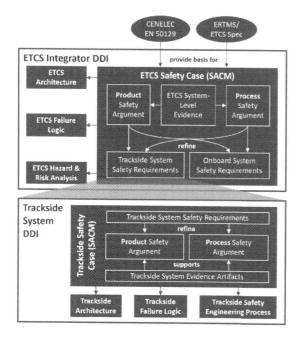

Fig. 4. High-level contents of ETCS and trackside DDIs

G3: *Hazard rate of trackside functions ("Trusted part") $\leq 0.67 \cdot 10^{-9}/h$ has been demonstrated.*

In order to analyze requirement G3 in a conventional safety assurance process (i.e. without DDIs), the ETCS *integration* safety engineer would have to perform the following steps:

S1 Determine, which activities and work products a standard-compliant satisfaction of the requirement implies

S2 Refine G3 according to the assurance strategy into interface safety requirements for all hazardous events (G5 and G6 as examples)

S3 Contact the *trackside* system's safety engineer and get documentation (e.g. documents or models) about evidence for the satisfaction of G5 and G6

S4 Identify the relevant parts within the provided documentation, in this case, the FTA models and analysis results (typically time-consuming due to different processes, tools and safety assurance perspectives)

S5 Sum up the supplier quantitative FTA results for the relevant hazardous events ($2 \cdot 10^{-11}/h$) and compare the result to the target failure rate demanded by G3 ($0.67 \cdot 10^{-9}/h$).

S6 If the requirement is fulfilled, link and archive evidence source to the requirement so that an assessor can find it easily.

Figure 5 shows how the engineering steps to verify requirement G3 listed above can be carried out automatically with the DDI framework. The starting points are the safety requirements G5 and G6, which are located in SACM

Argument packages of *both* ETCS and trackside DDIs, in the first as part of
the argument refinement, in the latter as explicit safety interface specification
(in Fig. 5, duplication was avoided). Thus, evidence produced for the trackside
system can be traced to from the ETCS safety argument during integration
by automatically matching. This automatic matching is currently done based
on tagged value content matching. However, more intelligent matching mechanisms such as semantic understanding of structured requirements and evidence
descriptions are to be explored. Having established traceability between ETCS
and trackside arguments, the main question is how to (a) relate G5 with the
failure logic model supporting the requirement and (b) how to perform steps S4-
S6 automatically, i.e. how to use the enriched data to produce the verification
result.

To support the understanding of a requirement by a machine, SACM provides the *Terminology* mechanism, which enables structured text definition. In
the example this means that G5 is enriched with semantic tags (called *Terms*)
representing the nature of the requirement:

RequirementType. The type of demand (=Failure Rate Demonstration with
Quantitative FTA), related to a DDI script encoding a safety standard activity consuming all required DDI models and producing the verification result.

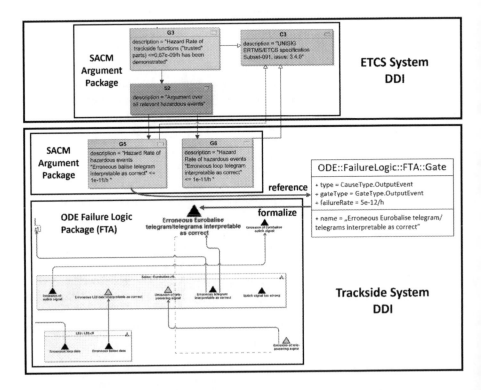

Fig. 5. ETCS failure rate consistency check with DDIs

ElementReference. Formal reference to the TopEvent element in the Track-side CFT representing the hazardous event described in the requirement. In general, this can be any element within the DDI.

VerificationCriteria. The target failure rate to be satisfied by the actual computed failure rate for the fault tree (assumed to be existent in the failureRate attribute of the top event's ODE representation). In general, these criteria should be defined with Boolean conditions to ensure decidability.

Based on a fully integrated DDI data model containing all required verification information, the missing piece is the encoded safety intelligence performing the automated verification. For this task, a script-based safety automation engine has been created in *DEIS* relying on the Eclipse Epsilon Framework [2]. It offers various task-specific languages for efficiently querying, manipulation and generation of models. For the ETCS verification task, DDI scripts have been created operating on the DDI models shown in Fig. 5. To that end, the *Epsilon Validation Language (EVL)* and the *Epsilon Object Language (EOL)* have been employed to navigate within and between the DDIs, generate new information such as analyzing the CFT (EOL) and checking structural constraints such as the verification criteria on it (EVL). Note that this paper's focus is on the conceptual idea of using DDIs for the evidence completeness analysis of different kinds of safety requirements. We plan to elaborate on its technical realization with the *Epsilon Framework* in a further publication. However, in our project deliverables [1], more details can be found.

For the ETCS example, the DDI script for checking failure rate satisfaction (G5) performs the following tasks:

1. Retrieve those claims in the SACM safety argument representing quantitative analysis requirements (indicated by the *RequirementType* Term).
2. For each identified claim, locate the referenced top event element in the FailureLogicPackage of the subsystem DDI and retrieve the actual failureRate attribute. If non-existent at that point, invoke another DDI script to perform an on-demand quantitative FTA for the component fault tree related to the top event.
3. Compare the actual failure rate with a target failure rate and report a violation to the safety engineer if the actual failure rate is higher than the actual failure rate.

The DDI script content outlined above is able to analyze the satisfaction of single budgeted failure rate requirements. Finally, summing up the actual failure rates of multiple contributing (sub)system parts (G3) is done in a separate DDI script orchestrating the *Failure Rate Demonstration Scripts* for all relevant contributing parts. This demonstrates, how higher-level requirement satisfaction can be analyzed by reuse of lower-level safety engineering DDI scripts.

---

[2] https://www.eclipse.org/epsilon/.

4.3   Automated Evidence Analysis of Process Safety Argument

For process-related safety requirements like G8 and G9 stated below, the engineering activities for requirement verification are similar to those described for product-related requirements in the previous section. The only difference is that the queried DDI contents are referring to model-based process execution documentation formally related to the safety artifacts (i.e. CFT models) produced by the respective process (i.e. standard-compliant FTA).

G8: *FTA is performed and its results have been documented.*

G9: *Independent reviews of FTA have been performed by two persons.* Figure 6 shows the relevant trackside DDI contents for verifying the above requirements resulting from ETCS process argument refinement. Evidence related to process execution can be captured in SACM *Artifact* packages along with the artifacts the process relates to. Therefore, *Events* and *Activities* including their *Participants* as well as used *Resources* and *Techniques* can be tracked for an *Artifact*. Within the DDI, SACM *Artifacts* may be formally connected to the product safety models, e.g. the CFT in the DDI's failure logic package.

In order to automatically verify the evidence of G8 and G9 the following logic has been codified in EVL DDI scripts:

G8 The FTA Artifact related to G8 should be associated with (a) the actual produced fault tree models as part of the DDI's failure logic package and (b) the Activity "Hazard or Failure analysis", where the used Technique is "FTA" and the used resource is the trackside system architecture referencing the DDI's trackside system architecture package including the safety-relevant trackside functions.

G9 The FTA Artifact related to G9 should be associated with (a) the actual produced fault tree models as part of the DDI's failure logic package and (b) an Event "Review", where there are at least two associated Participants being different people.

5   Related Work

Related work can be broadly categorized into the two different areas (a) the formalization of specific safety aspects into meta-models usable for automation and (b) the integration of multiple aspects for more comprehensive reasoning. Regarding a), common techniques have been formalized for the definition of system failure propagation (e.g. Component Fault Trees [4], HiP-HOPS [8]) and the corresponding safety argumentation supported by evidences (GSN, SACM) [5,7]. Using these techniques separately in different phases of the engineering process proved to be very valuable in the past, but their lack of integration with each other makes proper reaction to changes a nearly impossible task. Therefore, some initiatives aim at integrating safety aspects to allow more extensive safety reasoning supported by automation. In the SPES project series [9], the *Open Safety Metamodel* has been created enabling a modular, cross-tool and

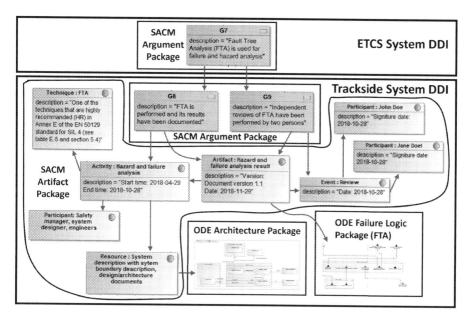

Fig. 6. ETCS FTA process evidence analysis with DDIs

cross-company safety certification. However, it only includes architectural view-points, safety analysis, and hazard models, missing the very important aspect of safety argumentation and evidence models, which is the backbone of a DDI. In the AMASS project, the focus rests on the organization of the safety argument and in particular the lifecycle of evidence, formalized in the *Common Assurance and Certification Metamodel* (CACM) [12]. Although this is very important in order to fulfill standard process compliance, the lack of product-related model semantics such as concrete architecture models, failure logic or hazard models disallows a proper product-related safety reasoning required for a complete compelling safety case. DDIs extend the state of the art in model-based safety certification in that they provide a dependability-specific integrated set of data models and an automation engine that together enable efficient and comprehensive safety reasoning across multiple safety aspects and supply chains.

6   Conclusion and Future Work

In this paper, we presented an approach to automatically verify safety requirements by model-based reasoning about multiple safety aspects at once that were only considered in isolation in the past. The automation is enabled by establishing formal traceability between safety argument and evidence supported by concrete product safety models all packaged together in the *Digital Dependability Identity (DDI)*. DDIs currently contain SACM safety case models integrated with hazard and risk models (HARA), architecture, failure propagation. Based

on DDIs and the corresponding DDI scripting framework, we showed that safety
requirements in the railway domain can be automatically verified.

Our approach reduces the effort for creation and maintenance of a system
safety case together with all relevant supporting models by first performing automated safety analysis, verification and safety artifact generation activities, second, supporting a model-based multi-tier safety engineering process and third,
eliminating the human error source by relying on DDI scripts to encode safety
engineering activities. The evaluation in the industrial case study suggested that
the DDI approach is feasible for performing safety engineering processes faster
and achieving a better process execution and safety case quality in general.

In the future, we will enrich DDIs with additional dependability aspects such
as security engineering (attack trees, threat and risk analysis). In addition, we are
currently performing a broader evaluation of the DDI framework in application
scenarios such as autonomous driving and health applications.

Acknowledgement. The work presented in this paper was created in context of the
DEIS Project funded by the European Commission (Grant No. 732242).

References

1. DEIS Project Consortium: Project Publications. http://www.deis-project.eu/dissemination/. Accessed 30 May 2019
2. European Committee for Electrotechnical Standardization (CENELEC): CENELEC EN 50129: Railway application - Communications, signaling and processing systems - Safety related electronic systems for signaling (2003)
3. International Organization for Standardization (ISO): ISO 26262: Road vehicles — Functional safety (2011)
4. Kaiser, B., Liggesmeyer, P., Mäckel, O.: A new component concept for fault trees. In: Proceedings of the 8th Australian Workshop on Safety Critical Systems and Software (2003)
5. Kelly, T.P.: Systematic approach to safety case management. In: Proceedings of SAE 2004 World Congress (2004)
6. Kelly, T., Weaver, R.: The goal structuring notation - a safety argument notation. In: Proceedings of the dependable systems and networks workshop (2004)
7. Object Management Group: Structured Assurance Case Metamodel 2.0 (SACM) (2018). https://www.omg.org/spec/SACM/
8. Papadopoulos, Y., McDermid, J.A.: Hierarchically performed hazard origin and propagation studies. In: Felici, M., Kanoun, K. (eds.) SAFECOMP 1999. LNCS, vol. 1698, pp. 139–152. Springer, Heidelberg (1999). https://doi.org/10.1007/3-540-48249-0_13
9. Pohl, K., Hönninger, H., Achatz, R., Broy, M. (eds.): Model-Based Engineering of Embedded Systems – The SPES 2020 Methodology. Springer, Heidelberg (2012). https://doi.org/10.1007/978-3-642-34614-9
10. Schneider, D., et al.: WAP: digital dependability identities. In: IEEE International Symposium on Software Reliability Engineering (ISSRE), pp. 324–329 (2015)
11. UNISIG: ETCS/ERTMS Safety Requirements for the Technical Interoperability of ETCS in Levels (Subset-091, Issue: 3.6.0) (2015)
12. de la Vara, J.L., et al.: Model-based specification of safety compliance needs for critical systems: a holistic generic metamodel. Inf. Softw. Technol. **72**, 16–30 (2016)

Interactive Systems and Design Validation

SafeDeML: On Integrating the Safety Design into the System Model

Tim Gonschorek[1]([envelope]) [ID], Philipp Bergt[2], Marco Filax[1] [ID], Frank Ortmeier[1] [ID], Jan von Hoyningen-Hüne[3], and Thorsten Piper[4]

[1] Otto von Guericke University, Universitätsplatz 2, 39106 Magdeburg, Germany
{tim.gonschorek,marco.fialx,frank.ortmeier}ovgu.de
[2] Xitaso Engineering GmbH, Werner-Heisenberg-Straße 1,
39106 Magdeburg, Germany
philipp.bergt@xitaso.com
[3] Conti Temic microelectronic GmbH, Dornierstrasse 1, 88677 Markdorf, Germany
jan.vonhuene@continental-corporation.com
[4] Continental Automotive GmbH, Siemensstraße 12, 93005 Regensburg, Germany
thorsten.piper@continental-corporation.com

Abstract. The safety design definition of a safety critical system is a complex task. On the one hand, the system designer must ensure that he addressed all potentially hazardous harwdware faults. This is often defined not(!) in the model but within extra documents (e.g., Excel sheets). On the other hand, all defined safety mechanisms must be transformed back into the system model. We think an improvement for the designer would be given by a modeling extension integrating relevant safety design artifacts into the normal design work-flow and supporting the safety design development directly from within the model.

To address this issue, we developed the UML-profile SafeDeML extending standard SysML such that it integrates the fault modeling into the system modeling. In addition, we defined a modeling process with special attention to the Iso 26262 standard. Therefore we introduce special elements for the diagnosis, modeling required safety mechanisms within the model and developed a library for standard Iso 26262 faults and corresponding hardware components, intended to lower the potential of missing important fault definitions.

Keywords: Model-based system design ·
SysML extension for the automotive domain ·
Safety design according to Iso 26262

1 The Need for Integrating the Safety Design

The job of a system designer is a hard task since the developed systems are getting more and more complex, integrating lots of sub-systems, designed by other designers, or delivered by suppliers with often only abstract descriptions

© Springer Nature Switzerland AG 2019
A. Romanovsky et al. (Eds.): SAFECOMP 2019, LNCS 11698, pp. 271–285, 2019.
https://doi.org/10.1007/978-3-030-26601-1_19

272 T. Gonschorek et al.

but no detailed design. Nevertheless, the designer must provide a design meeting all relevant requirements. In the context of safety-critical systems, this is even more complex, since safety-relevant requirements must be met. One specific requirement is that all hardware faults of the integrated elements must be analyzed. If such a fault has the potential of violating a given safety requirement with a unacceptable likelihood, potentially leading to a hazardous event, must be prevented by the system design.

Even though many system engineers, develop systems in a model-based methodology, the safety aspects of the design are managed within manually created and maintained documents with tools like Microsoft's Excel or Rational's Rhapsody and Doors. This means, that the enumeration of all potentially random hardware faults, their resulting effects, and further safety measure and mitigation strategies are kept not within the system model but within a separate document. Hence, there does not exist a deep, i.e., easily traceable, connection between the system component, especially the parts containing hazardous faults and corresponding safety measures, or fault definitions and design decisions made to prevent these faults or mitigate their effects. Further, especially for complex systems developed by several designer, the analysis of fault effects within the global system context and the corresponding failure propagation analysis requires huge effort and can introduce structural faults into the design process.

In our point of view, this leads to several problems regarding the quality of the safety design:

- No automatic consistency validation of the safety design based on the actual system model (e.g., Are all relevant faults addressed? Are the defined measures implemented?).
- Changes in the system model lead to a manual reworking of all analysis documents (even though nothing is changed a manual check is required).
- Safety mechanisms focusing on the system are calculated manually in an environment without information about the system model.
- Failure propagation through connected elements must manually be analyzed.

This means, the designer must take all relevant design information into account without direct support of the CASE tool (e.g., what are relevant faults defined by the standard or information on possible failure propagation due to component interfaces), project them into extra documents (e.g., an Excel sheet), make the safety design decisions on basis of these information (e.g., define proper fault prevention mechanisms), and transform this decisions back to design model. Even though the designer can handle this transformation process, it leaves space for potential structural failures (missed faults or overseen component links) and aggravates the traceability between system model and safety design decisions.

There exist already numerous approaches defining some safety design based on the system, but in our point of view, there is still a gap since most methods still require the building of parallel safety models or specific extensions that are not focused on the fault and failure propagation analysis. In contrast to that, our proposed *Safety Design Modeling Language* (SafeDeML) in addition handles the design of safety mechanisms and integrates directly into SysML. SafeDeML is designed to integrate the design decisions, i.e., the correlation between fault, failure, and safety mechanism, directly within the system model in the CASE tool. From this, we also derive tool support for the analysis if each defined fault has been processed by the designer and if all hazardous faults are prevented by a safety mechanism. Further, we defined a library based on the Iso 26262 standard containing all essential hardware elements (mentioned by the Iso 26262) and corresponding faults, itself providing a safety measure for the design process that the safety design does not miss relevant faults. Therefore, we developed (i) a SysML profile extension providing all necessary elements required for the analysis, (ii) a process proposal for the executing and integration the developed failure injection and analysis method, and (iii) developed a prototypical plugin for the CASE tool Enterprise Architect.

The remainder of the paper is structured as follows: In Sect. 2 we give a short background on SysML and relevant Iso 26262 terms. Section 3 handles related work to our modeling methodology. In Sect. 4 we introduce our developed UML-profile for SafeDeML, and Sect. 5 presents a corresponding modeling process. A conclusion of the work and planned future work is presented in Sect. 6.

2   Background

2.1   System Modeling Language

The UML [19] extension SysML, developed by the Object Modeling Group (OMG), is defined for modeling specific aspects of technical systems. For better understanding of the following discussion, we want to mention three basic elements: *Block*, *Port*, and *Requirements* [22].

SysML::Block is a basic element of the language and an extension of the UML::Class. It is applied for modeling basic entities of a system, e.g., hardware components or specific system functions. Like UML::Class elements, blocks can be hierarchically encapsulated by other classes for

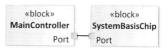

Fig. 1. Modeling system components in SysML.

providing several levels of system abstraction. Figure 1 presents two possible simple system components, a *MainController* and a *SystemBasisChip*, represented as a block each.

SysML::Port is a UML::Port providing an interface between a set of blocks. These can be input ports, output ports, or bidirectional ports. Ports are directly attached to a block (*cf.* Fig. 1). A modeled block component uses such a port to interact with its environments. Within basic SysML, the communication can also be defined only by using the interface and a corresponding association between blocks. In practice, however, ports are often designed to underline the character of the interaction with external components.

SysML::Requirement elements were introduced with SysML. Using requirement modeling has the advantage that we can directly within the system model assign requirements to the model implementing it and also represent all the refinement of the requirements between them. This means, using requirements as an element for the system modeling increases the comprehensibility and traceability of the model.

2.2 Error Modeling and Iso 26262 in a Nutshell

Even though known to our well-informed reader, we want to give some information about the Iso 26262 Standard *Road Vehicles – Functional Safety* [1] and the in this context often applied safety analysis technique *Failure Mode and Effect Analysis*. Since this gives only a very brief overview, we would like to refer interested readers to the given references [13, 18].

In general, the scope of the Iso 26262 is the development of an *item*, i.e., the vehicle part under development. This item consists of several *(sub-) systems*. Further, an item defines *functions* that are provided by the item and are realized by the systems it consists of. The system is also defined as an abstraction of *components* which are again an abstraction containing both *hardware parts* and *software units*.

The intended goal of the SafeDeML method is the support of the system designer, in particular during the safety design process. During safety design the designer must ensure concerning all events potentially leading to hazardous system states and addresses them in the design, i.e., implement specific diagnosis or handling mechanisms. *Safety Goal.*

Definition 1 (Safety Goal). *Safety goals are top-level safety requirements for the item under development, leading to the functional requirements that must be concerned for avoiding a hazardous event.*

To be compliant with the defined safety goals, the design must ensure that no safety goal could be violated by the malfunction of any element. Such a malfunction is in general defined as failure.

Definition 2 (Failure). *A failure is the termination of the ability of an element of item under development to perform a function as required (in particular regarding the set of safety goals).*

Failures are often defined as the inability of performing a required function or service, required on the outside of the element. The internal state causing the failure is often referred to as error.

Definition 3 (Error). *An error is a discrepancy between a computed, observed or measured value or condition, and the true, specified, or theoretically correct value or condition.*

Such an error can occur subsequent to an unforeseen condition during operation or to a fault within an element.

Definition 4 (Fault). *A fault is an abnormal condition that can cause an element or the complete item to fail.*

Further, according to [3], we assume that not every error occurring within an element leads to an observable failure and therefore not every fault has the potential of leading to a violation of the safety goal. The goal of our modeling method is to support the designer in concerning all relevant faults.

For preventing that a safety goal relevant fault leads to a failure and eventually to a potential hazard, *safety measures* are defined.

Definition 5 (Safety Measure). *A safety measure is an activity or technical solution to avoid or control systematic failures and to detect or control random hardware failures or to mitigate their harmful effects.*

Especially within the safety design, a system designer often applies a specialization of safety measures, *safety mechanisms*.

Definition 6 (Safety Mechanism). *A safety mechanism is a technical solution implemented to detect, or mitigate, or tolerate faults or to control or avoid failures in order to maintain intended functionality or a safe state.*

In correlation to safety mechanisms, often applied key properties are, e.g., *Diagnostic Coverage* (DC), *Detection and Reaction Time* (DT/RT), *Failure In Time* rate (FIT), or the *Fault Tolerant Time Interval* (FTTI). The DC is the rate of relevant failures of an element covered by a safety mechanism, the DT/RT is the time a safety mechanism requires for reacting to a fault, the FIT rate defines the occurrence likelihood of a fault, and the FTTI is a measure for the time span between the occurrence of a fault and the corresponding failure.

If a safety mechanism does not cover a specific failure, the failure propagates to another element. According to Iso 26262 and [3] they propagate either horizontally or vertically. Horizontal propagation means that a failure is propagated over an existing interface from the initial element, holding the fault, to another element on the same abstraction level (e.g., system or component level). Vertical propagation, in contrast, refers to the propagation to higher level abstraction, e.g., from a sub-component up to a parent component or to the outside of the element border. Due to this propagation, the system designer must not necessarily place a safety mechanism on the same element as the fault but can add new elements holding the particular safety mechanism.

In addition, Iso 26262 classifies faults into *single-point*, *residual*, *multi-point*, and *safe* faults. A fault is defined as single-point fault if it leads directly to the violation of a safety goal and no fault of the containing element is covered by any safety mechanism. Otherwise, no fault of that element is a single-point fault. If a fault does under no circumstances lead to a violation of the safety goal, it is a safe fault. Residual faults lead to the violation of a safety goal but are part of an element that implements a safety mechanism, however, no mechanism prevents the failure of the actual fault from violating the safety goal. Based on this, a multi-point fault leads to the violation of a safety goal and its failure is prevented by a safety mechanism. Depending on whether the corresponding failure is also detected, multi-point faults can be further classified as *detected*, if the corresponding failure is detected, *perceived*, if the failure is perceived, e.g., by the driver, or *latent*, if the corresponding failure is not detected.

3   Related Work

The essential uniqueness of SafeDeML is the direct integration of fault – failure – safety mechanism modeling into the standard system design life-cycle. In the literature, there also exist several works on the synthesis of system and safety design and also further safety analysis.

One of the currently most related works to our approach is SafeML [6,7]. Here, the authors provide an UML-profile extending standard SysML. This integration, however, is rather static than supporting the actual design process. That means that SafeML provides a set of elements like faults, failures, and hazards, but they are not used to support the design process by means of propagation analysis. They are instead used for integrating safety design results in the system model. However, there exist possible synergies, and if SafeML would be integrated into future SysML releases (cf. [5]), it could be an option to integrate the model elements with SafeDeML.

The work [15] from the Chess framework [8,21] also presents an approach to model the fault – failure relations on a system model. Further, they also provide propagation analysis based on the model structure [10]. This model, however, is intended to be used for the safety analysis rather than for the direct design purpose and therefore does not integrate essential design elements, e.g., the definition of safety mechanisms, into the model. Moreover, the model containing the failure definitions is defined in a separated modeling language and framework that must again be kept up to date with the system design.

HipHops [11,16,17] is a language and tool suite for failure modeling and propagation analysis. From a given system description they generate a parallel model used for failure definition and propagation analysis. This model, however, must again be kept up to date with the system model and does also not support the definition of related safety mechanisms for the system. This is the same for the Marte UML extension [20] which together with the DAM profile [4] provides a framework of defining dependability analysis specific extensions to the modeling language. In general, unfortunately, it is not provided to model the intended Fault – Failure – Diagnosis chain as it is desirable when executing a fault related safety measure.

Another work, focussing on the fault modeling and analysis, is the Component Fault Tree (CFT) [2,12] methodology providing an extended failure propagation and analysis mechanism based on the system component structure. Even a tool integration, the SafeT toolbox [14], exists. This methodology, however, again instead focus on the safety analysis than on the safety design. Only faults and corresponding failures are modeled but without the ability of the definition of preventing safety mechanisms which can directly be integrated into the design.

What, in our point of view, is still not sufficient covered by the approaches from the literature is (i) the propagation analysis of potentially critical faults with respect to defined safety and diagnosis mechanisms (directly within the system model) and (ii) the support of the designer in validating that all necessary faults have been addressed during the safety design process.

4 The Safety Design Modeling Language

For the model integration we introduce four basic elements *SafeDeML::Fault*, *SafeDeML::Failure*, *SafeDeML::Diagnosis*, and *SafeDeML::Safety Goal* as extensions to SysML. Therefor, we define an UML profile [9], intended to be integrateable into general UML\ SysML modeling tools.

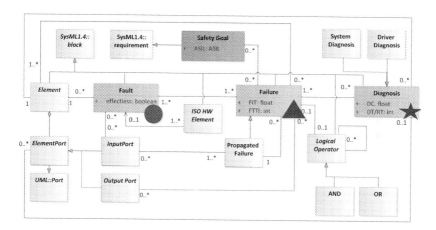

Fig. 2. UML-profile defining the extension of SysML by all relevant SafeDeML elements. For better readability we defined the SafeDeML elements without the corresponding name space.

As Fig. 2 shows, for ensuring the soundness of the integration into SysML, all elements are derived directly from SysML::Block. This ensures that the modeling extension is not restricted to one particular abstraction but can be used on all modeling levels, i.e., on hardware, software, and system level. Therefore the vertical propagation of failures can also be ensured as well as the failure modeling at the same level. We introduce further structure-related SysML extensions and logical operators. On component level the interface between local and global context is presented by the stereotypes *SafeDeML::Port*, *SafeDeML::InputPort*, and *SafeDeML::OutputPort*, derived from the SysML::Port class. In the following, we discuss the necessary elements in more detail.

4.1 SafeDeML::Fault

Figure 3a presents the basic visualization of a fault, as circle. A fault can per definition be active or is set as «effectless» if it is meant to be a safe fault that does not lead to a component failure. In most situations, the occurring faults correlate to hardware parts implemented within the specific component. Therefore, we provide in addition the definition of faults for specific atomic hardware parts, e.g., a power supply or particular memory types, or for the direct assignment to hardware elements. This hardware part definition is especially useful since often such atomic elements are not modeled on a system level, but their faults must be handled. By assigning the hardware parts to a component the fault definitions are directly imported into the component (*cf.* Fig. 3b). Moreover, for compliance with the ISO 26262 standard, we implemented all hardware parts and corresponding faults that are mentioned in the correlating standard *Part5 – Product development at the hardware level* Table D.1 to D.14. Further, the definition of faults can also be inherited from abstract component definitions.

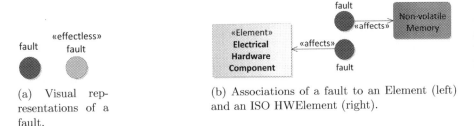

(a) Visual representations of a fault.

(b) Associations of a fault to an Element (left) and an ISO HWElement (right).

Fig. 3. Basic fault representations and associations to (ISO)HWElements.

4.2 SafeDeML::Failure

From the set of defined SafeDeML::Faults we define all relevant component failures. Therefor, SafeDeML::Failure elements (red triangle) are directly connected to corresponding SafeDeML::Faults (blue circle) or via a logical operator using the «results in» association (*cf.* Fig. 4). Safety-relevant properties, FIT and FTTI, are added as properties directly to the failure element. The horizontal propagation is defined by an association to available SafeDeML::OutputPorts using the «propagate by». External failures are included into an element by an SafeDeML::InputPort as a propagated failure.

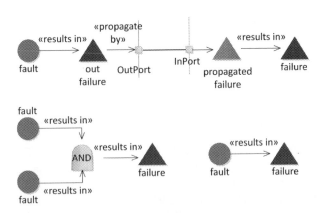

Fig. 4. Possible representations of the SafeDeML::Failure modeling. It shows a horizontal propagation (top), a SafeDeML::Failure with more than one correlated SafeDeML::Fault (left) and a single SafeDeML::Fault leading to a failure.

Further, we define the relation between a fault and a safety goal by failures. Therefore, we just defined a property for the SafeDeML::Failure element containing all possibly violated safety goals. Safety goals itself in our current state are directly derived from a corresponding safety requirement and imported directly within a SysML requirement diagram (Fig. 5).

4.3   SafeDeML::Safety Goal

A SafeDeML::Safety Goal can either be linked to a system component or directly to an occurring failure element. It is directly derived from a set of relevant safety requirements.

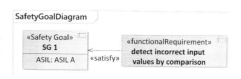

Fig. 5. Example of a safety goal modeling within the introduced `SafetyGoalDiagram`.

4.4   SafeDeML::Diagnosis

The SafeDeML::Diagnosis elements (visualized as star) are used to provide a safety mechanism for a given failure, e.g., a failure handling or detection. This is one of the key improvement of our method. We can directly correlate the safety mechanism to the corresponding failure and fault, but also it is directly connected to the system design model element that is meant to implement the defined measure. In our point of view, this provides an improvement since a possible source of errors, the transformation, and change between safety design documents and system model becomes obsolete. This can also be seen as a structural safety measure for the system development process.

If a SafeDeML::Diagnosis is defined as safety mechanism for a specific fault they are connected by a «detected by» association (cf. Fig. 6). Safety-related properties, e.g., DC, can directly be added as a property to the diagnosis element.

Fig. 6. Example of the SafeDeML::Diagnosis modeling with a system diagnosis (left) and a diagnosis perceived by the driver (right).

As mentioned in the background, faults are classified according to their potential of leading to a safety goal violation and designed safety and detection mechanisms. To enable the separation between detected and perceived faults, we also defined a *SafeDeML::Perceived Diagnosis* element. This defines that the detection is not implemented within the system but the occurrence of the corresponding SafeDeML::Failure can be perceived and further handled by the driver (in the Iso 26262 context).

5   Proposal of an Integratable Modeling Process

For integrating our developed modeling mechanism into the system design, we developed a step-wise modeling process. To verify this process, we developed an

Enterprise Architect plugin and applied it for extending a real system model. The basic process consists of five steps: *(A) Fault Modeling, (B) Failure Modeling, (C) Diagnosis* in the local component context and *(D) Global Analysis*, and *(E) Model Analysis* in the global context of the system (*cf.* Fig. 7). This process is developed according to the normal safety design workflow, starting with the definition of all faults for relevant elements, followed by the definition of correlated failures. After that, it is defined whether a safety measure is implemented on the component or the failure is propagated. This is what we define as local context. In the next step, what we see as the global context, all failure elements are propagated to the next adjacent components connected via available interfaces. There, they are again handled in the local component context as propagated failures. At the last step, it is checked whether all relevant faults are covered by a safety mechanism and if no safety goal is violated.

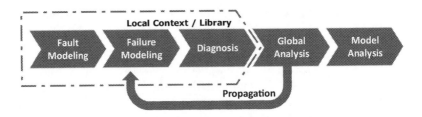

Fig. 7. A representation of the five process steps for the integration of the safety design elements into a given system model. The separation into local and global context represents the view change from a local into the global elements perspective also including all failures propagated from external connected elements.

In addition to the guided process, the provided integration into case tools is also an advantage in the direction of a safety measure. Proven-in-use processes, e.g., version control, and change management as well as user management and validation if and by whom a fault, failure, or diagnosis has been defined or changed can improve (a) the development and (b) the quality for the assessment.

Figure 8 shows an excerpt of our brake light system model representing the control of the brake lights of a car. The specific hazard of the system is that all brake lights are unavailable at the same time. The figure shows the two elements *MainController* and *SystemBasisChip*. The *MainController* generates the control signal for the brake lights and the *SystemBasisChip* is responsible for the communication to the brake light components.

5.1 Fault Modeling

Our defined fault modeling extension provides several mechanisms for assigning faults to model elements (*cf.* Fig. 9 No (1)). These are (i) the heir of fault definitions, (ii) the derivation of faults from specific atomic hardware parts, and (iii) standard definitions of additional faults.

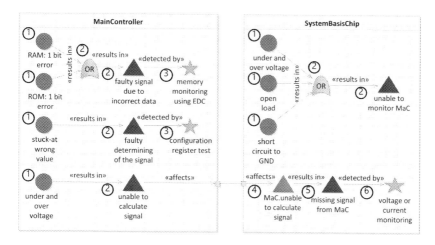

Fig. 8. Excerpt of the brake light system used to validate our modeling methodology. It contains the failure definitions for the *MainController (MaC)* and the *SystemBasis-Chip (SBC)* The numbers assigned to the elements indicate the different steps in which these elements are added to the fault modeling.

Inheritance from Parent Elements. In the first step all already defined faults from the parent component are added to the current component fault definition (of course, failure and diagnosis definitions as well).

Fault Assignments Inherit from Hardware Parts. In a high-level system design it is not desired to model the system in detail that all atomic hardware parts are included (e.g., a power supply, register, or a timer). For the analysis, however, it is essential to cover all critical failures coming from, more or less, the atomic parts of a component.

To overcome this, we provide the ability to associate atomic hardware parts to model elements (*cf.* Fig. 9) in a `Element Fault Diagram` and implement the corresponding faults in a `Fault Derivation Diagram`. In this context, we implemented all Iso 26262 hardware elements and corresponding faults as an entry point of a library, minimizing the possibility of overseeing the minimal set of required faults and also reuse already define hardware element – fault relations.

This is further essential since keeping track of all hardware parts potentially introducing new random hardware faults into the system requires a lot effort. In addition, even for the safety assessment process, the argumentation about which faults are analyzed and why gets more transparent if directly linked to available hardware model elements.

Specific Faults. In addition to the previous methods, it is, of course, possible to define specific faults the design must cover. This definition is done by linking the fault to the component at the same level as the hardware parts or directly within the fault definition diagram.

The basic idea behind these fault definition steps is that most of the necessary faults are automatically generated from specific system model information without much additional effort. These definition can be done in each block diagram of the structural architecture part of the SysML model.

After the fault definition, all associated faults are transferred into the internal fault diagram of the component. This step is marked with number (1) in Fig. 8.

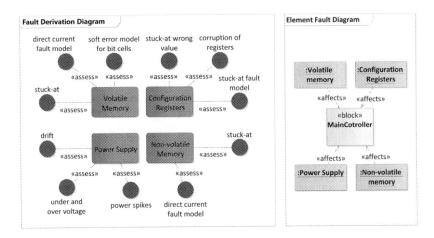

Fig. 9. Fault definitions of the MainController component. On the left side the associations of the faults to the ISO HWParts is shown and on the right side, instances of the HWElements are associated with the MainController block.

5.2   Failure Modeling

The task for this step is to analyze whether the occurrence of a fault leads to a failure (*cf.* number (2) in Fig. 8). If a fault is not relevant for the behavior of the component, it is marked as `effectless` in a `Internal Element Fault Diagram`. Further, we correlate the faults and the safety goal over the failure elements, i.e., we define for each failure element, whether and if so which safety goal(s) are affected by a specific fault. For this, the tool provides either the use of SafeDeML::Failure properties or an additional, automatically generated table, where the designer can enter if a failure violates a safety goal. Per default, a failure is defined violating all safety goals violated by other SafeDeML::Failure elements within each component reachable by propagation. This step is repeated until each fault is either assigned to a failure or marked as `effectless`. By this, it can be ensured that no fault has been forgotten until the safety assessment.

5.3   Diagnosis

In this step the specific safety mechanisms handling the occurrences of a specific failure (*cf.* step number (3) Fig. 8) within the `Internal Element Fault Diagram`. Further, we assign a particular diagnostic coverage for the diagnosis.

However, it can be possible that, for some failures, we do not implement a diagnosis on the same model element, e.g., if we want to analyze whether a fault is critical, if we implement the diagnosis on a different element, or if we just oversaw a failure. For the case we did not oversee a failure but do not want to handle it in the local context we can apply the propagation methodology. That means we define which port propagates a particular failure and associate them via «propagate by». By default, a not diagnosed failure is propagated over all available SafeDeML::OutputPorts.

5.4 Global Analysis

The scope of the global analysis is to verify the model elements with all side-effects that are introduced by failure propagation. Therefore, the first step is to propagate all SafeDeML::Failures associated with an SafeDeML::OutputPort over all connected SafeDeML::InputPort (*cf.* step number (4) Fig. 8). After that, we repeat step *(B)* and *(C)* of the process with the additional further propagated SafeDeML::Failures, i.e., to decide whether they introduce a safety goal violating failure (*cf.* step (5) Fig. 8) and design a diagnosis or propagate the new defined failure.

5.5 Model Analysis

The completeness of the system model's safety design, and therefore the integrity of all safety goals, is analyzed in this last step. Hence, it is checked whether (i) all SafeDeML::Faults had been handled at least once (set to `effectless` or are connected to a SafeDeML::Failure), (ii) all relevant SafeDeML::Failures are propagated or covered by a diagnosis, and (iii) if the minimal set of faults, according to the Iso 26262, has been concerned by a SafeDeML::Diagnosis.

If not, the tool integration can focus the designer's view directly to the element violating the integrity of a safety goal. From the model, of course, all relevant information as item element - fault - failure - diagnosis relations can be extracted from the model and provided within additional result tables.

6 Conclusion and Future Work

In this work, we presented our UML-profile SafeDeML, a SysML extension for integrating the safety design process into the model-based system design work-flow. Therefore we defined a set of modeling elements for fault, failure, and diagnosis definitions. In particular, the diagnosis provides an improvement since it enables the definition of generated safety mechanisms directly within the system model. Based on the SafeDeML fault definitions, we build a library integrating all Iso 26262 hardware fault definitions and corresponding hardware elements. We think that this decreases the effort necessary of ensuring that all relevant faults are addressed in the safety design and also serves as a starting point for the design.

In addition, we defined a structured process which integrates SafeDeML into the system modeling process. This process is intended to define a safety measure itself. Therefore it supports the designer during the safety analysis process by (i) addressing at least all potentially hazardous faults once in the model, (ii) ensuring that no information is lost by transforming the information from external safety design documents into the model, and (iii) providing a structured way of analyzing the elements in their local and global context by automatic failure propagation. In the next steps of our work, we plan to use the safety design definitions based on SafeDeML and execute Iso 26262 relevant safety analysis.

References

1. Road vehicles - Functional safety: Part(X): Standard
2. Adler, R., et al.: Integration of component fault trees into the UML. In: Dingel, J., Solberg, A. (eds.) MODELS 2010. LNCS, vol. 6627, pp. 312–327. Springer, Heidelberg (2011). https://doi.org/10.1007/978-3-642-21210-9_30
3. Avižienis, A., Laprie, J.-C., Randell, B.: Dependability and its threats: a taxonomy. In: Jacquart, R. (ed.) Building the Information Society. IFIP, vol. 156, pp. 91–120. Springer, Boston (2004). https://doi.org/10.1007/978-1-4020-8157-6_13
4. Bernardi, S., Merseguer, J., Petriu, D.C.: A dependability profile within MARTE. Softw. Syst. Model. **10**(3), 313–336 (2011)
5. Biggs, G., Juknevicius, T., Armonas, A., Post, K.: Integrating Safety and Reliability Analysis into MBSE: overview of the new proposed OMG standard. INCOSE Int. Symp. **28**(1), 1322–1336 (2018)
6. Biggs, G., Sakamoto, T., Kotoku, T.: 2A2-I06 SafeML: a model-based tool for communicating safety information (Robotics with Safety and Reliability). In: Proceedings of Robomec 2013(0), _2A2-I06_1-_2A2-I06_4 (2013)
7. Biggs, G., Sakamoto, T., Kotoku, T.: A profile and tool for modelling safety information with design information in SysML. Softw. Syst. Model. **15**(1), 147–178 (2016)
8. Cicchetti, A., et al.: CHESS: a model-driven engineering tool environment for aiding the development of complex industrial systems. In: Goedicke, M., Menzies, T., Saeki, M. (eds.) Proceedings of ASE, p. 362. IEEE, Piscataway (2012)
9. Fuentes-Fernández, L., Vallecillo-Moreno, A.: An introduction to UML profiles. UML Model Eng. **2**, 6–13 (2004)
10. Gallina, B., Javed, M.A., Muram, F.U., Punnekkat, S.: A model-driven dependability analysis method for component-based architectures. In: Proceedings of Euromicro DSD/SEAA, pp. 233–240 (2012)
11. Grunske, L., Kaiser, B., Papadopoulos, Y.: Model-driven safety evaluation with state-event-based component failure annotations. In: Heineman, G.T., Crnkovic, I., Schmidt, H.W., Stafford, J.A., Szyperski, C., Wallnau, K. (eds.) CBSE 2005. LNCS, vol. 3489, pp. 33–48. Springer, Heidelberg (2005). https://doi.org/10.1007/11424529_3
12. Kaiser, B., Liggesmeyer, P., Mäckel, O.: A new component concept for fault trees. In: Proceedings of SCS, pp. 37–46 (2003)
13. Langenhan, T.: Still basic guide to automotive functional safety. epubli, Berlin, version 2 edn. (2016)

14. Moncada, V., Santiago, V.: Towards proper tool support for component-oriented and model-based development of safety critical systems. In: Commercial Vehicle Technology 2016, pp. 365–374. Shaker Verlag, Aachen (2016)
15. Montecchi, L., Lollini, P., Bondavalli, A.: Dependability concerns in model-driven engineering. In: Proceedings of ISORC, pp. 254–263. IEEE (2011)
16. Papadopoulos, Y., McDermid, J.A.: Hierarchically performed hazard origin and propagation studies. In: Felici, M., Kanoun, K. (eds.) SAFECOMP 1999. LNCS, vol. 1698, pp. 139–152. Springer, Heidelberg (1999). https://doi.org/10.1007/3-540-48249-0_13
17. Papadopoulos, Y., et al.: Engineering failure analysis and design optimisation with HiP-HOPS. Eng. Fail. Anal. **18**(2), 590–608 (2011)
18. Ross, H.L.: Functional Safety for Road Vehicles. Springer International Publishing, Cham (2016)
19. Rumbaugh, J., Jacobson, I., Booch, G.: The Unified modeling language reference manual. Pearson Higher Education (2004)
20. Selic, B., Gérard, S.: Modeling and Analysis of Real-Time and Embedded Systems with UML and MARTE: Developing Cyber-Physical Systems. Elsevier (2013)
21. Mazzini, S., Favaro, J.M., Puri, S., Baracchi, L.: CHESS: an open source methodology and toolset for the development of critical systems. In: EduSymp/OSS4MDE@MoDELS (2016)
22. Weilkiens, T.: SysML–the systems modeling language. In: The MK/OMG Press (ed.) Systems Engineering with SysML/UML, pp. 223–270. Elsevier (2007)

Towards Trusted Security Context Exchange Protocol for SDN Based Low Latency Networks

Abdul Ghafoor[1,2(✉)], A. Qudus Abbasi[3], and Zaheer Khan[4]

[1] School of Electrical Engineering and Computer Science, Islamabad, Pakistan
[2] RISE AB, Isafjordsgatan 22, 164 40 Kista, Sweden
abdul.ghafoor@ri.se
[3] Department of Information Technology,
Quaid-i-Azam University, Islamabad, Pakistan
aqudus@qau.edu.pk
[4] University of the West of England, Frenchay Campus, Bristol, UK
Zaheer2.Khan@uwe.ac.uk

Abstract. To overcome the latency issue in real-time communication, a number of research based solutions and architectures are being proposed. In all these, security is not considered an important factor since it causes extra delay in the communication and introduces overhead. Therefore, a design decision is needed to assess tradeoff between efficiency and security mechanisms. In this respect, we designed a security approach in Software Defined Networks (SDN) based Vehicular Autonomous Ad hoc Network (VANET) where low latency and security are essential elements. VNAET provides a system of systems approach where various hybrid solutions are integrated and installed on number of network nodes managed by SDN. In such networks, our novel approach exchanges security context in a synchronized manner to serve as a baseline for network nodes to dynamically adopt security features as per security requirements of these nodes. Hence, various security contexts are designed and categorized based on the nature of information exchange between nodes, mainly, to offer authentication, secure and trustworthy communication services. These well-designed security contexts enable devices of different capabilities to securely communicate by using predefined security parameters and cryptographic functions. This eliminates the need to negotiate any secure communication parameters and hence results in less communication overhead. In addition, our approach is integrated with verifiable identities (Veidblock) concept which addresses privacy issues through anonymity. These security contexts are verified by using scyther by demonstrating that the trustworthiness is achieved by countering non-repudiation, impersonation, tampering, eavesdropping and replay attacks.

Keywords: Trust · Verifiable identities · SDN · Context · Security attributes · VANET

© Springer Nature Switzerland AG 2019
A. Romanovsky et al. (Eds.): SAFECOMP 2019, LNCS 11698, pp. 286–298, 2019.
https://doi.org/10.1007/978-3-030-26601-1_20

1   Introduction

Increasing demand of real time and/or latency sensitive applications encourages network operators to enhance their network infrastructure, for instance 5G network revolution [1]. It is anticipated that such networks would be capable to meet the demand of real-time applications e.g., IoT, autonomous vehicular systems, tele-surgery, industrial automation (industry 4.0), augmented reality and virtual reality, as such applications are highly sensitive to latency and demand high bandwidth [2]. There can be serious consequences in such applications due to delay in communication between devices; however, achieving <1 ms delay and acquiring 10–50 GB bandwidth are highly challenging and several solutions are being proposed e.g., Smart Energy System, Fieldbus System and Industrial Ethernet [3, 28]. This becomes more challenging when it is predicted that trillion of devices and sensors will be connected to the internet to generate & collect data and then exchange data between devices for real-time processing [4, 27]. This will require underlying network infrastructures to be highly efficient, provide high data transfer rates, dependable, trusted, ultra-reliable and secure communication.

To overcome the latency issue in real-time communication, a number of architectural solutions are being proposed, for example, Edge computing model [29]. In edge computing, storage and processing services are kept close to the users' proximity to reduce payload for communication and hence low latency but such an infrastructure causes extra management issues by replicating some services in edge environment. One of the solutions to handle these issues and efficiently manage edge and main data centers is programmable networks or Software Defined Networks (SDN) [5]. Current SDN developments are mainly focused on automating and orchestrating existing network facilities [6]. In literature, it is observed that only few network automation solutions are proposed for low latency networks, which are focusing on per-routing path calculation, segregation between small and large flows, categorization in control and data flows, identification of efficient routes based on network state which is derived by using regular network monitoring mechanisms and others techniques [7, 8]. However, despite these solutions research community has varying views on the provision of autonomous and efficient connectivity that is mainly based on the pre-configurations and introduces extra delay in network connectivity. Further, introducing security features can causes more delays in the system; therefore, current implementations of SDN and security protocols do not meet the requirements of latency sensitive applications such as autonomous vehicular network.

Without inclusion of security features in low latency network, it is hard to deploy a trustworthy infrastructure and applications but, as mentioned above, it causes extra delay which can be reduced by minimizing number of security messages, preprocessing and reducing message overheads.

In the above context, a novel solution is proposed that exchanges security context in a synchronized manner that serves as a baseline to dynamically adopt security features and fulfill security requirements of the deployed network. In our solution, various security contexts are designed and categorized based on the nature of information exchange between nodes (resources), mainly, to offer authentication; and secure and trustworthy communication services. These well-designed security contexts enable the devices of different capabilities to securely communicate by using the predefined security parameters and cryptographic functions. This eliminates the need to negotiate any secure communication parameters and hence results in less communication overhead. In our previous work we focused on secure SDN applications [9]; now we extend our work to secure SDN for low latency network and applications. In [9], we designed verifiable identities (Veidblock) for devices and users and published it in a Distributed Ledger Technology (DLT). The Veidblock is used to simplify authenticity process and establishing trust between various resources involved in communication without verifying the direct legitimacy of sender and receiver and hence reduces extra communication overhead. This makes Veidblock a suitable candidate for secure latency sensitive applications.

After deigning our solution, it has following main features:

- Eliminates security context exchange time to reduce network communication and increase in message processing time;
- Security context are synched with each node therefor they are secure and interoperable;
- Reduces message size which decreases communication overhead;
- Reduces authentication time through verifiable identities; and,
- Introduces security contexts which are categorized to facilitate every node with diverse capabilities.

2   Background and Case Study

In recent years, researchers have been focusing on designing network infrastructure to facilitate current and future secure and delay sensitive applications [28]. For instance, fifth generation (5G) of mobile communication network is considered to facilitate low latency applications designed either in 2020 or beyond [10]. Similarly, edge and fog computing are also playing a key role to minimize the data transmission time, efficiently utilization of bandwidth and resources [11]. Such enabling technologies target tactile internet and low latency applications to provide greater throughput and higher capacity that is not achievable through existing mobile networks. Furthermore, they focus on to functional requirement by achieving lower communication delay, providing high reliability and supporting higher connection density without compromising the non-functional requirements such as security, trust, identity and privacy.

2.1   Secure Software Defined Networks

Due to the growing network size and increasing devices on the internet, network automation through virtualization and software components plays an important role to manage such scaling infrastructures. Other organisations have already started investigating SDN to benefit businesses through high elastic nature of the virtual computing resources [12]. Though such systems can provide economic, management, maintenance and extensibility benefits, but thorough testing is needed to measure and understand limitations and associated risks before wider adoption by business organisations [30]. Among other challenges, researchers highlighted security of orchestrator and controllers in and SDN environment as one of the major concerns. For Network Function Virtualisation (NFV), SDN and cloud-based networks, European Telecommunication Standards Institute (ETSI) is playing an important role and actively contributing and defining new standards to secure SDN and NFVs. The ETSI [13] focused on defining basic security services such as AAA (Authentication, Authorization, and Accountability) services. They highlighted the need to consider privacy in authentication, anti-privilege escalation techniques, authorization and accountability through network infrastructure. The ETSI also mentioned security monitoring and management requirements in [14] but their standards do not provide technical details on how these security related services can be implemented.

In [15], other researchers have presented security challenges of SDN and mentioned that along with conventional security challenges, leakage of sensitive information is easy in SDN. They recommend that a security protocol and suitable techniques must be considered to protect SDN from information disclosure attack when programmable components are used to manage networks. The Open Networking Foundation (ONF) described security analysis of OpenFlow switch specification in [16]. They recommended certificate-based authentication and secure communication. For trust development, they assume that the certificate is issued (to both communicating components) by same domain; otherwise, communicating virtual switch/host are considered untrusted.

In addition to the above challenges, combination of SDN with low latency network introduces new challenges. In this respect, there are many solutions proposed in literature, which claim that SDN can be suitable to minimize delays in packet delivery [7]. In [17], other researchers contributed to overcoming the delay caused by SDN controller when it interacts with virtual switches to install new flows and rules. For their study, they categorized flow types into large volume data carrier (bulk data) and small data carrier (short messages). In most of the cases, small flows required frequent transmission and needed frequent controller invocation which caused delays. To overcome this problem, authors in [7] suggested that the system must be able to predict frequent communication pairs in advance instead of at run time. Data collected from switches is maintained and future flows are predicted on maintained data. Though this solution is reasonable but it is yet unknown how this will behave when security interventions are introduced in the network. Similarly in [18], other researchers described a network coding technique to reduce retransmission delays and implemented it in a virtual router. Their results are promising and indicate that they achieved desired objectives. Among others, security issues in an SDN are discussed in the [17, 18] where other researchers discussed about various attacks and services required by different components of an SDN. For instance, two of these components are directly related to the secure flow of information: (i) Secure Communication (SC) Component, and (ii) Policy Based Communication (PBC) Component. In SC component they provide solutions for IP-level packets and replaced weak authentication between backhaul devices with better authentication solutions.

2.2 Case Study: Security Issues in Vehicular Ad-hoc Networks

We consider Vehicular Ad hoc Networks (VANET) as a case study to demonstrate a viable application of low latency network. In VANETs, user authentication and privacy are the major concerns along with latency issue [19]. To ensure security of the VANETs, appropriate security protocols and low latency network are the key requirements. In [20], other researchers discussed privacy and security related challenges of VANETs; for example, they highlighted various forms of attacks, defined security primitives and mitigation techniques to support vehicular network applications and provide a secure and trusted propagation of road information with other drivers. Similar privacy and security related issues are discussed in [21]. They highlighted various security protocols, which can be used to protect the vehicular network from various attacks.

In VANETs like highly mobile and ad hoc network environment, broadcasting of safety messages requires low latency and high reliability. In [22], other researchers have provided technical details of techniques for user's authentication which uses identity based signature schemes and recommended RSA and ECDSA algorithms for signature creation and verification. In contrast, batch verification is the most commonly adopted scheme in VANETs which verifies multiple signature at once rather than verifying individual signatures [23]. Furthermore in this, privacy issues are handled by three approaches which include pseudonymous authentication schemes, group signature based schemes and hybrid schemes. Trust based authentication technique is described in [24] where verifier nodes are responsible to verify a node for trust based authentication in VANET by using certificates. Recently, most of low latency applications are using Blockchain or DLTs for trust and authentication services, for example, in [25] and [26] VANET based application is presented.

2.3 Research Gap Analysis

After analyzing existing approaches in SDN and low latency applications such as VANET, we found following limitations:

- Current security solutions for SDN are only applicable in standard SDN environment. These existing solutions do not cater for underlying non-physical network and low latency applications on these networks.
- VANET only considers security solutions which are suitable for VANET and meets the requirements of low latency networks.
- Analysis of the above literature reveals that when these both technologies are integrated to form an SDN based Vehicular Network; it raises new security requirements and needs new solutions which must be suitable for various nature of messages.

3 The Proposed Solution: Adaptable Security Contexts

To fill the above gap, this paper introduces a novel approach that defines security contexts for applications which are able to synchronize security primitives according to the capabilities of resources available in Vehicular Networks. Our proposed approach introduces two main characteristics in the SDN based Networks:

- *Adaptability:* It adapts security solution and cryptographic functions by considering the sensitivity of data and aims to meet the basic security criteria.
- *Dynamicity:* It supports security context development and synchronization of the security parameters between the various devices (of different capabilities) installed in Vehicular Network.

3.1 Initial Setup with VeidBlock Based Authentication

In [9], we introduced IAV (Identify Authority & Validation) component in SDN to issue, register and verify identities of various resources in the network. Here we reuse IAV component and each resource in the system must be registered with IAV and it possess required security credentials like Veidblock and key pair (public and private key). Veidblock is a cryptographically digitally signed block which contains randomly generated identity of the owner, public key of the owner along with required parameters which are used for its verification. These all attributes are digitally signed by IAV which provide information to verifier that the Veidblock is valid and issued to a trusted resource. Since basic authentication is achieved through Veidblock therefore there is a need of a secure and trusted protocol which will help resources to develop security context for secure communication.

3.2 Security Context Exchange Protocol

In our approach, admin of orchestrator is responsible to create security context and publish it in the DLT. Each security context has following three attributes:

- *Version:* is used to indicate version of the security context.
- *Context-Id:* indicates the context which reflects security requirements of a message
- *Cryptographic-Functions:* various cryptographic functions and sequence of the cryptographic functions used to generate and process contents of the message.

All recommended security contexts with their associated type of messages are shown in Table 1. Our solution is customizable and extendable therefore Table 1 can be extended with more secure and suitable options according to the requirements of their networks.

Publication of security contexts in the DLT provides immutability, trust and availability of transactional data for each node. Publication process follows the standard blockchain transaction process as defined in [22]. In this respect, Admin of SDN Orchestrator (referred as Admin in this paper) creates security contexts, digitally signs security contexts and Veidblock and then publishes them in the DLT. After that Admin submits it to the network where certain rules are applied (which is implemented in the

Table 1. Recommended security context and suggested operations used in each security context

Ver	Context Id		Cryptographic Functions
1	1		No Crypto
1	2		$E(S_{pr}, H(M \mid n) \mid V_h) \mid M \mid n$
1	3	Exchange SK	$SK` = E(R_{pu}, SK)$ $M` = E(S_{pr}, H(SK` \mid n) \mid Vh) \mid SK` \mid n$
		Message	$M` = E(SK`, M \mid H(M \mid n) \mid Vh) \mid n$
1	4		$M` = E(S_{pr}, H(E (R_{pu}, M) \mid n) \mid Vh) \mid E(R_{pu}, M) \mid n$

Where E = Encryption, R_{pu} = Public key of the recipient, SK = Symmetric Key, S_{pr} = Private key of sender, H = SHA-256 Hash function, SK` = Encrypted symmetric key, n = nonce and Vh = Hash value of Veidblock, already calculated

form of smart contract). For example, it checks double publication and verifies Veidblock for Admin authenticity. Similarly each category of security context will be published in the DLT.

3.3   Categorization of Security Context

Categorization of security context is dependent on the types of security services required by the resources in a network. Each message must be transmitted with ctx number and hash of Veidblock (Vh) as a header value of the communication protocol. There are following possible scenarios:

No Security Services (ctx-1.1): If security services are not required during communication then its context number should be '*1.1*'. For example, if a car wants to share general information like music or simple chat messages to other cars then such message does not need any type of security. These are not critical messages and any attack on such messages will not be a threat for the VANET. Similarly, if orchestrator or controller sends general messages, like checking heartbeat, to other components then they also do not need severe security measures. Therefore, in these situations such resources will use message type 1.1 which represents protocol version along with its context id.

Trusted Messages (ctx-1.2): These are trusted messages and are implemented by using applying following cryptographic function:

$$M' = E(S_{pr}, H(M|n)|V_h)|M|n \tag{1}$$

By using this context, content of a message and nonce value is hashed by using hashing algorithms like SHA-256 and then hash value and the hashed value of Veidblock is signed with private key of the sender. Digitally singed value and actual message with nonce will be payload of a Secure Message. The recipient of this message will verify signature. In this the digital signature and hash value of Vh indicates that the message is coming from legitimate source because only the owner of the private key can digitally sign the message. These cryptographic functions protect the protocol against repudiation, tampering, spoofing and impersonation attacks because the Veidblock owner is a trusted user which has its own trusted public key while nonce in the message protects it from replay attacks and hash is used to ensure the integrity of the messages.

These types of the messages are normally broadcast types of informative messages which provide information about weather, accidents, road conditions, etc. Such messages must be verifiable that it should be coming from trusted source and must provide authentic information.

Confidential Bulk Messages (ctx-1.3): This type of security context is used to exchange bulk messages between two resources in peer-to-peer fashion. Normally these resources are fixed and are not part of the dynamic network. In our framework such resources are orchestrator, controller or may be some other resources with fixed and high bandwidth network. In this case, both peers share a symmetric key by using following cryptographic operation. Public key of the recipient is acquired from the DLT which is the part of Veidblock architectural configuration and is already trusted.

$$SK' = E(R_{pu}, SK) \tag{2}$$

$$M' = E(S_{pr}, H(SK'|n) | Vh) | SK' | n \tag{3}$$

The protected key is then used (Eq. 3) to generate key exchange message and these are same as described in the security context (Eq. 1). Once key is shared then, the peers can use following cryptographic operations for exchanging bulk messages in secure way (Eq. 4). These operations provide protection of messages against information disclosure (eavesdropping) because SK is encrypted by using the using the public key of the recipients. The tampering, spoofing, replay attacks and provides trusted communication between resources by using digital signature, verification of Veidblock and inclusion of none in the message.

$$M' = E(SK', M | H(M|n)|Vh) |n \tag{4}$$

Confidential Light Messages (ctx1.4): This type of security context is recommended to use for light weight messages exchanged between two low latency devices. Example of such message are sharing location information with a friend, exchanging codes between peers, etc. In short, this type of context is used when a peer to peer secure and trusted communication is required. As depicted in Eq. 5, in this security context, sender encrypts the message with public key of the recipient and then digitally signs it by using the Eq. 1.

$$M' = E(S_{pr}, H(E(R_{pu}, M) | n) | Vh) | E(R_{pu}, M) | n \tag{5}$$

4   Mapping of the Proposed Solution to VANET Case Study

As shown in the Fig. 1, various components are configured installed and they are connected with each other. Each node is also synched with the DLT and stores various security context in local storage. In this the Orchestrator is responsible to manage controller therefore they can exchange bulk messages for updated controller configuration, installing new policies and routes. Since these messages are bulk messages therefore they mention ctx1.3 in the header of a message. Rest of operations are automatically synched according to the ctx requirements. Similarly, the controller needs to transfer updated state to orchestrator therefore it also uses ctx1.3.

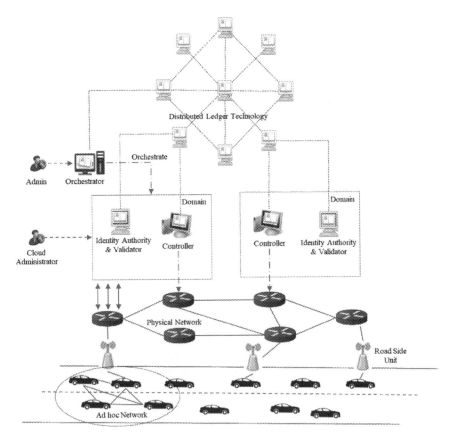

Fig. 1. Architectural view of the use case and interaction between various nodes

On the other hand, if a vehicle sends its current location to the Road Side Unit (RSU) then it uses sctx1.4 because these are light messages and vehicle does not have fixed connection with RSU. Similarly, if a vehicle wants to exchange information messages like road condition, air pressure, weather status or urgent help message then such messages needs only source authentication and data integrity which leads to the trusted communication. Such types of messages are normally broadcasted in ad hoc network and vehicle only specifies ctx1.2 in the message header. Recipients can process messages according to the crypto functions specified in ctx specification.

5 Evaluation and Discussion

In this section, various designed message contexts are evaluated by using scyther, a tool for formal verification of security protocols which already has a built-in adversary model. In this evaluation, two main security contexts are considered because the others are subset of these two. These are ctx1.2 and ctx 1.3. In addition to that, in scyther model, V1 represents a sender Vehicle while the V2 represents a receiver vehicle.

In ctx 1.2, we focused on a *match* event to ensure that the Veidblock is correct and authentic therefore it is defined as a global variable since it is fetched from DLT. Other relevant four claims are: (i) *Nisynch*, is used to ensure that the communication between sender and receiver is synched and sent by the sender, (ii) *Alive*, required for authentication to ensure that the recipient received messages and processed it, (iii) *Commit*, is used for commitments between sender and receiver and makes effective claim against impersonation attack. (iv) *Niagree*, ensures that the non-injective property is achieved to protect protocol from replay attack. As shown in Fig. 2 that all claims verified by scyther and only one claim 'Alive' at the V2 failed because our solution provides reduction of messages exchanged between V1 and V2 by pre-establishing generalized security context therefore V1 is not receiving any response message.

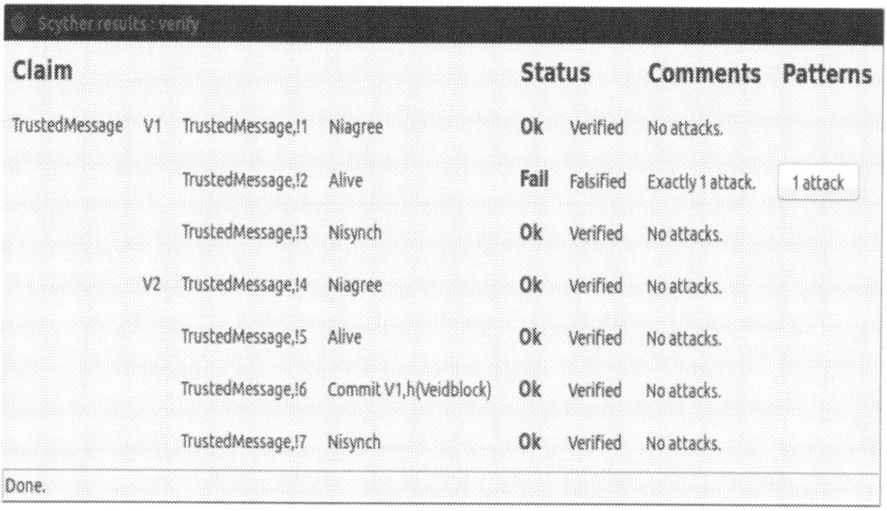

Claim				Status		Comments	Patterns
TrustedMessage	V1	TrustedMessage,!1	Niagree	Ok	Verified	No attacks.	
		TrustedMessage,!2	Alive	Fail	Falsified	Exactly 1 attack.	1 attack
		TrustedMessage,!3	Nisynch	Ok	Verified	No attacks.	
	V2	TrustedMessage,!4	Niagree	Ok	Verified	No attacks.	
		TrustedMessage,!5	Alive	Ok	Verified	No attacks.	
		TrustedMessage,!6	Commit V1,h(Veidblock)	Ok	Verified	No attacks.	
		TrustedMessage,!7	Nisynch	Ok	Verified	No attacks.	

Fig. 2. Formal verification results of designed ctx1.2 for Trusted Messages

The ctx1.3 messages which is used for confidential bulk messages. This type of security context is also used to exchange a share secret and then by using that secret encrypted bulk messages are exchanged. Figure 3 shows the results of ctx1.3. In this we can view that the '*Alive*' claim is also successful since more than one message are involved in this verification. In addition to the above claims, we also claimed '*Secret*' in which to verify that a shared key is exchanged securely and then messages level confidentiality is also achieved.

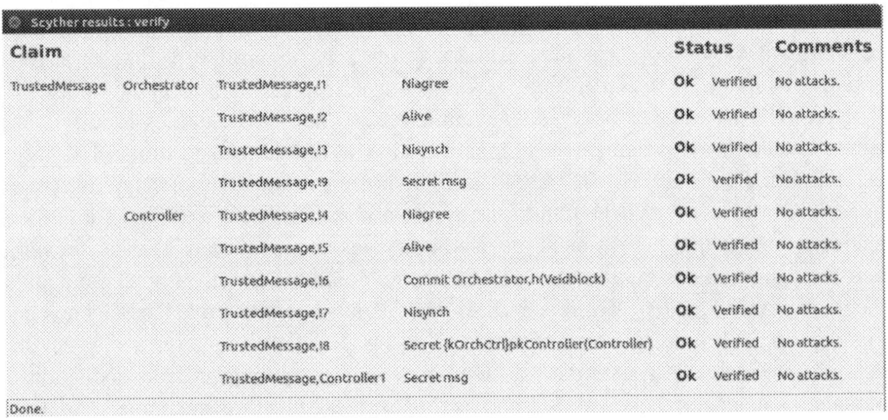

Claim				Status		Comments
TrustedMessage	Orchestrator	TrustedMessage,t1	Niagree	Ok	Verified	No attacks.
		TrustedMessage,t2	Alive	Ok	Verified	No attacks.
		TrustedMessage,t3	Nisynch	Ok	Verified	No attacks.
		TrustedMessage,t9	Secret msg	Ok	Verified	No attacks.
	Controller	TrustedMessage,t4	Niagree	Ok	Verified	No attacks.
		TrustedMessage,t5	Alive	Ok	Verified	No attacks.
		TrustedMessage,t6	Commit Orchestrator,h(Veidblock)	Ok	Verified	No attacks.
		TrustedMessage,t7	Nisynch	Ok	Verified	No attacks.
		TrustedMessage,t8	Secret {kOrchCtrl}pkController(Controller)	Ok	Verified	No attacks.
		TrustedMessage,Controller1	Secret msg	Ok	Verified	No attacks.

Fig. 3. Formal verification results of designed ctx1.3 for confidential bulk messages

Our evaluation results show that the designed security context provides data integrity, confidentiality, non-reputation and freshness services for SDN based VANET use case.

6   Conclusions

To overcome the latency issue in real-time communication, a number of research based solutions and various architectures are being proposed. In this paper, a novel solution is proposed for such networks to exchange security context in a synchronized manner to serve as a baseline for nodes to dynamically adopt security features and fulfill security requirements of deployed nodes. Various security contexts are designed, proposed and categorized based on the nature of information exchange between nodes (resources) ensure trustworthy communication services. We verified our security contexts operations by using scyther and verified that the designed security contexts provide message authentication, data confidentiality, data integrity and secure key exchange mechanisms for hybrid network (based on fixed and ad hoc network). In addition to that we also, discussed that the more suitable security context can be used according to the requirements of network which makes it adaptable and more flexible. Our future objective is to extend existing solution and introduce more complex cryptographic functions with alternative options to make it more adaptable and customizable. To practically demonstrate the realization of the solution and comparing its network latency and efficiency with existing solution, VEINS simulator based solution (Proof of Concept) will be implemented in near future.

Acknowledgment. This research activity is partially supported by TOUCHES ICT-TNG project and KP for Cybersecurity at RISE. We are also thankful to prof. Panos for technical discussion on initial topic at KTH.

References

1. Chen, M., Qian, Y., Hao, Y., Li, Y., Song, J.: Data-driven computing and caching in 5G networks: architecture and delay analysis. IEEE Wirel. Commun. **25**(1), 70–75 (2018)
2. IEEE 5G and beyond technology roadmap. https://futurenetworks.ieee.org/images/files/pdf/ieee-5g-roadmap-white-paper.pdf. Accessed 13 June 2019
3. Accenture Consulting. Tactile Internet enabled by pervasive networks. http://technodocbox.com/Computer_Networking/69821120-Tactile-internet-enabled-by-pervasive-networks.html. Accessed 12 Feb 2019
4. van Kranenburg, R., Bassi, A.: IoT challenges. mUX: J. Mob. User Exp., 1–9 (2012). https://doi.org/10.1186/2192-1121-1-9
5. Kreutz, D., Ramos, F., Veríssimo, P.E., Rothenberg, C.E., Azodolmolky, S., Uhlig, S.: Software-defined networking: a comprehensive survey. IEEE. **103**(1), 14–76 (2015)
6. Truong, N.B., Lee, G.M., Ghamri-Doudane, Y.: Software defined networking-based vehicular Adhoc Network with Fog Computing. In: Proceedings of the IFIP/IEEE International Symposium on Integrated Network Management (IM), Ottawa, ON, Canada (2015)
7. Su, Z., Wang, T., Xia, Y., Hamdi, M.: CheetahFlow: towards low latency software-defined network. In: Proceedings of IEEE International Conference on Communications (ICC), Sydney, NSW, Australia (2014)
8. Requena, J.C., et al.: SDN and NFV integration in generalized mobile network architecture. In: Proceedings of European Conference on Networks and Communications (EuCNC), Paris, France (2015)
9. Abbasi, A.G., Khan, Z.: VeidBlock: verifiable identity using blockchain and ledger in a software defined network. In: Proceedings of SCCTSA2017 Co-located 10th IEEE/ACM Utility and Cloud Computing Conference, Austin, Texas, USA, pp. 173–179 (2017)
10. Kirichek, R.: 5G and Tactile Internet. Network and Services Decentralization. https://www.itu.int/en/ITU-T/Workshops-and-Seminars/20160921/Documents/Presentations/S1_2_Ruslan_Kirichek_v3.pdf. Accessed 13 June 2019
11. Hu, P., Dhelim, S., Ning, H., Qiu, T.: Survey on fog computing: architecture, key technologies, applications and open issues. J. Network Comput. Appl. **98**, 27–42 (2017)
12. Ramel, D.: SDN a game changer but slow out of the gate, survey shows. https://gcn.com/Articles/2015/01/13/SDN-adoption.aspx. Accessed 13 June 2019
13. ETSI. Network Functions Virtualisation (NFV); NFV Security; Security and Trust Guidance, https://www.etsi.org/deliver/etsi_gr/NFV-SEC/001_099/003/01.02.01_60/gr_nfv-sec003v010201p.pdf. Accessed 13 June 2019
14. ETSI. Network Functions Virtualisation (NFV); NFV Security; Problem Statement, http://www.etsi.org/deliver/etsi_gs/NFV-SEC/001_099/001/01.01.01_60/gs_NFV-SEC001v010101p.pdf. Accessed 13 June 2019

15. Wen, X., Chen, Y., Hu, C., Shi, C., Wang, Yi.: Towards a secure controller platform for openflow applications. In: Proceedings of 2nd ACM SIGCOMM Workshop on Hot Topics in Software Defined Networking (HotSDN 2013), Hong Kong, China, pp. 171–172 (2013)

16. Wasserman, M., Hartman, S., Zhang, D.: Security analysis of the Open Networking Foundation (ONF) OpenFlow Switch Specification. https://tools.ietf.org/id/draft-mrw-sdnsec-openflow-analysis-00.html. Accessed 12 June 2019

17. Szabo, D., Gulyas, A., Fitzek, F.H., Lucani, D.E.: Towards the tactile internet: decreasing communication latency with network coding and software defined networking. In: Proceedings of 21st European Wireless Conference, Budapest, Hungary, pp. 1–6 (2015)

18. Liyanage, M., et al.: Enhancing security of software defined mobile networks. IEEE Access 5, 9422–9438 (2017)

19. Parno, B., Perrig, A.: Challenges in securing vehicular networks. https://netsec.ethz.ch/publications/papers/cars.pdf. Accessed 13 June 2019

20. Al-Raba'nah, Y., Samara, G.: Security Issues in Vehicular Ad Hoc Networks (VANET): a survey. Int. J. Sci. Appl. Res. 2(4), 50–55 (2015)

21. Zaidi, K., Rajarajan, M.: Vehicular internet: security & privacy challenges and opportunities. Future Internet 7, 257–275 (2015)

22. Qu, F., Wu, Z., Wang, F.-Y., Cho, W.: A security and privacy review of VANETs. IEEE Trans. Intell. Transp. Syst. 16(6), 2985–2996 (2015)

23. Shrestha, R., Bajarachary, R., Nam, S.Y.: Challenges of future VANET and cloud-based approaches. Hindawi Wirel. Commun. Mob. Comput. 2018, 15 (2018)

24. Sugumar, R., Rengarajan, A., Jayakumar, C.: Trust based authentication technique for cluster based vehicular ad hoc networks (VANET). Wirel. Netw. 24(2), 373–382 (2018)

25. Kaiser, C., Steger, M., Dorri, A., Festl, A., Stocker, A., Fellmann, M., Kanhere, S.: Towards a privacy-preserving way of vehicle data sharing – a case for blockchain technology? In: Dubbert, J., Müller, B., Meyer, G. (eds.) AMAA 2018. LNM, pp. 111–122. Springer, Cham (2019). https://doi.org/10.1007/978-3-319-99762-9_10

26. Sharma, P.K., Moon, S.Y., Park, J.H.: Block-VN: a distributed blockchain based vehicular network architecture in smart city. J. Inform. Process. Syst. 13(1), 184–195 (2017)

27. Bogue, R.: Towards the trillion sensors market. Sens. Rev. 34(2), 137–142 (2014)

28. Aijaz, A., Sooriyabandara, M.: The tactile internet for industries: a review. IEEE 107(2), 414–435 (2018). https://doi.org/10.1109/JPROC.2018.2878265

29. Varghese, B., Wang, N., Barbhuiya, S., Kilpatrick, P., Nikolopoulos, D.S.: Challenges and opportunities in edge computing. In: IEEE International Conference on Smart Cloud (SmartCloud), New York, NY, USA (2016). https://doi.org/10.1109/smartcloud.2016.18

30. Sezer, S., et al.: Are we ready for SDN? implementation challenges for software-defined networks. IEEE Commun. Mag. 51(7), 36–43 (2013)

Devil's in the Detail: Through-Life Safety and Security Co-assurance Using SSAF

Nikita Johnson[(✉)] and Tim Kelly

Department of Computer Science, University of York, York, UK
{nikita.johnson,tim.kelly}@york.ac.uk

Abstract. Regulatory bodies, industry and academia present a plethora of approaches for risk analysis and engineering for safety and security. However, few standards and approaches discuss the management of both safety and security risks. Fewer yet provide detail on how the two attributes interact within a given system. In this paper, the Safety-Security Assurance Framework (SSAF) is presented as a candidate solution to many of the extant challenges of attribute co-assurance. It is a holistic approach, based on the concept of *independent co-assurance*, that considers both the technical risk impact and the socio-technical impact on assurance. The Framework's Technical Risk Model (TRM) is applied and evaluated against a case study of an insulin pump. It is argued that SSAF TRM is not only a plausible and practical approach, but also more effective for co-assurance than many existing approaches alone.

Keywords: System safety · Cyber security · Co-assurance framework

1 Introduction

Advancements in technology have caused an exponential increase in the complexity and interconnectedness of systems that are used by society. These systems range from autonomous aircraft, to critical national infrastructure and household appliances. Indeed, these new capabilities allow society to improve in many ways. However, the challenge is how to ensure that safety and security risk is managed whilst reaping the benefits of innovation, and how to assess the impact of change and make the trade-off for a particular risk.

There are many technical risk reduction approaches that consider both safety and security to different extents; these include, but are not limited to security-aware HAZOPs, security-aware STPA, integrated attack-fault trees, dependability analysis and architectural methods - all of these have been surveyed in [17]. Even with these approaches to unified risk management, problems with co-assurance of the attributes remain. Too often, analysis techniques during development do not capture the level of detail required to assess the impact of change during operation. This is particular true for security assurance, which has the presence of an intelligent adversary as a distinguishing factor. The lack of detail

© Springer Nature Switzerland AG 2019
A. Romanovsky et al. (Eds.): SAFECOMP 2019, LNCS 11698, pp. 299–314, 2019.
https://doi.org/10.1007/978-3-030-26601-1_21

and paucity of assurance information gives rise to issues with the attributes' technical risk arguments, *e.g.* conflicts between safety and security have the potential to undermine or undercut assurance claims made in a single domain, possibly causing a reduction in the accuracy of an assurance claim, and a reduction in the level of confidence we can have in it.

The Safety-Security Assurance Framework (SSAF) [16] is a candidate solution to address the challenges of co-assurance. It is a two-part approach that considers both the technical risk arguments for the attributes, and the socio-technical factors affecting co-assurance. SSAF is based on the new paradigm of *independent co-assurance*, that is, maintaining separate assurance processes, but sharing the right information, with the right people, at the right time. Thus, gaps in assurance can be managed in a more systematic and demonstrable way than simply unifying co-assurance processes and artefacts.

In this paper, the challenges and key concepts are introduced in Sect. 1; Sect. 2 explores the SSAF Technical Risk Model, and Sects. 3 and 4 summarise and conclude the findings of the case study.

1.1   Safety-Security Co-assurance Primer

This introduction to co-assurance concepts is not meant to be exhaustive or complete, but provide the key concepts and terms that will be used in subsequent discussion. *Assurance* will refer to the rationale of why a system has certain quality attributes *e.g.* safety or security, and the process of building that rationale and gaining confidence. *Safety* will refer to systems safety, and look at the interaction of software components within a wider technological system. *Security* refers to cyber-security, which consists of information assurance, as well as physical security and the interactions within a technological system. An *assurance case* is a structured argument of claims supported by evidence, in a given context and under specified assumptions. *Co-assurance*, therefore, is the process and rationale that a system has at least two attributes. The difficulty in discussing assurance may already be apparent, as the word can be both a verb and a noun - either referring to the outcome of an activity, or to the process by which assurance is gained. This difficulty is reflected in the existing standards and frameworks for supporting safety and security assurance.

Safety assurance, for the most part, follows the *4 + 1 Assurance Principles* described in [11]. The Principles 1–3 are concerned with the definition, decomposition and satisfaction of safety requirements. Principle 4 is concerned with ensuring that no hazards have been introduced as a result of the preceding principles. Finally, Principle 4 + 1 is orthogonal to the first four, and it deals with confidence of each of the principles. To a lesser or greater extent, most standards and codes of practice conform to these principles.

Security assurance, however, is currently process based, and most security standards and codes of practice conform to the Plan-Do-Check-Act (PDCA) model described in the security standard ISO 27001 [15]. The Check-Act parts of the PDCA model can be mapped to the 4 + 1 Principles, however the sense of dynamic change and temporal significance is lessened. In addition, the 4 + 1 Principles can be regarded as reductionist in their approach, this is problematic for security where an intelligent adversaries may exploit *emergent properties* of a system to achieve a goal thereby making decomposition impossible.

Independent Co-Assurance is a paradigm that begins to resolve these assurance conflicts. At its core, it allows for separate safety and security assurance processes, separate teams, separate artefacts and different timescales for assurance. To many this might appear to be a step in the wrong direction, *i.e.* a model of siloed assurance. However, what makes independent co-assurance different is that it requires the structure for the "separateness" of the attributes to be determined beforehand. Therefore the right information for assurance activities can be given to the right people at the right time. Determining this structure is non-trivial. The Safety-Security Assurance Framework provides guidelines as to how this might be achieved.

2   SSAF - Technical Risk Model

The Safety-Security Assurance Framework is a two-part, independent co-assurance solution comprised of:

The Socio-Technical Model (STM) – This recognises that the SSAF Technical Risk Model, or indeed any technical approach, is limited by the socio-technical factors that influence it. The STM considers five dimensions - Conceptual, Structure, People, Process and Tools based on the interacting variable classes identified for management information systems [3]. Even though the trade-off decisions made on the socio-technical abstraction level are fundamental to having assurance, for example, deciding the frequency of security patches versus maintaining safety certification stability, they are mostly beyond the (necessarily limited) scope of this research paper.

The Technical Risk Model (TRM) – This is the meta-process and meta-model for integrated technical co-assurance. It is based on the explicit modelling of the causal relationships between attributes, which link the artefacts from activities in one domain to those of the other. In this paper, focus will be on the SSAF Technical Risk Model process which has previously been introduced in [16]; the following subsections will provide further detail. The input, activities and output of each step are shown in Table 1.

Insulin Pump Case Study. To better understand the framework, and to capture the detail of the modelling, a case study of an insulin pump will be used. Insulin pumps are portable medical devices whose primary purpose is to deliver correct dosages of insulin to a diabetic patient. This option is often chosen instead of multiple insulin injections a day. The technology used in the pump introduces new avenues for harm to occur. Therefore, risk must be explicitly considered and safety must be engineered into the system. The components, described in Hu & Li's paper on intelligent insulin pump design [13], consist of an embedded controller which receives input from the patient (such as last meal data via the keyboard), and delivers a dosage of fast or slow-acting insulin by controlling the motor and infusion.

Table 1. Activities, inputs and outputs of SSAF steps.

	Prerequisites.	Activities.	Outcome.

Step 1: Ontology	- Assurance process
	- Key concepts and terms
	- Information needs
		- Establish
		    Sync points
		    Minimal common language
		- Create initial causal model
			- Agreed sync points
			- Shared ontology/dictionary
			- Understand info needs

Step 2: Process	(Single Domain)
	- Assurance process model
	- Activity info requirements
	- Relationship to SDLC
		- Plan
		    Tasks & assign resources
		    Task info requirements
		- Assign techniques to tasks
		- Record or resolve gaps
			- Linked artefacts to process
			- Gaps in assurance that require
			    Resolution or Justification
			- Aligned assurance to SDLC

Step 3: Argument	(Single Domain) - Initial assurance argument - Evidence requirements	- Develop risk argument - Create confidence argument	- Linked argument, artefacts and process that generated them
Step 4: Link	- Ontology of terms - (Single domain) Causal model	- Link conditions and artefacts - Develop causal model	- Integrated causal model - Evidence for integration claims

Step 5: Update	- Assurance arguments
	- Causal models
		- Update artefacts to reflect
		    new information
		- Activities triggered in
		    response to change impact
			- Up-to-date and more dynamic
			    assurance arguments
			- Systematically managed
			    attribute interaction uncertainty

The following sections will apply the Safety-Security Assurance Framework - Technical Risk Model (SSAF TRM) process to the Insulin Pump. As far as possible, existing assurance artefacts in the literature will be used (*e.g.* assurance context [28,35], hazard analyses and safety arguments [5,12,39], security analyses [4,24,25,36], system weaknesses [33,34], *etc.*). The focus of this case study is not the accuracy of the artefacts themselves, but the creation of a shared meta-model of the interactions between artefacts. Having correct risk analyses is a fundamental part of attribute integration, however the assumption is made that the artefacts presented here are plausible enough to demonstrate the application of the TRM.

2.1   Step 1: Establish an Ontology and Synchronisation Points

This initial SSAF step is characterised by the creation of a shared language for assurance across the domains. This may seem trivial, however the similarity of the domains can lead to a false sense of homogeneity, when there exist potentially irreconcilable differences. An example is the concept of *harm*. Within the safety domain harm is understood, in the strictest sense, to be injury or loss of life. Security harm is less clear - significant financial impact is often given as a measure for security harm, however it has been demonstrated that major data breaches often do not depress stock market prices for the affected company longer than a week [21]. This is in stark contrast to the severe impact and in-depth investigation after an accident or safety incident. Security loss events require more deliberate trade-off analysis against the benefits of accepting the risk because many more factors are considered for security risk such as business reputation, resources available, political climate, competitive advantage, *etc.* Furthermore, because the effects of safety harm are perceived to be so egregious, safety often takes precedence when trade-off decisions must be made during development, which limits options for security during operation.

On industrial projects, under the pressure of delivery, there may also be different pressures and expectations from safety and security practitioners. Thus, it is paramount to the success of co-assurance activities to establish a common dictionary early in the development process. A common ontology does not imply unified terminology - it is acceptable to define *safety risk* and *security risk* separately, or where there are intractable disagreements. What is important is to understand the minimal number of terms required for communication and their relation to each other. This is fundamental to communication whether using SSAF or any other methodology. For illustrative purposes, Firesmith's Survivability model [7] will be used for this case study.

Another important aspect of this step is establishing *synchronisation points* and *information needs*. What is meant by this, is explicit agreement between practitioners in each domain about *what* information shall be exchanged and *when*. Guidance might be found in existing standards for the system being developed. For the insulin pump example, AAMI guidance on security risk management for medical devices [2] provides a process that is matched to the safety risk process in ISO 14971 [14]. Specified interaction points are shown in the process, *e.g.* security controls affect safety, safety controls affect security, and security risk has a potential safety impact. Note that SSAF does not advocate how many sync points should be present. It is possible to instantiate sync points in a variety of models *e.g.* aligned with a project's frequent weekly meetings to limit divergence of the attributes or aligned with project milestones, *etc.*; each alignment model has different advantages and disadvantages.

2.2   Step 2: Model Risk and Assurance Process

SSAF Step 2 - Process Modelling and *Step 3 - Argument Modelling* are performed within a single domain. This separation accommodates different delivery timescales that are often present on industrial projects, and removes the need to try to unify assurance processes completely. The steps are presented sequentially, however it is more likely that modelling the assurance process and assurance argument will be done in parallel and incrementally. Specific information is required at synchronisation points agreed in Step 1, outside of that, there is flexibility for the single attribute assurance to be optimised *e.g.* to meet their individual concerns of certification or accreditation. For most safety-related systems there is already an existing standard that provides a risk management process, and this is increasingly the case for application-specific security standards, as with ISO 14971 [14] and AAMI TIR57 [2] for medical devices.

The purpose of this SSAF step is to resolve any issues regarding the information requirements for a single attribute. Conflicts arise between traditional "V" assurance process and modern agile development processes where there are differences in the information needed and the information available. For example, Functional Failure Analysis requires information about all the functions of a system to be available at the start of the analysis, if an iterative and incremental model-based system development process is being used such as MBSE, then all the failures required may not be available at the time the FFA is performed. This could lead to an incomplete analysis. This gap in assurance should be recorded and either resolved when the system model is more mature or the reasons why it is acceptable should be argued in the assurance case. Modelling the tasks explicitly allows for strategic assignment of methods, people and time to meet assurance goals.

2.3   Step 3: Model Assurance Argument

The objective for this SSAF step is to link the artefacts generated in the previous step to the assurance argument for a single attribute. The benefit of this is that the *meaning* of the artefacts is explained. Artefacts generated from a risk management processes *e.g.* Hazard List, remain unexplained until an argument is built about how and why that artefact is relevant, and what it contributes to the top level claim of safety or security. Table 2 shows an example safety assurance argument for the insulin pump. It is divided into six levels of claims (denoted by G*), context elements (C*) and argument strategies (St*). The contents of the the the argument are derived from the structure shown in [12] and from the hazard lists contained in [8]. The risk argument presented is decompositional, and argues over each of the safety hazards for the insulin pump. The leaf claim *G1.4.2.3.2 Commanded excess infusion adequately mitigated.* is supported by evidence during a Fault Tree analysis. Part of that Fault Tree is shown in Figure 2 and discussed in the next section.

There are several questions that may arise at this step, such as why not have a unified co-assurance argument, or why perform the step at all considering the resource overhead that might be better spent on technical risk reduction. Both these questions are valid, however a unified assurance argument would be difficult to construct because of the differing goals of the attributes. This separate approach to the arguments also allows for work to progress in a single domain, *e.g.* if safety risk management begins several months before the security programme then valuable progress can be made and security results incorporated. This only works if SSAF Step 1 – establishing information needs and synchronisation points has been completed. Not explicitly modelling the assurance argument means that during operation it is difficult to understand the impact of change *via* the artefacts; this is especially important for security where there is the potential for tens of vulnerabilities to be added daily for complex systems.

Table 2. Example safety argument structure for insulin pump

G1. Insulin pump is adequately safe for routine use
C1. Definition of adequately safe & routine use (ISO 14971)
C2. Pump design documentation & system model
C3. Details of patient types and usage environments
St1. Argument mitigation of system hazards
C4. Complete set of hazards
G1.1 Traumatic injury mitigated
G1.2 Biological/chemical contamination mitigated
G1.3 Incorrect therapy mitigated
G1.4 Infusion delivery error mitigated
G1.4.1 Risk of hyperglycaemia adequately mitigated
G1.4.2 Risk of hypoglycaemia adequately mitigated
St2. Argument over delivery modes
G1.4.2.1 Excess insulin during basal infusion mitigated
G1.4.2.2 Excess insulin during pump priming mitigated
G1.4.2.3 Excess insulin during meal/correction bolus infusion mitigated
St3. Argument over commanded *vs.* uncommanded infusions
G1.4.2.3.1 Uncommanded excess infusion mitigated
G1.4.2.3.2 Commanded excess infusion adequately mitigated

2.4   Step 4: Link Artefacts

This SSAF Step is deceptively simple, but is in fact, the *core contribution* of the
SSAF Technical Risk Model. The activity is to link the artefacts generated in the
previous steps with those of the other domain at the set synchronisation points.
This might be in the form of experts from safety and security teams meeting
to reconcile requirements, or to determine which vulnerabilities contribute to a
hazard. The difference with SSAF artefact linking is that the causal model is
modelled explicitly.

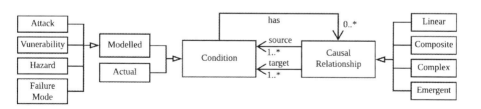

Fig. 1. SSAF causal model meta-model (Partial)

Figure 1 shows part of the SSAF TRM causal model meta-model. It is based on conditions being linked to conditions through a causal relationship. *Condition* here can refer to a safety condition such as a hazard, failure of a safety function, accident; equally it can refer to a security condition such as a threat, vulnerability, attack, *etc.* The beauty of this abstraction is that it enables the relationship between safety and security to be explicitly analysed. For many of the current co-engineering and co-assurance methods the causal link is implied, and the assurance gaps that the relationship introduces are obfuscated. This lack of clarity is counter-productive to the goal of successful and rigorous integration of the two attributes. The Technical Risk Model does not prescribe particular causal relationships, however through the meta-model, it provides a way of explicitly structuring the causal relationships so that they can be reasoned about regardless of how the modelled relationship was reached, *i.e.* it is independent of methodologies for establishing causal links.

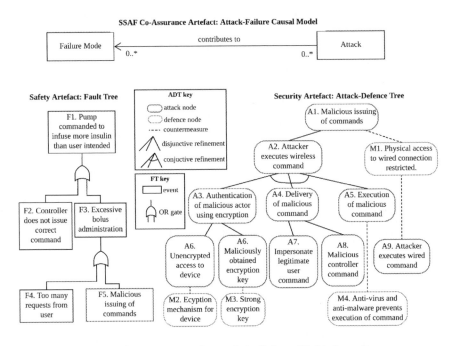

Fig. 2. Assurance artefacts. *Left.* Safety. *Right.* Security.

Figure 2 shows one instance of the causal link for the insulin pump example. On the left is the safety artefact - the Fault Tree which has information about failure behaviour from a safety perspective. On the right, the security artefact - the attack defence tree (ADT), which is a directed, acyclic graphs that is based on fault trees [20], however it contains much more information such as potential mitigations to prevent reaching a particular node. For this SSAF step, expert judgement is used to determine the causal link between failure event *F5. Malicious issuing of commands* is connected to the attack node *A1. Malicious issuing of command* node. The artefacts are derived directly from examples in the literature [1,4,25,30,36], and do not necessarily provide the strongest evidence for safety or security arguments; however it is especially important to form a meta-model of the links for weak arguments and artefacts so that the relationship can be examined further, for example, if a safety claim is related to a weak security artefact this could be revealed in the SSAF analysis and model.

The primary benefit of approaching the problem in this way is that, due to the implicit causal model represented by the fault tree and the ADT, the link between the attributes instantly provides the analysts with more information without having to know the details of the other domain. For example, if there was a new attack vector discovered where a wired command could be executed that by-passed mitigation *M1. Physical access to wired connection restricted*, then the causal link allows us to know that safety event *F5. Malicious issuing of commands* would return true. Through the fault tree failure path, *F1. Pump commanded to infuse more insulin than user intended* would be true. If this fault tree was used as a solution to the claim *G1.4.2.3.2 Commanded excess infusion adequately mitigated* from Table 2, then that claim is now undercut by that evidence. Thus, it is possible to see, in a semi-automated way, the impact propagation of adding another security condition. This enables better complexity and risk management in the real-world context of hundreds of vulnerabilities being added to vulnerability databases daily. The SSAF causal link provides a way of seeing the impact of one attribute on another without the requirement to resolve the issue *i.e.* in the insulin example, it is now demonstrated *how* claims in safety argument may be invalidated, therefore resources can be allocated proportional to severity - if the risk of excess insulin infusion is too great then the pump manufacturers might recall the product.

The example in Fig. 2 is just one instance of an artefact link. Table 3 shows more examples of causal links. SSAF TRM methodology is agnostic to the ontology and condition definitions used; for illustrative purposes Firesmith's Survivability model and explanation of the conditions are used [7]. There are many ways to create the causal relationship, some of the methods used in the literature are included in the Table.

Bi-Directional Link. *CR1* and *CR2* are an example of a bi-directional link using the Architecture Trade-Off Analysis Method (ATAM)[19]. ATAM relies on stakeholder for a system having a structured meeting and evaluating the benefits of using different architectures, then negotiating the best architecture based on a set of scenarios. This method was found to be effective in meeting its goals, and good at creating open communication channels, including between government and contractors [18]. A limitation of this method however is that it is resource intensive (the case study in [18] took two days and not all scenarios were covered).

Security Condition Influencing System Safety. *CR3* shows how Systems Theoretic Process Analysis (STPA)[23] has been adapted to STPA-Sec [38] and

Table 3. Causal relationship examples.

ID	Condition		Causal relationship	
	Source	Target	Label	Method
CR1	Safety requirements	Security requirements	trade-off	ATAM
CR2	Security requirements	Safety requirements	trade-off	ATAM
CR3	Threat condition	Safety requirements	influence	STPA-Sec, STPA-SafeSec
CR4	Vulnerabilities	Failure	cause	FFA
CR5	Vulnerabilities	Hazards	contribute to	SAHARA, DDA, UML, FTA
CR6	Safety effect	Attack	motivates	ADT
CR7	Threat condition	Hazard	safety impact	Standard
CR8	Security controls	Safety requirements	conflict with	ad-hoc

STPA-SafeSec [9] to integrate security conditions to system level hazards and safety requirements. Like many other techniques that have been adapted from safety, there are few industrial evaluations currently available and initial evaluations have found that Security-Aware STPA has limitations with regards to analysis of security concerns such as privacy or confidentiality.

Vulnerabilities Contributing to Failure and Hazards. *CR4* and *CR5* show the different ways in which vulnerabilities can contribute to hazards or failures. The methods used: Functional Failure Analysis (FFA), SAHARA [26] and DDA [6] are based on the *bowtie model* (in this case, security condition leading to a safety hazard). They rely on using expert judgement and guide words to structure the discovery of the effects of one attribute on another. Note that a causal link can be defined in UML [27], for example using expert knowledge of a particular application domain to describe a complex relationship.

Safety-Informed Security. There a many methods currently that investigate the impact of security on safety. However, the reverse relationship: the impact of safety on security is just as worthy of study. With increased threat from well-resourced adversaries, and the increased integration of technology into critical national infrastructure, how a safety risk might motivate a particular attack and thus increase security risk is worth analysis in its own right. *CR6* shows one example of this, by incorporating safety effects (possibly from a Failure Modes and Effects Analysis) into an Attack Defence Tree.

Domain- and Project-Specific Links. *CR7* demonstrates how causal relationships can be derived from the standards. *CR7* shows the *safety impact* relationship between threat conditions and hazards that is defined in the aerospace safety and security complementary standards ARP 4754A [32]/DO-326A [31]. The last causal relationship *CR8* shows how the interaction between the attributes can be analysed in an ad-hoc way, for example a domain expert doing an analysis in a spreadsheet. The reasons for a this are many and varied, however the most common might be that there does not exist a causal relationship in the standards or with existing techniques that allows for the link to be made. Performing this ad-hoc analysis using a text-based tool is discouraged, a modelling environment would be better suited for future update of the link.

The causal relationships discussed in this section are a small subset of examples of the relationships that can exist between safety and security. It is unlikely that any one method will sufficiently address all the concerns for both attributes, especially when they are sometimes conflicting (even within a single domain). With its causal link meta-model, SSAF proposes a way forward that enables work to continue under uncertainty. Compared to existing techniques for integration, it allows for updates in knowledge to be more easily incorporated. Borrowing the idea of an attack surface from security, SSAF enables the *assurance surface*, *i.e.* all the ways that safety and security uncertainty and risk can be reduced, to be managed in a systematic, strategic and rigorous way.

2.5   Step 5: Update the Model

The purpose of the Safety-Security Assurance Framework is to provide the structure for through-life co-assurance. This kind of structure is fundamental to the success of any co-assurance activities during the operational phase of a system. Without knowledge of the assurance arguments for both safety and security, or the causal relationship between the two, the problem of determining the impact and meaning of change becomes intractable. However, stating that a change structure is a necessary for effective co-assurance does not show *how* or *why* this is the case, so an illustrative example of change for the insulin pump is discussed in the subsequent section.

Insulin Pump Example: New Vulnerabilities. In October 2016, three new vulnerabilities for the Animas OneTouch Ping Insulin Pump were released [29]. It was revealed that the insulin pump used cleartext rather than encrypted communications; in addition, a weak pairing between the pump and its set-up device enabled a remote adversary to connect with, and spoof the pump to trigger patient uncommanded insulin infusion.

Considering the impact of these new vulnerabilities in the context of the ADT in Fig. 2 - both vulnerabilities enable an adversary to bypass the mitigations and lower levels of the tree, and exploit new paths to reach the node *A2. Attacker executes wireless command.* These vulnerabilities challenge and undermine the assumptions made about the attack vectors that an adversary could exploit at the time when the ADT analysis was performed. Thus there is a path to malicious issuing of commands which affects the "mitigated excessive infusion" safety claim. If the artefacts are in a model-based environment, then the new vulnerabilities can be added to the ADT and the impact propagated and flagged in the safety argument. The propagation does not indicate how the change should be managed, however it does give a clear indication where the assurance argument has been affected, therefore allowing expert time to be spent on determining the best course of action rather than attempting to assess impact.

Of course, these are two vulnerabilities, and it is possible for a complex system to have hundreds disclosed daily. The SSAF causal models do not trivialise the need to manage the gaps in assurance once they are known. They do, however, allow for more effective impact propagation and SSAF provides a practical structure to manage the assurance gaps *i.e.* the known unknowns.

3   SSAF Discussion and Way Forward

In this Section, the theory underlying SSAF will be briefly discussed and evaluated, then armed with knowledge from the development of SSAF, Sect. 3.1 provides recommendations for Safety-Security standards of the future.

A major difficulty in integrating safety and security is the lack of an underlying *theory of integration* or conceptual framework of the connections and trade-offs. This makes using traditional notions of validity, based on the scientific method less effective; as there is little information about *how* integration works, there is reduced confidence in the hypothesis formation phase, let alone hypothesis testing. To ameliorate the effects of this issue, the development of SSAF used diverse sets of data[1] together with theory-building methodologies[2] to create an underlying model for safety-security interactions.

SSAF TRM theoretical framework was evaluated against three criteria: fit, workability and modifiability [22]. **Fit** - The TRM framework closely fits with the co-assurance concepts and relationships it is representing because it is predominantly based on the incremental application of existing techniques (condition and process modelling, argumentation, *etc.*) on large-scale industrial projects. **Workability** - The workability of using the TRM approach was demonstrated on a small scale using the insulin pump case study. Further testing is required of the full SSAF model (TRM and STM) in an industrial setting to fully evaluate the workability of the methodology described in Sect. 2. Finally, the **Modifiability** - This too was evaluated on a small scale when the effects of adding new conditions were discussed (Sect. 2.5). What is still missing is a full evaluation of the effects of using the TRM meta-model in different application domains.

The SSAF TRM theoretical framework clearly requires further verification in an industrial context. However, unlike extant techniques, the TRM offers a unique way of explicitly modelling and reasoning about integration claims, therefore enabling the systematic construction of a stronger co-assurance case.

3.1   What Might Safety-Security Standards Look Like?

The difficulty with standardising co-assurance processes is the dynamic security landscape. For any one system, risk reduction for security would need to take into account the threat landscape for that system and the organisation developing/operating it, the assumptions about adversaries, the modes of attack, to name but a few factors. All this variation is difficult to capture in a standardised form because, by their nature, standards attempt to abstract from particular

---

[1] Industrial experience at BAE Systems, research literature, and workshop results.

[2] Social science approaches: Grounded Theory [10] and Yin-style Case Studies [37].

instances. Furthermore, safety standards aim for stability but the changes from security require constant adaptation.

Instead of attempting to create generic standards that perfectly unify assurance, and in the process lose information that is valuable for security, potentially a better way forward would be to have a generic description of an assurance process that refers to particular *assurance profiles i.e.* integration strategies and methods. Such a standard could describe the benefits and limitations of each integration strategy, and require particular strategies for systems that need high assurance levels for both attributes. The SSAF models would be one way to capture the integration models and strategies. Safety-security co-assurance should be developed as a discipline in its own right, with the aim of investigating and resolving the particular integration challenges that are not addressed in either safety or security domains.

4 Conclusion

There exist real-world challenges that pose barriers to developing and assuring complex, interconnected systems for safety and security. It is insufficient to disregard this real-world detail in order to make the assurance processes more tractable. Therefore, to address the challenges, a systematic and rigorous approach must be adopted to manage the interaction between safety and security.

The Safety-Security Assurance Framework (SSAF) was presented as a candidate solution to provide the structure and *deliberateness* required for co-assurance. SSAF is a two-part framework that consists of a Technical Risk Model (TRM) and a Socio-Technical Model (STM). The TRM is more effective at through-life co-assurance than many existing techniques because of its capacity to propagate the impact of change across domains during all phases of a system. A key enabler for impact propagation is creating explicit models of the causal relationships between attributes. However, even with technical models of causal relationships assurance gaps exist. SSAF TRM or, any other technical model alone, cannot address wider socio-technical factors affecting assurance.

The aim of this paper is primarily to explore the safety-security framework TRM and demonstrate the plausibility of such an approach. The scope was set to just the technical assurance because of the novelty of the approach and underlying theoretical framework. Rather than over-simplifying and reducing the problem, SSAF proposes a novel way of looking at the problem - by embracing the complexity and uncertainty, but doing so in a transparent and reasoned manner. In this way, it is possible to continue to manage the safety-security interactions and trade-offs in a deliberate way, thereby systematically improving co-assurance.

Acknowledgements. Research and development of SSAF supported by the University of York, the Assuring Autonomy International Programme (AAIP), and BAE Systems. UK Engineering and Physical Sciences Research Council Award Ref EPSRC iCASE 1515047.

References

1. AlTawy, R., Youssef, A.M.: Security tradeoffs in cyber physical systems: a case study survey on implantable medical devices. IEEE Access **4**, 959–979 (2016)
2. Association for the Advancement of Medical Instrumentation: AAMI TIR57:2016 Principles for medical device security - Risk management. Technical report, June 2016
3. Bostrom, R.P., Heinen, J.S.: MIS problems and failures: a socio-technical perspective part I: the causes. MIS Q. **1**, 17–32 (1977)
4. Camara, C., Peris-Lopez, P., Tapiador, J.E.: Security and privacy issues in implantable medical devices: a comprehensive survey. J. Biomed. Inform. **55**, 272–289 (2015)
5. Chen, Y., Lawford, M., Wang, H., Wassyng, A.: Insulin pump software certification. In: Gibbons, J., MacCaull, W. (eds.) FHIES 2013. LNCS, vol. 8315, pp. 87–106. Springer, Heidelberg (2014). https://doi.org/10.1007/978-3-642-53956-5_7
6. Despotou, G., Alexander, R., Kelly, T.: Addressing challenges of hazard analysis in systems of systems. In: 2009 3rd Annual IEEE Systems Conference, pp. 167–172. IEEE (2009)
7. Firesmith, D.G.: Common concepts underlying safety security and survivability engineering. Software Engineering Institute, Carnegie-Mellon University, Pittsburgh PA, Technical report (2003)
8. Food and Drug Administration (FDA): Infusion Pumps Total Product Life Cycle: Guidance for Industry and FDA Staff. Technical report, U.S. Department of Health and Human Services, December 2014
9. Friedberg, I., McLaughlin, K., Smith, P., Laverty, D., Sezer, S.: STPA-SafeSec: safety and security analysis for cyber-physical systems. J. Inf. Secur. Appl. **34**, 183–196 (2017)
10. Glaser, B.G., Strauss, A.L.: Discovery of Grounded Theory: Strategies for Qualitative Research. Routledge, New York (2017)
11. Hawkins, R., Habli, I., Kelly, T.: Principled construction of software safety cases. In: SAFECOMP 2013-Workshop SASSUR (Next Generation of System Assurance Approaches for Safety-Critical Systems) of the 32nd International Conference on Computer Safety, Reliability and Security (2013)
12. Hawkins, R., Kelly, T., Knight, J., Graydon, P.: A new approach to creating clear safety arguments. In: Dale, C., Anderson, T. (eds.) Advances in Systems Safety, pp. 3–23. Springer, London (2011). https://doi.org/10.1007/978-0-85729-133-2_1
13. Hu, R., Li, C.: The design of an intelligent insulin pump. In: 2015 4th International Conference on Computer Science and Network Technology (ICCSNT), vol. 1, pp. 736–739. IEEE (2015)
14. ISO 14971:2007 Medical devices - Application of risk management to medical devices. Standard, International Organization for Standardization, Geneva, CH, September 2007
15. ISO/IEC 27001:2013 Information technology - Security techniques - Information security management systems - Requirements. Standard, International Organization for Standardization, Geneva, CH, October 2013
16. Johnson, N., Kelly, T.: Safety-security assurance framework (SSAF) in practice. In: 37th International Conference on Computer Safety, Reliability, & Security SAFECOMP2018 (Abstract Paper) (2018)

17. Johnson, N., Kelly, T.: An assurance framework for independent co-assurance of safety and security. In: Muniak, C. (ed.) Journal of System Safety. International System Safety Society (January 2019), presented at: the 36th International System Safety Conference (ISSC), Arizona, USA, August 2018

18. Jones, L.G., Lattanze, A.J.: Using the architecture tradeoff analysis method to evaluate a wargame simulation system: a case study. Technical report, Carnegie Mellon University; Software Engineering Institute (SEI), Pittsburg, PA, USA (2001)

19. Kazman, R., Klein, M., Barbacci, M., Longstaff, T., Lipson, H., Carriere, J.: The architecture tradeoff analysis method. In: Proceedings Fourth IEEE International Conference on Engineering of Complex Computer Systems (Cat. No. 98EX193), pp. 68–78. IEEE (1998)

20. Kordy, B., Mauw, S., Radomirović, S., Schweitzer, P.: Foundations of attack–defense trees. In: Degano, P., Etalle, S., Guttman, J. (eds.) FAST 2010. LNCS, vol. 6561, pp. 80–95. Springer, Heidelberg (2011). https://doi.org/10.1007/978-3-642-19751-2_6

21. Lange, R., Burger, E.W.: Long-term market implications of data breaches, not. J. Inf. Priv. Secur. **13**(4), 186–206 (2017)

22. Lazenbatt, A., Elliott, N., et al.: How to recognise a 'quality' grounded theory research study. Aust. J. Adv. Nurs. **22**(3), 48 (2005)

23. Leveson, N.G.: A new approach to hazard analysis for complex systems. In: International Conference of the System Safety Society (2003)

24. Li, C., Raghunathan, A., Jha, N.K.: Hijacking an insulin pump: security attacks and defenses for a diabetes therapy system. In: 2011 IEEE 13th International Conference on e-Health Networking, Applications and Services, pp. 150–156. IEEE (2011)

25. Luckett, P., McDonald, J.T., Glisson, W.B.: Attack-graph threat modeling assessment of ambulatory medical devices. In: Proceedings of the 50th Hawaii International Conference on System Sciences (2017)

26. Macher, G., Sporer, H., Berlach, R., Armengaud, E., Kreiner, C.: SAHARA: a security-aware hazard and risk analysis method. In: Proceedings of the 2015 Design, Automation & Test in Europe Conference & Exhibition, pp. 621–624. EDA Consortium (2015)

27. OMG Unified Modeling Language. Standard, Object Management Group, December 2017. https://www.omg.org/spec/UML/About-UML/

28. Piggin, R.: Cybersecurity of medical devices: addressing patient safety and the security of patient health information. Technical report, BSI Group ANZ Pty Ltd. (2017)

29. Radcliffe, J., Beardsley, T.: R7-2016-07: Multiple vulnerabilities in animas One-Touch ping insulin pump. Technical report, Rapid7, October 2016. https://blog.rapid7.com/2016/10/04/r7-2016-07-multiple-vulnerabilities-in-animas-onetouch-ping-insulin-pump/

30. Rathore, H., Mohamed, A., Al-Ali, A., Du, X., Guizani, M.: A review of security challenges, attacks and resolutions for wireless medical devices. In: 2017 13th International Wireless Communications and Mobile Computing Conference (IWCMC), pp. 1495–1501. IEEE (2017)

31. RTCA: RTCA DO-326: Revision A Airworthiness Security Process Specification. Technical report, Washington, DC, USA, August 2014

32. SAE International: SAE ARP4754: Rev A Guidelines for Development of Civil Aircraft and Systems. Technical report, December 2010

33. U.S. Cybersecurity and Infrastructure Security Agency (CISA): Advisory (ICSMA-16-279-01): Animas OneTouch Ping insulin pump vulnerabilities. Technical report, National Cybersecurity and Communications Integration Center (NCCIC) Industrial Control Systems, October 2016

34. U.S. Cybersecurity and Infrastructure Security Agency (CISA): Advisory (ICSMA-18-219-02): Medtronic MiniMed 508 insulin pump. Technical report, National Cybersecurity and Communications Integration Center (NCCIC) Industrial Control Systems, August 2018. https://ics-cert.us-cert.gov/advisories/ICSMA-18-219-02

35. U.S. Food & Drug Administration (FDA): Postmarket Management of Cybersecurity in Medical Devices: Guidance for Industry and Food and Drug Administration Staff. Technical report, Center for Devices & Radiological Health, December 2016

36. Wu, F., Eagles, S.: Cybersecurity for medical device manufacturers: ensuring safety and functionality. Biomed. Instrum. Technol. **50**(1), 23–34 (2016)

37. Yin, R.K.: Case Study Research and Applications: Design and Methods. Sage publications, Thousand Oaks (2017)

38. Young, W., Leveson, N.G.: An integrated approach to safety and security based on systems theory. Commun. ACM **57**(2), 31–35 (2014)

39. Zhang, Y., Jones, P.L., Jetley, R.: A hazard analysis for a generic insulin infusion pump. J. Diabetes Sci. Technol. **4**(2), 263–283 (2010)

Author Index

Printed in the United States
By Bookmasters